Praise for *Mastering Marketing Data Science*

"In Mastering Marketing Data Science, *Iain Brown has meticulously crafted a seminal text that stands as a cornerstone for modern marketers. This comprehensive guide not only demystifies the complexities of data science in the marketing realm but also provides actionable insights and practical examples that bridge the gap between theoretical understanding and real-world application. From the foundational principles of marketing data science to the cutting-edge applications of generative artificial intelligence, Brown navigates through the nuances of data collection, analytics, machine learning, and ethical considerations with unparalleled clarity and expertise. This book is an indispensable resource for marketers seeking to harness the power of data science to drive innovation, enhance customer engagement, and achieve competitive advantage in today's digital landscape. A must-read for both seasoned professionals and those aspiring to transform their marketing strategies through data science."*

—Bernard Marr, Bestselling Author and International Keynote Speaker on Business and Technology

"This is an outstanding and timely book on marketing data science as it provides a unique blend of foundational as well as emerging topics. The author has a proven track record in the field and his extensive experience tops off the book in a splendid way. A must-read for anyone seeking to gain competitive advantage through marketing data science!"

—Prof. dr. Bart Baesens, Professor KU Leuven, Lecturer Southampton Business School

*"*Mastering Marketing Data Science *redefines the landscape of modern marketing, offering a compelling roadmap for harnessing the power of data science. With practical use cases and expert insights, this book equips practitioners with the tools they need to navigate the complexities of the digital age and drive transformative marketing strategies."*

—Professor Ganna Pogrebna, Lead for Behavioural Data Science at the Alan Turing Institute (UK); Executive Director at AI and Cyber Futures Institute and Honorary Professor at the University of Sydney Business School (Australia)

"Dr. Iain Brown expertly blends his expertise in financial and credit systems with his strong credentials in data science and analytics to deliver a remarkably thorough guidebook for those who are looking to bring data-driven analytic and algorithmic methods to marketing. This highly practical and thoroughly educational book goes both wide and deep into many data science methods, algorithms, and techniques (including exploratory data analytics, predictive analytics, and generative AI), clearly demonstrating how each of those augments, accelerates, and amplifies a broad spectrum of traditional marketing applications (such as A/B testing, customer segmentation, attribution, customer journey, churn, propensity)."

—Kirk Borne, Founder and Owner of Data Leadership Group LLC

"Mastering Marketing Data Science *is an invaluable resource for marketers and data enthusiasts seeking to navigate the dynamic landscape of modern marketing where data is critical. Iain integrates key marketing and data science concepts well, including relevant examples to bring the concepts to life. This book would be very useful to our MSc Digital Marketing students to empower them in the journey towards a data-driven decision-making world."*

—Dr Anabel Gutierrez, Director of the MSc Digital Marketing Programme and Senior Lecturer in Digital Marketing and Innovation – Royal Holloway, University of London.

"Iain Brown's Mastering Marketing Data Science *meticulously navigates the entire data journey in marketing, offering a deep dive into data collection, ingestion, and modeling, alongside the practical application of AI and analytics in the marketing field. This book stands as an invaluable roadmap for newcomers to the intersection of data, marketing, analytics, and AI, including the optimization with neural networks and generative AI. It demystifies the complexities and provides actionable knowledge that's crucial for anyone stepping into the data-analytics-marketing arena."*

—Yves Mulkers, Data Strategist and Thought Leader, Founder of 7wData

Mastering Marketing Data Science

Wiley and SAS Business Series

The Wiley and SAS Business Series presents books that help senior level managers with their critical management decisions.

Titles in the Wiley and SAS Business Series include:

Analytics: The Agile Way by Phil Simon

The Analytics Lifecycle Toolkit: A Practical Guide for an Effective Analytics Capability by Gregory S. Nelson

Artificial Intelligence for Marketing: Practical Applications by Jim Sterne

Business Analytics for Managers: Taking Business Intelligence Beyond Reporting (Second Edition) by Gert H. N. Laursen and Jesper Thorlund

Business Forecasting: The Emerging Role of Artificial Intelligence and Machine Learning by Michael Gilliland, Len Tashman, and Udo Sglavo

Fraud Analytics Using Descriptive, Predictive, and Social Network Techniques: A Guide to Data Science for Fraud Detection by Bart Baesens, Veronique Van Vlasselaer, and Wouter Verbeke

Intelligent Credit Scoring: Building and Implementing Better Credit Risk Scorecards (Second Edition) by Naeem Siddiqi

Leaders and Innovators: How Data-Driven Organizations Are Winning with Analytics by Tho H. Nguyen

A Practical Guide to Analytics for Governments: Using Big Data for Good by Marie Lowman

Statistical Thinking: Improving Business Performance (Third Edition) by Roger W. Hoerl and Ronald D. Snee

Style and Statistics: The Art of Retail Analytics by Brittany Bullard

Text as Data: Computational Methods of Understanding Written Expression Using SAS by Barry deVille and Gurpreet Singh Bawa

For more information on any of the above titles, please visit www.wiley.com.

Mastering Marketing Data Science

A Comprehensive Guide for Today's Marketers

Iain Brown

WILEY

Registered Office(s)
John Wiley & Sons Ltd, The Atrium, Southern Gate, Chichester, West Sussex, PO19 8SQ, UK
John Wiley & Sons, Inc., 111 River Street, Hoboken, NJ 07030, USA

For details of our global editorial offices, customer services, and more information about Wiley products visit us at www.wiley.com.

Wiley also publishes its books in a variety of electronic formats and by print-on-demand. Some content that appears in standard print versions of this book may not be available in other formats.

Library of Congress Cataloging-in-Publication Data is Available

ISBN 9781394258710(Cloth)
ISBN 9781394258734(epdf)
ISBN 9781394258727(epub)

Cover Design: Wiley
Cover Image: © queezz/Shutterstock

Set in 10/14pt Meridien LT Std by Straive, Chennai, India

SKY10073121_042424

Contents

Preface

NAVIGATING THE INTERSECTION OF MARKETING AND DATA SCIENCE

In the rapidly evolving landscape of marketing, the fusion of traditional strategies with cutting-edge data science has opened new frontiers for innovation, efficiency, and personalization. Over the past decade, both as a practitioner and professor, I recognized a palpable gap in the literature that adequately bridges the gap between theoretical data science concepts and their practical application in marketing. This book is my endeavor to fill that void, offering a comprehensive guide that reflects the latest advancements in the field.

This book is meticulously tailored for:

1. Master's level students in marketing, data science, or related fields, seeking a solid foundation and practical insights into marketing data science.
2. Marketing professionals, including managers, digital marketing specialists, and marketing analysts, aiming to harness data-driven practices to enhance their strategies.
3. Data scientists and analysts looking to pivot their skills towards marketing applications, offering a unique blend of technical expertise and market acumen.

Spanning 13 chapters, this book covers a breadth of essential topics:

- Fundamental principles of marketing data science and its pivotal role in modern marketing strategies.
- Data collection, preparation, and the art of transforming raw data into actionable insights.
- From descriptive and inferential analytics to predictive models and machine learning, we delve into techniques that power decision-making and strategy optimization.
- The application of natural language processing, social media, and web analytics, unlocking the potential of unstructured data in crafting compelling narratives and understanding consumer behavior.
- Advanced topics such as marketing mix modeling, customer journey analytics, experimental design, and the burgeoning field of generative AI in marketing.

Each chapter is enriched with practical examples and exercises designed to bridge theory with practice, enabling readers to apply these concepts in real-world scenarios. *Mastering Marketing Data Science* aims to:

- Equip readers with a deep understanding of marketing data science fundamentals and their application in driving business value.
- Foster proficiency in data collection, preparation, and analytical techniques tailored for marketing data.
- Empower readers to leverage data-driven insights for informed decision-making and optimization of marketing strategies.

Embark on this journey with an open mind and a keen spirit of inquiry. The field of marketing data science is vast and ever-changing, offering endless opportunities for innovation and impact. Through this book, I invite you to explore, experiment, and excel. Whether you are a student stepping into the world of data-driven marketing, a professional seeking to elevate your practice, or a data scientist venturing into the marketing domain, let this guide be your compass. Together, let's navigate the complexities of marketing data science and harness its potential to redefine the future of marketing.

Acknowledgments

My journey in writing this book has been supported by many, but none more so than my wife and two children. Their patience, encouragement, and unwavering support have been my anchor. I extend my gratitude to my wider family and the community of colleagues, students, and professionals who have inspired and contributed to my work in countless ways.

About the Author

Dr. Iain Brown is the Head of Data Science for SAS Northern Europe and an Adjunct Professor of Marketing Data Science at the University of Southampton. With over a decade of experience spanning various sectors, he is a thought leader in Marketing, Risk, AI, and Machine Learning. His work has not only contributed to significant projects and innovations but also enriched the academic and professional communities through publications in prestigious journals and presentations at internationally renowned conferences.

CHAPTER 1

Introduction to Marketing Data Science

1.1 WHAT IS MARKETING DATA SCIENCE?

In the modern landscape, marketing data science stands at an intriguing intersection, intricately weaving the sophisticated methodologies and instruments of data science with the profound realm of marketing wisdom. What lies at the core of this juncture? A pursuit to mine deep-seated insights, catalyze organizational growth, and refine marketing blueprints (Wedel & Kannan, 2016). As data continuously flows from diverse sources—encompassing customer engagements, the vast expanse of social media, and intricate web metrics—there's a pressing call for astute navigation and interpretation (Kelleher et al., 2015).

Within the realm of marketing, data science plays a critical role in unlocking valuable insights and driving strategic decision-making. This dynamic field encompasses a variety of key factors that collectively contribute to its power and effectiveness. These factors include the collection and preparation of high-quality data from diverse sources, the application of advanced analytical techniques such as descriptive, predictive, and prescriptive analytics, and the ability to communicate findings in a clear and actionable manner. Furthermore, data science in marketing requires an understanding of consumer behavior, market trends, and competitive landscape, as well as the ability to leverage this knowledge to inform and optimize marketing strategies. As a result, the marriage of marketing expertise and data science capabilities creates a potent combination that can significantly enhance a company's competitive advantage and drive business growth.

The key factors include the following, which will be discussed in detail in this book:

1. **Data collection.** Amassing pertinent data, extracted from diverse origins such as internal databases, customer relationship management systems, social media landscapes, web analytics instruments, and third-party purveyors (Chapter 2: Data Collection and Preparation).

2. **Data preparation.** Scrubbing, preprocessing, and transforming raw data into an analysis-ready format. This stage often grapples with the challenges of missing or discordant data, feature engineering, and data normalization or standardization (Chapter 2: Data Collection and Preparation).

3. **Data analysis.** Employing descriptive, inferential, and predictive analytics techniques to scrutinize data, unveiling insights, patterns, and trends that can guide marketing strategies and decision-making processes (Chapter 3: Descriptive Analytics in Marketing and Chapter 4: Inferential Analytics and Hypothesis Testing).

4. **Model development.** Architecting, examining, and validating machine learning models, spanning classification, regression, or clustering algorithms, with an aim to forecast customer behavior, segment customers, or optimize marketing endeavors (Chapter 5: Predictive Analytics and Machine Learning).

5. **Visualization and communication.** Conveying the findings and insights gleaned from data analysis and models through clear, compelling visualizations,

reports, and presentations, thoughtfully tailored for an array of stakeholders, be it marketing executives, product managers, or data scientists (Chapter 3: Descriptive Analytics in Marketing).

6. **Implementation and optimization.** Incorporating insights and models into marketing strategies, campaigns, and processes to propel business growth and augment marketing performance. In this phase, a continuous cycle of monitoring, evaluating, and refining models and strategies unfolds, responsive to feedback, outcomes, and the ever-evolving marketplace (throughout all chapters).

In the journey of applying data science to marketing problems, practitioners encounter various challenges at different stages, ranging from data collection to implementation. Table 1.1 outlines these challenges and proposes common solutions and approaches, presenting them not as sequential steps, but as interconnected aspects of the data science process.

Marketing data science equips organizations with the power to make data-driven decisions, optimize marketing expenditures, elevate customer experiences, and secure a competitive edge. By harnessing advanced techniques, such as machine learning (see Chapter 5), natural language processing (NLP) (see Chapter 6), and big data analytics (see Chapter 11), marketing data scientists can discover latent opportunities, foresee customer behavior, and devise personalized marketing strategies that resonate with target audiences (Ngai et al., 2009).

Table 1.1 Challenges and Solutions in Data Science Processes.

Stage	Challenges	Common Solutions and Approaches
Data collection	• Fragmented data sources • Inconsistencies in data • Unstructured data	• Integration tools and platforms • Data validation checks • Web scrapers and parsers
Data preparation	• Missing data • Noisy data • Duplicate records	• Imputation techniques • Data filtering and cleaning • Deduplication methods
Data analysis	• Incorrect assumptions • Overfitting or underfitting • Irrelevant features	• Hypothesis testing • Cross-validation • Feature selection and extraction
Model development	• Choosing wrong model types • Model validation challenges • Scalability issues	• Model benchmarking • K-fold validation • Cloud and distributed computing solutions
Visualization and communication	• Misrepresentative visuals • Overwhelming complexity • Loss of nuance in simplification	• Use of standard visualization guidelines • Iterative design • Annotation and context
Implementation and optimization	• Difficulty in real-time application • Feedback loop challenges • Integration with existing systems	• Streaming data solutions • Continuous monitoring tools • Middleware and APIs

1.2 THE ROLE OF DATA SCIENCE IN MARKETING

The world of data science has surged as an indispensable catalyst of expansion and ingenuity in the marketing landscape. Amidst technology's evolution and the intricate maze of customer behavior, marketers must harness data-driven insights to outpace the competition (Wedel & Kannan, 2016). Herein, we explore the pivotal roles data science plays in marketing:

- **Customer insights and preferences.** Analyzing customer data, encompassing purchase history, demographic details, and online behavior, empowers data scientists to discern trends, tastes, and patterns, subsequently informing marketing strategies tailored to satisfy customer needs (Ngai et al., 2009).

- **Customer segmentation and profiling.** Employing clustering algorithms and other machine learning techniques, data scientists carve meaningful customer segments based on shared characteristics, facilitating targeted campaigns, personalized messaging, and customized offers that bolster engagement and conversion rates (Hastie et al., 2009).

- **Marketing spend optimization.** Data science methodologies unveil the efficacy of different marketing channels, campaigns, and tactics. By pinpointing impactful marketing activities, organizations optimize marketing spend and allocate resources more wisely (Kotler et al., 2017).

- **Campaign effectiveness and A/B testing.** Campaign effectiveness refers to the measure of how successfully a marketing campaign achieves its objectives, often evaluated through key performance indicators (KPIs) such as conversion rates or return on investment. One of the primary methods used by data scientists to assess campaign effectiveness is A/B testing. A/B testing, also known as *split testing*, involves comparing two versions of a marketing variable (e.g., ad creatives, email subject lines, landing page designs) to determine which one performs better. Through such experimentation, data scientists can analyze the efficacy of different marketing strategies, enabling marketers to continually refine their campaigns and make decisions based on data. This approach is essential in today's data-driven marketing landscape (Provost & Fawcett, 2013).

- **Sentiment analysis and social media monitoring.** NLP techniques analyze customer sentiment, feedback, and online conversations surrounding a brand or product. This equips organizations to comprehend customer perceptions, pinpoint potential issues, and unearth opportunities for improvement or innovation (Kelleher et al., 2015).

- **Recommender systems and personalization.** Data scientists can develop algorithms recommending products or content based on customer preferences, browsing history, and other behavioral data. This bolsters customer engagement, amplifies sales, and enhances the overall customer experience (Shmueli et al., 2011).

- **Forecasting and demand planning.** Leveraging time series analysis and predictive modeling techniques, data scientists can forecast sales, customer demand, and other crucial marketing metrics, empowering organizations to effectively plan marketing strategies, inventory management, and resource allocation (Few, 2009).

- **Churn prediction and customer retention.** By dissecting customer behavior and identifying churn-contributing factors, data scientists can create models predicting customer attrition risks. This enables organizations to proactively retain valuable customers and augment overall customer satisfaction (Wedel & Kannan, 2016).

- **Marketing mix modeling and attribution.** Data scientists gauge the influence of diverse marketing variables on sales or other marketing objectives and attribute marketing success to particular channels or tactics. This guides organizations in making informed decisions about their marketing mix and optimizing strategies for maximum impact (Provost & Fawcett, 2013).

In summary, data science has become an essential facet of marketing, aiding organizations in understanding customers, optimizing marketing approaches, and propelling business growth. As data continues to multiply in volume, variety, and velocity, data science's role in marketing will grow increasingly critical and ubiquitous.

1.3 MARKETING ANALYTICS VERSUS DATA SCIENCE

Amidst the paramount roles marketing analytics and data science play in steering organizations toward data-driven decisions, these functions diverge in scope, techniques, objectives, skill set, and integration with marketing strategies (Wedel & Kannan, 2016). In this section, we delve into these disparities in greater detail.

- **Scope.** Although marketing analytics primarily focuses on the measurement, analysis, and reporting of marketing data to fathom marketing effort efficacy, identify trends, and inform marketing decisions, data science envelops a more extensive array of techniques and methodologies exceeding traditional analytics to create profound insights, predictions, and recommendations (Ngai et al., 2009).
  - **Marketing analytics.** A major sports brand, for instance, might use marketing analytics to measure the effectiveness of its Super Bowl ad campaign by monitoring metrics such as views, click-through rates, and direct sales resulting from the ad.
  - **Data science.** The same sports brand might employ data science to analyze customer purchase behaviors, social media sentiments, and other complex data sources to predict which type of product will be the next big hit or which celebrity endorsement might resonate best with their target audience.

Techniques. Marketing analytics typically hinges on descriptive and inferential statistics to analyze data and draw conclusions, employing techniques such as data visualization, summary statistics, hypothesis testing, and regression analysis. Data science, however, delves into more advanced techniques such as machine learning, NLP, and network analysis to unearth hidden patterns, make predictions, and devise data-driven solutions to complex marketing conundrums (Hastie et al., 2009).

- **Marketing analytics.** An e-commerce retailer might employ descriptive statistics to understand which products are the best-sellers, based on historical data, and visualize these trends using bar charts or heat maps.
- **Data science.** For the same e-commerce retailer, data science might be employed to develop a recommendation system using machine learning. This system can predict and display products a customer might be interested in based on their browsing history, significantly improving upsell and cross-sell opportunities.

Objectives. Marketing analytics seeks primarily to understand and evaluate past and current marketing performance, involving the measurement of KPIs, trend identification, and the evaluation of marketing campaign return on investment (ROI). Data science, by contrast, aims to comprehend past performance while also predicting future outcomes and optimizing marketing strategies. This may involve crafting models to forecast customer behavior, segmenting customers based on preferences, and generating recommender systems for personalized marketing endeavors (Kotler et al., 2017).

- **Marketing analytics.** A coffee shop chain might evaluate the performance of a new loyalty program by analyzing the frequency of repeat customers and average sales per visit after the program's introduction.
- **Data science.** The same coffee shop chain could use data science to forecast stock demand for specific beverages, predict peak times based on historical data and weather patterns, or segment customers into clusters to tailor marketing offers to individual preferences.

Skill set. Marketing analysts often boast backgrounds in marketing, business, or economics and wield robust analytical and quantitative skills. They are proficient in statistical analysis, data visualization, and reporting tools, such as Excel, Tableau, and Google Analytics. Data scientists, conversely, generally possess backgrounds in computer science, statistics, or related fields and are adept in programming languages (e.g., SAS, Python), machine learning libraries (e.g., scikit-learn, TensorFlow), and big data platforms (e.g., Hadoop, Spark) (Provost & Fawcett, 2013).

- **Marketing analytics.** A skin care brand might hire a marketing analyst with a background in business analytics to interpret sales data, understand which products are performing well in specific regions, and identify market trends using tools such as Excel and Tableau.

- **Data science.** The skin care brand might also hire a data scientist with a background in machine learning to create models predicting which new products will become best-sellers based on ingredient trends, customer reviews, and other related datasets.

Integration with marketing strategies. Marketing analytics frequently informs marketing strategies by offering insights into customer preferences, campaign performance, and market trends. Data science surpasses mere insight provision, actively engaging in the development and optimization of marketing strategies. Data scientists often collaborate with marketing teams to design experiments, develop predictive models, and implement data-driven solutions (Shmueli et al., 2011).

- **Marketing analytics.** An online fashion store might analyze data on best-selling outfits and use these insights to guide the design of the next season's collection, ensuring alignment with customer preferences.
- **Data science.** The same fashion store could employ data science techniques to A/B test different website layouts, optimizing user experience to drive sales. They could also use predictive models to identify customers likely to churn, subsequently sending these customers targeted promotional offers.

Notwithstanding these differences, marketing analytics and data science serve as complementary disciplines that, in unison, enable organizations to attain a comprehensive understanding of their customers, markets, and marketing performance. By capitalizing on both disciplines' strengths, marketers can make more informed decisions, optimize strategies, and propel business growth (Wedel & Kannan, 2016).

1.4 KEY CONCEPTS AND TERMINOLOGY

As the business landscape evolves, so too does the sophistication and complexity of marketing techniques. Now more than ever, marketing is intricately intertwined with the evolving paradigms of data, technology, and algorithms. Navigating the labyrinth of modern marketing necessitates not just an awareness but a deep understanding of the language of data science as it applies to marketing. This is not just about mastering jargon, but rather ensuring you have the foundational knowledge to harness the immense power of data-driven marketing strategies. Terms such as *machine learning* and *predictive analytics* aren't mere buzzwords—they represent transformative methodologies that have revolutionized how businesses interact with consumers, shape products, and chart out their future strategies. For anyone embarking on a journey in marketing data science, the road map begins with a clear comprehension of the fundamental terms and concepts. In this section, we identify some of the most pivotal terms you'll encounter, serving as the building blocks for your journey into the depths of marketing data science.

1.4.1 Data Science

Data science is an interdisciplinary field combining computer science, statistics, and domain expertise to distil knowledge and insights from structured and unstructured data. Data science techniques help identify patterns, trends, and relationships that inform decision-making and bolster business growth (Dhar, 2013). This topic will be explored in detail throughout this text.

1.4.2 Data Visualization

Data visualization refers to employing graphical representations, including charts, graphs, and maps, to exhibit data and simplify understanding, exploration, and analysis. Data visualization tools such as Tableau and Power BI enable marketers to convey insights, trends, and patterns in visually appealing and easily digestible manners (Few, 2009). The topic of data visualization will be explored fully in Chapter 3.

1.4.3 Customer Segmentation

Customer segmentation is the act of segregating customers into groups or segments based on shared characteristics, such as demographics, behaviors, or preferences. Customer segmentation permits organizations to craft targeted marketing campaigns, personalized messaging, and tailored offers resonating with each customer group (Dolnicar & Grün, 2008). The topic of customer segmentation will be explored fully in Chapter 4.

1.4.4 Predictive Analytics

Predictive analytics is the use of statistical and machine learning techniques to analyze historical data and prognosticate future events or trends. Predictive analytics aids organizations in anticipating customer behavior, optimizing marketing strategies, and pinpointing potential opportunities or risks (Shmueli & Koppius, 2011). The topic of predictive analytics will be explored fully in Chapter 5.

1.4.5 Machine Learning

Machine learning is a subset of data science and artificial intelligence (AI) employing algorithms to learn from data, discern patterns, and make predictions or decisions. Machine learning encompasses supervised learning (e.g., regression, classification), unsupervised learning (e.g., clustering, dimensionality reduction), and reinforcement learning (Hastie et al., 2009). The topic of machine learning will be explored fully in Chapter 5.

1.4.6 Natural Language Processing

An AI branch addressing the interaction between computers and human language, empowering computers to comprehend, interpret, and generate human language. NLP techniques serve various marketing applications, such as sentiment analysis, topic modeling, and chatbot development (Liu, 2012). The topic of NLP will be explored fully in Chapter 6.

1.4.7 Marketing Mix Modeling

Marketing mix modeling is a technique gauging the impact of distinct marketing variables (e.g., price, promotion, product, place) on sales or other marketing objectives. Marketing mix modeling assists organizations in assessing their marketing effort efficacy, efficiently allocating resources, and optimizing marketing strategies for maximal impact (Leeflang et al., 2009). The topic of machine learning will be explored fully in Chapter 8.

1.4.8 Big Data

Large and intricate datasets that traditional data processing techniques struggle to efficiently manage. Big data is often typified by volume (data amount), variety (data types), and velocity (data generation and processing speed). Big data technologies, such as Hadoop and Spark, facilitate real-time processing and analysis of massive data quantities (Chen et al., 2014). The topic of big data will be explored fully in Chapter 11.

Cultivating a robust understanding of these key concepts and terminology will better prepare you to delve into the diverse techniques and methodologies employed in marketing data science and their practical applications in real-world marketing scenarios.

1.5 STRUCTURE OF THIS BOOK

Chapter 1 has served as an introduction to marketing data science, emphasizing its critical role in modern marketing strategies and underscoring the need to refine data to unlock its intrinsic value. By diving deep into the intricacies of data science methodologies, key concepts, and their applications in marketing, readers are offered a comprehensive understanding of the field. The chapter distinguishes traditional marketing analytics from data science, and two real-world examples showcase the tangible impact of data-driven decision-making in marketing scenarios. This chapter sets the stage for an in-depth exploration of the transformative power of marketing data science in subsequent sections of the book.

Chapter 2 delves into the essential techniques and tools involved in gathering and preparing data for marketing data science. This chapter introduces various data collection methods, from surveys and web scraping to API use, while emphasizing the importance of data integrity. It explores data cleaning, transformation, and feature engineering, ensuring that the data is ready for analysis. Readers will come away with an understanding of how to manage the challenges associated with handling missing and inconsistent data, illustrated by real-world examples.

Chapter 3 offers a deep dive into descriptive analytics in marketing, focusing on the techniques used to summarize and visualize data. This chapter guides the reader through exploratory data analysis, including data visualization and descriptive statistics. By exploring the foundations of these techniques, readers will be equipped with the knowledge to understand customer behaviors and market trends through practical examples.

Chapter 4 dives into inferential analytics, focusing on the statistical concepts and tests required for making predictions and inferences from sampled data. By exploring sampling techniques, confidence intervals, customer segmentation, and A/B testing, this chapter equips the reader with tools to validate marketing hypotheses and make informed decisions. This knowledge will empower marketers to generate actionable insights from their data.

Chapter 5 provides an in-depth exploration of predictive analytics using machine learning algorithms. From understanding supervised and unsupervised learning to churn prediction and market basket analysis, this chapter offers insights into cutting-edge predictive models. Practical examples and case studies will illustrate these concepts, preparing the reader to apply predictive analytics to real-world marketing problems.

Chapter 6 unveils the potential of NLP in the realm of marketing. From basics to advanced techniques such as sentiment analysis and topic modeling, the chapter explores how NLP can extract valuable insights from text data. Readers will learn about the role of chatbots and voice assistants in modern marketing, with practical examples to guide implementation.

Chapter 7 is dedicated to the intersection of marketing with social media and web analytics. Readers will discover how to leverage social network analysis and conversion rate optimization to drive online engagement. Practical insights into web analytics tools and social media tracking will empower marketers to measure and improve their online strategies.

Chapter 8 delves into the data-driven approach of marketing mix modeling and attribution. By understanding these concepts, readers will be able to measure and optimize the effect of various marketing channels. Case studies on multi-touch attribution and return on marketing investment (ROMI) will enable readers to evaluate marketing performance with precision.

Chapter 9 guides readers through the multifaceted realm of customer journey mapping and touchpoint analysis. By focusing on cross-channel marketing optimization and the path to purchase, this chapter offers invaluable insights into understanding customer behavior across various touchpoints. Practical examples will help readers build effective customer journey strategies.

Chapter 10 explores the robust methodology of experimental design in marketing, providing readers with a foundation in design of experiments and multi-armed bandits. Emphasizing both online and offline experiments, this chapter empowers marketers to test hypotheses and optimize strategies effectively, using real-world examples to illustrate key concepts.

Chapter 11 demystifies big data technologies, introducing distributed computing frameworks such as Hadoop and Spark and cloud computing. By exploring real-time analytics tools and personalization techniques, readers will learn to handle vast datasets and provide immediate insights. This chapter lays the groundwork for harnessing big data to drive real-time marketing decisions.

Chapter 12 offers a cutting-edge exploration of generative AI and its impact on marketing. From content creation to predictive analytics and ethical considerations, readers will learn how generative AI is shaping the future of marketing. Practical guidance and case studies will help readers to understand and harness this transformative technology in their own marketing efforts.

Finally, Chapter 13 tackles the critical considerations of ethics and privacy in marketing data science. By examining regulations such as GDPR (general data protection regulation) and CCPA (California Consumer Privacy Act) and exploring concepts of bias, fairness, and transparency, this chapter guides readers through the ethical landscape. Insights into emerging trends and the future of the field will prepare readers for the evolving world of marketing data science.

1.6   PRACTICAL EXAMPLE 1: APPLYING DATA SCIENCE TO IMPROVE CROSS-SELLING IN A RETAIL BANK MARKETING DEPARTMENT

A retail bank, which for illustrative purposes we will call *NexaTrust Bank*, wants to improve its cross-selling efforts by offering targeted financial products to existing customers. The marketing department decides to use data science techniques to enhance their approach, aiming to increase customer satisfaction and boost revenue.

1.6.1   Data Collection

NexaTrust Bank gathers relevant data from various sources, including customer demographics, account types, transaction history, credit scores, and customer service interactions.

1.6.2 Data Preparation

The raw data is cleaned, preprocessed, and transformed into a suitable format for analysis. This step involves handling missing or inconsistent data, feature engineering, and data normalization or standardization.

1.6.3 Customer Segmentation

Using clustering algorithms, NexaTrust Bank segments its customers based on their financial behavior, product use, and demographic information. This results in distinct customer segments, such as young professionals, families, high-net-worth individuals, and retirees.

1.6.4 Product Recommendation Modeling

NexaTrust Bank develops a recommender system using machine learning algorithms, such as collaborative filtering or content-based filtering, to identify the most relevant financial products for each customer segment based on their preferences, needs, and financial behavior.

1.6.5 Campaign Design

NexaTrust Bank designs targeted marketing campaigns for each customer segment, focusing on the recommended financial products. These campaigns include personalized messaging, customized offers, and tailored communication channels (e.g., email, SMS, in-app notifications).

1.6.6 A/B Testing and Evaluation

NexaTrust Bank conducts A/B testing to evaluate the effectiveness of different marketing variables, such as ad creatives, offer types, and communication channels. This enables NexaTrust Bank to continuously optimize its campaigns based on data-driven insights.

1.6.7 Monitoring and Refinement

NexaTrust Bank closely monitors the performance of its cross-selling campaigns, tracking metrics such as conversion rates, customer satisfaction, and revenue. Based on these insights, the bank refines its product recommendation models, customer segmentation, and marketing strategies to maximize the effectiveness of its cross-selling efforts (see Figure 1.1).

By leveraging data science techniques, NexaTrust Bank can offer more relevant and personalized financial products to its customers, improving customer satisfaction and increasing the success of its cross-selling efforts.

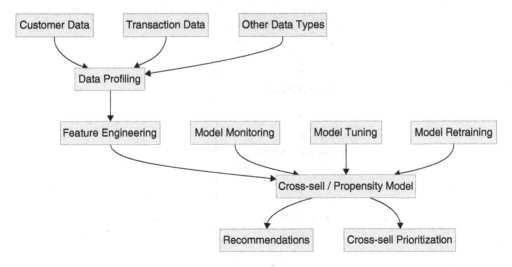

Figure 1.1 Using Data Science to Improve Cross-Selling in NexaTrust Bank's Marketing Department.

1.7 PRACTICAL EXAMPLE 2: THE IMPACT OF DATA SCIENCE ON A MARKETING CAMPAIGN

Let us consider LuxeVogue Retailers, a hypothetical retail company eager to enhance the performance of its email marketing endeavors. Historically, like many others in the retail space, LuxeVogue Retailers used a one-size-fits-all email strategy, sending the same promotions to all customers. However, to stay competitive and increase the efficacy of their marketing campaigns, the team at LuxeVogue Retailers turns to data science.

The first step involves the meticulous collection of data, which becomes the life-blood of their data-driven strategy. This data isn't just a random assortment of numbers and facts; it's a rich tapestry of customer stories told through their demographic profiles, their past purchasing behaviors, and their interactions with previous emails. With this treasure trove of data at their fingertips, LuxeVogue's marketing analysts employ sophisticated machine learning algorithms to sift through this information, identifying patterns that the human eye would likely miss.

Figure 1.2 provides a graphical depiction of this nuanced process. It illustrates how data flows from the collection phase into the analytical engines of machine learning, which then churns out actionable customer segments.

With these segments identified, LuxeVogue Retailers embarks on a journey of personalized marketing. This isn't just about addressing customers by their first names; it's about crafting offers that resonate with their unique preferences and sending emails that align with their specific behaviors. For instance, one segment might consist of customers who have shown interest in premium products, and another is more price sensitive and responsive to discount offers.

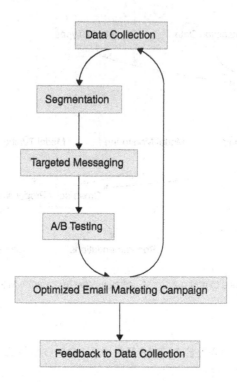

Figure 1.2 Using Data Science to Optimize Email Marketing Campaigns for LuxeVogue Retailers.

LuxeVogue Retailers doesn't stop there. Armed with the power to personalize, they take it a step further with A/B testing. They craft various email campaigns with different subject lines—some straightforward, some using intrigue, and others with a sense of urgency. Email layouts are tweaked, some with vibrant images and others with a focus on text and clarity. The content itself is varied to see what storytelling style resonates best with their audience.

Each campaign iteration is meticulously monitored. The team measures how many customers opened the emails (open rates), how many clicked on the links within them (click-through rates), and, most important, how many took the desired action, such as making a purchase (conversion rates). This process is not a one-off; it is an ongoing cycle of hypothesizing, testing, learning, and refining.

Through this iterative process of testing and analysis, LuxeVogue Retailers is not just sending emails; they are cultivating a deeper understanding of their customer base. They are learning what inspires customers to act, what time of the day they are most likely to engage with emails, and what content drives not just clicks but meaningful engagement that contributes to the bottom line.

The outcome? A more informed marketing team that can demonstrate a clear link between specific campaign elements and customer responses. The email marketing campaigns become more than just a tool for promotion—they become a dynamic conversation between LuxeVogue Retailers and their customers. This strategic approach, powered by data science, ultimately results in higher engagement rates, fostering an increase in sales and a robust ROI for their marketing efforts.

1.8 CONCLUSION

In the opening chapter of this book, we've set the stage by unveiling the intricacies of marketing data science, clarifying its essence, and drawing distinctions between it and the more conventional marketing analytics. Through a pair of illustrative examples, we aimed to shed light on the tremendous benefits that can be reaped when integrating data science approaches to address intricate marketing dilemmas.

As we progress further into the subsequent chapters, our focus will shift to a deeper exploration of the specific methodologies, instruments, and techniques that form the backbone of marketing data science. Our journey will span across a wide spectrum of subjects. We will dive into the mechanics of data gathering, the foundational principles of various analytics forms, the art of interpreting human language through machines, the realm of social media and website data analysis, and the intricate dance of marketing strategies, among others.

Throughout this book, readers will be presented with concrete examples coupled with illustrative depictions, aimed at explaining the tangible applications of the discussed techniques in the real business world. To enhance comprehension and contextual relevance, each chapter will be interspersed with real-world scenarios and case studies, meticulously curated to bridge the gap between theoretical concepts and their practical manifestations.

By the time you turn the final page of this book, it's the author's aspiration that you'll possess a comprehensive toolkit of knowledge, enabling you to adeptly employ marketing data science. This, in turn, will empower you to unearth critical business insights that can inform and enrich your marketing endeavors, subsequently driving business expansion and success.

1.9 REFERENCES

Chen, M., Mao, S., & Liu, Y. (2014). Big data: A survey. *Mobile Networks and Applications*, *19*(2), 171–209.

Dhar, V. (2013). Data science and prediction. *Communications of the ACM, 56*(12), 64–73.

Dolnicar, S., & Grün, B. (2008). Challenging "Factor-cluster segmentation." *Journal of Travel Research, 47*(1), 63–71.

Few, S. (2009). *Now you see it: Simple visualization techniques for quantitative analysis*. Analytics Press.

Hastie, T., Tibshirani, R., Friedman, J. H., & Friedman, J. H. (2009). *The elements of statistical learning: data mining, inference, and prediction* (Vol. 2). Springer.

Kelleher, J. D., Mac Namee, B., & D'Arcy, A. (2015). *Fundamentals of machine learning for predictive data analytics: Algorithms, worked examples, and case studies*. MIT Press.

Kotler, P., Keller, K. L., Ancarani, F., & Costabile, M. (2017). *Marketing management*. Pearson.

Leeflang, P.S.H., Wittink, D. R., Wedel, M., & Naert, P. A. (2009). *Building models for marketing decisions*. Springer Science & Business Media.

Liu, B. (2012). Sentiment analysis and opinion mining. *Synthesis Lectures on Human Language Technologies*, 5(1), 1–167.

Ngai, E.W.T., Xiu, L., & Chau, D.C.K. (2009). Application of data mining techniques in customer relationship management: A literature review and classification. *Expert Systems with Applications*, 36(2), 2592–2602.

Provost, F., & Fawcett, T. (2013). *Data science for business: What you need to know about data mining and data-analytic thinking*. O'Reilly Media.

Shmueli, G., & Koppius, O. R. (2011). Predictive analytics in information systems research. *MIS Quarterly*, 35(3), 553–572.

Shmueli, G., Patel, N. R., & Bruce, P. C. (2011). *Data mining for business intelligence: Concepts, techniques, and applications in Microsoft Office Excel with XLMiner*. Wiley.

Wedel, M., & Kannan, P. K. (2016). Marketing analytics for data-rich environments. *Journal of Marketing*, 80(6), 97–121.

CHAPTER 2

Data Collection and
Preparation

2.1 INTRODUCTION

The journey of data in the realm of marketing is reminiscent of the evolution of a diamond. Much like how a diamond begins as a lump of coal, subjected to heat and pressure to emerge as a brilliant gem, data too starts as a vast, often chaotic raw resource. With the right processes, it transforms into a treasure trove of insights. The comparison, however, goes further. Just as the value of a diamond is not merely in its discovery but in its careful cutting and polishing, the true power of data is not just in its collection but its diligent preparation.

Yet, in the race to keep up with an increasingly digitized marketplace, the importance of this meticulous collection and preparation process is often overlooked. Marketers are eager to jump into the deep waters of analytics, sometimes bypassing the foundational steps that ensure the quality of their results. But much like constructing a skyscraper on shaky ground, skipping or glossing over the data collection and preparation phase can result in unsteady, unreliable outcomes.

One might wonder, why is this process often sidelined? The reasons are multifaceted:

- **Ubiquity of data.** The omnipresence of data might give an illusion that it's always ready for use. With every click, like, share, purchase, and even scroll being recorded, there's a misconception that this data is instantly actionable.
- **Misplaced focus.** There's a certain allure to the advanced analytical tools and algorithms that promise immediate insights and results. The spotlight often shines brighter on these tools, leaving the foundational data processes in the shadow.
- **Underestimation of complexity.** Data collection and preparation is not merely about gathering vast quantities. It's about obtaining the *right* data and ensuring it's in the *right* form. This involves intricate decisions and steps that many underestimate.

However, these oversights can have significant repercussions. Faulty data collection or inadequate preparation can lead to biases, inaccuracies, and misconceptions, muddying the waters of insight and potentially leading to costly marketing mistakes. It is thus paramount to ensure that the data at hand is not only abundant but also well curated and aptly prepared for the analysis.

In this chapter, we delve into the heart of the marketing data science process—data collection and preparation. The quality, accuracy, and relevance of the data form the bedrock on which robust and effective marketing strategies are built. And although data is abundantly available in our digital world, its sheer volume and diversity can be both an advantage and a challenge.

The diversity and volume of data available in today's digital world offer a wealth of opportunities for informed decision-making in marketing. However, understanding the landscape of data sources is crucial for effective data collection and preparation. Figure 2.1 provides a visual representation of the estimated distribution of data sources used by organizations today. This figure helps illustrate the variety and prevalence of

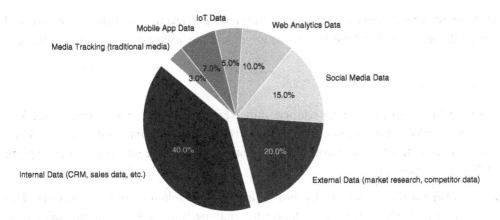

Figure 2.1 Estimated Distribution of Data Sources Used by Organizations Today.

different data types, highlighting where marketers often gather the information that forms the foundation of their data-driven strategies.

In this chapter, we will cover the following topics:

- **The variety of data sources.** Dive deep into myriad data reservoirs accessible to marketing data scientists, including internal organizational records, customer databases, external market research, social media feeds, and more.
- **Data collection techniques.** Understand the diverse methods available for data gathering—from traditional surveys to more modern tools such as web scraping, application programming interfaces (APIs), and even strategic data purchasing.
- **Data preparation best practices.** Discover how to transform raw data into a polished gem, ready for insights extraction. This encompasses data cleaning, data integration from multiple sources, transformation for better compatibility, and data reduction to focus on what truly matters.

Throughout this chapter, real-world case studies and examples will illuminate the principles discussed, providing a theoretical and practical understanding of each concept. These examples will offer a glimpse into how top-tier companies harness the power of well-collected and impeccably prepared data to drive their marketing strategies.

As you delve into the following sections, remember that the insights derived are only as good as the data they are based on. Much like a master jeweler would emphasize the importance of a diamond's cut and clarity, as marketing data scientists, our focus must be on the collection and refinement of our most valuable asset: data.

2.2 DATA SOURCES IN MARKETING: EVOLUTION AND THE EMERGENCE OF BIG DATA

Before diving into data collection, it is essential to understand the various sources of data that marketing data scientists can leverage. The evolution of data sources over the years has transformed the marketing landscape, with the emergence of big data and advanced analytics techniques opening new opportunities for marketers. In this section, we will discuss the traditional and modern data sources and the impact of big data on marketing.

2.2.1 Traditional Data Sources

In the realm of marketing data science, understanding and leveraging traditional data sources is critical. These sources, categorized as internal, external, and media tracking, have historically played a pivotal role in shaping marketing strategies. Let's explore each of these in detail:

- **Internal data.** Historically, organizations have relied heavily on internal data sources, such as customer relationship management (CRM) systems, sales data, and customer feedback, to inform their marketing strategies. These sources provide valuable insights into customer behavior, preferences, and purchase patterns (Kumar & Reinartz, 2018).
- **External data.** External data sources, such as market research reports, industry publications, and competitor information, have also played a crucial role in shaping marketing strategies. These sources offer insights into market trends, competitive landscapes, and customer demographics.
- **Media tracking.** Before the advent of the digital age, traditional media was the primary channel for mass communication. This included print publications, television broadcasts, and radio programs. Organizations placed immense value on tracking mentions and coverage in these mediums. By monitoring these sources, companies could gauge their brand presence, understand public perception, and evaluate the impact of their advertising campaigns. This was typically done with the help of media monitoring services and clipping agencies, which would provide businesses with compilations of all mentions or advertisements across various traditional media platforms. Analyzing this data helped in measuring campaign effectiveness, reputation management, and understanding the reach of their brand message in the broader market. Tracking media mentions also served as an early indicator of potential public relations issues or emerging trends in the industry. In many ways, media tracking was a precursor to today's social listening tools, emphasizing the timeless importance of understanding how a brand or product is perceived in the wider world.

2.2.2 The Emergence of Modern Data Sources

With the rapid growth of the internet, social media, and mobile technologies, new data sources have emerged, transforming the marketing data landscape (see Table 2.1):

- **Social media data.** Social media platforms, such as X (formerly Twitter), Facebook, and LinkedIn, generate vast amounts of user-generated content, likes, shares, and comments. This data can be used to analyze customer sentiment, preferences, and brand perception (Schultz & Peltier, 2013).

- **Web analytics data.** Web analytics tools, such as Google Analytics or Adobe Analytics, track user behavior, page views, bounce rates, and other website performance metrics. This data provides insights into customer engagement, user experience, and the effectiveness of online marketing efforts.
- **IoT data.** Internet-connected devices, such as smartwatches, sensors, and beacons, generate real-time data on customer behavior and preferences. This data can be used to personalize marketing efforts, optimize pricing strategies, and improve product development (Perera et al., 2015).
- **Mobile app data.** In the era of smartphones, mobile apps have become an integral part of consumers' daily lives. From social networking and online shopping to fitness tracking and entertainment, apps cater to a wide range of user needs. With this surge in mobile app use, the data generated from user interactions with apps has become a goldmine for marketers. Every tap, swipe, and action on an app provides insights into user preferences, behavior patterns, and engagement levels.

Table 2.1 Features, Advantages, and Limitations of Traditional Versus Modern Data Sources.

Aspect	Traditional Data Sources	Modern Data Sources
Features	Surveys Census Face-to-face interviews	Web analytics CRM systems Social media analytics
Advantages	Tried and tested Qualitative insights Direct feedback	Real-time insights Wide scope Quantitative data
Limitations	Time-consuming Limited scope Not real-time	Requires tech infrastructure Privacy concerns Misses qualitative insights

2.2.3 Big Data and Its Impact on Marketing

Big data refers to the massive and complex datasets that traditional data processing techniques cannot handle efficiently. It is often characterized by its volume (amount of data), variety (different types of data), and velocity (speed of data generation and processing). The emergence of big data has significantly affected the marketing landscape in several ways:

- **Enhanced customer understanding.** Big data enables organizations to collect and analyze diverse data sources, providing a more comprehensive and nuanced understanding of customers. This helps marketers develop more targeted and personalized marketing strategies (Russom, 2011).
- **Real-time decision-making.** With the ability to process and analyze data in real time, marketers can make data-driven decisions more quickly, enabling them to adapt and optimize their strategies in response to changing customer behavior or market conditions.

- **Advanced analytics techniques.** The growth of big data has led to the development of advanced analytics techniques, such as machine learning, natural language processing, and predictive analytics, which help marketers uncover deeper insights, make predictions, and optimize their strategies for maximum impact (Kelleher et al., 2020).

Although big data has undeniably opened new avenues and capabilities for marketers, it has also brought forth several challenges that organizations must address:

- **Data privacy issues.** With the accumulation of massive amounts of data, especially personal user data, comes the heightened responsibility of protecting that data. Data breaches can harm consumers and companies, leading to financial losses, reputational damage, and legal repercussions. Moreover, regulations such as General Data Protection Regulation (GDPR) in the European Union and California Consumer Privacy Act (CCPA) in the US impose stringent guidelines on data collection, storage, and use, requiring businesses to ensure that they are compliant (Fan et al., 2014).

- **Need for specialized skills.** The complexity and sheer volume of big data mean that traditional data analysis methods and tools are often inadequate. This has created a demand for specialized skills, such as expertise in advanced analytics, machine learning, and big data technologies. Hiring or training staff members with these competencies can be resource-intensive (Davenport, 2013).

- **Data accuracy and reliability concerns.** The vastness of big data sources increases the likelihood of encountering inaccurate, outdated, or misleading data. Relying on such data can lead to flawed insights and misguided marketing strategies. Organizations need robust data validation and cleansing processes to ensure the integrity of their data. Furthermore, due to the decentralized nature of data collection in a big data environment, there can be inconsistencies and redundancy in data, which pose challenges in achieving a single source of truth (Cai & Zhu, 2015).

In navigating the big data landscape, organizations must strike a balance. Although harnessing the power of big data can offer unparalleled insights and competitive advantages, it's crucial to address these challenges head-on, ensuring that data-driven marketing strategies are effective and responsible. It's worth noting that we will delve deeper into the intricacies, applications, and challenges of big data in Chapter 11, offering a comprehensive understanding for those keen to master its impact on modern marketing.

By understanding the evolution of data sources and the impact of big data on marketing, you will be better equipped to identify the most relevant data sources for your marketing data science projects and leverage them effectively to drive data-driven marketing strategies.

2.3 DATA COLLECTION METHODS

There are various methods to collect marketing data, each with its unique advantages and challenges. Choosing the right method depends on the specific data requirements of your marketing data science project, available resources, and the desired level of data quality and granularity. In this section, we will discuss the most common data collection methods in more detail.

2.3.1 Surveys and Questionnaires

Historically rooted in marketing research, surveys and questionnaires continue to be pivotal. Administered through a plethora of channels—from traditional methods such as telephonic routes, mail, or face-to-face to modern digital survey tools such as SurveyMonkey or Google Forms—such tools offer structured insights into consumer thought processes (Malhotra et al., 2017). Although cost-effective and scalable, they're potentially marred by biases, such as self-selection and nonresponse, often not offering a window into implicit consumer tendencies. However, the advantages of surveys include their relatively low cost, scalability, and the ability to collect structured data.

2.3.2 Web Scraping

Web scraping involves extracting data from websites and online platforms using automated tools and scripts. This method can be useful for collecting data on product listings, customer reviews, competitor pricing, and other publicly available information. Web scraping tools such as Beautiful Soup or Scrapy in Python are popular choices for this purpose (Mitchell, 2018). Although web scraping can yield large volumes of data, it may require technical expertise, and the quality and structure of the data may vary significantly across websites. There may be ethical and/or legal concerns when scraping certain websites without permission, which is also worth noting.

2.3.3 Application Programming Interfaces

APIs are a more structured and reliable way of accessing data from online platforms. Examples of widely used APIs include the Twitter API, which allows access to tweets, user profiles, and other public content; the Google Maps API, enabling the embedding of Google Maps on web pages with customized layers and markers; and the YouTube Data API, which lets developers retrieve YouTube content for integration into their own applications. These APIs, among others, cater to platforms such as social media sites, search engines, or e-commerce websites. APIs enable programmatic access to data, allowing developers to query and retrieve specific data points directly from the source. Although APIs often come with use limits and might require authentication, they typically provide more accurate, up-to-date, and structured data compared to web scraping.

2.3.4 Data Purchase

Purchasing data from third-party providers, such as market research firms, data brokers, or industry-specific data providers, can offer valuable external insights to complement internal data. These providers often have access to large, high-quality datasets that may be difficult or time-consuming to collect independently. However, purchasing data can be expensive, and the relevance and quality of the data must be carefully assessed before making a decision (Duhigg, 2012).

2.3.5 Observational Data

In some cases, data collection may involve observing customer behavior, interactions, or other activities, either in-person or through digital channels. Examples of observational data include in-store customer behavior, website user interactions, or social media engagement (Kotler & Keller, 2015). Observational data can provide valuable insights into customer preferences and behavior, but it may be time-consuming to collect and may require specialized tools or expertise to analyze.

▌ CASE STUDY: APPLE STORE OBSERVATIONAL STUDY

To better understand the customer experience and improve their in-store design and service, Apple conducted observational studies in its retail stores. Observers took note of how customers interacted with the products on display, the flow of traffic within the store, the points where customers seemed confused or needed assistance, and the areas where they congregated the most.

From these observations, Apple identified that customers often sought assistance right where they were standing, rather than approaching the designated counters. This insight led to the introduction of the "Genius Bars" positioned centrally in the store. Furthermore, they realized that customers appreciated being able to freely touch and try out devices, which solidified the open table design concept without enclosures for products.

This observational study directly influenced Apple's store layout and service model, optimizing the customer experience and store efficiency (Miles et al., 2019).

By understanding the strengths and limitations of each data collection method, you can choose the most appropriate approach for your marketing data science project, ensuring that you have access to accurate, relevant, and high-quality data to inform your analysis and decision-making (see Table 2.2).

Table 2.2 Data Collection Methods with Pros, Cons, Use Cases, and an Example.

Method	Pros	Cons	Use Cases	Example
Interviews	Deep insights Flexibility	Time-consuming Bias risks	Product feedback User experience	Job exit interviews
Focus groups	Group dynamics Multiple viewpoints	Hard to manage, Expensive	New product ideas Brand perception	Discussion on a new ad campaign
Online surveys	Wide reach Cost-effective	Low response rates Online bias	Market research Customer satisfaction	Feedback form on a website
Offline surveys	No internet dependency Physical presence	Logistically challenging Time-consuming	Rural studies In-person feedback	Survey in a local community event
Observational studies	Natural behavior Real context	Observer effect Subjectivity risks	User behavior Sociological studies	Watching shoppers in a store
Web scraping	Large-scale data Automation	Legal concerns Inconsistency	Competitor analysis Data mining	Extracting data from competitor websites
Sensors/IoT	Real-time data, Specific metrics	Expensive setup, Maintenance required	Smart homes, Health tracking	Wearable fitness trackers
Database queries	Structured data Consistency	Data might be outdated Limited scope	Business reports Performance metrics	Monthly sales query in a CRM
Archival research	Historical context Comprehensive	Not always digitized Can be fragmented	Historical studies Policy research	Researching old newspapers

2.4 DATA PREPARATION

Once the data is collected, it is crucial to prepare it for analysis to ensure its quality, accuracy, and relevance. Data preparation is a critical step in the marketing data science process, because it directly affects the effectiveness and reliability of the insights derived from data analysis. It's the process where raw, noisy, and often scattered data is transformed into a structured, clean, and usable format, ready for analysis or model training. The quality of the data fed into a machine learning algorithm significantly influences the model's performance. Thus, investing time in thorough data preparation often leads to more accurate and insightful results. In this section, we will explore the key steps involved in data preparation in more detail.

In Figure 2.2 the clean data is represented by the dark gray line, which follows a sine wave pattern, and the noisy data is shown in light gray, including random variations to represent the noise added to the clean signal.

2.4.1 Data Cleaning

Data cleaning is the process of identifying and addressing issues in the data, such as missing values, duplicate records, or incorrect data entries. Techniques for data cleaning include the following:

- **Imputation.** Filling in data gaps is essential to ensure the wholeness of a dataset. Although basic techniques such as replacing with means or medians are

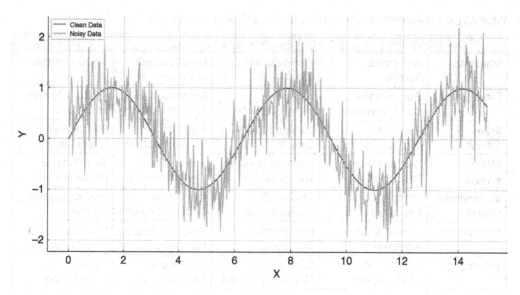

Figure 2.2 Noisy Versus Cleaned Data.

common, advanced machine learning algorithms can predict missing values
with higher accuracy (Batista & Monard, 2003).

- **Record linkage.** This technique ascertains that entries referring to the same
  real-world entity are represented as one, ensuring data consistency and reducing redundancy (Christen, 2012).
- **Outlier detection.** Outliers can skew results and interpretations. Although
  some outliers are genuine anomalies, others might be data errors. Techniques
  range from simple statistical measures to advanced clustering algorithms (Hodge
  & Austin, 2004).

As we explore the techniques used in data cleaning, it's important to visualize their
impact. Figure 2.3 presents a box plot that illustrates data before and after the removal
of outliers. This visual representation is key to understanding how outlier detection
techniques can significantly alter the structure and interpretation of a dataset, demonstrating the practical effects of these cleaning processes.

2.4.2 Data Integration

Data integration involves combining data from multiple sources, ensuring consistency,
accuracy, and completeness across all datasets. Techniques for data integration include
the following:

- **Data mapping.** A foundational step to ensure datasets speak the same language,
  data mapping harmonizes common fields across sources (Rahm & Do, 2000).
- **Data transformation.** Ensuring uniformity across datasets, transformation
  may involve standardizing units, formats, or scales. This step guarantees consistency and comparability of data (Kimball & Ross, 2013).

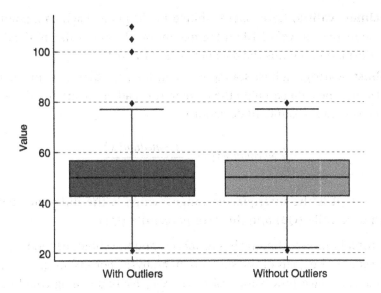

Figure 2.3 Data Before and After Outlier Removal.

- **Data deduplication.** Redundancies can cloud analysis. Deduplication ensures each data entry is distinct and unambiguous, optimizing the data structure for analysis (Elmagarmid et al., 2006).

2.4.3 Data Transformation

Data transformation involves converting the raw data into a format suitable for analysis. This step may include various operations, such as described in the next sections.

2.4.3.1 Normalization

Normalization, in the context of data preparation, refers to the process of adjusting numeric variables so that they can be compared on a common scale. This is pivotal for several machine learning algorithms, because they can be sensitive to variables measured at different scales. Different methods for normalization cater to various analytical needs and data distributions:

- **Min-max scaling.** This is perhaps the most intuitive form of normalization. For each data point, this method subtracts the minimum value of its feature and then divides by the range of that feature. As a result, the entire dataset is bounded within [0, 1]. The formula is

$$Normalized(x) = \frac{x - \min(x)}{\max(x) - \min(x)},$$

where x is a particular value, $\min(x)$ is the smallest value in that feature, and $\max(x)$ is the largest.

- **Decimal scaling.** Here, data is shifted by decimals. Each data point is divided by the highest power of 10 for the maximum absolute value in the dataset. This transformation bounds the data between −1 and 1.
- **Robust scaling.** Robust scaling is useful for data that contains many outliers and scales the data based on the median (instead of mean) and the interquartile range (instead of standard deviation).

$$Normalized(x) = \frac{x - median(x)}{IQR(x)},$$

where IQR is the interquartile range, which is the difference between the 75th percentile (Q3) and the 25th percentile (Q1).

Each normalization technique has its merits, and the choice depends on the nature of the dataset and the goals of the subsequent analysis. For instance, min-max scaling might be apt for image processing tasks, whereas decimal scaling could be beneficial when you want to reduce the order of magnitude of data points, making the dataset more manageable (Schneider, 2010).

2.4.3.2 Standardization

Standardization is the process of scaling features so they have the properties of a standard normal distribution with a mean of 0 and a standard deviation of 1. It's especially useful when working with algorithms sensitive to the scale of features, such as

USE CASE: MARKETING SPEND AND CLICK-THROUGH RATE ANALYSIS

Imagine a marketing department at a retail company is assessing the efficiency of its advertising channels. They've collected data on two primary metrics for each channel: the total marketing spend and the resulting click-through rate (CTR). The marketing spend is in thousands of dollars (ranging from $1,000 to $100,000) and the CTR is a percentage (ranging from 0% to 3%).

To understand which channel is providing the best return on investment, a machine learning model is being designed to predict the CTR based on the marketing spend. However, given the vast difference in the scales of these two metrics, a direct application of a model might lead to it being unduly influenced by the marketing spend figures due to their higher magnitude.

By applying min-max scaling, both the marketing spend and the CTR are normalized between 0 and 1. This ensures that the machine learning algorithm treats both features fairly, enabling a more accurate assessment of the relationship between marketing spend and CTR.

The outcome of this analysis, backed by a properly normalized dataset, might reveal that certain channels, though costlier, deliver a significantly better CTR, guiding the marketing team's future budget allocation decisions.

k-means clustering, support vector machines, or any algorithms that rely on distance calculations or gradient descent optimization.

- **Z-score normalization.** This is the most common form of standardization. For each feature, the mean is subtracted from each data point, and the result is divided by the standard deviation. The resulting z-score indicates how many standard deviations a data point is from the mean.

$$Z = \frac{X - \mu}{\sigma},$$

where

- Z is the standardized value.
- X is the original feature value.
- μ is the mean of the feature.
- σ is the standard deviation of the feature.
- **Robust scaling.** In the presence of outliers, standard z-score normalization might not work as intended because the mean and standard deviation are sensitive to extreme values. Robust scaling overcomes this by using median and interquartile range (IQR) instead.

$$X_{scaled} = \frac{X - X_{median}}{IQR},$$

where

- IQR is the interquartile range, which is the difference between the 75th percentile and the 25th percentile.
- **Unit vector scaling.** This approach scales the components of a feature vector such that the complete vector has a length of one. It's often used in text classification or clustering for sparse data.

$$X_{unit} = \frac{X}{\|X\|},$$

where

- $\|X\|$ is the Euclidean norm of the feature vector.

When deciding to standardize data, it's crucial to fit the scaler only to the training data and then apply the same transformation to the training and test datasets. This prevents data leakage, where information from the test set could influence the model during training, potentially leading to overly optimistic performance estimates.

In summary, standardization is an essential preprocessing step that can greatly improve the performance and stability of many machine learning algorithms by ensuring that features are on a consistent scale (Kelleher & Tierney, 2018).

■ **USE CASE: CREDIT SCORING MODEL IN BANKING**

Consider a bank that wants to develop a machine learning model to predict the creditworthiness of loan applicants. The dataset contains various features like annual income, credit utilization rate, and age:

- Annual income of the applicants ranges from $10,000 to $1,000,000.

- Credit utilization rate, which is the fraction of an individual's available credit they currently use, ranges between 0% to 100%.

- Age of the applicants ranges from 18 to 80 years.

When trying to cluster similar applicants using the k-means clustering algorithm (see Section 4.6.1), which is sensitive to the scale of data, the vast differences in the ranges of these features can skew the results. Specifically, the algorithm might prioritize annual income over other features simply due to its higher numeric values.

By standardizing these features using Z-score normalization, annual income, credit utilization rate, and age are adjusted to have a mean of 0 and a standard deviation of 1. This ensures that each feature contributes equally to the distance metric used in k-means.

After standardization, the bank finds that their clustering algorithm now identifies groups of applicants that have similar financial behaviors, making it easier to assign appropriate credit scores or interest rates.

Moreover, when the bank uses a model such as support vector machines (see Section 5.3.1.4) to predict loan defaults, standardized data ensures that the decision boundary is not disproportionately influenced by the scale of any single feature, leading to more accurate predictions.

Figure 2.4 displays two histograms representing the frequency distribution of a dataset before and after z-score normalization:

- The histogram on the left shows the frequency distribution of the original right-skewed data, with a concentration of values on the left side and a long tail to the right.

- The histogram on the right shows the frequency distribution after z-score normalization, where the data has been scaled to have a mean of 0 and a standard deviation of 1. This transformation does not change the shape of the distribution but centers the data on the mean and expresses the values in terms of standard deviations from the mean.

2.4.3.3 Encoding Categorical Variables

Before diving into the techniques of encoding categorical variables, it's essential to understand why this step is indispensable in data preprocessing. Categorical variables are ubiquitous in datasets, often representing qualitative attributes such as gender, nationality, product type, and more. Although these categories carry significant

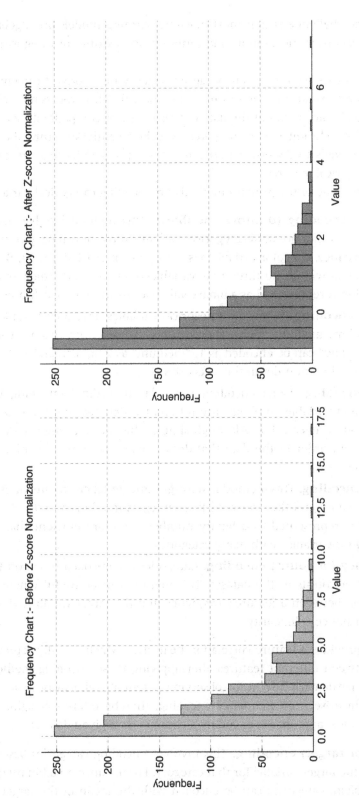

Figure 2.4 Data Before and After Z-Score Normalization.

information, the challenge is that most machine learning models are algebraic. This means they expect numerical inputs and cannot process strings or categorical data in their raw form.

To bridge this gap, we turn to encoding strategies, which convert categorical variables into numeric formats that algorithms can work with. This process not only retains the informative characteristics of the data but also ensures compatibility with various machine learning techniques. Encoding preserves the essential structure of categorical data, enabling models to discern patterns and make predictions that are contingent upon these categorical features.

Let's explore some of the primary methods for encoding categorical variables:

- **One-hot encoding (dummy variables).** This method involves converting each category of a nominal categorical variable into a new binary column (0 or 1). For instance, if a color variable has three categories (Red, Green, Blue), one-hot encoding will create three new variables—one for each color, where each observation is represented as a binary value across these new columns.

- **Ordinal encoding.** When the categorical variables have a clear rank or order (such as low, medium, high), they can be encoded with ordinal values. For example, "low" can be encoded as 1, "medium" as 2, and "high" as 3. This preserves the inherent order in the categories.

- **Label encoding.** Label encoding is similar to ordinal encoding but used for nominal variables without any inherent order. Every unique category is assigned an integer value. Although simple, this method might inadvertently introduce an order in the data that doesn't exist, potentially confusing some algorithms.

- **Binary encoding.** This method first assigns integer labels to categories (such as label encoding) and then converts these integers into binary code. Hence, each category is represented as a binary number. It's more efficient than one-hot encoding for variables with many categories.

- **Frequency (or count) encoding.** Categories are encoded based on their frequencies or counts in the dataset. This method can be useful when there's a correlation between a feature's frequency and the target variable. However, it might introduce collinearity.

Figure 2.5 provides a feature correlation heat map, which visually represents the correlations between different features after applying these encoding methods. This visualization is particularly useful for observing potential collinearity issues, such as those that might arise from frequency encoding, thereby offering insights into the selection of the most appropriate encoding technique for a given dataset.

- **Mean (or target) encoding.** This involves encoding categories based on the mean of the target variable for that category. For instance, in a binary classification problem, categories can be encoded with the mean of the target variable

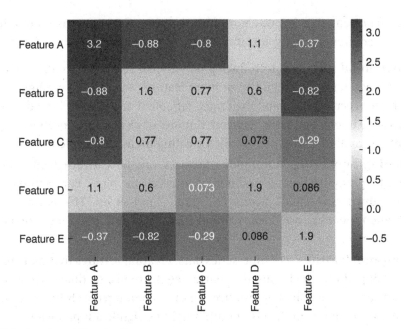

Figure 2.5 Feature Correlation Heat Map.

(0 or 1) for each category. Although powerful, it can lead to overfitting, so care must be taken, and it's essential to use techniques such as regularization or adding noise to the encoded values.

- **Embedding layers.** Deep learning models, especially neural networks, allow for the use of embedding layers to handle categorical variables. An embedding layer learns a multidimensional representation of each category during the training process, which can be especially useful for handling high cardinality categorical variables.

When encoding categorical variables, it's essential to consider the algorithm's nature and the data. Some algorithms can handle categorical data directly, and others might be sensitive to the numerical values assigned through encoding, potentially leading to misinterpretations. Properly encoding categorical variables is crucial for building a predictive model that accurately captures underlying patterns and relationships in the data (Kuhn & Johnson, 2019). By applying these encoding techniques, we facilitate a smooth transition from non-numeric data to formats that can be readily processed by statistical models, paving the way for more accurate and insightful data analysis.

2.4.3.4 Feature Engineering

Feature engineering is the art of creating new features from existing ones, enhancing the predictive power of machine learning models. By converting raw data into more suitable or representative forms, algorithms can often find patterns more effectively. This process requires creativity, intuition, and domain expertise.

- **Polynomial features.** Introducing polynomial terms (squared, cubed, etc.) or interaction terms between two or more features can capture nonlinear relationships between features and the target variable. For instance, if predicting house prices, an interaction term between 'number of rooms' and 'location' might capture the combined effect better than treating them independently.

- **Binning/bucketing.** Continuous features can be converted into categorical ones by grouping them into different intervals or 'bins'. For example, age can be grouped into 'child', 'teenager', 'adult', and so on. This is especially useful when there are nonlinear relationships across different ranges of a continuous variable.

- **Temporal features.** For time-series data, creating features that capture seasonality (day of the week, month, quarter, etc.), trends, or time since a particular event can be valuable. For instance, for an e-commerce website, 'days since last visit' or 'purchases in the last month' might be significant predictors.

- **Text features.** Text data can be transformed into numerical features using techniques such as TF-IDF (term frequency-inverse document frequency), word embeddings (for example Word2Vec), or bag-of-words. These methods capture the semantics and context of the text in a form that algorithms can work with.

- **Geospatial features.** If dealing with location data, new features such as 'distance from a particular landmark', 'density of a specific amenity in the vicinity', or 'proximity to a public transit route' can be insightful.

- **Aggregation.** Creating summarized features over a set, like 'mean transaction value over the past six months', 'maximum heart rate in the last 10 minutes', or 'frequency of a particular event' can add significant predictive power.

- **Decomposition.** Techniques like PCA (principal component analysis) or T-SNE can be used to reduce the dimensionality of the data, creating new features that retain the maximum variability of the original data.

- **Domain-specific features.** Depending on the specific problem or industry, certain custom features may be created. For instance, in finance, features such as P/E ratios or moving averages might be used. In health care, BMI (body mass index) can be calculated from height and weight.

Incorporating feature engineering can substantially enhance model performance (see Figure 2.6). However, it's essential to ensure that the features are not overly complex, which can lead to overfitting. Regular consultation with domain experts and iterative model testing can help in refining and validating the efficacy of engineered features (Kuhn & Johnson, 2019).

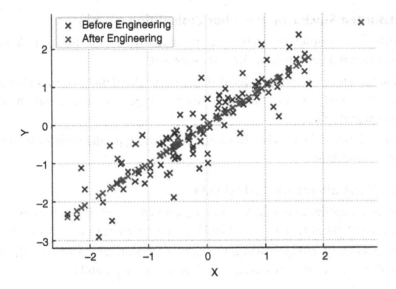

Figure 2.6 Data Before and After Feature Engineering.

2.4.4 Data Reduction

Data reduction involves reducing the complexity and size of the dataset while retaining its key information. Techniques for data reduction include the following.

2.4.4.1 Dimensionality Reduction

Dimensionality reduction refers to the process of transforming high-dimensional data into a lower-dimensional form while retaining as much of the relevant information as possible. This reduction can lead to simpler models, improved performance, and better interpretability. Here's a more detailed breakdown:

Principal Component Analysis (PCA)

- PCA is a linear technique that identifies the "principal components" of the data, which are orthogonal (perpendicular) to each other and capture the maximum variance in the data.
- It reprojects the data onto these principal components, often reducing the dimensionality considerably.
- Although the first few principal components usually capture the bulk of the variance in the dataset, they may not always be interpretable in the context of the original features.
- PCA is particularly useful for continuous variables and when there's a need to eliminate multicollinearity.

t-Distributed Stochastic Neighbor Embedding (t-SNE)

- t-SNE is a nonlinear technique particularly useful for visualizing high-dimensional data in two or three dimensions.
- It emphasizes retaining the local structure of the data, ensuring that instances that are close in the high-dimensional space remain close in the low-dimensional space.
- Although powerful for visualization, t-SNE isn't typically used for feature reduction in modeling.

Linear Discriminant Analysis (LDA)

- LDA is a classifier and a dimensionality reduction technique. It aims to find the linear combinations of features that best separate two or more classes in a dataset.
- It is particularly effective when the classes are well separated, and the objective is both to reduce dimensions and maintain class separability.

Autoencoders

- Autoencoders are neural networks used for dimensionality reduction. They're designed to learn efficient codings or compressions of input data, then decode or reconstruct the data from these codings.
- The middle layer represents the compressed form of the input data. Autoencoders are versatile and can capture linear and nonlinear patterns in the data.

Feature Selection

- Although not a transformation technique like the others, feature selection involves retaining a subset of the original features based on their importance, variance, or relevance to the target variable.
- Techniques include backward elimination, forward selection, recursive feature elimination, and using tree-based models (such as decision trees or random forests) to rank feature importance.
- It's worth noting that feature selection retains the original, interpretable features, unlike methods such as PCA.

The choice of dimensionality reduction technique often depends on the nature of the problem, the characteristics of the data, and the goals of the analysis.

2.4.4.2 Sampling

Sampling is the technique of selecting a subset from a larger dataset to make data analysis more manageable or cost-effective. Different sampling methods serve various needs:

- **Simple random sampling.** Every data point has an equal chance of being selected, which is useful when there's no need to focus on specific subgroups. *Example:* Imagine a bowl containing 1,000 colored marbles (each representing a data point). Close your eyes and pick 100 marbles. This is your random sample.

- **Stratified sampling.** The dataset is divided into subgroups, and samples are taken from each. This is great for ensuring all subgroups are represented, such as age or gender categories. *Example:* Suppose you have a school with 1,000 students, 500 males and 500 females. If you want to sample 100 students, you could take 50 from each gender group to ensure both genders are equally represented.

- **Cluster sampling.** Data is divided into clusters, and a few clusters are randomly picked for study. This is handy when data spans large areas, such as studying shoppers in certain cities. *Example:* If you're studying retail buying habits in a country with 50 cities, you might randomly select 5 cities (clusters) and then survey all customers or a random sample of customers in each of those selected cities.

- **Systematic sampling.** Choose every nth item from a list. This is useful for regular intervals, such as checking every 10th product off an assembly line. *Example:* You're quality checking items on a production line that produces 1,000 items a day. You decide to check every 10th item, so you'll inspect the 10th, 20th, 30th item, and so on.

- **Convenience sampling.** This helps to choose data that's easiest to get. The method is quick but can be biased. It is often used for preliminary studies. *Example:* A soft drink company sets up a tasting booth at a mall and asks passersby to taste and give feedback. Here, they're sampling whoever comes to the booth, which is convenient but not necessarily representative of the broader market.

- **Quota sampling.** Select samples based on certain criteria or quotas. This method is used to ensure certain categories, such as age groups, are covered in the sample. *Example:* A TV network wants feedback on a new show. They decide they need 100 viewers from each age group: 18–30, 31–50, and 51+. They then sample viewers until they meet this quota for each group.

When sampling, it's essential to pick the right method and size to ensure your sample represents the larger dataset accurately.

2.4.4.3 Aggregation

Aggregation is the process of transforming raw data into a summarized or higher-level form to make it more comprehensible and to reduce its size for analysis. It is particularly useful in cases where detailed data is more granular than needed for specific analyses. Here's a deeper look:

Purpose of Aggregation

- **Simplification.** Aggregated data is more manageable and easier to analyze.
- **Reduction.** By summarizing data, you reduce the volume, making processing and visualization quicker.

- **Enhanced privacy.** Aggregating data can help in anonymizing personal details, protecting individuals' privacy.

Common Aggregation Techniques

- **Sum.** Total of a particular set of numbers.
- **Average.** Mean value of a set.
- **Max/min.** Highest and lowest values in a set.
- **Count.** Number of occurrences or items in a set.
- **Median.** The middle value in a sorted list.
- **Mode.** Most frequently occurring value in a set.

Temporal Aggregation

- This involves summarizing data over time. For example, daily sales figures can be aggregated to give monthly or yearly totals.
- This is useful for spotting longer-term trends and patterns.

Spatial Aggregation

- This means summarizing data over spatial regions. For instance, city-level data might be aggregated to provide a view at the country level.
- This helps in analyzing geographical trends and patterns.

Categorical Aggregation

- This groups data based on categories, for example, aggregating sales data by product type.
- It is useful for understanding how different categories perform relative to each other.

Challenges

- **Loss of detail.** Aggregation can cause a loss of finer details. Although this is often the intent, it's important to ensure the granularity is still appropriate for the analysis.
- **Risk of misinterpretation.** Aggregated data can sometimes mask outliers or anomalies that might be significant.
- **Balancing act.** It's crucial to strike a balance between over-aggregation, which can hide useful insights, and under-aggregation, which can overwhelm with too much detail.

Aggregation is a fundamental concept in data science, especially in marketing where there's often a need to present data in a digestible and actionable format. Deciding on the level of aggregation requires a keen understanding of the data and the business questions being addressed.

By following these best practices for data preparation, you can ensure that your marketing data science projects are built on a solid foundation of accurate, relevant, and high-quality data, enabling you to derive reliable insights and make data-driven decisions that drive significant business value.

Data preparation can be a time-consuming and complex process, but investing the necessary effort and resources in this stage will pay dividends in the long run by improving the accuracy, relevance, and effectiveness of your marketing data science initiatives. By using the right tools, techniques, and best practices, you can transform raw, unstructured data into valuable information that empowers your organization to make better decisions and achieve its marketing goals.

In summary, the process of data preparation involves cleaning, integrating, transforming, and reducing data to ensure that it is accurate, relevant, and ready for analysis. By carefully preparing your data, you will lay the foundation for successful marketing data science projects and ensure that the insights you derive from your data are reliable, actionable, and impactful.

2.5 PRACTICAL EXAMPLE: COLLECTING AND PREPARING DATA FOR A CUSTOMER CHURN ANALYSIS

A telecommunications company wants to analyze customer churn by studying patterns in customer behavior and use data. As we delve into the meticulous process of data preparation for customer churn analysis, it's illustrative to examine a snapshot of the raw data that the telecommunications company encounters. Table 2.3 presents a sample of such raw data, showcasing a subset of records that include potential problems to be addressed in the data preparation steps. This table provides a real-world perspective of the types of challenges commonly faced, such as missing values, duplicates, and incorrect entries, and sets the stage for understanding how these issues are identified and rectified. To collect and prepare the necessary data, they follow these steps:

1. **Data collection.** The company collects customer data from their CRM system, billing records, call detail records, and customer feedback surveys. Additionally, they collect data on competitors' pricing and promotions through web scraping and third-party providers.

2. **Data integration.** They merge the collected data into a unified dataset, ensuring consistency and accuracy across all sources.

3. **Data cleaning.** The company identifies and addresses issues such as missing values, duplicates, and incorrect data entries.

4. **Data transformation.** They transform the raw data into a format suitable for analysis, normalizing numeric variables, encoding categorical variables, and engineering new features, such as average call duration, monthly spend, and the number of customer service interactions.

5. **Data reduction.** The company reduces the complexity and size of the dataset by selecting relevant features, using dimensionality reduction techniques, and aggregating data where appropriate.

Table 2.3 Sample Raw Data for the Customer Churn Analysis, Showing a Subset of Records That Include Potential Problems to Be Addressed in the Data Preparation Steps.

Customer ID	Age	Subscription Duration (days)	Average Monthly Usage	Last Login	Feedback Score	Churned
1	62.0	100	78	2022–01–31	4.0	False
2	18.0	118	73	2022–02–28	1.0	False
3	21.0	344	10	2022–03–31	2.0	True
4	NaN	223	21	2022–04–30	4.0	False
5	57.0	69	81	2022–05–31	NaN	True
6	27.0	117	70	2022–06–30	4.0	True
7	37.0	204	80	2022–07–31	4.0	False
8	39.0	118	48	2022–08–31	1.0	False
9	54.0	195	65	2022–09–30	2.0	True
10	41.0	55	83	2022–10–31	2.0	False

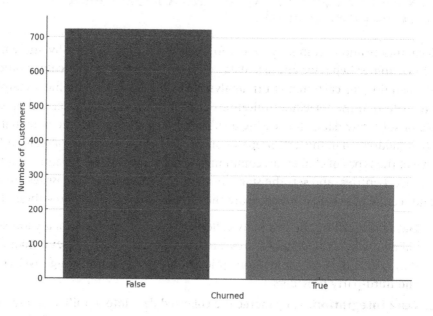

Figure 2.7 Distribution of Churned Versus Retained Customers in the Cleaned and Prepared Dataset.

Figure 2.7 shows the distribution of churned versus retained customers in the cleaned and prepared dataset.

- The True bars represent customers who churned.
- The False bars represent customers who were retained.

From the visualization, we can infer that a larger proportion of customers were retained, and a smaller proportion was churned.

By collecting and preparing the data effectively, the telecommunications company can ensure that their marketing data science team has access to accurate, relevant, and high-quality data for their customer churn analysis. This, in turn, will enable them to develop data-driven strategies to reduce churn and improve customer retention.

2.6 CONCLUSION

In conclusion, the intricate process of data collection and preparation forms the backbone of effective marketing data science. The initial chapters of this book have laid out a road map through the multifaceted terrain of data sources, providing clarity on how the advent of big data has revolutionized the marketing landscape. As we dissected the various methodologies for data acquisition—from the traditional surveys to the cutting-edge APIs and beyond—we illuminated the strengths and potential pitfalls inherent in each approach.

The latter part of the chapter served as a deep dive into the meticulous art of data preparation. This crucial phase, often underestimated, is where raw data is refined into a strategic asset. Through cleaning, integration, transformation, and reduction, data ceases to be a mere by-product of business operations and becomes the lifeblood of strategic decision-making.

It is here, in the trenches of data wrangling, that the foundation for sophisticated analytics is laid. By mastering these initial steps, the marketing data scientist transforms noise into a symphony of insights, paving the way for actionable strategies that resonate with precision and efficacy.

As we turn the page to subsequent chapters, we carry with us the understanding that thorough data preparation is not a mere preliminary step but a continuous process that runs parallel to all marketing data science activities. The diligence and foresight applied here echo through the life cycle of data analysis, influencing the accuracy of predictions, the relevance of insights, and the potency of marketing strategies.

Therefore, let this chapter serve as a testament and a guide to the transformative power of well-harvested and meticulously curated data. As we venture deeper into the realms of advanced analytics, machine learning, and beyond, the lessons learned here will be the guiding stars that ensure the integrity and success of your data-driven marketing endeavors.

2.7 REFERENCES

Batista, G. E., & Monard, M. C. (2003). An analysis of four missing data treatment methods for supervised learning. *Applied Artificial Intelligence, 17*(5–6), 519–533.

Cai, L., & Zhu, Y. (2015). The challenges of data quality and data quality assessment in the big data era. *Data Science Journal, 14*, article 2.

Christen, P. (2012). *Data matching: Concepts and techniques for record linkage, entity resolution, and duplicate detection.* Springer Science & Business Media.

Davenport, T. H. (2013). Analytics 3.0. *Harvard Business Review, 91*(12), 64–72.

Duhigg, C. (2012). How companies learn your secrets. *New York Times Magazine*, February 16. http://www.nytimes.com/2012/02/19/magazine/shopping-habits.html

Elmagarmid, A. K., Ipeirotis, P. G., & Verykios, V. S. (2006). Duplicate record detection: A survey. *IEEE Transactions on Knowledge and Data Engineering, 19*(1), 1–16.

Fan, J., Han, F., & Liu, H. (2014). Challenges of big data analysis. *National Science Review, 1*(2), 293–314.

Hodge, V. J., & Austin, J. (2004). A survey of outlier detection methodologies. *Artificial Intelligence Review, 22*(2), 85–126.

Kelleher, J. D., Mac Namee, B., & D'arcy, A. (2020). *Fundamentals of machine learning for predictive data analytics: Algorithms, worked examples, and case studies.* MIT Press.

Kelleher, J. D., & Tierney, B. (2018). *Data science.* MIT Press.

Kimball, R., & Ross, M. (2013). *The data warehouse toolkit: The definitive guide to dimensional modeling.* Wiley.

Kotler, P., & Keller, K. L. (2015). *Framework for marketing management.* Pearson.

Kuhn, M., & Johnson, K. (2019) *Feature engineering and selection: A practical approach for predictive models.* CRC Press.

Kumar, V., & Reinartz, W. (2018). *Customer relationship management.* Springer-Verlag Germany.

Malhotra, N. K., Nunan, D., & Birks, D. F. (2017). *Marketing research: An applied approach.* Pearson.

Miles, D. A., Garcia, J., Olagundoye, E., Brown, J., Clay, J., Cook, L., . . . & Platt, P. (2019). Market research and applied statistics: The Apple Store vs. the Microsoft Store—A market research study on consumer behavior and retailer sales behavior. *Journal of Marketing Perspectives, 1*, 75–99.

Mitchell, R. (2018). *Web scraping with Python: Collecting more data from the modern web.* O'Reilly Media.

Perera, C., Liu, C. H., & Jayawardena, S. (2015). The emerging internet of things marketplace from an industrial perspective: A survey. *IEEE Transactions on Emerging Topics in Computing, 3*(4), 585–598.

Rahm, E., & Do, H. H. (2000). Data cleaning: Problems and current approaches. *IEEE Data Eng. Bulletin, 23*(4), 3–13.

Russom, P. (2011). Big data analytics. *TDWI Best Practices Report, 19*(4), 1–34.

Schultz, D. E., & Peltier, J. J. (2013). Social media's slippery slope: Challenges, opportunities and future research directions. *Journal of Research in Interactive Marketing, 7*(2), 86–99.

Schneider, T. D. (2010). A brief review of molecular information theory. *Nano Communication Networks, 1*(3), 173–180.

EXERCISE 2.1: DATA CLEANING AND TRANSFORMATION

Objective: Clean and transform a dataset to prepare it for analysis.

Tasks:

1. Handle missing values (**NaN**) in the "**data_cleaning_transfomation.csv**" dataset.
2. Convert the 'Last Login Date' from a string to a datetime object.
3. Create a new feature, 'Monthly Spend per Day', by dividing 'Monthly Spend' by 'Subscription Length'.

Steps:

1. **Importing Required Libraries:**

```
1. import pandas as pd
```

- **pandas** is used for data manipulation and analysis.

2. **Loading the Data:**

```
2. data_exercise_1 = pd.read_csv('path_to_csv_file')
```

This line of code reads the CSV file containing the data into a Pandas DataFrame, enabling us to work with the data in Python.

3. **Handling Missing Values:**

- **Filling Missing 'Age' Values:**

```
3. mean_age = data_exercise_1['Age'].mean()
4. data_exercise_1['Age'].fillna(mean_age, inplace=True)
```

Here, we calculate the mean of the 'Age' column and fill missing values (**NaN**) in the 'Age' column with this mean. This approach is chosen as age data typically follows a normal distribution, making the mean a good estimate for missing values.

- **Filling Missing 'Monthly Spend' Values:**

```
5. median_monthly_spend = data_exercise_1['Monthly Spend ($)'].median()
6. data_exercise_1['Monthly Spend ($)'].fillna(median_monthly_spend, inplace=True)
```

We fill missing values in 'Monthly Spend ($)' with the median, because financial data often has outliers, and the median is less sensitive to them compared to the mean.

- **Filling Missing 'Feedback Score' Values:**

```
7. mode_feedback = data_exercise_1['Feedback Score'].mode()[0]
8. data_exercise_1['Feedback Score'].fillna(mode_feedback, inplace=True)
```

For the 'Feedback Score' we use the mode (the most frequently occurring value) to fill in missing values, because this score likely represents categorical or ordinal data.

4. **Converting 'Last Login Date' to DateTime:**

```
9. data_exercise_1['Last Login Date'] = pd.to_datetime(data_
exercise_1['Last Login Date'])
```

The 'Last Login Date' is initially read as a string. This line converts it to a Pandas DateTime object, making it easier to perform any date-related operations later.

5. **Creating New Feature: 'Monthly Spend per Day':**

```
10. data_exercise_1['Monthly Spend per Day'] = data_
exercise_1['Monthly Spend ($)'] / data_exercise_1['Subscription
Length (days)']
```

We create a new column, 'Monthly Spend per Day' by dividing the 'Monthly Spend ($)' by 'Subscription Length (days)'. This new feature gives additional insight into customer spending habits on a per-day basis.

These steps comprehensively cover the data cleaning and feature engineering processes necessary for preparing the dataset for further analysis.

EXERCISE 2.1: OUTPUT

The output of the Python code for Exercise 2.1 is as follows.

The DataFrame now reflects the changes made during the data cleaning and transformation process:

```
# Display the first few rows of the dataset
data.head()
```

Customer ID	Age	Subscription Length (days)	Monthly Spend ($)	Last Login Date	Feedback Score	Monthly Spend per Day
1	62.00	260	112.89	2022–01–01	5.0	0.434
2	42.95	180	288.36	2022–01–02	5.0	1.602
3	18.00	60	72.97	2022–01–03	1.0	1.216
4	21.00	285	199.07	2022–01–04	3.0	0.698
5	21.00	49	194.15	2022–01–05	5.0	3.962

Here's a brief summary of the transformations:

- **Handling Missing Values:** Missing values in 'Age', 'Monthly Spend ($)', and 'Feedback Score' were filled with the mean, median, and mode of their respective columns.

- **Date Conversion:** 'Last Login Date' was converted from a string to a DateTime object for better handling of date-related operations.
- **New Feature Creation:** A new column, 'Monthly Spend per Day', was added to the DataFrame, calculated by dividing 'Monthly Spend ($)' by 'Subscription Length (days)'. This new feature provides additional insights into customer spending behavior.

EXERCISE 2.2: DATA AGGREGATION AND REDUCTION

Objective: Perform data aggregation and dimensionality reduction on a marketing dataset.

Tasks:

1. Aggregate the "**data_aggregation_reduction.csv**" data by 'Region' and calculate the average 'Monthly Spend' and total 'Purchase Frequency' per region.
2. Perform a principal component analysis (PCA) to reduce the dimensions of the data while retaining key information.

Steps:

1. **Importing Required Libraries:**

```
1. import pandas as pd
2. from sklearn.decomposition import PCA
3. import matplotlib.pyplot as plt
```

- **pandas** is used for data manipulation and analysis again.
- **PCA** from **sklearn.decomposition** is a dimension reduction technique.
- **matplotlib** is used for visualization.

2. **Loading the Data:**

```
4. data_exercise_2 = pd.read_csv('path_to_csv_file')
```

This line reads the CSV file containing the data for Exercise 2.2 into a Pandas DataFrame, enabling data manipulation and analysis.

3. **Data Aggregation:**

- **Aggregating by 'Region':**

```
5. region_aggregated_data = data_exercise_2.groupby('Region').
agg( Average_Monthly_Spend=pd.NamedAgg(column='Monthly
Spend ($)', aggfunc='mean'), Total_Purchase_Frequency=pd.
NamedAgg(column='Purchase Frequency', aggfunc='sum') ).reset_
index()
```

Here, we group the data by the 'Region' column and calculate two aggregate metrics: the average 'Monthly Spend ($)' and the total 'Purchase Frequency' for each region. The **groupby** and **agg** functions in Pandas are used to achieve this, providing a summary of spending and purchasing behavior by region.

4. **Data Reduction using Principal Component Analysis (PCA):**

■ **Preparing Data for PCA:**

```
6. pca_data = data_exercise_2[['Monthly Spend ($)', 'Purchase
Frequency']]
```

We select only the numeric columns 'Monthly Spend ($)' and 'Purchase Frequency' for PCA.

■ **Standardizing the Data:**

```
7. pca_data_standardized = (pca_data-pca_data.mean()) / pca_
data.std()
```

PCA is sensitive to the scale of the data so we standardize the features to have a mean of 0 and a standard deviation of 1.

■ **Performing PCA:**

```
8. pca = PCA(n_components=2)
9. principal_components = pca.fit_transform(pca_data_
standardized)
```

We instantiate a PCA object to reduce the data to two dimensions. The **fit_transform** method computes the principal components and transforms the data accordingly.

■ **Creating DataFrame with Principal Components:**

```
10. principal_df = pd.DataFrame(data=principal_components,
columns=['Principal Component 1', 'Principal Component 2'])
```

The resulting principal components are stored in a new DataFrame. These components are the transformed data points in the new two-dimensional space.

The first part of the code provides an aggregated view of the data by region, useful for regional analysis. The second part, PCA, reduces the dimensionality of the data, enabling easier visualization and potentially revealing intrinsic patterns or relationships not evident in the high-dimensional space.

EXERCISE 2.2: OUTPUT

The output of the Python code for Exercise 2.2 is as follows:

1. **Data Aggregation Result:** This table shows the aggregated data by region, including the average monthly spend and the total purchase frequency per region.

Region	Average Monthly Spend	Total Purchase Frequency
East	273.57	2,423
North	264.17	2,645
South	290.11	2,712
West	265.98	2,464

2. The table provides a summary of consumer behavior in different regions, highlighting differences in spending and purchasing frequency.

3. **Principal Component Analysis (PCA) Result:** The following table shows the first five rows of the dataset after applying PCA, reducing the data to two principal components.

Principal Component 1	Principal Component 2
−0.559	−0.955
0.364	1.279
−0.096	−2.208
−0.313	−0.413
−0.354	0.155

4. These two principal components represent the transformed dataset in a two-dimensional space. This transformation helps in visualizing and analyzing the data in a reduced form, making it easier to identify patterns or clusters.

CHAPTER **3**

Descriptive Analytics in Marketing

3.1   INTRODUCTION

Descriptive analytics serves as the cornerstone of the marketing data science process. It involves a meticulous examination of historical data to discern and illustrate key patterns, trends, and relationships. This foundational analytical technique is essential for marketers who seek to obtain a panoramic understanding of customer behavior, market conditions, and the efficiency of marketing initiatives. By leveraging descriptive analytics, marketers can unearth insights that drive informed decision-making and fine-tune their marketing strategies for enhanced impact (Chaffey & Ellis-Chadwick, 2019; Wedel & Kannan, 2016).

This chapter unfolds the multifaceted aspects of descriptive analytics within the marketing realm, blending theory with practical application. We shall dissect key concepts, delve into robust techniques, and showcase the pivotal applications of descriptive analytics in marketing. Each section is fortified with practical examples and illustrative visual aids, bringing to life the principles and techniques discussed.

The strategic advantage conferred by descriptive analytics cannot be overstated. It is the analytical bedrock that sets the stage for more sophisticated approaches, such as predictive and prescriptive analytics. These advanced stages of analytics, which anticipate future events and recommend optimal marketing actions, build on the insights gleaned from descriptive analysis (Sharda et al., 2021). Mastery of descriptive analytics is not just about understanding the past—it's about shaping the future. It empowers marketers with the acumen to identify areas ripe for improvement, seize on burgeoning trends, and amplify the efficacy of marketing endeavors (Kotler et al., 2016).

Our journey through this chapter will encompass an exploration of descriptive statistics, which reveal the central tendencies, dispersion, and shape of your data distributions. We will also navigate the realm of data visualization, illustrating the power of graphs, charts, and interactive platforms to communicate complex information clearly and effectively. Furthermore, we will critically analyze the performance of marketing campaigns, learning how to measure and interpret their success accurately.

We will immerse ourselves in the real-world application of these concepts, learning not just the what but the how of applying these techniques in marketing data science projects. By understanding the various facets of descriptive analytics, you will be equipped to transform raw data into actionable insights that propel your marketing strategies forward. This chapter serves as a comprehensive guide through the vibrant landscape of descriptive analytics, providing not only a foundational understanding but also practical insights into how these techniques can be applied effectively in marketing data science projects. By delving into the role of descriptive analytics in marketing, you'll learn to transform raw data into actionable insights, thereby laying a solid groundwork for the more advanced analytics topics that will be explored in subsequent chapters of this book.

3.2 OVERVIEW OF DESCRIPTIVE ANALYTICS

3.2.1 The Role of Descriptive Analytics in Marketing

Descriptive analytics plays a vital role in the marketing data science process by providing a comprehensive understanding of historical data. It enables marketers to summarize, visualize, and interpret key patterns, trends, and relationships in their data, laying the groundwork for more advanced analytics techniques, such as predictive and prescriptive analytics. Descriptive analytics is essential for the following reasons:

- Understanding customer behavior and preferences
- Identifying market trends and competitive dynamics
- Evaluating the effectiveness of marketing campaigns and strategies
- Informing data-driven decision-making in marketing

By providing a clear picture of historical data, descriptive analytics enables marketers to gain insights into the factors that drive customer engagement, loyalty, and sales, so they can make better-informed decisions and optimize their marketing efforts. As we explore the impact of descriptive analytics on marketing, it is enlightening to compare it with other types of analytics—predictive and prescriptive—that are also crucial in this domain. Table 3.1 offers a comprehensive comparison of these three types of analytics: descriptive, predictive, and prescriptive. It outlines their key features, uses in marketing, and the distinct roles they play. This table not only clarifies the definition and purpose of each type but also details the methods and techniques involved, along with the outcomes and specific use cases in marketing. Such a comparison provides a clear framework for understanding where descriptive analytics fits within the wider

Table 3.1 Different Types of Analytics—Descriptive, Predictive, and Prescriptive—with Their Key Features and Uses in Marketing.

Dimensions	Descriptive Analytics	Predictive Analytics	Prescriptive Analytics
Definition	Analyzes historical data to understand what has happened	Uses historical data to predict future outcomes	Recommends actions based on analysis to achieve desired outcomes
Purpose	To summarize and understand past behavior	To forecast future events or behaviors	To advise on potential future actions
Methods/ techniques	Statistics Data aggregation Visualization	Regression Machine learning Time series analysis	Optimization Simulation Decision trees
Outcome	Reports Dashboards Charts	Predictions Probability scores	Recommendations Decision models
Use cases in marketing	Market trend analysis Customer segmentation Sales performance analysis	Sales forecasting Customer churn prediction Lead scoring	Pricing optimization Campaign targeting Inventory management

analytics spectrum and how it complements other analytical approaches in driving effective marketing strategies.

3.2.2   Key Techniques in Descriptive Analytics

Descriptive analytics employs various techniques to analyze and summarize marketing data:

- **Descriptive statistics.** These are mathematical measures used to summarize and describe key characteristics of a dataset, such as measures of central tendency (mean, median, mode), measures of dispersion (range, variance, standard deviation), and measures of association (correlation, covariance).
- **Data visualization.** This involves the graphical representation of data using charts, plots, and maps to help marketers quickly identify patterns, trends, and relationships in their data. Common data visualization techniques include bar charts, line charts, scatterplots, and heat maps.
- **Data aggregation.** This is the process of summarizing data at a higher level of granularity, such as aggregating daily sales data to a monthly level or customer-level data to a segment level. Data aggregation helps marketers simplify their data and focus on the most important trends and patterns.

3.2.3   The Importance of Data Visualization

Data visualization is a critical component of descriptive analytics, because it enables marketers to quickly and effectively communicate complex data in a visually appealing and easily digestible format. By using data visualization techniques, marketers can accomplish the following:

- Identify patterns and trends in their data more easily and intuitively.
- Compare different data points, variables, or segments more effectively.
- Communicate their findings and insights to stakeholders in a compelling manner.
- Facilitate data-driven decision-making by making complex data more accessible and actionable.

In the following sections, we will delve deeper into the specific techniques and applications of descriptive analytics in marketing, including descriptive statistics, data visualization, and the analysis of marketing campaign performance. Through practical examples and relevant illustrations, we will demonstrate the real-world value of descriptive analytics in driving data-driven marketing strategies and decisions.

3.3   DESCRIPTIVE STATISTICS FOR MARKETING DATA

Descriptive statistics provide a summary of key characteristics of a dataset, helping marketers understand the data's central tendencies, dispersion, and associations

DESCRIPTIVE ANALYTICS IN MARKETING ◀ 53

between variables (Hair et al., 2019). These measures serve as a starting point for more advanced data analysis and are essential for making informed decisions in marketing.

3.3.1 Measures of Central Tendency

Measures of central tendency describe the central or typical value in a dataset. The most common measures of central tendency are the mean, median, and mode (Wedel & Kannan, 2016; see Figure 3.1):

- **Mean.** The arithmetic average of all data points
- **Median.** The middle value in a dataset when ordered from smallest to largest
- **Mode.** The most frequently occurring value in a dataset

Understanding the central tendency of marketing data, such as customer demographics or sales metrics, helps marketers identify the "typical" customer or sales performance and make better-informed decisions (Kotler et al., 2016).

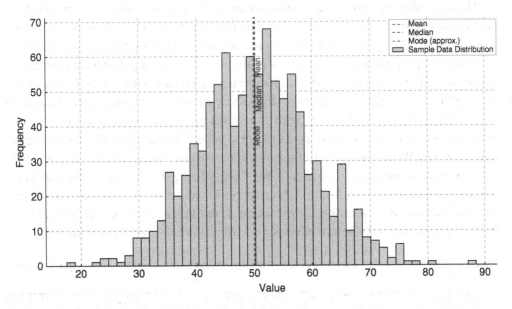

Figure 3.1 Various Measures of Central Tendency (Mean, Median, Mode) on a Sample Data Distribution.

3.3.2 Measures of Dispersion

Measures of dispersion describe the spread or variability of data points in a dataset. The most common measures of dispersion are range, variance, and standard deviation (Hair et al., 2019):

- **Range.** The difference between the highest and lowest values in a dataset
- **Variance.** The average squared difference between each data point and the mean

- **Standard deviation.** The square root of the variance, representing the average distance of each data point from the mean

Understanding the dispersion of marketing data helps marketers evaluate the variability and risk in their marketing campaigns and strategies (Wedel & Kannan, 2016).

3.3.3 Measures of Association

Measures of association describe the relationship between two or more variables in a dataset. The most common measures of association are correlation and covariance (Chaffey & Ellis-Chadwick, 2019):

- **Correlation.** A standardized measure of the linear relationship between two variables, ranging from −1 (perfect negative relationship) to +1 (perfect positive relationship)
- **Covariance.** A measure of the joint variability of two variables, indicating the direction of their relationship

Understanding the associations between marketing variables, such as customer behavior and sales performance, helps marketers identify key drivers of customer engagement, loyalty, and sales, informing their marketing strategies and tactics (Kotler et al., 2016).

Table 3.2 presents key descriptive statistics for a marketing dataset, illustrating a strong, almost one-to-one, correlation between ad spend and clicks, with both exhibiting significant variability. By contrast, clicks show a moderate positive correlation with sales, which are more consistent with much less variation, suggesting other factors may influence the conversion of clicks to sales. Table 3.2 underlines the importance of understanding the distribution and relationship between different marketing metrics.

In summary, descriptive statistics play a crucial role in understanding and interpreting marketing data, providing a foundation for more advanced data analysis and decision-making. By mastering these measures, marketers can gain valuable insights into their data and make better-informed decisions in their marketing efforts.

Table 3.2 A Sample Marketing Dataset with Calculations for Measures of Central Tendency, Dispersion, and Association.

Variable	Mean	Median	Mode	Range	Variance	Standard Deviation	Correlation with Next Variable
Ad Spend	2880.72	2856.57	1022.09	3925.46	1415999.00	1189.96	0.98
Clicks	145.35	147.50	188.00	236.00	3817.06	61.78	0.55
Sales	2.85	2.00	2.00	11.00	4.82	2.19	0.53

3.3.4 Symmetry and Skewness

Understanding the distribution of your data is critical in data analysis. Two crucial aspects of this are symmetry and skewness, which provide insights into the nature and shape of the distribution.

3.3.4.1 Symmetry

Symmetry refers to a situation in which one-half of the data is a mirror image of the other half. For example, consider the heights of adults in a large population. If most people have an average height (with equal numbers being taller or shorter than the average), the distribution of heights will be symmetrical. A perfectly symmetrical distribution will have its mean, median, and mode at the same value.

3.3.4.2 Skewness

Skewness measures the degree of asymmetry in the distribution of data. A distribution can be negatively skewed (left-skewed), positively skewed (right-skewed), or have no (or zero) skewness (symmetrical) (see Figure 3.2).

- **Positive skewness.** Positive skewness occurs when the tail on the right side (higher end of values) is longer than the left tail, indicating that the data has more outliers on the right. Consider the distribution of wealth in a society. A few individuals might have extremely high net worth, pulling the mean to the right, but the majority will be clustered around a lower average value.
- **Negative skewness.** Negative skewness occurs when the tail on the left side (lower end of values) is longer than the right tail, indicating that the data has more outliers on the left. Think about the time it takes to run a marathon. A few professional athletes might finish the race exceptionally quickly, but most participants will finish in a longer average time, leading to a left-skewed distribution.
- **Zero skewness.** Zero skewness indicates a perfectly symmetrical distribution.

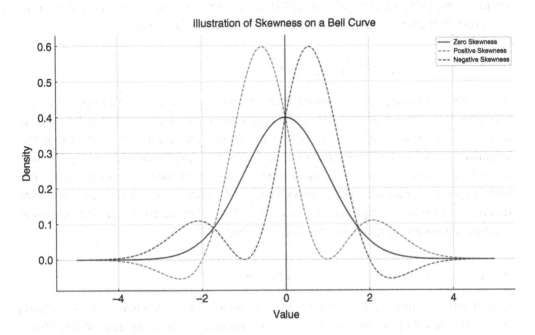

Figure 3.2 Positive, Negative, and Zero Skewness.

3.3.4.3 Implications

Skewness in data distribution has far-reaching implications for analytical accuracy and the interpretation of marketing data.

- **Statistical analysis.** The degree and direction of skewness can affect the choice and outcome of statistical tests. Some tests assume normally distributed data, and significant skewness can violate this assumption.
- **Data transformation.** In situations where skewness might be problematic, various data transformation techniques, such as logarithmic or square root transformations, can be applied to make the distribution more symmetrical.
- **Descriptive statistics.** Depending on skewness, the mean might not be the most representative measure of central tendency. In skewed distributions, the median might offer a better central value.

Understanding the symmetry and skewness of a dataset offers insights into its structure, guiding appropriate analytical approaches and aiding in interpreting results effectively.

3.4 DATA VISUALIZATION TECHNIQUES

Data visualization plays a crucial role in descriptive analytics, enabling marketers to quickly and effectively communicate complex data in a visually appealing and easily digestible format (Few, 2009). By using data visualization techniques, marketers can identify patterns and trends in their data more easily and intuitively, compare different data points or segments more effectively, and communicate their findings to stakeholders in a compelling manner (Cairo, 2012). In this section, we will discuss some of the most common data visualization techniques used in marketing analytics.

3.4.1 Bar Charts and Histograms

Bar charts and histograms are widely used in marketing analytics to display the distribution of a categorical variable or the frequency of occurrences within intervals of a continuous variable, respectively (Yau, 2013). Bar charts represent data using rectangular bars, with the height or length of each bar proportional to the value it represents. Histograms, however, use adjacent bars to represent the frequency of data points within specified intervals. These visualizations are particularly useful for comparing different categories or segments in marketing data, such as customer demographics, product categories, or geographic regions (see Figure 3.3).

3.4.2 Line Charts and Time Series Plots

Line charts and time series plots are used to display data trends over time, helping marketers identify patterns, seasonality, and fluctuations in their data (Tufte, 2001).

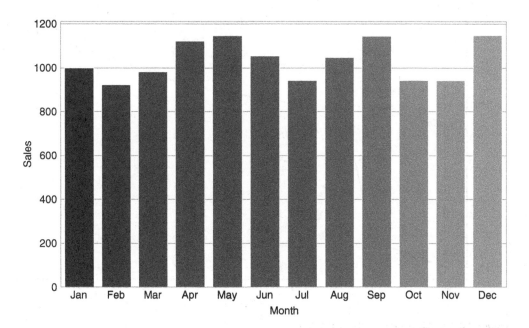

Figure 3.3 Frequency Distributions of a Product's Monthly Sales.

By connecting data points with lines, these charts enable marketers to visualize changes in variables over time, making it easier to spot trends and make forecasts. Time series plots are particularly useful in marketing for tracking key performance indicators (KPIs), such as sales, website traffic, or customer acquisition, over time (see Figure 3.4).

3.4.3 Scatterplots and Bubble Charts

Scatterplots and bubble charts are used to display the relationship between two or more variables in a dataset (Cleveland & McGill, 1984). Scatterplots represent data points as individual dots on a Cartesian plane, with the position of each dot determined by the values of two variables. Bubble charts extend scatterplots by adding a third dimension, represented by the size of the data points. These visualizations are useful for exploring correlations, trends, and clusters in marketing data, such as the relationship between customer demographics and sales performance or the association between marketing spend and revenue (see Figure 3.5).

3.4.4 Heat Maps and Geographic Maps

Heat maps and geographic maps are used to visualize data in a spatial context, helping marketers understand geographic patterns and trends in their data (Harrower & Brewer, 2003). Heat maps use color gradients to represent the density or intensity of data points within a specific area, whereas geographic maps display data on a map, often using color-coding, symbols, or proportional symbols to represent data values.

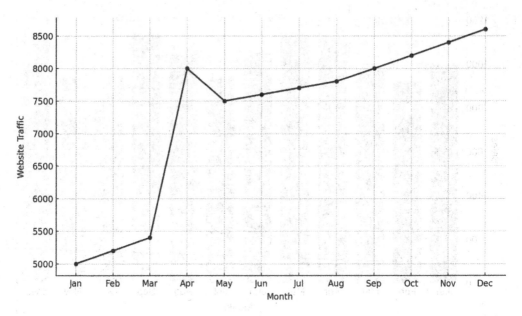

Figure 3.4 Monthly Website Traffic over a Year.

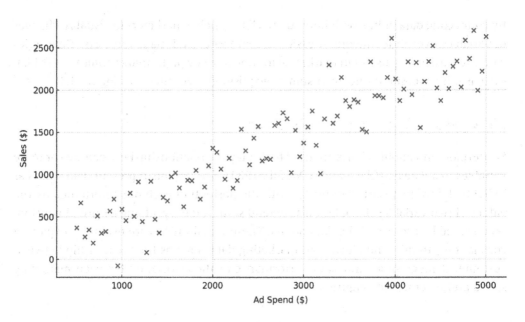

Figure 3.5 Correlation Between Ad Spend and Sales for a Product.

These visualizations are particularly useful for analyzing the spatial distribution of customers, sales performance, or marketing campaign effectiveness across different regions or markets (see Figure 3.6).

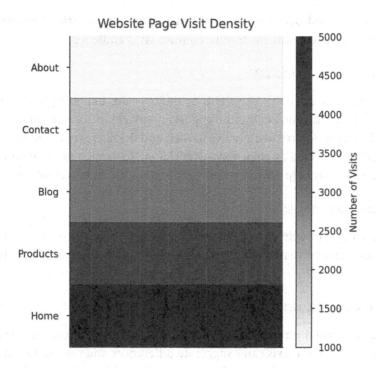

Figure 3.6 Website Page Visit Density.

3.4.5 Visualization Best Practices

Data visualization is an art as much as it is a science. When executed effectively, it can transform complex datasets into intuitive, insightful visuals that communicate a clear message. However, poor visualization practices can lead to confusion or even misinterpretation. Here are some best practices to ensure your visualizations convey the intended message accurately and effectively.

3.4.5.1 Simplicity Is Key

Always start with a clear purpose in mind. What story do you want your data to tell? Each visualization should convey one primary message or insight. Eliminate clutter; remove any unnecessary elements such as excessive gridlines, labels, or decorations. A cleaner chart is often a more effective chart. Tufte's principle of maximizing the "data-ink ratio" emphasizes reducing non-data ink (Tufte, 2001).

3.4.5.2 Choose the Right Chart Type

Different chart types emphasize different kinds of data and relationships. For example, bar charts are effective for comparing discrete quantities, and line charts are ideal for showing trends over time. Pie charts, for instance, can be problematic when comparing many categories, and 3D charts can distort perceptions of value. Ensure that your choice doesn't inadvertently mislead or confuse your audience.

3.4.5.3   Use Colors Judiciously

Colors should have purpose. Use them to differentiate items, highlight specific data points, or indicate categories. Avoid using too many colors, because they can be visually overwhelming. Approximately 8% of men and 0.5% of women of Northern European descent are affected by color vision deficiency. Tools such as Color Oracle (https://colororacle.org/) can help ensure your visualizations are interpretable by everyone.

3.4.5.4   Maintain Consistency

When comparing multiple charts, ensure that the scales are consistent so the comparisons are valid. Ensure that symbols, colors, and terminology remain consistent across all visualizations.

3.4.5.5   Prioritize Data Integrity

Ensure that the visual representation of data points is proportional to the actual data values. Cutting off the y-axis can exaggerate differences and can be misleading. If you must truncate, always clearly label the axis to indicate it's not starting from zero.

3.4.5.6   Interactive Visualizations

Tools such as SAS Visual Analytics or D3.js enable creation of interactive visualizations, helping users to dive deeper into specific parts of the data, providing a broad overview and detailed insights. When using interactive tools, guide the user through the data story by providing cues or focused pathways.

3.4.5.7   Test and Iterate

Share your visualizations with a diverse group, gather feedback, and be ready to adjust. A visualization that seems clear to you might be confusing to someone else. As with all skills, your proficiency in data visualization will improve with practice and ongoing learning. Stay updated with new techniques, tools, and best practices.

In conclusion, effective visualization is a powerful tool for marketers, enabling them to convey complex data in an easily digestible format. By following these best practices, marketers can ensure their visualizations not only look good but also communicate their message effectively, leading to better decision-making and more impactful presentations.

3.5   EXPLORATORY DATA ANALYSIS IN MARKETING

Exploratory data analysis (EDA) is a fundamental step in the marketing data science process, acting as the bridge between raw data and more intricate analytical techniques. It involves a comprehensive and systematic examination of datasets to discover patterns, spot anomalies, test hypotheses, and understand data structures—all with the aid of visual methods and descriptive statistics. For marketers, EDA is crucial because it offers a preliminary glance at data, helping to uncover insights, determine the right analytical tools to use, and shape data modeling strategies.

3.5.1 Data Distribution Analysis

Before delving into advanced analytical methods, it's vital for marketers to first understand the distribution of their data.

- **Univariate distribution.** This looks at one variable at a time. Tools such as histograms, box plots, and density plots can help visualize the distribution, central tendency, and spread of data. For instance, a histogram might reveal how customer ages are distributed across various age groups, shedding light on the demographics of a customer base.
- **Multivariate distribution.** When marketers want to observe the interactions between multiple variables, techniques such as scatterplots come into play. For example, a scatterplot could illustrate how website traffic (one variable) relates to sales (another variable).

Understanding the distribution of data is a fundamental step in any analytical process, and visual tools play a key role in this understanding. Figure 3.7 showcases box plots and histograms of a sample marketing dataset, illustrating how these tools can vividly depict data distributions. Box plots provide insights into the central tendency and spread of data, and histograms effectively demonstrate the frequency distribution of a variable, such as customer age groups. By examining these visual representations, marketers can gain a clearer understanding of the nature of their data, identify outliers, and assess the need for any data transformation techniques.

Understanding data distribution aids in determining the nature of the data, spotting outliers, and deciding if any data transformation techniques (such as normalization or standardization) are necessary.

3.5.2 Correlation and Covariance

To understand relationships between variables, marketers turn to measures of association such as correlation and covariance:

- **Correlation.** This is a standardized measure, which provides the strength and direction of a linear relationship between two variables. A correlation of 1 indicates a perfect positive linear relationship, −1 a perfect negative relationship, and 0 no linear relationship. For instance, there might be a strong positive correlation between advertising spend and sales, indicating that as one goes up, the other tends to as well.

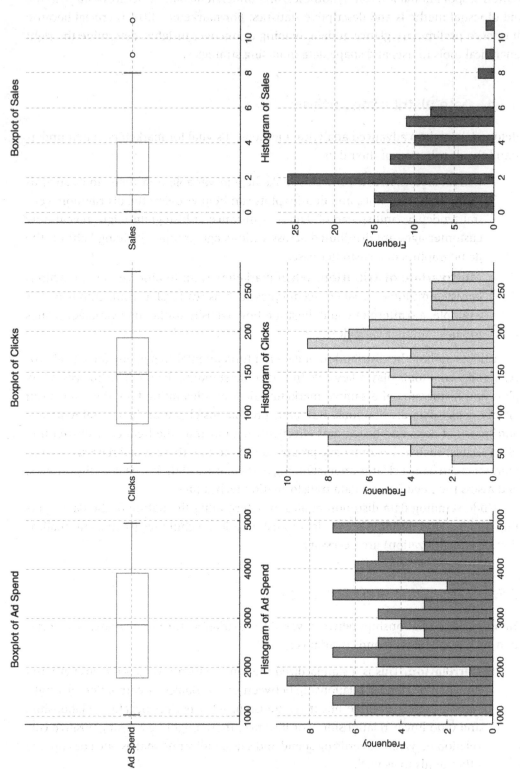

Figure 3.7 Sample Marketing Dataset Showcasing Data Distributions.

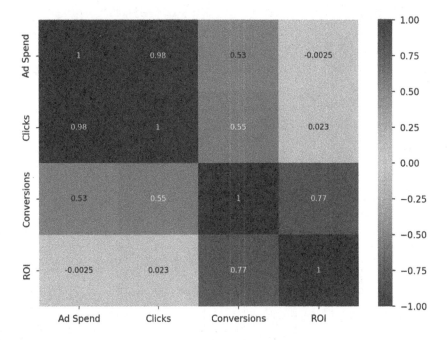

Figure 3.8 Relationships Among Various Marketing Variables.

- **Covariance.** While also indicating the direction of a relationship, covariance isn't standardized. Thus, although it can suggest the direction of a linear relationship (positive or negative), it cannot, by itself, quantify the strength of that relationship.

To further illuminate the concepts of correlation and covariance in the realm of marketing data, Figure 3.8 presents a correlation matrix that visually illustrates the relationships among various marketing variables. This matrix not only shows the direction but also the strength of linear relationships between pairs of variables, offering a clear, comprehensive view that can be more informative than numerical values alone. Such a visualization is particularly useful for marketers in identifying potential relationships, aiding in feature selection, detecting multicollinearity, and refining predictive models. By providing a bird's-eye view of how different marketing variables interrelate, this figure exemplifies the practical application of correlation and covariance in data-driven marketing strategies.

Both these measures are instrumental for marketers because they aid in feature selection, multicollinearity detection, and model refinement in subsequent analyses.

3.5.3 Visual Exploratory Techniques

Visualization is at the heart of EDA. It translates intricate datasets into comprehensible visuals, aiding in data interpretation and decision-making (see Figure 3.9).

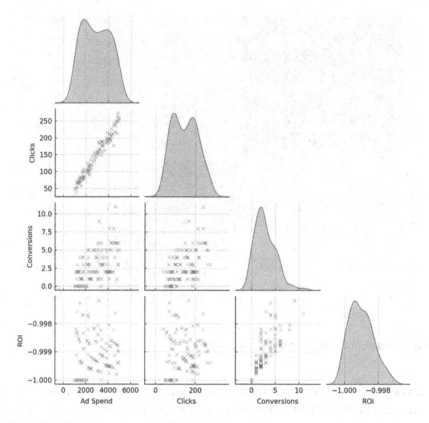

Figure 3.9 Relationship Patterns Among Multiple Marketing Variables.

- **Histograms and box plots.** Although histograms depict frequency distributions, box plots provide a glimpse into a dataset's quartiles, showcasing data spread and outliers.

- **Scatterplots.** Ideal for spotting trends, scatterplots visually depict relationships between two variables. They're especially helpful in examining potential causality or seeing clusters.

- **Heat maps.** These are great for understanding correlations between multiple variables at once. For instance, a marketer might use a heat map to see how various digital marketing metrics correlate with one another.

- **Pair plots.** This technique offers a holistic view by plotting pairwise relationships in a dataset. By using pair plots, marketers can instantly observe distributions and relationships between multiple variables.

In the context of marketing, visual exploratory techniques can shed light on questions such as: Which marketing channels are most strongly correlated with high customer lifetime value? Are there any unexpected patterns in the distribution of customer purchase frequencies?

In marketing, where understanding customer behavior, market dynamics, and campaign outcomes is paramount, EDA emerges as an invaluable tool. By combining statistical and visual techniques, EDA equips marketers with a holistic view of their data, paving the way for more sophisticated analyses and, ultimately, more informed decision-making. Whether one is trying to pinpoint key customer segments, determine the most effective marketing channels, or predict future sales, the journey often begins with exploratory data analysis.

3.6 ANALYZING MARKETING CAMPAIGN PERFORMANCE

Evaluating the performance of marketing campaigns is essential for marketers to understand the effectiveness of their strategies, tactics, and channels, and to optimize their marketing efforts based on data-driven insights. In this section, we will discuss the key metrics, techniques, and approaches used to analyze marketing campaign performance, as well as the importance of using descriptive analytics in this process.

3.6.1 Key Performance Indicators

KPIs are quantifiable measures used to evaluate the success of marketing campaigns in achieving their objectives. KPIs may vary depending on the marketing channel, campaign objectives, and target audience, but some common KPIs used in marketing analytics include the following:

- Sales revenue
- Return on investment (ROI)
- Customer acquisition cost
- Conversion rate
- Customer lifetime value
- Click-through rate (CTR)

Selecting the right KPIs is crucial for accurately measuring campaign performance and making data-driven decisions to optimize marketing efforts (Kotler et al., 2016; see Table 3.3).

3.6.2 Techniques for Analyzing Marketing Campaign Performance

Several techniques can be employed to analyze marketing campaign performance, including cohort analysis, segmentation, and lift analysis:

- **Cohort analysis.** This approach involves analyzing the performance of different groups of customers who share a common characteristic (e.g., acquisition channel, sign-up date) over time. Cohort analysis helps marketers identify trends and

Table 3.3 Common KPIs in Marketing with Definitions and Methods of Calculation.

KPI	Definition	Method of Calculation
Return on investment	Measures the profitability of a campaign	$\frac{Net\ Profit}{Cost\ of\ Campaign} \times 100$
Cost per acquisition	Average cost to acquire a customer through a campaign	$\frac{Total\ Campaign\ Cost}{Number\ of\ Acquisitions}$
Conversion rate	Percentage of visitors who take a desired action	$\frac{Number\ of\ Conversions}{Total\ Visitors} \times 100$
Customer lifetime value	Predicted net profit from a customer over the lifetime	$Avg\ Purchase\ Value \times Avg\ Purchase\ Frequency \times Avg\ Customer\ Lifespan$
Click-through rate	Percentage of people who clicked on an ad after seeing it	$\frac{Total\ Clicks}{Total\ Impressions} \times 100$
Bounce rate	Percentage of visitors who navigate away after viewing only one page	Calculated by web analytics tools such as Google Analytics

patterns in customer behavior, as well as the effectiveness of different marketing campaigns or channels.

- **Segmentation.** Segmentation involves dividing customers into groups based on shared characteristics, such as demographics, preferences, or behavior. By analyzing the performance of different customer segments, marketers can identify target audiences, tailor their marketing strategies, and allocate resources more effectively (Wedel & Kamakura, 2000) (see Section 4.4).

- **Lift analysis.** Lift analysis compares the performance of a marketing campaign to a baseline or control group. This technique helps marketers determine the incremental impact of a campaign on key metrics, such as sales or conversion rate, and calculate the ROI of their marketing efforts.

As we explore the various techniques for analyzing marketing campaign performance, it's crucial to have a tool that visually encapsulates the results in a concise and clear manner. Figure 3.10 provides just that—a dashboard-style visualization presenting multiple KPIs from a sample marketing campaign. By displaying various metrics and insights in one consolidated visual, this figure exemplifies how complex data can be synthesized into actionable intelligence, aiding marketers in making informed decisions about their strategies and investments.

3.6.3 The Role of Descriptive Analytics in Marketing Campaign Performance Analysis

Descriptive analytics plays a critical role in analyzing marketing campaign performance by providing a comprehensive understanding of historical data, helping marketers identify trends, patterns, and relationships in their data (Chaffey & Ellis-Chadwick, 2019).

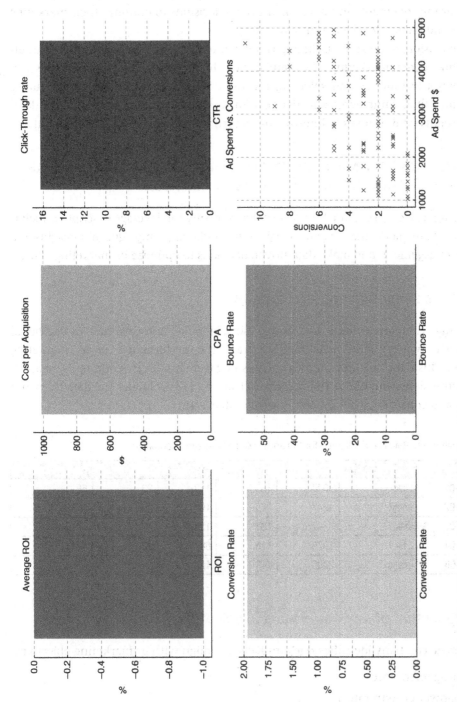

Figure 3.10 Multiple KPIs from a Sample Marketing Campaign.

67

By leveraging descriptive statistics, data visualization techniques, and other analytical tools, marketers can gain valuable insights into campaign performance, identify opportunities for improvement, and make data-driven decisions to optimize their marketing strategies and tactics (Wedel & Kannan, 2016).

In conclusion, analyzing marketing campaign performance is essential for marketers to optimize their marketing efforts and achieve better results. By employing descriptive analytics techniques and selecting the right KPIs, marketers can gain valuable insights into their campaigns' effectiveness, make informed decisions based on data-driven insights, and ultimately improve the return on their marketing investments.

3.7 PRACTICAL EXAMPLE: DESCRIPTIVE ANALYTICS FOR A BEVERAGE COMPANY'S SOCIAL MEDIA MARKETING CAMPAIGN

In this example, we will explore how a beverage company can leverage descriptive analytics to evaluate the performance of its social media marketing campaign, gain insights into customer engagement, and make data-driven decisions to optimize its marketing efforts.

3.7.1 Data Collection and Preparation

The beverage company collects data from its social media platforms, such as Facebook, X (formerly Twitter), and Instagram, to track the performance of its marketing campaign. This data includes metrics such as engagement (likes, comments, shares), reach, impressions, and CTRs. The company cleans and consolidates the data to ensure accuracy and consistency before analysis (see Table 3.4).

Table 3.4 Simulated Raw Data Collected for the Social Media Marketing Campaign.

Date	Post Type	Reach	Clicks	Likes	Shares	Comments
2023–01–01	Link	3047	133	113	23	66
2023–01–02	Image	4547	225	192	55	76
2023–01–03	Link	3747	187	128	40	75
2023–01–04	Link	1975	115	88	20	44
2023–01–05	Image	2806	146	126	24	61

3.7.2 Selection of Key Performance Indicators

The beverage company identifies relevant KPIs that align with its marketing objectives:

- Engagement rate
- Follower growth rate
- Conversion rate (clicks to website or online purchases)
- Cost per engagement.

3.7.3 Descriptive Analytics

The company employs descriptive analytics techniques, such as descriptive statistics and data visualization, to analyze its social media marketing data and identify patterns, trends, and relationships.

- **Descriptive statistics.** The company calculates the average, median, and standard deviation of its engagement rate, follower growth rate, and conversion rate to identify the central tendency and dispersion of its social media performance.
- **Data visualization.** The company uses bar charts to compare the performance of its social media platforms and line charts to track the performance of its KPIs over time. For example, a line chart could show how engagement rate varies throughout the campaign, revealing any spikes or drops in engagement that might warrant further investigation.

3.7.4 Segmentation Analysis

The beverage company segments its audience based on factors such as demographics, geography, and engagement behavior to better understand customer preferences and tailor its marketing efforts accordingly. For example, the company could analyze engagement rates by age group or location to identify the most responsive target audience for its marketing efforts (see Figure 3.11).

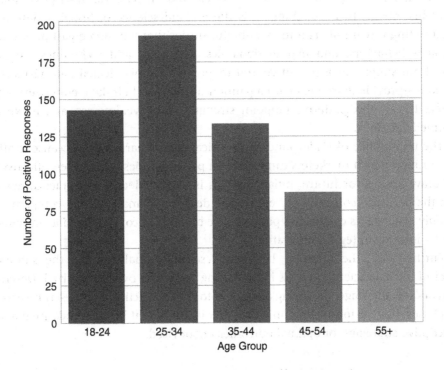

Figure 3.11 Segmentation Analysis Results (Responses Segmented by Age Groups).

3.7.5 Insights and Optimization

Based on the insights gained from descriptive analytics, the beverage company can make data-driven decisions to optimize its social media marketing campaign. For instance, if the analysis reveals that Instagram has the highest engagement rate among its target audience, the company might allocate more resources to this platform. Additionally, the company could adjust its content strategy based on audience segmentation insights, tailoring its messaging and creative elements to better resonate with specific customer segments.

In conclusion, leveraging descriptive analytics techniques can help the beverage company evaluate the performance of its social media marketing campaign, gain valuable insights into customer engagement, and make informed decisions to optimize its marketing efforts.

3.8 CONCLUSION

Descriptive analytics stands as the cornerstone of data-driven marketing, acting as the bedrock on which all subsequent analytical methodologies are built. In this chapter, we embarked on an enlightening journey through the realm of descriptive analytics in marketing, underscoring its pivotal role in elucidating the narratives hidden within the vast sea of data.

Through our discussions, it becomes clear that at its core, descriptive analytics is not just about data crunching. It is the art and science of bringing data to life, transforming raw numbers into meaningful stories that illuminate past performance, customer behaviors, and market dynamics. The tools and techniques we delved into—from simple measures of central tendency to sophisticated data visualization methods—provide marketers with a panoramic view of their data, empowering them to decode complex patterns, pinpoint strengths, and weaknesses, and make more informed decisions.

The importance of understanding historical data is paramount because it offers a lens through which marketers can reflect on past strategies, gauge their effectiveness, and draw lessons for future initiatives. This is exemplified in our practical example with the beverage company. By employing descriptive analytics, the company could not only evaluate its campaign's performance but also uncover actionable insights that directly inform strategic optimizations.

Furthermore, the interplay between descriptive analytics and the subsequent stages of the data science process in marketing cannot be overemphasized. Descriptive analytics sets the stage, preparing marketers for the predictive and prescriptive analytical phases. It is the foundation on which predictions about future trends are made and prescriptive strategies for optimal outcomes are devised.

As the digital marketing landscape continues to evolve and become more complex, the imperative for marketers to embrace and master descriptive analytics grows stronger. In a world inundated with data, the ability to effectively summarize, visualize, and interpret this data is no longer just an advantage but a necessity.

In closing, as marketers progress in their data science journey, they must remember the adage, "You cannot know where you are going until you know where you have been." Descriptive analytics offers that very knowledge, ensuring marketers not only know where they have been but also understand the intricacies of their journey, enabling them to chart a more informed and successful path forward.

3.9 REFERENCES

Cairo, A. (2012). *The functional art: An introduction to information graphics and visualization.* New Riders.

Chaffey, D., & Ellis-Chadwick, F. (2019). *Digital marketing.* Pearson.

Cleveland, W. S., & McGill, R. (1984). Graphical perception: Theory, experimentation, and application to the development of graphical methods. *Journal of the American Statistical Association, 79*(387), 531–554.

Few, S. (2009). *Now you see it: Simple visualization techniques for quantitative analysis.* Analytics Press.

Hair, J. F., Black, W. C., Babin, B. J., & Anderson, R. E. (2019). *Multivariate data analysis.* Cengage Learning.

Harrower, M., & Brewer, C. A. (2003). ColorBrewer.org: An online tool for selecting colour schemes for maps. *The Cartographic Journal, 40*(1), 27–37.

Kotler, P., Keller, K. L., Brady, M., Goodman, M., & Hansen, T. (2016). *Marketing management.* Pearson.

Sharda, R., Delen, D., & Turban, E. (2021). *Analytics, data science, & artificial intelligence: Systems for decision support.* Pearson.

Tufte, E. R. (2001). *The visual display of quantitative information* (Vol. 2, p. 9). Graphics Press.

Wedel, M., & Kamakura, W. A. (2000). *Market segmentation: Conceptual and methodological foundations.* Springer Science & Business Media.

Wedel, M., & Kannan, P. K. (2016). Marketing analytics for data-rich environments. *Journal of Marketing, 80,* 97–121.

Yau, N. (2013). *Data points: Visualization that means something.* Wiley.

EXERCISE 3.1: DESCRIPTIVE ANALYSIS OF MARKETING DATA

Objective: Understand and describe the central tendencies, dispersion, and associations in the marketing data.

Tasks:

1. **Calculate Descriptive Statistics:** Compute mean, median, and mode for variables such as 'Ad Spend', 'Clicks', and 'Sales'.

2. **Visualization:** Create bar charts for engagement metrics, line charts for ad spend over time, and scatterplots to show relationships between ad spend and conversions.

3. **Interpretation:** Analyze the results, discussing any interesting findings or patterns.

Steps:

1. **Import Libraries:**

```
1. import pandas as pd
```

   - We import the Pandas library, which is essential for data manipulation and analysis.

2. **Load the Dataset:**

```
2. marketing_data = pd.read_csv('path_to_csv_file')
```

   - Replace **'path_to_csv_file'** with the actual path of the marketing_ data CSV file.
   - This line reads the CSV file into a Pandas DataFrame, which is a two-dimensional labeled data structure.

3. **Calculate Descriptive Statistics:**

```
3. descriptive_stats = marketing_data.describe()
```

   - The **describe()** function in Pandas provides a summary of the central tendency, dispersion, and shape of the dataset's distribution, excluding NaN values. It calculates statistics such as mean, standard deviation, minimum, and maximum values for each column.

Visualization:

1. **Import Visualization Library:**

```
4. import matplotlib.pyplot as plt
```

   - We import Matplotlib, a widely used library for creating static, animated, and interactive visualizations in Python.

2. **Create a Bar Chart for 'Total Engagement Metrics':**

```
5. marketing_data[['Likes', 'Shares', 'Comments']].sum().
plot(kind='bar')
```

```
6. plt.title('Total Engagement Metrics')
7. plt.ylabel('Total Count')
8. plt.show()
```

- This code snippet creates a bar chart representing the total counts of 'Likes', 'Shares', and 'Comments'.
- The **sum()** function is used to calculate the total for each engagement metric.
- **plot(kind='bar')** generates a bar chart, and **plt.title**, **plt.ylabel**, and **plt.show()** are used to set the title, label the y-axis, and display the plot, respectively.

3. **Create a Line Chart for 'Ad Spend Over Time':**

```
9. marketing_data.plot(x='Date', y='Ad Spend', kind='line')
10. plt.title('Ad Spend Over Time')
11. plt.ylabel('Ad Spend')
12. plt.xlabel('Date')
13. plt.show()
```

- This line of code generates a line chart showing how 'Ad Spend' varies over time.
- The x-axis represents dates, and the y-axis shows the 'Ad Spend' for each date.

4. **Scatterplot to Show Relationship Between 'Ad Spend' and 'Conversions':**

```
14. marketing_data.plot(x='Ad Spend', y='Conversions',
kind='scatter')
15. plt.title('Ad Spend vs Conversions')
16. plt.xlabel('Ad Spend')
17. plt.ylabel('Conversions')
18. plt.show()
```

- This code creates a scatterplot to visualize the relationship between 'Ad Spend' and 'Conversions'.
- Each point on the plot represents a pair of values from the dataset.

EXERCISE 3.1: OUTPUT

The descriptive statistics for the dataset are as follows:

- **'Ad Spend':**
  - Mean: $1208.58
  - Standard Deviation: $451.45
  - Minimum: $508.28
  - Maximum: $1980.33

- **'Impressions':**
  - Mean: 3096.93
  - Standard Deviation: 1104.78
- **'Clicks':**
  - Mean: 123.28
  - Standard Deviation: 48.49
- **'Conversions':**
  - Mean: 27.97
  - Standard Deviation: 13.48
- **Engagement Metrics ('Likes', 'Shares', 'Comments'):**
  - Likes: Mean – 148.49, Standard Deviation –83.67
  - Shares: Mean – 48.63, Standard Deviation –30.86
  - Comments: Mean – 85.52, Standard Deviation –46.24

Visualization Results

1. **Bar Chart—'Total Engagement Metrics':**
   - This chart shows the total counts for 'Likes', 'Shares', and 'Comments'. 'Likes' are the highest, followed by 'Comments' and 'Shares'.

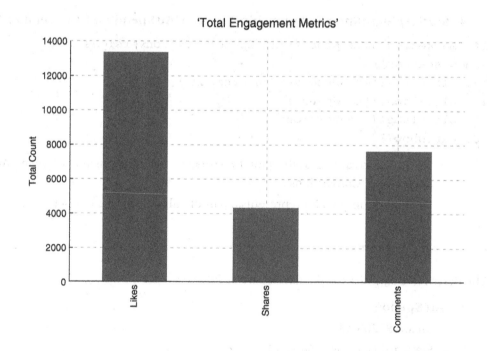

2. **Line Chart—'Ad Spend Over Time':**
   - The line chart displays the trend of 'Ad Spend' over the three-month period. It helps to visualize fluctuations in spending over time.

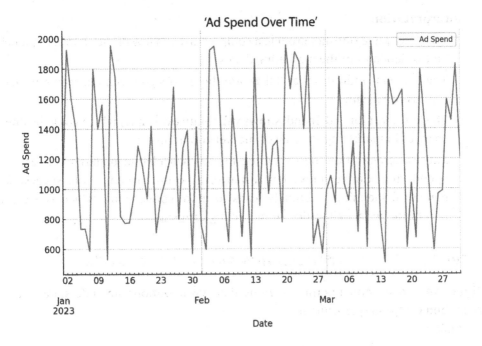

3. **Scatterplot—'Ad Spend' vs 'Conversions':**

  ▪ The scatterplot illustrates the relationship between 'Ad Spend' and 'Conversions'. Each point represents a day's data, showing how conversions vary with different levels of ad spending.

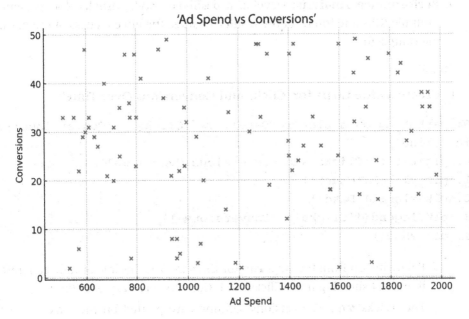

Interpretation

- The descriptive statistics provide a comprehensive view of the central tendencies and variabilities in the marketing data.

- The bar chart indicates that 'Likes' are the most significant engagement metric for this campaign.

- The line chart for 'Ad Spend' shows variability over time, which could be due to changes in marketing strategy or market conditions.

- The scatterplot could be examined for any correlation patterns between 'Ad Spend' and 'Conversions'. For instance, a positive trend would suggest that higher ad spending potentially leads to more conversions, which is a crucial insight for budget allocation in marketing campaigns.

EXERCISE 3.2: DATA VISUALIZATION AND INTERPRETATION

Objective: Create and interpret various data visualizations to understand market trends and campaign performance.

Tasks:

1. **Time Series Analysis:** Use line charts to analyze trends in 'Clicks' and 'Conversions' over time.

2. **Segmentation Analysis:** Create a heat map to visualize engagement metrics across different customer segments.

3. **Performance Analysis:** Develop a dashboard-style visualization presenting multiple KPIs and interpret the results to gauge the effectiveness of the marketing campaign.

Steps:

1. **Create a Line Chart for 'Clicks and Conversions Over Time':**

```
19. marketing_data.plot(x='Date', y=['Clicks', 'Conversions'],
kind='line')
20. plt.title('Clicks and Conversions Over Time')
21. plt.ylabel('Count')
22. plt.xlabel('Date')
23. plt.legend(['Clicks', 'Conversions'])
24. plt.show()
```

- Following on from the steps run for Exercise 3.1, this line of code generates a line chart showing how 'Clicks' and 'Conversions' vary over time.

- The 'Clicks' and 'Conversions' columns are plotted on the *y*-axis, and the 'Date' column is used for the *x*-axis.

■ The **legend** function is used to differentiate between the two lines ('Clicks' and 'Conversions').

2. **Create a Heat Map for Engagement Metrics Across Different Days of the Week:**

   ■ First, we'll create a new column to represent the 'Day of the Week', and then group the data accordingly.

```
25. import seaborn as sns
26. # Creating a new column for the day of the week
27. marketing_data['Day of Week'] = marketing_data['Date'].
dt.day_name()
28. # Grouping data by the day of the week and summing
29. engagement metrics engagement_by_day = marketing_data.
groupby('Day of Week')[['Likes', 'Shares', 'Comments']].sum()
30. # Creating a heatmap
31. plt.figure(figsize=(10, 6))
32. sns.heatmap(engagement_by_day, annot=True, fmt="d",
cmap='viridis')
33. plt.title('Engagement Metrics by Day of the Week')
34. plt.show()
```

   ■ The **groupby** function is used to group data by the 'Day of Week'.
   ■ **sns.heatmap** from Seaborn library creates a heat map to visualize engagement metrics for each day of the week.

3. **Create a Dashboard-Style Visualization Presenting Multiple KPIs:**

   ■ We'll select a few KPIs and create a combined visualization.

```
35. fig, axes = plt.subplots(nrows=2, ncols=2, figsize=(15, 10))
36. # Plotting Ad Spend over time
37. marketing_data.plot(x='Date', y='Ad Spend', ax=axes[0,0])
38. axes[0,0].set_title('Ad Spend Over Time')
39. axes[0,0].set_ylabel('Ad Spend ($)')
40. # Plotting Impressions over time
41. marketing_data.plot(x='Date', y='Impressions',
ax=axes[0,1], color='green')
42. axes[0,1].set_title('Impressions Over Time')
43. axes[0,1].set_ylabel('Impressions')
44. # Plotting Clicks over time marketing_data.plot(x='Date',
y='Clicks', ax=axes[1,0], color='orange')
45. axes[1,0].set_title('Clicks Over Time')
46. axes[1,0].set_ylabel('Clicks')
```

```
47. # Plotting Conversions over time marketing_data.
plot(x='Date', y='Conversions', ax=axes[1,1], color='red')
48. axes[1,1].set_title('Conversions Over Time')
49. axes[1,1].set_ylabel('Conversions')
50. plt.tight_layout()
51. plt.show()
```

- This code creates a 2×2 grid of plots, each displaying a different KPI over time.
- The **subplots** function is used to create a grid layout, and individual plots are created using the **plot** method with specified axes.

This code, when executed using the dataset, will provide a comprehensive view of the marketing campaign's performance, highlighting trends and patterns crucial for strategic decision-making. Let's run this code and observe the outputs.

EXERCISE 3.2: OUTPUT

1. **Line Chart—'Clicks Over Time' and 'Conversions Over Time':**
   - This chart displays the trends in 'Clicks' and 'Conversions' over the three-month period, enabling us to observe how these metrics have changed over time and to identify any patterns or anomalies.

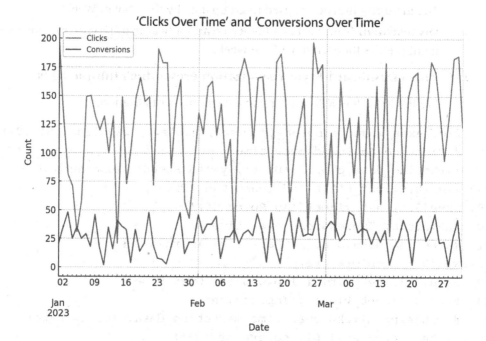

2. **Heat Map—Engagement Metrics by 'Day of the Week':**
   - ▦ The heat map visualizes the total counts of 'Likes', 'Shares', and 'Comments' for each day of the week. This can help identify which days tend to have higher engagement, potentially informing content scheduling and marketing strategies.

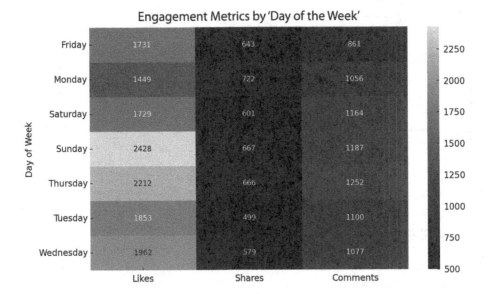

3. **Dashboard-Style Visualization—Multiple KPIs:**
   - ▦ The 2×2 grid of plots showcases 'Ad Spend', 'Impressions Over Time', 'Clicks Over Time', and 'Conversions Over Time'. This comprehensive view helps to quickly assess the performance of different aspects of the marketing campaign, highlighting trends and areas that may need attention.

Interpretation

- ▦ From the time series analysis, it's possible to understand the correlation between different activities, such as the impact of ad spending on 'Clicks' and 'Conversions'.

- ▦ The heat map provides insights into the effectiveness of social media engagement across different days, which can be crucial for planning and optimizing social media marketing strategies.

- ▦ The dashboard-style visualization offers a holistic view of the campaign's performance, enabling a quick assessment of how different KPIs have evolved over time.

These visualizations, drawn from the dataset, provide a deeper understanding of market trends and campaign performance, crucial for informed decision-making in marketing.

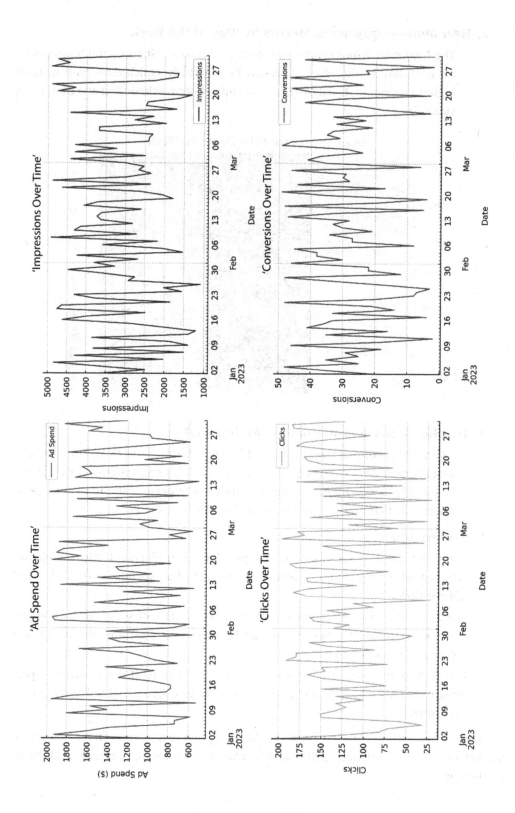

CHAPTER 4

Inferential Analytics and Hypothesis Testing

4.1 INTRODUCTION

Inferential analytics and hypothesis testing are paramount pillars of marketing data science, enabling professionals to transcend mere observation and move toward proactive, data-informed decision-making. As businesses are inundated with vast amounts of data, the pressing question becomes, How can this data be transformed into actionable insights? The answer lies in the ability to infer broader trends from sample data and validate assumptions through rigorous hypothesis testing.

This chapter delves deep into the world of inferential analytics, revealing its pivotal role in marketing. By examining statistical techniques that enable marketers to generalize findings from samples to larger populations, we aim to spotlight the tremendous value these techniques offer. Beyond mere theory, the chapter highlights real-world applications, showcasing how businesses employ these tools to drive results. From understanding customer behavior, preferences, and trends at a macroscopic level to verifying the impact of specific marketing interventions, inferential analytics and hypothesis testing emerge as invaluable assets in a marketer's arsenal.

Through an exploration of key concepts, techniques, and practical examples, this chapter provides readers with a comprehensive understanding of inferential analytics and hypothesis testing in the context of marketing. Armed with this knowledge, marketing professionals will be better equipped to navigate the complex data landscape, making decisions that are not only informed but also impactful.

As we embark on a detailed exploration of inferential analytics within the marketing domain, it's important to visualize the entire process from start to finish. Figure 4.1 offers a flowchart that precisely represents this journey, from the initial stages of data collection to the final steps of drawing meaningful conclusions. By presenting these steps in a clear and organized manner, the figure helps demystify the process, providing readers with a road map of how inferential analytics is applied to transform raw data into actionable insights. It underscores the systematic approach required in hypothesis testing and inferential analysis, which are critical in making data-driven marketing decisions.

4.2 INFERENTIAL ANALYTICS IN MARKETING

4.2.1 Overview of Inferential Analytics

Inferential analytics is a branch of statistics that deals with drawing conclusions about a population based on a smaller sample of data (Starnes et al., 2014). In the context of marketing, inferential analytics enables organizations to understand customer behavior, preferences, and trends at a broader level, providing valuable insights for making informed decisions and optimizing marketing strategies (Winston, 2014).

Unlike descriptive analytics, which focuses on summarizing and visualizing data from a single dataset, inferential analytics aims to generalize findings from a sample

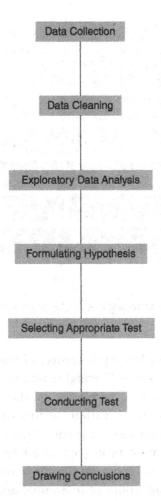

Figure 4.1 A Process of Inferential Analytics, from Data Collection to Drawing Conclusions.

to a larger population (Leek & Peng, 2015). This is particularly useful in marketing because it is often impractical or impossible to collect data from every customer or prospect. By using inferential analytics, marketers can gain insights into a larger population's characteristics, such as average spending, preferences, and buying patterns, based on a smaller, more manageable sample (Larose & Larose, 2014).

Inferential analytics involves the use of probability theory and various statistical techniques to estimate population parameters, such as means, proportions, and variances, based on sample data (Freedman et al., 2007). These techniques enable marketers to quantify the uncertainty associated with their estimates and make predictions with a certain level of confidence (Field et al., 2012). For instance, a marketer might use inferential analytics to estimate the average revenue generated by a specific customer segment, along with a confidence interval that provides a range within which the true population mean is likely to lie.

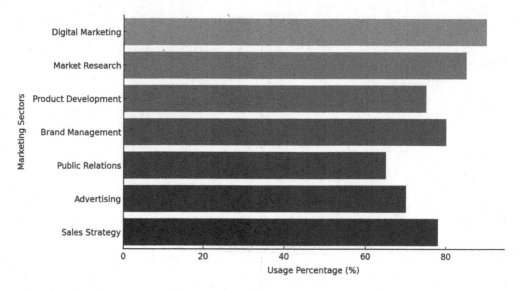

Figure 4.2 The Various Sectors Within Marketing That Employ Inferential Analytics Most Frequently.

As we conclude our discussion on the power of inferential analytics in shaping data-driven marketing decisions, it is enlightening to examine where these techniques are most frequently applied within the marketing industry. Figure 4.2 presents a bar chart that showcases the various sectors within marketing that employ inferential analytics with the greatest frequency. This visualization helps to contextualize the real-world application of inferential analytics, highlighting the sectors where these techniques are making a significant impact. From this chart, readers can appreciate the widespread utility of inferential analytics across different marketing domains, providing a clear picture of how these methods are integrated into various marketing strategies to drive deeper customer insights and improve marketing outcomes.

In summary, inferential analytics is a powerful tool that enables marketers to make data-driven decisions and optimize their marketing efforts based on insights gleaned from a sample of data. By understanding and applying inferential analytics techniques, marketing professionals can gain deeper insights into customer behavior, preferences, and trends, leading to better marketing outcomes (Hair et al., 2018).

4.2.2 Basics of Probability

Probability is the foundation on which inferential analytics is built, offering a mathematical means to quantify uncertainty. In essence, probability provides a measure of the likelihood of a particular event occurring, typically expressed as a number between 0 and 1, inclusive. This section will introduce core concepts in probability that underpin many of the analytical techniques discussed later in this chapter.

4.2.2.1 *Definition of Probability*

Probability (P) of an event E is defined as:

$$P(E) = \frac{number\ of\ favorable\ outcomes\ for\ E}{total\ number\ of\ possible\ outcomes},$$

where

The probability of an impossible event is 0.

The probability of a certain event is 1.

For any event $E, 0 \leq P(E) \leq 1$.

WORKED EXAMPLE: PROBABILITY OF CLICKING AN AD

Imagine you're a digital marketer for a company that sells sports equipment. You have designed two different banner ads (Ad A and Ad B) for the same product, and you want to determine the probability that a website visitor will click on each ad.

Let's assume that your website has a steady stream of traffic, and you have historical data indicating that out of 1,000 visitors, 50 clicked on Ad A, and 75 on Ad B.

Calculating the Probability

For Ad A:

- The number of favorable outcomes (clicks) is 50.
- The total number of possible outcomes (visitors) is 1000.

Using the formula for probability:

$$P(Clicking\ Ad\ A) = \frac{number\ of\ favourable\ outcomes\ for\ Ad\ A}{total\ number\ of\ possible\ outcomes}$$

$$P(Clicking\ Ad\ A) = \frac{50}{1000} = 0.05$$

So, the probability that a visitor clicks on Ad A is 0.05, or 5%.
For Ad B:

- The number of favorable outcomes (clicks) is 75.
- The total number of possible outcomes (visitors) is 1000.

$$P(Clicking\ Ad\ B) = \frac{75}{1000} = 0.075$$

Thus, the probability that a visitor clicks on Ad B is 0.075, or 7.5%.

Interpreting the Results

- The probability of a certain event, such as a user visiting the website (assuming it's accessible and online), is 1 (or 100%).
- The probability of an impossible event, such as a click from a nonexistent ad, is 0.
- The calculated probabilities for clicking on Ad A and Ad B are between 0 and 1, which aligns with the principle that the probability of any event E must satisfy $0 \leq P(E) \leq 1$.

Using this probability information, you can deduce that Ad B currently has a higher chance of being clicked on by any given visitor to your website. This could inform your decision on which ad to allocate more resources to or whether to redesign Ad A.

4.2.2.2 Sample Space and Events

The sample space, denoted as S, represents the set of all possible outcomes of a random experiment. An event is a subset of this sample space. For instance, in a coin toss, the sample space is $S = \{Head, Tail\}$, and an event might be getting a head.

4.2.2.3 Basic Probability Rules

- **Complementary events.** The probability of an event E not happening, denoted by $P(E')$, is given by:

$$P(E') = 1 - P(E)$$

- **Addition rule.** For any two events E and F:

$$P(E \, or \, F) = P(E) + P(F) - P(E \, and \, F)$$

  If E and F are mutually exclusive (they can't both happen at the same time), then:
$$P(E \, or \, F) = P(E) + P(F)$$

- **Multiplication rule.** For any two independent events E and F (the occurrence of one does not affect the probability of the other):

$$P(E \, and \, F) = P(E) \times P(F)$$

4.2.2.4 Conditional Probability

Conditional probability is the probability of an event E happening given that another event F has already occurred, represented as $P(E|F)$ It is calculated as:

$$P(E|F) = \frac{P(E \, and \, F)}{P(F)}$$

4.2.2.5 Bayes's Theorem

Bayes's theorem is a fundamental concept in probability theory and statistics, providing a way to find a probability when certain other probabilities are known. It's represented as:

$$P(E|F) = \frac{P(F|E) \times P(E)}{P(F)},$$

where

$P(E|F)$ is the posterior probability.

$P(F|E)$ is the likelihood.

$P(E)$ is the prior probability of E.

$P(F)$ is the total probability of F.

Bayes's theorem has wide applications in fields like medical testing, machine learning, and, indeed, marketing analytics.

CASE STUDY: PERSONALIZING EMAIL CAMPAIGNS FOR AN ONLINE RETAILER

Let's take the example of an online retailer, ShopStream, which offers a range of products from electronics to clothing. ShopStream has a vast customer base, and they send weekly promotional emails. They noticed that the engagement rate of their general promotional emails is dwindling. To address this, they want to personalize their email campaigns based on users' probable interests.

Objective: To predict the likelihood that a customer is interested in a specific product category (e.g., electronics) given their past behavior and use this information to send targeted email promotions.

Application of Bayes's Theorem

1. **Prior Probability $\left(P(E)\right)$:**

   ▪ This represents the overall probability that a random customer is interested in electronics, based on historical data. Let's say 20% of their customers have shown interest in electronics in the past.

2. **Likelihood $\left(P(F|E)\right)$:**

   ▪ This is the probability that a customer who is interested in electronics exhibits a certain behavior. For instance, from past campaigns, they've noticed that 60% of users interested in electronics clicked on electronics-related content in their emails.

3. **Total Probability of $F\left(P(F)\right)$:**

   ▪ This is the overall probability that any customer, irrespective of their interest, clicks on electronics-related content. Suppose this is 25%.

Using Bayes's theorem, they want to find the posterior probability, $P(E|F)$, that is, the probability that a customer is interested in electronics given they clicked on electronics-related content.

Plugging in the numbers:

$$P(E|F) = \frac{P(F|E) \times P(E)}{P(F)}$$

$$P(E|F) = \frac{(0.6 \times 0.2)}{(0.25)}$$

$$P(E|F) = 0.48 \, or \, 48\%$$

Interpretation. Given a customer clicked on electronics-related content, there's a 48% chance they're interested in electronics, which is significantly higher than the initial 20% prior probability.

Outcome. Based on this enhanced understanding, ShopStream started sending more electronics-specific promotions to users who clicked on electronics content. This resulted in a 15% increase in click-through rates for this segment, proving the effectiveness of the Bayesian approach in refining their marketing strategy.

Conclusion. Bayes's theorem enabled ShopStream to update its beliefs about customers based on new data, optimizing their marketing efforts. By grounding decisions in Bayesian probability, they achieved a more personalized and effective email campaign. This showcases the power of Bayes's theorem in turning data into actionable marketing insights.

4.2.2.6 Importance to Marketing Data Science

Understanding the basics of probability equips marketers to interpret data more intuitively. For instance, by assessing the probability of customers purchasing a product after viewing an advertisement, marketers can optimize ad placements. Or, using Bayes's theorem, they can update their beliefs about customer preferences based on new data.

In conclusion, probability offers a robust framework to understand uncertainty and variability, essential for making informed, risk-assessed decisions in the realm of marketing. As we progress through this chapter, the importance of these foundational concepts will become even clearer, laying the groundwork for advanced inferential analytics techniques.

4.2.3 Parametric Versus Nonparametric Tests

Statistical tests serve as the backbone of inferential analytics, helping marketers make decisions based on sample data. Generally, these tests can be categorized into two main types: parametric and nonparametric tests. This section will delve into the differences between these two categories and explore their implications for marketing data science.

4.2.3.1 What Are Parametric Tests?

Parametric tests are statistical tests that make specific assumptions about the parameters of the population distribution from which the samples are drawn.

Characteristics of Parametric Tests

- Assume data follows a certain distribution (e.g., normal distribution)
- Expect data should be measured at least at the interval or ratio scale
- Assume homogeneity of variances when comparing two or more groups
- Sensitive to outliers

Common Parametric Tests

- t-test (for comparing means) (see Section 4.5.2.1)
- Analysis of variance (ANOVA) (see Section 4.5.2.3)
- Linear regression (see Section 4.5.2.4)

4.2.3.2 What Are Nonparametric Tests?

Nonparametric tests, often called *distribution-free tests*, do not make any strict assumptions about the population parameters.

Characteristics of Nonparametric Tests

- Do not assume a specific distribution for the data
- Suitable for ordinal, nominal, interval, or ratio data
- Robust against heterogeneity of variances
- Less sensitive to outliers

Common Nonparametric Tests

- Mann-Whitney U test
- Wilcoxon signed-rank test
- Kruskal-Wallis test
- Spearman's rank correlation

4.2.3.3 Choosing Between Parametric and Nonparametric Tests

The decision on which type of test to use depends on the following:

- **Data distribution.** If your data is normally distributed, parametric tests are preferable due to their greater statistical power; otherwise, consider nonparametric tests.

- **Scale of measurement.** Nonparametric tests are more versatile and can handle various data scales, including nominal and ordinal.
- **Sample size.** For small sample sizes, nonparametric tests are often more appropriate because they don't rely on distributional assumptions.
- **Presence of outliers.** If your data has significant outliers, nonparametric tests might be more appropriate because they're less sensitive to extreme values.

Table 4.1 provides a clear and concise comparison between parametric and non-parametric tests, highlighting their basic differences, advantages, and disadvantages. This table serves as an invaluable reference for marketers and data scientists, aiding them in making informed decisions based on the nature of their data, such as distribution, scale of measurement, sample size, and the presence of outliers. Understanding these aspects is vital in selecting the most appropriate statistical test that aligns with the characteristics of the data and the objectives of the analysis.

Table 4.1 Differences, Advantages, and Disadvantages of Parametric Versus Nonparametric Tests.

	Parametric Tests	Nonparametric Tests
Basic differences	Assume data follows a specific distribution, often the normal distribution	Do not assume data follows a specific distribution
Advantages	Powerful, with greater sensitivity to detect significant results when assumptions are met	More robust, can be used when data does not meet parametric assumptions
Disadvantages	Sensitive to outliers, require data to meet certain assumptions (e.g., normality, equal variance)	Generally less powerful, may not detect subtle differences in data

4.2.3.4 Implications for Marketing Data Science

In marketing data science, the choice between parametric and nonparametric tests can greatly affect the conclusions drawn from the data. For instance:

- When assessing the effect of a new advertisement on sales, if the sales data is normally distributed, a parametric test might be used to determine if there's a significant difference in means before and after the ad campaign.
- However, if a marketer is analyzing ordinal data, such as customer satisfaction ratings from 1 to 5, a nonparametric test might be more suitable.

In essence, understanding the underlying assumptions and characteristics of these tests enables marketers to select the most appropriate analysis method, ensuring robust and meaningful conclusions.

Both parametric and nonparametric tests have their advantages and limitations. The key is understanding when to apply each, based on the nature of the data and the research question at hand. As we move forward in this chapter, we will explore various statistical techniques in detail, emphasizing their applicability in real-world marketing scenarios.

4.2.4 Key Concepts in Inferential Analytics

To effectively apply inferential analytics in marketing, it is essential to understand several key concepts that underpin this statistical approach. In this section, we will cover these concepts, including populations, samples, sampling techniques, and sampling distributions, as well as margin of error, confidence intervals, and standard error.

4.2.4.1 Populations and Samples

A population refers to the entire group of individuals or entities of interest in a particular study or analysis (Triola, 2017). In marketing, this might include all customers, prospects, or users of a product or service. A sample, however, is a smaller subset of the population, selected to represent the broader group (Levy & Lemeshow, 2013).

4.2.4.2 Sampling Techniques

Sampling techniques are methods used to select a representative sample from a population (Lohr, 2019). Common sampling techniques include simple random sampling, stratified sampling, and cluster sampling (see Section 2.4.4.2). Each technique has its advantages and disadvantages, and the choice of the appropriate method depends on the research objectives and the nature of the population.

4.2.4.3 Sampling Distributions

A sampling distribution is the probability distribution of a given statistic based on random samples drawn from a population (Hogg et al., 2005). The central limit theorem, a fundamental result in probability theory, states that the sampling distribution of the sample mean approaches a normal distribution as the sample size increases, regardless of the shape of the population distribution (Wasserman, 2004).

4.2.4.4 Margin of Error

The margin of error quantifies the uncertainty associated with an estimate obtained from a sample (Agresti & Coull, 1998). It represents the range within which the true population parameter is likely to lie, given the observed sample statistic. The margin of error is typically expressed as a percentage and depends on the sample size, the level of confidence, and the variability of the population (Kish, 1965).

4.2.4.5 Confidence Intervals

A confidence interval is a range of values within which the true population parameter is likely to lie, with a specified level of confidence (Cumming & Calin-Jageman, 2016). For example, a 95% confidence interval means that if repeated samples were taken and the confidence interval calculated for each sample, 95% of these intervals would contain the true population parameter (see Section 4.3 for a detailed breakdown).

4.2.4.6 *Standard Error*

The standard error is a measure of the variability of a sample statistic, such as the mean or proportion, across different samples drawn from the same population (Kenney & Keeping, 1962). The standard error is used to calculate confidence intervals and is inversely proportional to the sample size—as the sample size increases, the standard error decreases, resulting in narrower confidence intervals and more precise estimates (Field et al., 2012).

4.3 CONFIDENCE INTERVALS

Confidence intervals (CIs) are a fundamental concept in statistics and are essential for making informed decisions based on sample data. They offer a range of values that is likely to contain the population parameter of interest. This section provides a deep dive into confidence intervals, particularly focusing on their significance in estimating population parameters.

4.3.1 Estimating Population Mean

When conducting research or analyzing data, we often use a sample to make inferences about an entire population. The sample mean is a good point estimate of the population mean, but it's beneficial to provide a range within which we believe the true population mean lies.

Formula:

$$\bar{x} \pm z\left(\frac{\sigma}{\sqrt{n}}\right),$$

where

- $\bar{x}$ = sample mean
- z = z-value, which corresponds to the desired confidence level (e.g., for a 95% confidence level, z is approximately 1.96)
- σ = population standard deviation
- n = sample size

In many real-world scenarios, the population standard deviation (σ) is not known. In such cases, while trying to estimate the population mean from a sample, we rely on the sample standard deviation (s) as an estimate for σ. Instead of the z-distribution, which assumes the population standard deviation is known, we turn to the t-distribution, which is more suitable for these situations.

The t-distribution is like the z-distribution in shape but has heavier tails. This makes it more accommodating for the variability expected when estimating both the population mean and standard deviation from a sample.

The formula for estimating the population mean using the t-distribution is:

$$\bar{x} \pm t\left(\frac{s}{\sqrt{n}}\right),$$

where

- $\bar{x}$ = sample mean
- t = t-value, which corresponds to the desired confidence level and degrees of freedom (df). The degrees of freedom for this test is $n-1$. For example, for a 95% confidence level and a sample size of 30, you would refer to a t-table to find the appropriate t-value.
- s = sample standard deviation (used as an estimate for σ)
- n = sample size

Key point. The reason for using the t-distribution over the z-distribution when the population standard deviation is unknown is to provide a more accurate range (confidence interval) for the population mean. Because the sample standard deviation may not be a perfect estimate for the population standard deviation, the t-distribution compensates for this uncertainty, especially when the sample size is small. As the sample size increases, the t-distribution approaches the shape of the z-distribution.

4.3.2 Margin of Error and Level of Confidence

The margin of error (MOE) gives the amount by which we expect our sample estimate to vary from the true population value. The larger the MOE, the less precise our estimate is.

Formula:

$$MOE = z\left(\frac{\sigma}{\sqrt{n}}\right),$$

where the components are as defined previously.

The level of confidence specifies the probability that the method of constructing the interval will encompass the population parameter. Common confidence levels are 90%, 95%, and 99%. The choice of confidence level affects the width of the CI: higher confidence levels result in wider intervals.

4.3.3 Interpreting Confidence Intervals

Understanding how to correctly interpret a confidence interval is crucial for making informed decisions.

- **Interval range.** If a 95% CI for the population mean is (50, 60), it means that we are 95% confident that the true population mean lies between 50 and 60.

■ **Not a probability statement about the parameter.** A common misconception is thinking that there's a 95% chance that the true mean lies in the interval. This is incorrect. The true mean either lies within the interval or it doesn't. The confidence level refers to the method of interval construction. If we were to repeat our sampling process numerous times, we expect about 95% of the constructed intervals to contain the population mean.

■ **Wider versus narrower intervals.** A wider interval suggests more uncertainty about the population parameter, while a narrower interval indicates greater precision. However, obtaining a narrower interval may require increasing the sample size.

■ **Practical implications.** In a business context, the width of the CI can influence decision-making. For instance, if a marketing campaign's ROI has a 95% CI between 5% and 15%, there's more uncertainty compared to a CI between 8% and 10%.

Figure 4.3 presents a bell curve (normal distribution) showcasing confidence intervals and highlighting regions under the curve. This visual aids in illustrating the interval range, the meaning of wider versus narrower intervals, and the practical implications of these intervals in decision-making.

Confidence intervals serve as a bridge between sample statistics and population parameters, providing a range where we believe the true value lies. They integrate the sample's point estimate, the variability of the data, and our desired level of confidence. By understanding and correctly interpreting CIs, professionals across fields, including marketing, can make more informed and evidence-based decisions.

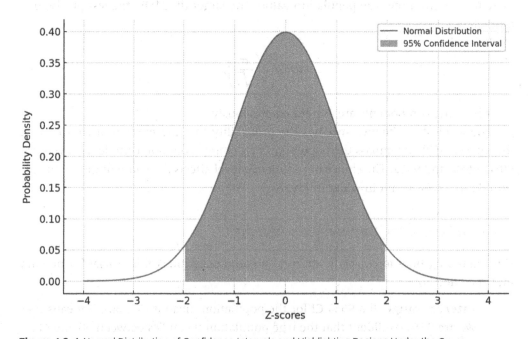

Figure 4.3 A Normal Distribution of Confidence Intervals and Highlighting Regions Under the Curve.

4.3.4 Practical Example: Confidence Interval in Marketing Campaign Evaluation

Let's reconsider our e-commerce company, ShopStream, that's planning to launch a new marketing campaign. Before rolling it out on a large scale, they decide to test it on a sample of 1,000 customers. The goal is to estimate the average increase in sales due to the campaign and to make projections for the broader customer base.

Data Collection. After the campaign, ShopStream records the increase in sales for the sampled customers. They find a sample mean ($\bar{x}$) increase of $50 and a sample standard deviation (s) of $15.

Constructing the Confidence Interval Using the T-Distribution. Because the population standard deviation is unknown, ShopStream uses the t-distribution. With 1,000 customers, the degrees of freedom is $df = 1,000 - 1 = 999$. Referring to a t-table for a 95% confidence level, they find the t-value close to 1.96 (very similar to the z-value due to the large sample size).

Using the formula:

$$CI = \bar{x} \pm t\left(\frac{s}{\sqrt{n}}\right)$$

$$CI = 50 \pm 1.96\left(\frac{15}{\sqrt{1000}}\right)$$

$$CI = (49.08, 50.92)$$

Interpretation. The 95% confidence interval for the increase in sales due to the marketing campaign lies between $49.08 and $50.92. This means that ShopStream is 95% confident that the average increase in sales for the entire customer base, due to the campaign, will fall within this range.

Business decision. Given this narrow interval, ShopStream's marketing team can confidently predict the campaign's impact on the broader customer base. If this projected increase aligns with their return on investment (ROI) targets, they can decide to implement the campaign for all customers.

This practical example showcases the applicability of confidence intervals in making informed business decisions. By testing their campaign on a sample first, ShopStream was able to gauge the potential outcomes without fully committing, thus optimizing resources, and ensuring the campaign's effectiveness.

4.4 A/B TESTING IN MARKETING

A/B testing, sometimes known as *split testing*, has become a cornerstone tool in the marketing world. With the increasing emphasis on data-driven decision-making, it offers a scientific method to test and optimize various marketing efforts. In this section, we will

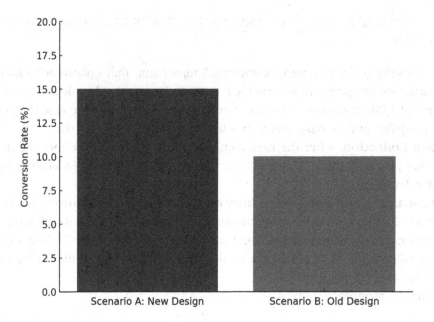

Figure 4.4 Comparing the Results of Two Different A/B Testing Scenarios.

delve deep into the realm of A/B testing, specifically tailored to marketing. Figure 4.4 offers a visual aid in this regard, presenting a bar graph that compares the results of two different A/B testing scenarios. This comparison not only illustrates the effectiveness of each scenario but also underscores the importance of carefully designed tests in deriving meaningful insights.

4.4.1 Basics and Importance

A/B testing is a method of comparing two versions (A and B) of a web page, advertisement, or other marketing assets to determine which one performs better in achieving a given objective, such as increasing click-through rates, sales, or any other conversion metric.

The significance of A/B testing in modern marketing cannot be overstated, because it offers a methodical approach to enhancing marketing strategies across various dimensions. Key aspects of its importance include the following:

- **Data-driven decisions.** Instead of relying on intuition, marketers can use empirical evidence to decide which version of a marketing asset is more effective.
- **Optimize campaigns.** Through iterative testing, marketers can continually refine and enhance their campaigns, leading to improved ROI.
- **Reduce risks.** Before committing to large-scale changes or campaigns, marketers can test variations to ensure they're moving in the right direction.

4.4.2 Experimental Design for A/B Tests

- **Control and variation.** For an A/B test, one version acts as the control, and the other is the variation with the proposed changes.
- **Random assignment.** It's crucial to randomly assign users to either the control or variation group. This ensures that the groups are comparable, and any observed differences can be attributed to the changes made rather than external factors.
- **Sample size.** The size of the sample can influence the reliability of the results. A larger sample can provide more accurate results, but it's also important to ensure a minimum sample size to detect meaningful differences.
- **Duration.** Running the test for an appropriate duration ensures that results aren't skewed due to day-of-week effects or other short-term factors.

Table 4.2 provides a simplified outline of an experimental design for A/B testing, including the variables involved, the expected outcomes, and the key metrics used for measurement.

Table 4.2 A Simplified Experimental Design for A/B Testing Including Variables, Outcomes, and Metrics.

	Variables	Outcomes	Key Metrics
Test 1	Website design (old vs. new)	Increase in website engagement	Time spent on website, bounce rate
Test 2	Ad placement (top vs. bottom)	Click-through rate on ads	Number of clicks, impressions
Test 3	Call-to-action text (buy now vs. add to cart)	Increase in product purchases	Conversion rate, cart abandonment rate

4.4.3 Setting Up A/B Tests: A Step-by-Step Guide

Setting up a successful A/B test requires meticulous planning and attention to detail. Here's a structured step-by-step guide to help you navigate the process:

1. **Define the objective.** Before anything else, have a clear understanding of what you're trying to achieve with the test. It could be increasing email open rates, boosting product sales, or enhancing user engagement on a specific web page.
2. **Identify the variable.** Decide on the specific element or feature you want to test. This could range from button colors, website copy, and product images to email subject lines.
3. **Develop the hypothesis.** Formulate a clear hypothesis based on your objective and the chosen variable. For instance, "Changing the call-to-action button from blue to red will increase click-through rates."
4. **Choose your tools.** Depending on the platform and the scale, you might use tools such as Google Optimize, Optimizely, VWO, or others for web-based tests. For email campaigns, platforms such as Mailchimp or HubSpot might be suitable.

5. **Segment your audience.** Divide your audience into two groups. One group (the control group) will see the current version, and the other (the variation group) will see the new version.

6. **Random assignment.** Ensure that users are randomly assigned to each group to avoid selection bias.

7. **Set test duration and sample size.** Before starting the test, calculate the required sample size to achieve statistical significance. Also, determine the test duration, ensuring you capture complete business cycles.

8. **Launch the test.** With everything in place, launch your test. Ensure real-time monitoring to check for any anomalies or issues.

9. **Analyze results.** At the end of the test period, collect and analyze the data. Calculate metrics like conversion rates for both groups, the difference in those rates, and the statistical significance of that difference.

10. **Draw conclusions**. Based on the analyzed results, decide whether the hypothesis was supported or refuted.

11. **Implement learnings.** If the new version outperformed the old one and you achieved statistical significance, consider implementing the change. If the test was inconclusive or the new version didn't perform well, use the insights gained to inform future tests.

12. **Document everything.** For future reference and to build an organizational learning curve, document the test setup, hypothesis, results, and key takeaways.

13. **Rinse and repeat.** The beauty of A/B testing lies in its iterative nature. Use the insights from one test to inform future ones, continuously improving and optimizing your marketing efforts.

Proper setup is crucial for the success of an A/B test. It ensures that the results obtained are valid, actionable, and aligned with business objectives. By systematically following the outlined steps, marketers can harness the power of A/B testing to make informed, data-driven decisions.

4.4.4 Statistical Significance in A/B Tests

Statistical significance indicates how confident we can be that the observed results in the A/B test aren't due to random chance.

- *P*-value. This is a commonly used metric in A/B testing. A low p-value (typically < 0.05) suggests that the results are statistically significant.

- **Type I and Type II errors.** It's important to be aware of the potential for false positives (believing there's an effect when there isn't) and false negatives (believing there isn't an effect when there is).

- **Power of the test.** This refers to the probability of detecting a difference if one exists. A standard desired power is 0.8 or 80%.

4.4.5 Advanced A/B Testing Techniques

As businesses become more data-driven and the digital landscape evolves, the realm of A/B testing has seen the introduction of more sophisticated techniques. Let's dive deeper into these advanced methods and understand how they differ from the basic A/B testing approach.

4.4.5.1 Multivariate Testing

What is it? Unlike A/B testing, in which only one variable is changed at a time, multivariate testing (MVT) involves testing multiple changes/variations concurrently to see which combination produces the best result.

How does it differ from A/B testing? Although A/B testing compares version A to version B, MVT might compare a combination of version A1, B1, C1 to A2, B2, C2, and so on, exploring the interactions between variables.

Application. For instance, if an e-commerce site wanted to test the color of a call-to-action button and the text within it simultaneously, MVT would assess various combinations of color and text to identify the most effective mix.

4.4.5.2 Sequential Testing

What is it? Sequential testing is a dynamic method in which the sample size isn't fixed beforehand. The test is continuously monitored, and based on the incoming results, decisions to stop (due to significant findings) or continue are made.

How does it differ from A/B testing? Traditional A/B tests have a predetermined sample size and duration. In sequential testing, the test might end earlier if a clear winner is identified or might extend if the results remain inconclusive.

Application. If a company is testing a crucial website feature, and early results already show significant improvements with the new variant, they might decide to stop the test and implement the change sooner, saving resources and time.

4.4.5.3 Bayesian A/B Testing

What is it? Bayesian A/B testing is an approach that updates the probability of a hypothesis being true as more data becomes available, providing a more intuitive and flexible analysis.

How does it differ from A/B testing? Traditional A/B testing, based on frequentist statistics, provides a p-value indicating if there's a statistically significant difference. Bayesian testing, however, provides a probability distribution, showing how likely a particular result or effect size is.

Application. If a marketing team wants to understand the potential impact of two ad designs, a Bayesian approach would tell them not just if one ad is better, but how much better it is and the certainty level of that estimate.

4.4.5.4 *Personalization and Segment-Based Testing*

What is it? This approach focuses on creating tests tailored for specific audience segments instead of treating the entire audience as a single entity.

How does it differ from A/B testing? Although basic A/B testing might give results for the average user, segment-based testing delves deeper, uncovering insights for specific groups such as new visitors, returning customers, or users from a particular location.

Application. A streaming service might conduct segment-based tests to understand content preferences. Instead of generalizing that a new UI is better for all users, they might find that younger users prefer one style, whereas older users have different inclinations.

Conclusion. Although traditional A/B testing offers valuable insights, these advanced techniques allow for a more nuanced understanding, optimizing multiple aspects of a campaign and catering to diverse audience needs. As businesses grow and datasets expand, integrating these advanced methodologies can lead to more refined, effective, and personalized marketing strategies.

4.4.6 Potential Pitfalls in A/B Testing

Although A/B testing is a powerful methodology, there are common pitfalls that marketers need to be wary of to ensure valid and actionable results:

- **Carryover effects.** Sometimes, users who were exposed to one version (e.g., Version A) might later be exposed to the other version (Version B), leading to potential biases in their behaviors.
- **Novelty effect.** New designs or features might initially perform better simply because they are new and capture attention, not because they are inherently better.
- **External factors.** Events outside of the test, such as holidays, news events, or technical issues, can skew results.
- **Peeking early.** It's tempting to stop a test early when results look promising, but this can lead to incorrect conclusions. A test should run its full course to ensure statistical validity.
- **Testing too many elements at once.** Although multivariate testing can be valuable, testing too many changes simultaneously can make it difficult to pinpoint which change led to the observed results.
- **Ignoring business cycles.** Not considering weekly or monthly business cycles can lead to skewed data. For example, an online retailer might see different behaviors on weekdays compared to weekends.

4.4.7 Interpreting A/B Test Results

Once the test is concluded, interpretation and application of the results are paramount:

- **Effect size.** Even if a result is statistically significant, it's crucial to determine if the difference is practically significant. For instance, a 0.01% increase in click-through might not be worth the investment, even if it's statistically significant.
- **Confidence intervals.** Instead of just looking at point estimates, check the range in which the true metric lies with a certain confidence. This provides a more holistic view of potential outcomes.
- **Contextualize results.** Always interpret results in the context of the business and audience. A change that works for one demographic or product might not work for another.
- **Follow-up tests.** If a test result is unexpected or counterintuitive, consider running follow-up tests to validate the findings or explore the phenomenon further.
- **Document and share.** Maintaining a repository of past tests, their designs, results, and learned lessons can be invaluable for future campaigns and for educating the broader team.

A/B testing, when executed correctly, can unveil deep insights into customer behavior, preferences, and motivations. Although it's a technical process, it's also an art that requires marketers to balance statistical rigor with intuitive understanding of their audience and market context. By being aware of potential pitfalls, regularly updating testing methodologies, and placing results in the right business context, marketers can significantly elevate their strategies and execution.

In summary, A/B testing is a potent tool in the marketer's arsenal. By employing rigorous scientific techniques, marketers can ensure that their decisions are data-driven, reducing risks and amplifying returns on their marketing investments.

4.5 HYPOTHESIS TESTING IN MARKETING

4.5.1 Introduction to Hypothesis Testing

Hypothesis testing is a fundamental technique in inferential statistics that enables researchers to evaluate the validity of their assumptions and make data-driven decisions (Cohen, 1994). In the context of marketing, hypothesis testing can be employed to assess the effectiveness of marketing campaigns, compare customer segments, or evaluate the impact of pricing changes, among other applications (Kotler & Keller, 2015).

The process of hypothesis testing involves formulating a null hypothesis (H0) and an alternative hypothesis (H1) (Moore et al., 2009). The null hypothesis represents the assumption of no effect or relationship between variables, and the alternative hypothesis posits that there is an effect or relationship (Romano & Lehmann, 2005). For example, a marketer might want to assess whether a new promotional campaign has a positive impact on sales. In this case, the null hypothesis would state that there is no difference in sales between the new campaign and the old one, and the alternative hypothesis would assert that there is a difference.

To assess the hypotheses, researchers use sample data and compute a test statistic, such as the t-statistic or the chi-square statistic, which quantifies the difference between the observed data and the null hypothesis (Wilcox, 2011). The test statistic is then compared to a critical value, which is determined based on the chosen significance level (α) and the probability distribution associated with the test statistic (Rice, 2006). If the test statistic exceeds the critical value, the null hypothesis is rejected in favor of the alternative hypothesis, suggesting that there is evidence to support the claim that the new marketing campaign has an impact on sales (Field et al., 2012).

Hypothesis testing has been widely used in marketing research and practice to evaluate marketing strategies and make data-driven decisions (Hair et al., 2018). By applying hypothesis testing techniques, marketers can gain valuable insights and optimize their marketing efforts, ultimately leading to improved outcomes and increased ROI.

Figure 4.5 provides a graphical representation of a two-tailed hypothesis test, with highlighted regions indicating the rejection and non-rejection zones. This visual aid is particularly useful for illustrating how the test statistic is compared against critical values to determine whether to reject or retain the null hypothesis.

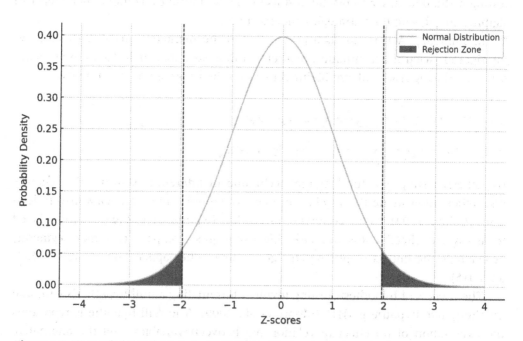

Figure 4.5 A Two-Tailed Hypothesis Test with Highlighted Regions Indicating Rejection and Non-Rejection Zones.

4.5.2 Common Hypothesis Tests in Marketing

In marketing, various hypothesis tests are employed to analyze data and derive insights. Some of the most common hypothesis tests include *t*-tests, chi-square tests, ANOVA, and correlation and regression tests. In this section, we will briefly discuss each of these tests and their applications in marketing, with relevant references (see Table 4.3).

4.5.2.1 T-*tests*

T-tests are a family of statistical tests used to compare the means of two groups (Student, 1908). In marketing, *t*-tests can be applied to compare the average sales or customer satisfaction scores between two different marketing campaigns or customer segments (Kotler & Keller, 2015). There are several types of *t*-tests, including independent samples *t*-test, paired samples *t*-test, and one-sample *t*-test, each designed for specific research scenarios (Field et al., 2012).

4.5.2.2 *Chi-square tests*

Chi-square tests are non-parametric tests used to examine the relationship between two categorical variables (Pearson, 1900). In marketing, chi-square tests can be employed to analyze the association between customer demographics (e.g., age, gender, income) and their preferences for a particular product or service (Hair et al., 2018). The test statistic, chi-square ($\chi2$), is calculated based on the observed and expected frequencies in a contingency table and is compared to a critical value to determine the significance of the relationship (Agresti, 2018).

4.5.2.3 *Analysis of Variance*

ANOVA is a statistical technique used to compare the means of three or more groups (Fisher, 1970). In marketing, ANOVA can be used to analyze the effectiveness of multiple marketing campaigns, pricing strategies, or promotional offers (Kotler & Keller, 2015). ANOVA decomposes the total variation in the data into between-group and

Table 4.3 Common Hypothesis Tests in Marketing with Their Applications and Assumptions.

Hypothesis Test	Applications	Assumptions
t-test	Compare means of two groups (e.g., control vs. treatment)	Normally distributed data, equal variances
Chi-square test	Test relationships between categorical variables (e.g., ad type vs. click-through rate)	Observed frequencies are sufficiently large
Analysis of variance	Compare means of three or more groups	Normally distributed, equal variances, independent observations
Regression analysis	Predict the value of a variable based on the value of one or more other variables	Linear relationship, multivariate normality, no multicollinearity

within-group variations and calculates an *F*-ratio to test the null hypothesis that all group means are equal (Field et al., 2012).

4.5.2.4 Correlation and Regression Tests

Correlation and regression tests are powerful analytical tools that unveil relationships between continuous variables (Cohen et al., 2013). In marketing analytics, these tests not only ascertain relationships but also predict future outcomes based on various influencing factors (Kotler & Keller, 2015).

Correlation analysis. Pearson's correlation coefficient (*r*) quantifies the strength and direction of a linear relationship between two variables. This can be particularly useful in marketing to do the following:

- Identify if there's a relationship between advertising spend and sales.
- Understand the correlation between customer satisfaction scores and repeat purchases.

However, although correlation can reveal that two variables move together, it doesn't necessarily imply causation. A high correlation between advertising spend and sales doesn't prove that the advertising caused the sales to increase.

Regression analysis. Regression takes this a step further by establishing a predictive model. In marketing, regression analysis is an indispensable tool because of its ability to forecast outcomes based on changes in predictor variables.

- **Simple linear regression.** This involves one independent variable predicting a dependent variable, for instance, predicting sales (dependent variable) based on the marketing budget (independent variable).
- **Multiple regression.** Here we model the relationship between a dependent variable and multiple independent variables. Consider an e-commerce firm. They might want to predict product sales (dependent variable) using multiple predictors such as online ad spend, the number of reviews, product pricing, and website traffic (Hair et al., 2018).

Application of Regression in Marketing

- **Budget allocation.** By understanding which marketing activities (online ads, influencer campaigns, email marketing) are driving sales, businesses can optimize their budget allocation for maximum ROI.
- **Pricing strategy.** If product price is one of the independent variables in a regression model, businesses can analyze its impact on sales and thereby refine pricing strategies.
- **Customer lifetime value prediction.** Using regression, firms can predict the total net profit from a customer throughout their relationship. Predictors might include average purchase value, purchase frequency, and customer life span.

■ **Product recommendations.** By analyzing purchase behaviors and other customer data, regression models can help in predicting which products a customer might be interested in next, driving upsell and cross-sell strategies.

In conclusion, although correlation provides insights into relationships, regression is a robust tool in a marketer's arsenal to predict outcomes and optimize strategies. It's not just about understanding what happened but also leveraging data to shape future strategies and decisions.

4.5.3 Significance Levels and *P*-Values

In hypothesis testing, the significance level (α) and *p*-values play crucial roles in determining whether to reject or retain the null hypothesis. These concepts help researchers quantify the likelihood of obtaining the observed results if the null hypothesis is true (Romano & Lehmann, 2005). In this section, we will discuss the significance levels and *p*-values in detail, with relevant references.

4.5.3.1 Significance Level (α)

The significance level, denoted by α, is the probability of rejecting the null hypothesis when it is actually true (Type I error) (Cohen, 1994). Commonly used significance levels in research are 0.05, 0.01, and 0.001, which represent the maximum acceptable probability of making a Type I error (Field et al., 2012). The chosen significance level dictates the critical value, against which the test statistic is compared. If the test statistic exceeds the critical value, the null hypothesis is rejected in favor of the alternative hypothesis (Rice, 2006).

4.5.3.2 P-Values

P-values, which stand for probability values, represent the probability of obtaining a test statistic as extreme or more extreme than the observed value, assuming that the null hypothesis is true (Romano & Lehmann, 2005). Smaller *p*-values indicate stronger evidence against the null hypothesis, whereas larger *p*-values suggest weaker evidence (Wilcox, 2011). To determine the outcome of a hypothesis test, the *p*-value is compared to the chosen significance level (α) (Moore et al., 2009). If the *p*-value is less than or equal to α, the null hypothesis is rejected, indicating that the observed results are statistically significant and provide evidence in favor of the alternative hypothesis.

The concepts of significance levels and *p*-values are essential for making informed decisions in hypothesis testing. By setting an appropriate significance level and interpreting *p*-values correctly, researchers can control the risk of making erroneous conclusions and increase the reliability of their findings (Cohen, 1994). In marketing, understanding these concepts is crucial for evaluating the effectiveness of marketing strategies and making data-driven decisions (Kotler & Keller, 2015).

4.6   CUSTOMER SEGMENTATION AND PROCESSING

As we transition from hypothesis testing to customer segmentation, it might seem as though we're making a leap from one realm to another. However, in the intricate web of data-driven marketing, these two areas are interconnected and complementary.

Inferential analytics as the foundation. At its core, inferential analytics, especially through tools such as A/B testing, enables marketers to draw conclusions about specific strategies or assets. We hypothesize, test, and then infer based on sample data what might be true for our entire target population. It equips marketers with the knowledge of what works and what doesn't in engaging a specific audience.

Enter customer segmentation. Although inferential analytics helps marketers understand the effectiveness of specific strategies, customer segmentation focuses on understanding the audience itself. It categorizes the vast array of consumers into more manageable and coherent groups based on various attributes such as behaviors, needs, or demographics. But why is this relevant in the context of inferential analytics?

- **Tailored hypotheses.** With a better grasp on distinct customer segments, marketers can formulate more precise hypotheses. For example, instead of hypothesizing a strategy's effectiveness for the entire user base, one could focus on its impact on a particular segment, such as millennials or repeat customers.

- **Enhanced testing relevance.** Inferential analytics, when applied to specific segments, ensures that the tests are more relevant. Testing a new feature for tech-savvy users might yield different results compared to testing it for users who aren't as technologically inclined.

- **Driving personalization.** As tests validate which strategies work for which segments, it paves the way for personalized marketing campaigns. Instead of a one-size-fits-all approach, businesses can cater to the unique needs and preferences of each segment.

- **Optimized resource allocation.** By understanding which segments respond best to which strategies, businesses can allocate their resources more effectively. This ensures higher ROIs and minimizes wasted effort on less responsive segments.

In essence, although inferential analytics provides marketers with the tools to test and validate strategies, customer segmentation offers a lens to view their audience in a nuanced manner. Together, they empower businesses to not just engage their audience but to engage them in the most effective way possible. As we delve deeper into customer segmentation in this section, keep in mind the inferential foundation we've built, and consider how each segment might respond differently to various marketing strategies.

In the digital age, understanding customers on a granular level is essential for marketing success. However, with a deluge of customer data available, processing and segmenting this information in a meaningful manner becomes a challenging endeavor. Customer segmentation is the process of dividing a vast customer base into more manageable and homogenous groups, based on certain criteria or behaviors, to tailor marketing efforts effectively. This chapter will delve into various powerful method-ologies for customer segmentation and data processing. We'll begin by understanding the intricacies of k-means clustering, a partitioning method that segments data into distinct clusters. Following that, we'll explore the hierarchical structure of customer groups through hierarchical clustering, providing a multitiered view of customer segments. Last, the chapter will dissect the RFM (recency, frequency, monetary) analysis, a behavioral segmentation method that offers a comprehensive lens into customer value and engagement. Through these techniques, marketers can achieve a nuanced under-standing of their audience, ensuring marketing strategies are precise and impactful.

4.6.1 K-Means Clustering

K-means clustering is one of the most popular partitioning methods in unsupervised learning, especially in the context of marketing for customer segmentation (Jain, 2010). The core idea behind k-means clustering is to divide a dataset into k number of mutually exclusive clusters where each data point belongs to the cluster with the nearest mean.

4.6.1.1 Process of K-Means Clustering

1. **Initialization.** Choose k initial cluster centers (usually k data points from the dataset).
2. **Assignment.** Assign each data point to the nearest cluster center.
3. **Recomputation.** Compute the new mean for each cluster.
4. **Repeat.** Repeat the assignment and recomputation steps until the cluster assignments no longer change.

4.6.1.2 Benefits for Marketers

Segmentation efficiency. Using k-means, large customer datasets can be quickly seg-mented based on chosen characteristics or behaviors, aiding in target marketing (Punj & Stewart, 1983).

Flexibility. Marketers can determine the number of desired customer segments (k) based on business needs, although it's essential to choose an optimal k using tech-niques such as the elbow method.

Profiling. Once clusters are defined, marketers can profile each segment to under-stand its defining characteristics, driving personalized marketing efforts (Wedel & Kamakura, 2000).

4.6.1.3 Considerations

Feature scaling. Feature scaling, which encompasses standardization and normal-ization techniques, is a critical preprocessing step when employing algorithms such as k-means clustering. The reason for this necessity is deeply embedded in how the algorithm operates:

- **Distance-based algorithms.** K-means clustering is fundamentally a distance-based algorithm, where data points are grouped based on their distance from the centroid of a cluster. If one feature has a broad range of values (e.g., annual income ranging from thousands to millions) and another has a narrow range (e.g., age ranging from 20 to 70), the algorithm may unduly weight the feature with the broader range more heavily. This disproportionate weighting can distort the formation of clusters.

- **Uniformity in measurement.** Features in a dataset may be measured in various units (e.g., kilograms, miles, dollars). Directly comparing these without scaling could yield meaningless clusters. By scaling features, we ensure they are on a uniform measurement scale, allowing for meaningful comparisons.

- **Improving convergence.** Many optimization algorithms (such as gradient descent) used in machine learning converge faster with standardized or normalized data. In the context of k-means, feature scaling can help in achieving faster convergence to the optimal centroids.

- **Enhanced interpretability.** Post clustering, if you aim to profile or understand the characteristics of each cluster, having scaled features can ease the interpretability. The relative importance of each feature in determining cluster membership becomes more apparent.

In essence, for k-means clustering to yield meaningful and accurate results, it's essential to ensure that each feature contributes approximately proportionately to the computation of distances. Feature scaling ensures this balance, making it a necessary step in the clustering process.

- **Random initialization trap.** K-means can produce different results depending on initial cluster centers. This can be mitigated using techniques such as k-means++ for smarter initialization.

- **Choosing *k*.** Finding the right number of clusters is critical. Techniques such as the elbow method or silhouette analysis can help in this determination.

- **Application in marketing.** A retail company might use k-means clustering to segment its customers based on purchasing behavior, frequency, and product preferences. By doing so, they could tailor promotional offers or advertisements specific to each segment's characteristics, maximizing the chances of positive customer responses.

4.6.2 Hierarchical Clustering in Customer Segmentation

Hierarchical clustering is a method used to construct a hierarchy or a tree of clusters. Unlike k-means clustering, which partitions data into distinct clusters with no intrinsic order or relation, hierarchical clustering establishes a multilevel hierarchy of clusters. This can provide a more granular view of customer segmentation.

4.6.2.1 Basics of Hierarchical Clustering

Hierarchical clustering operates on the principle of grouping similar data points together into clusters, ensuring data points in a single cluster are more alike compared to those in other clusters. There are two primary approaches to this:

- **Agglomerative clustering.** This is a bottom-up approach where each data point starts as an individual cluster. These clusters are then iteratively merged based on their similarity until there's just one large cluster containing all data points.
- **Divisive clustering.** Opposite to the agglomerative approach, divisive clustering starts with one large cluster containing all data points. It then splits the cluster iteratively into smaller ones based on dissimilarity, continuing until each data point stands alone as a single cluster.

4.6.2.2 How It Works

- **Similarity matrix creation.** The first step is to compute a matrix containing distances (or dissimilarities) between each pair of data points.
- **Cluster formation.** Using the distance matrix, clusters are formed using a linkage criterion. Common linkage criteria include the following:
  - **Single linkage.** The distance between two clusters is the shortest distance between two data points in each cluster.
  - **Complete linkage.** The distance between two clusters is the longest distance between two data points in each cluster.
  - **Average linkage.** The distance between two clusters is the average distance between data points in the two clusters.
- **Tree (dendrogram) creation.** A tree-like diagram called a *dendrogram* is created, representing how clusters are merged (agglomerative) or split (divisive).
- **Cutting the dendrogram.** By cutting the dendrogram at a specific level, a marketer can decide the number of clusters they want for segmentation.

4.6.2.3 Application in Marketing

Hierarchical clustering offers a multi-resolution perspective of customer segmentation. For instance, an e-commerce business can cluster customers based on their purchasing behavior:

- At a higher level, they might identify clusters such as 'Frequent Shoppers', 'Seasonal Shoppers', and 'Rare Shoppers'.
- Drilling down, 'Frequent Shoppers' might further divide into 'High Spenders' and 'Bargain Hunters'.

By visualizing this in a dendrogram, the business gets a clear hierarchical view of customer segments, leading to more nuanced marketing strategies.

4.6.2.4 Advantages and Limitations

Advantages

- **Hierarchical structure.** One of the primary benefits of hierarchical clustering is the ability to visualize and understand nested groupings. This is often valuable in real-world scenarios where hierarchical relationships matter, such as categorizing products or understanding organizational structures.
- **No need for predefined clusters.** Unlike some other clustering methods that require a predefined number of clusters, hierarchical clustering does not demand this input, making it easier to commence without prior assumptions.

Limitations

- **Computationally intensive.** Hierarchical clustering is more computationally demanding than some other clustering algorithms, especially for larger datasets. The algorithm must evaluate and merge data points or clusters in a stepwise manner, leading to a higher computational cost.
- **Lack of reproducibility and determinism.** Hierarchical clustering does not incorporate randomness in its process. Therefore, one might assume it should always produce the same result for the same dataset. However, the catch is in the nuances:
  - Different software or tools may implement hierarchical clustering with slight variations, leading to different results.
  - The order in which data points are presented to the algorithm, or the order of merges, can influence the resulting hierarchy. This means that unless the process is carefully controlled to be deterministic (i.e., the same actions are taken in the same order every time), different runs or applications might yield different cluster hierarchies.
- **Complexity of dendrograms.** A dendrogram is the primary tool for visualizing the results of hierarchical clustering. Although dendrograms can provide a wealth of information, they come with challenges:
  - **Interpretability.** As the number of data points or clusters grows, dendrograms can become complex and challenging to interpret. Deciding where to cut the dendrogram to define clusters is not always straightforward.
  - **Scale sensitivity.** Dendrograms can be sensitive to the scale of the data. If data isn't properly standardized or normalized, the dendrogram might misrepresent the true hierarchical relationships.
  - **Overwhelming detail.** Especially for large datasets, dendrograms can display an overwhelming amount of detail, making it tough to discern meaningful patterns or relationships immediately.

In conclusion, although hierarchical clustering offers unique advantages, it's essential to be aware of its limitations, especially when dealing with larger datasets or when requiring consistent, reproducible results. Properly interpreting dendrograms also requires a level of expertise and experience.

4.6.2.5 Real-World Example: Media Consumption Habits

A streaming service wanted to understand the viewing habits of its audience. Using hierarchical clustering, they segmented their users based on genres watched. At a broader level, clusters such as 'Action Lovers', 'Drama Enthusiasts', and 'Documentary Watchers' were identified. Delving deeper, 'Action Lovers' split into 'Superhero Movie Fans' and 'Classic Action Film Buffs'. Based on these insights, the service could recommend more curated content to users, enhancing user engagement.

Hierarchical clustering offers a unique approach to understanding customer behaviors and preferences. Its ability to provide a multitiered segmentation perspective makes it invaluable for businesses seeking in-depth insights. Although it has its challenges, when applied judiciously, it can significantly augment marketing strategies, ensuring they're both tailored and targeted.

4.6.3 Recency, Frequency, Monetary Analysis in Marketing

RFM analysis is a cornerstone method in the world of customer segmentation based on behavioral attributes. Recency, frequency, and monetary value represent three critical dimensions to understand and predict customer behavior. By analyzing and segmenting customers based on these parameters, businesses can tailor their marketing strategies more effectively and enhance customer engagement. Figure 4.6 presents a 3D scatterplot showing the result of applying RFM segments to a sample customer dataset. This visual representation effectively illustrates the distribution of customers across the three RFM dimensions, providing a clear and comprehensive view of how these parameters intersect to form distinct customer segments. By observing this 3D scatterplot, marketers can gain a deeper understanding of their customer base, observing patterns and trends that inform targeted marketing strategies and contribute to enhanced customer engagement. Such visual tools are essential in translating the theoretical aspects of RFM analysis into actionable insights.

4.6.3.1 Understanding Recency, Frequency, Monetary

- **Recency (R).** Refers to the time since the last transaction or interaction of a customer. Customers who have interacted or purchased recently are more likely to respond positively to new offers and are generally considered more loyal.
- **Frequency (F).** Signifies how often a customer transacts or interacts with the brand within a specified time frame. High-frequency customers are consistent buyers and are crucial for business sustenance.

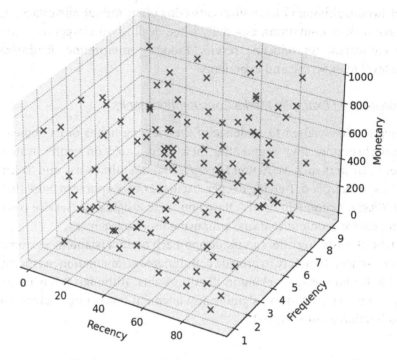

Figure 4.6 Result of RFM Segments on a Sample Customer Dataset.

- **Monetary (M).** Represents the total amount of money a customer has spent with the brand during a particular period. Customers with high monetary values are high spenders, often forming the segment that contributes a large chunk to the business revenue.

4.6.3.2   Benefits of Recency, Frequency, Monetary Analysis

- **Targeted marketing.** By segmenting the customer base on RFM criteria, businesses can craft highly targeted campaigns. For example, customers with high recency but low frequency might be targeted with specific campaigns to increase their purchase frequency.
- **Enhanced customer retention.** Understanding which customers are at risk of churning enables businesses to take preventive actions, offering specialized promotions or loyalty benefits to retain them.
- **Optimized marketing budgets.** Instead of spending indiscriminately, businesses can channel their marketing budget more effectively toward segments that will yield the highest ROI.
- **Personalization.** RFM analysis can drive personalization strategies, ensuring that customers receive content and offers most relevant to their behavior and spending patterns.

4.6.3.3 Determining Recency, Frequency, Monetary Scoring Thresholds

Determining the thresholds for RFM scoring is crucial because it influences how customers are segmented and targeted. Here's how businesses typically set these thresholds:

- **Percentile-based scoring.** One common method is to divide the dataset into percentiles. For instance, the top 20% of customers in terms of recency (i.e., the most recent) might be assigned a score of 5, the next 20% a score of 4, and so on. This method ensures that scoring is relative to the current dataset and can adjust as the business grows or customer behavior shifts.

- **Business rules.** Some businesses might have specific benchmarks or targets. For example, if a business believes that any customer who hasn't purchased in the last 30 days is at risk of churning, they might assign those customers a recency score of 1, irrespective of how that aligns with percentiles.

- **Standard deviation.** Another method involves calculating the mean and standard deviation for recency, frequency, and monetary values. Customers might be scored based on how many standard deviations away from the mean their behavior falls.

- **Historical analysis.** Looking at past data, businesses can identify patterns or benchmarks. If historically, customers who purchase more than five times in a month tend to be loyal, a frequency above this might be scored as a 5.

- **Iterative approach.** Some businesses might start with an initial scoring system, then adjust over time based on outcomes. If a scoring threshold isn't effectively segmenting valuable customers, it can be recalibrated.

- **Engaging with stakeholders.** Especially for setting monetary thresholds, businesses might engage with finance or sales teams to understand what constitutes a "high" spender.

Importance of calibration. It's essential to revisit and recalibrate these thresholds regularly. Customer behavior, business models, and external factors can evolve, necessitating adjustments to scoring.

By understanding and setting these thresholds thoughtfully, businesses can ensure that their RFM analysis is tuned to their unique needs and can generate actionable insights. It's not just about the numbers; it's about understanding what those numbers mean in the context of the business's goals and challenges.

4.6.3.4 Implementing Recency, Frequency, Monetary Analysis

1. **Data collection.** Collate customer transaction data. Ensure it's clean, updated, and accurate.

2. **Scoring.** Assign scores typically from 1 to 5 (with 5 being the highest) based on RFM values. A customer with a score of 555 is a high-value customer, having interacted recently, frequently, and has spent a significant amount.

3. **Segmentation.** Based on the RFM scores, segment customers into categories such as 'Champions', 'At Risk', 'Can't Lose Them', 'New Customers', 'Lost', and so on. Each segment will correspond to a unique combination of RFM scores.

4. **Tailored marketing strategies.** Develop and deploy marketing strategies specific to each segment. For instance, 'At Risk' customers might benefit from exclusive offers or loyalty points to reengage them.

5. **Continuous monitoring.** RFM isn't a one-time analysis. Continuously monitor and adjust scores as customer behaviors evolve.

4.6.3.5 Case Study: E-Commerce Implementation

An e-commerce business noticed dwindling sales and an increasing customer churn rate. On implementing RFM analysis, they identified a segment of customers (scored as 515) who had made significant purchases in the past, but it had been a while since their last transaction, even though they purchased fairly regularly. Realizing these customers were 'At Risk', the e-commerce site launched a "We Miss You" email campaign with exclusive discounts. This resulted in a 25% reengagement rate from that segment, boosting sales.

4.6.3.6 Considerations and Limitations

RFM is a quantitative analysis and might not factor in qualitative aspects of customer behavior. It's vital to choose the right time frame for analysis, which might vary based on the business model and industry. Not all high spenders are profitable. RFM should be combined with profitability analysis for a holistic view.

RFM analysis, with its simplicity and effectiveness, remains a vital tool for modern businesses. By focusing on three key metrics, it helps unravel the intricacies of customer behavior, enabling businesses to forge stronger, more personalized relationships with their clientele. In the vast universe of data analytics and marketing strategies, RFM stands out as a beacon, guiding businesses toward more meaningful customer interactions and heightened profitability.

Although RFM analysis offers a straightforward and effective approach to customer segmentation, it's also valuable to consider how it compares to other segmentation methods such as k-means and hierarchical clustering. Table 4.4 presents a comprehensive comparison of these three techniques, covering criteria such as the type of data each method is best suited for, the size of the dataset they can handle, scalability, interpretability, and specific use cases. This comparative view enables us to appreciate the unique strengths and limitations of each approach and understand where RFM analysis fits within the broader landscape of data-driven segmentation strategies. By examining this table, businesses can make more informed decisions about which segmentation method aligns best with their specific needs and the nature of their data, thereby enhancing the effectiveness of their marketing strategies.

Table 4.4 Comparison of K-Means, Hierarchical Clustering, and RFM Analysis.

Criteria	K-Means Clustering	Hierarchical Clustering	RFM Analysis
Type of data	Numerical, often standardized or normalized	Numerical, can handle mixed data types in some variations	Transactional data (dates, frequencies, amounts)
Size of dataset	Works well with large datasets	More suitable for smaller datasets due to computational complexity	Relatively flexible; can handle both small and large datasets
Business problem	General segmentation based on customer attributes or behavior	Understanding nested groupings or hierarchy in data; producing dendrograms for visual representation	Customer value segmentation based on purchase behavior
Number of clusters	Needs to be specified in advance (though methods such as the elbow method can help determine an optimal number)	No need to specify upfront; creates a tree of clusters	Segments typically based on score combinations (e.g., 111 to 555)
Scalability	Highly scalable	Less scalable due to computational intensity	Highly scalable, especially with automated tools
Interpretability	Depends on the features used; might require profiling post clustering	Dendrograms can be challenging to interpret, especially with large datasets	Highly interpretable due to its straightforward scoring and focus on three critical parameters
Use case examples	Segmenting website visitors based on behavior; identifying customer segments based on product preferences	Understanding hierarchical relationships in product categories, grouping similar items in content recommendation systems	Targeting high-value customers with premium offers, reengaging customers who haven't purchased recently
Deterministic results	May not be deterministic due to random initialization of centroids	Deterministic because it doesn't have a randomness element	Deterministic, based on fixed scoring of RFM parameters
Flexibility	General-purpose clustering; adaptable to various datasets and problems	More specific, especially when there's a hierarchical structure in the data	Tailored for transactional data; less adaptable to non-transactional scenarios

4.7 PRACTICAL EXAMPLES: INFERENTIAL ANALYTICS FOR CUSTOMER SEGMENTATION AND HYPOTHESIS TESTING FOR MARKETING CAMPAIGN PERFORMANCE

4.7.1 Inferential Analytics for Customer Segmentation

Customer segmentation is a fundamental marketing strategy that involves dividing a customer base into smaller groups with similar characteristics, preferences, or behaviors (Kotler & Keller, 2015). Inferential analytics plays a vital role in

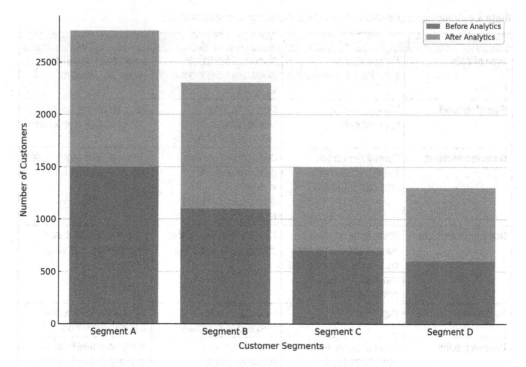

Figure 4.7 How Inferential Analytics Improved Customer Segmentation for a Particular Brand.

customer segmentation because it enables marketers to identify underlying patterns and relationships within customer data, test hypotheses about different segments, and make informed decisions about targeting and personalization (Wedel & Kamakura, 2000). In this section, we will discuss the application of inferential analytics in customer segmentation, with relevant references. In illustrating the significant role of inferential analytics in enhancing customer segmentation, Figure 4.7 presents a compelling case study. This graph showcases how the application of inferential analytics methods has markedly improved customer segmentation for a specific brand.

4.7.1.1   Identifying Key Customer Attributes

The first step in customer segmentation is to identify the key attributes that differentiate customers, such as demographics, psychographics, purchase behaviors, and preferences (Smith, 1956). Inferential analytics techniques, such as correlation and regression analysis, can help marketers determine which attributes are significantly related to customer value, loyalty, or satisfaction (Hair et al., 2018). By understanding the relationships between customer attributes and marketing outcomes, marketers can select the most relevant variables for segmentation and tailor their strategies accordingly.

4.7.1.2 Cluster Analysis for Segmentation

Cluster analysis is a widely used inferential analytics technique for customer segmentation, which aims to group customers based on their similarities across selected attributes (Aldenderfer & Blashfield, 1984). Various clustering algorithms, such as hierarchical clustering, k-means, and model-based clustering, can be applied to partition customer data into homogeneous segments (Wedel & Kamakura, 2000). By comparing the statistical properties (e.g., means, variances) of the resulting clusters, marketers can derive insights about the distinct customer segments and develop targeted marketing strategies for each group.

4.7.1.3 Hypothesis Testing for Segmentation Validation

Once the customer segments are identified, hypothesis testing can be employed to validate the segmentation results and ensure that the differences between segments are statistically significant (Hair et al., 2018). *T*-tests, ANOVA, or chi-square tests can be used to compare the means or proportions of key marketing outcomes (e.g., sales, customer satisfaction, conversion rates) across different segments (Romano & Lehmann, 2005). If the null hypothesis of equal means or proportions is rejected, marketers can have greater confidence in the segmentation results and implement targeted strategies to address the unique needs and preferences of each customer segment.

4.7.2 Hypothesis Testing for Marketing Campaign Performance

Evaluating the performance of marketing campaigns is crucial for optimizing marketing strategies, budget allocation, and ROI (Kotler & Keller, 2015). Hypothesis testing plays a key role in this evaluation process, enabling marketers to assess the statistical significance of observed differences in marketing outcomes between campaigns, channels, or customer segments. In this section, we will discuss the application of hypothesis testing for marketing campaign performance, with relevant references. Figure 4.8 provides a graphical representation that compares the performance of marketing campaigns before and after the application of hypothesis testing techniques.

4.7.2.1 A/B Testing and Experimental Design

A/B testing, also known as *randomized controlled trials* or *split testing*, is a popular approach for evaluating the effectiveness of different marketing tactics, such as ad creatives, landing pages, or email subject lines (Kohavi et al., 2007). In A/B testing, a sample

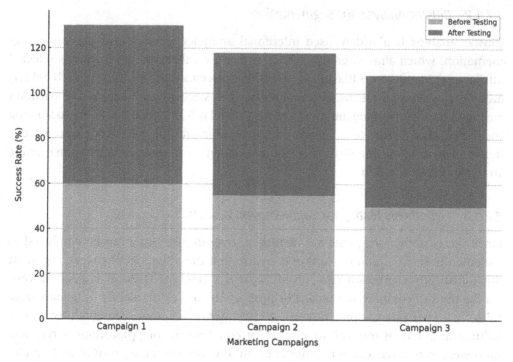

Figure 4.8 Comparing Marketing Campaign Performances Before and After Employing Hypothesis Testing.

of customers is randomly divided into two or more groups, each exposed to different versions of the marketing stimulus (e.g., treatment vs. control). Hypothesis tests, such as t-tests or chi-square tests, are used to compare the mean or proportion of key performance indicators (KPIs), such as conversion rates, click-through rates, or revenue, between the groups. If the null hypothesis of equal means or proportions is rejected, marketers can conclude that the observed differences are statistically significant and implement the more effective marketing tactic.

4.7.2.2 Marketing Mix Modeling and Regression Analysis

Marketing mix modeling is an inferential analytics technique that employs multiple regression analysis to quantify the impact of various marketing activities on sales or other marketing outcomes (Hanssens et al., 2003). By estimating the coefficients of marketing variables (e.g., advertising, promotions, pricing) in the regression model, marketers can determine the relative contribution of each activity to the overall performance and test hypotheses about their significance (Romano & Lehmann, 2005). Based on these insights, marketers can optimize their marketing mix and allocate resources more efficiently to maximize ROI.

4.7.2.3 Time Series Analysis for Marketing Performance

Time series analysis, such as autoregressive integrated moving average models or exponential smoothing state space models, can be used to forecast marketing performance and assess the significance of marketing interventions over time (Hyndman & Athanasopoulos, 2018). By incorporating hypothesis tests, such as intervention analysis or Granger causality tests, marketers can evaluate whether specific marketing events (e.g., product launches, promotions, or advertising campaigns) have a significant impact on sales or other KPIs. These findings can help marketers understand the effectiveness of their marketing efforts and make data-driven decisions to improve future performance.

4.7.2.4 Attribution Modeling and Hypothesis Testing

Attribution modeling is a method used to analyze the customer journey and assign credit to different marketing touchpoints that contributed to a conversion or sale (Kotler & Keller, 2015). Various attribution models, such as last-touch, first-touch, or multi-touch models, can be employed to allocate credit to marketing channels or campaigns (Ghose & Todri-Adamopoulos, 2016). Hypothesis testing can help marketers determine whether the observed differences in the performance of marketing channels or campaigns, as measured by the attribution models, are statistically significant (Romano & Lehmann, 2005). By validating the attribution results, marketers can optimize their marketing mix and make data-driven decisions to improve the efficiency of their marketing investments.

4.8 CONCLUSION

In the rapidly evolving landscape of marketing, leveraging data to derive actionable insights has never been more paramount. The chapter delved deep into the realms of inferential analytics and hypothesis testing, unearthing their critical roles in the marketing discipline. Inferential analytics, with its prowess to extrapolate insights from a sample to a larger population, enables businesses to make robust decisions without the impracticality of surveying entire customer bases. It grants businesses the statistical clout to understand customer behaviors, preferences, and patterns on a macro level, shaping the direction of holistic marketing strategies.

Hypothesis testing, however, is the bedrock of validating marketing assumptions. As the marketing world gets increasingly data-driven, this method offers a structured way to test and either adopt or discard strategies. It's not just about making choices, but about making choices rooted in evidence, providing an empirical foundation to marketing decisions.

The practical implementations discussed, ranging from customer segmentation with cluster analysis to the evaluation of marketing campaign effectiveness, further solidify the pertinence of these techniques. These are not mere theoretical constructs but actionable tools that marketers can deploy, whether it's to dissect a customer base into actionable segments or to gauge the impact of a new advertising campaign.

It's also worth noting the inherent challenges that come with these techniques. From deciding the optimal number of clusters in k-means clustering to circumventing the pitfalls of random initialization, practitioners must approach these tools with a blend of analytical rigor and mindful consideration.

In summation, as the intersections of marketing and data science grow more intertwined, professionals equipped with the knowledge of inferential analytics and hypothesis testing will be better poised to navigate this confluence. They will be the torchbearers, leading businesses toward more informed, impactful, and innovative marketing strategies. As we journey deeper into the age of data, let this chapter serve as a compass and a catalyst, guiding and galvanizing marketers to harness the true potential of data science in their craft.

4.9 REFERENCES

Agresti, A. (2018). *An introduction to categorical data analysis* (3rd ed.). Wiley.

Agresti, A., & Coull, B. A. (1998). Approximate is better than "exact" for interval estimation of binomial proportions. *The American Statistician, 52*(2), 119–126.

Aldenderfer, M. S., & Blashfield, R. K. (1984). *Cluster analysis*. SAGE Publications.

Cohen, J. (1994). The earth is round ($p<.05$). *American Psychologist, 49*(12), 997–1003.

Cohen, J., Cohen, P., West, S. G., & Aiken, L. S. (2013). *Applied multiple regression/correlation analysis for the behavioral sciences*. Routledge.

Cumming, G., & Calin-Jageman, R. (2016). *Introduction to the new statistics: Estimation, open science, and beyond*. Routledge.

Field, A. P., Miles, J., & Field, Z. (2012). *Discovering statistics using R*. SAGE Publications.

Fisher, R. A. (1970). Statistical methods for research workers. *Breakthroughs in statistics: Methodology and distribution* (pp. 66–70). Springer.

Freedman, D., Pisani, R., & Purves, R. (2007). *Statistics* (4th ed.). W. W. Norton & Company.

Ghose, A., & Todri-Adamopoulos, V. (2016). Toward a digital attribution model: Measuring the impact of display advertising on online consumer behaviour. *MIS Quarterly, 40*(4), 889–910.

Hair, J. F., Black, W. C., Babin, B. J., & Anderson, R. E. (2018). *Multivariate data analysis* (8th ed.). Cengage Learning.

Hanssens, D. M., Parsons, L. J., & Schultz, R. L. (2003). *Market response models: Econometric and time series analysis* (Vol. 2). Springer Science & Business Media.

Hogg, R. V., McKean, J. W., & Craig, A. T. (2005). *Maximum likelihood estimation: Introduction to mathematical statistics* (6th ed., p. 313). Pearson Prentice Hall.

Hyndman, R. J., & Athanasopoulos, G. (2018). *Forecasting: Principles and practice* (2nd ed.). OTexts.

Jain, A. K. (2010). Data clustering: 50 years beyond k-means. *Pattern Recognition Letters, 31*(8), 651–666.

Kenney, J. F., & Keeping, E. S. (1962). Linear regression and correlation. *Mathematics of Statistics, 1,* 252–285.

Kish, L. (1965). *Survey sampling.* Wiley.

Kohavi, R., Henne, R. M., & Sommerfield, D. (2007). Practical guide to controlled experiments on the web: Listen to your customers not to the HiPPO. *Proceedings of the 13th ACM SIGKDD International Conference on Knowledge Discovery and Data Mining,* pp. 959–967.

Kotler, P., & Keller, K. L. (2015). *Marketing management* (15th ed.). Pearson.

Larose, D. T., & Larose, C. D. (2014). *Discovering knowledge in data: An introduction to data mining.* Wiley.

Leek, J. T., & Peng, R. D. (2015). What is the question? *Science, 347*(6228), 1314–1315.

Levy, P. S., & Lemeshow, S. (2013). *Sampling of populations: Methods and applications* (4th ed.). Wiley.

Lohr, S. L. (2019). *Sampling: Design and analysis* (3rd ed.). Chapman & Hall/CRC.

Moore, D. S., McCabe, G. P., & Craig, B. A. (2009). *Introduction to the practice of statistics* (6th ed.). W. H. Freeman.

Pearson, K. (1900). On the criterion that a given system of deviations from the probable in the case of a correlated system of variables is such that it can be reasonably supposed to have arisen from random sampling. *The London, Edinburgh, and Dublin Philosophical Magazine and Journal of Science, 50*(302), 157–175.

Punj, G., & Stewart, D. W. (1983). Cluster analysis in marketing research: Review and suggestions for application. *Journal of Marketing Research, 20*(2), 134–148.

Rice, J. A. (2006). *Mathematical statistics and data analysis.* Cengage Learning.

Romano, J. P., & Lehmann, E. L. (2005). *Testing statistical hypotheses.* Springer.

Smith, W. R. (1956). Product differentiation and market segmentation as alternative marketing strategies. *Journal of Marketing, 21*(1), 3–8.

Student. (1908). The probable error of a mean. *Biometrika, 6*(1), 1–25.

Starnes, D. S., Tabor, J., Yates, D., & Moore, D. S. (2014). *The practice of statistics.* W. H. Freeman.

Triola, M. F. (2017). *Elementary statistics* (13th ed.). Pearson.

Wasserman, L. (2004). *All of statistics: A concise course in statistical inference.* Springer.

Wedel, M., & Kamakura, W. A. (2000). *Market segmentation: Conceptual and methodological foundations.* Springer Science & Business Media.

Wilcox, R. R. (2011). *Introduction to robust estimation and hypothesis testing* (3rd ed.). Academic Press.

Winston, W. L. (2014). *Marketing analytics: Data-driven techniques with Microsoft Excel.* Wiley.

EXERCISE 4.1: BAYESIAN INFERENCE FOR PERSONALIZED MARKETING

Objective: Use Bayesian inference to estimate the likelihood of customers being interested in electronics based on their past behavior and demographics.

Tasks:

1. **Data Exploration:** Analyze the dataset to understand customer demographics and past behaviors.

2. **Bayesian Analysis:**
   a. Calculate the prior probability (general interest in electronics).
   b. Compute the likelihood (probability of clicking on electronics-related content).
   c. Calculate the posterior probability using Bayes's theorem.

3. **Interpretation:** Interpret the results to understand which customer segment is more likely to be interested in electronics.

4. **Application:** Suggest personalized email campaign strategies based on the Bayesian inference results.

Steps:

1. **Importing Required Libraries:**

```
1. import pandas as pd
```

- **pandas** is used for data manipulation and analysis.

2. **Loading and Displaying the Data—Bayesian_Inference_Customer_Data.csv:**

```
2. # Loading the data for Exercise 1: Bayesian Inference for
Personalized Marketing
3. df_bayesian = pd.read_csv('path_to_csv_file')
4. # Displaying the first few rows of the DataFrame
5. df_bayesian.head()
```

- **pd.read_csv()**: Reads the CSV file into a pandas DataFrame.
- **df_bayesian.head()**: Displays the first five rows of the DataFrame for a quick overview of the data structure.

With the data loaded, the next steps will involve calculating the prior probability, likelihood, and posterior probability using Bayes's theorem. Let's proceed to perform these calculations.

3. **Calculate the Prior Probability:**

The next step is to calculate the prior probability. This is the general likelihood of a customer being interested in electronics based on the historical data we have. Here's how we calculate it:

```
6. # Total number of customers who clicked on electronics email
7. total_clicked_electronics = df_bayesian['ClickedOnElectronics
Email'].sum()
```

```
8. # Total number of customers
9. total_customers = len(df_bayesian)
10. # Prior probability: P(E)—Probability of being interested
in electronics
11. prior_probability = total_clicked_electronics / total_
customers
```

- **df_bayesian['ClickedOnElectronicsEmail'].sum()**: Counts the number of customers who clicked on electronics-related emails.
- **len(df_bayesian)**: Determines the total number of customers in the dataset.
- **prior_probability**: The ratio of customers who showed interest in electronics to the total number of customers, giving us the prior probability $P(E)$.

In our dataset, the prior probability $P(E)$ of a customer being interested in electronics is approximately 0.312, or 31.2%.

Next, we'll calculate the likelihood and the total probability of clicking on electronics-related content, which are necessary to find the posterior probability using Bayes's theorem.

4. **Likelihood Calculation:**

The likelihood $P(F|E)$ is the probability of a customer clicking on electronics-related emails given they are interested in electronics. For this example, let's assume that customers interested in electronics are twice as likely to click on electronics emails compared to the average customer. Here's how we calculate it:

```
12. # Likelihood: P(F|E)—Probability of clicking on electronics
email given they are interested in electronics
13. # Assuming customers interested in electronics are twice as
likely to click on electronics emails
14. likelihood = 2 * prior_probability
```

5. **Total Probability Calculation:**

The total probability $P(F)$ is the overall probability of any customer clicking on electronics-related content. This is essentially the average click rate on electronics emails within our dataset:

```
15. # Total Probability: P(F)—Overall probability of clicking
on electronics email
16. # This is the average click rate on electronics emails
17. total_probability = df_bayesian['ClickedOnElectronicsEmail'].
mean()
```

Based on our data:
- The likelihood $P(F|E)$ is about 0.624, or 62.4%.
- The total probability $P(F)$ is about 0.312, or 31.2%.

Next, we'll use these values to compute the posterior probability, which will tell us the probability of a customer being interested in electronics given that they clicked on electronics-related content.

The final step is to calculate the posterior probability using Bayes's theorem. The posterior probability $P(E|F)$ represents the probability of a customer being interested in electronics, given that they have clicked on electronics-related content. Here's the formula and the calculation:

6. **Bayes's Theorem**

$$P(E|F) = \frac{P(F|E) \times P(E)}{P(F)}$$

- $P(E|F)$: Posterior probability (what we want to find)
- $P(F|E)$: Likelihood of clicking on electronics email given they are interested in electronics (likelihood)
- $P(E)$: Prior probability of being interested in electronics
- $P(F)$: Total probability of clicking on electronics email

```
18. # Calculating the Posterior Probability using Bayes's Theorem
19. posterior_probability = (likelihood * prior_probability) /
total_probability
```

In our dataset, the posterior probability $P(E|F)$ is approximately 0.624, or 62.4%. This means that given a customer clicked on electronics-related content, there is a 62.4% chance that they are interested in electronics. This is a significant increase from the prior probability of 31.2%, indicating that clicking on electronics-related content is a strong indicator of interest in electronics.

This completes the Bayesian inference exercise, demonstrating how to use Python to apply Bayes's theorem for marketing analytics. This approach enables marketers to refine their strategies based on updated beliefs about customer preferences, leading to more effective and targeted marketing campaigns.

EXERCISE 4.2: A/B TESTING FOR MARKETING CAMPAIGN EVALUATION

Objective: Evaluate the effectiveness of the two marketing campaigns using A/B testing.

Tasks:

1. **Experimental Design:** Understand the design of the A/B test (random assignment, duration, sample size).

2. **Statistical Analysis:**
   - Calculate key performance metrics for both campaigns.
   - Perform hypothesis testing (e.g., *t*-test) to determine if there's a statistically significant difference in the effectiveness of the two campaigns.

3. **Result Interpretation:** Analyze and interpret the results of the A/B test.

4. **Decision-Making:** Make recommendations on which campaign should be adopted based on the test results.

Steps:

1. **Importing Required Libraries:**

```
1. import pandas as pd
```

- **pandas** is used for data manipulation and analysis.

2. **Loading and Displaying the Data—B_Testing_Campaign_Data.csv:**

```
2. # Loading the data for Exercise 2: A/B Testing for Marketing
Campaign Evaluation
3. df_ab_testing = pd.read_csv('path_to_csv_file')
4. # Displaying the first few rows of the DataFrame
5. df_ab_testing.head()
```

- **pd.read_csv()**: Reads the CSV file into a pandas DataFrame.
- **df_ab_testing.head()**: Displays the first five rows of the DataFrame for an overview of the data structure.

The data consists of campaign groups 'A' and 'B', with metrics that will help us compare the effectiveness of these campaigns. Next, we will separate the data for each campaign group and calculate key performance metrics. Let's proceed with these calculations.

The next step in the A/B testing analysis involves separating the data for each campaign and calculating key performance metrics. Here's how we do it in Python:

3. **Separating Campaign Data:**

We first divide the data into two subsets, one for each campaign group (A and B):

```
6. # Separating the data for Campaign A and Campaign B
7. df_campaign_a = df_ab_testing[df_ab_testing['CampaignGroup']
== 'A']
8. df_campaign_b = df_ab_testing[df_ab_testing['CampaignGroup']
== 'B']
```

4. **Calculating Key Metrics:**

We then calculate the mean 'Click-Through Rate (CTR)' and 'Conversion Rate' for each campaign:

```
9. # Mean Click-Through Rate (CTR) and Conversion Rate for each
campaign
```

```
10. mean_ctr_a = df_campaign_a['ClickThroughRate'].mean()
11. mean_ctr_b = df_campaign_b['ClickThroughRate'].mean()
12. mean_conversion_rate_a = df_campaign_a['ConversionRate'].
mean()
13. mean_conversion_rate_b = df_campaign_b['ConversionRate'].
mean()
```

Based on the data:

- **Campaign A:**
  - Mean 'Click-Through Rate (CTR)': Approximately 0.1108 (or 11.08%)
  - Mean 'Conversion Rate': Approximately 0.0264 (or 2.64%)
- **Campaign B:**
  - Mean 'Click-Through Rate (CTR)': Approximately 0.1048 (or 10.48%)
  - Mean 'Conversion Rate': Approximately 0.0243 (or 2.43%)

These metrics give us an initial indication of each campaign's performance. Next, we will conduct a statistical test (like a t-test) to determine if the differences observed in these metrics between the two campaigns are statistically significant. Let's proceed with this analysis.

To determine the statistical significance of the differences observed between the two campaigns, we perform t-tests on both the 'Click-Through Rate (CTR)' and 'Conversion Rate'. Here's the breakdown of this part of the analysis:

5. **Performing T-Tests:**

   We use the **ttest_ind** function from the **scipy.stats** module, which performs an independent two-sample t-test. This test compares the means of two independent groups (in this case, Campaign A and Campaign B) to determine if there is a statistically significant difference between them.

```
14. from scipy import stats
15. # T-test for Click-Through Rates
16. t_stat_ctr, p_value_ctr = stats.ttest_ind(df_campaign_
a['ClickThroughRate'], df_campaign_b['ClickThroughRate'])
17. # T-test for Conversion Rates
18. t_stat_conversion, p_value_conversion = stats.ttest_ind(df_
campaign_a['ConversionRate'], df_campaign_b['ConversionRate'])
```

- **stats.ttest_ind()**: Conducts the t-test for the mean of two independent samples.
- **t_stat_ctr, p_value_ctr**: The t-statistic and p-value for the 'Click-Through Rate' comparison.
- **t_stat_conversion, p_value_conversion**: The t-statistic and p-value for the 'Conversion Rate' comparison.

Based on the data:

- The t-statistic for the 'Click-Through Rate' comparison is approximately 1.231 with a p-value of about 0.219.

- The t-statistic for the 'Conversion Rate' comparison is approximately 1.654 with a p-value of about 0.099.

6. **Interpretation:**

The p-values indicate the probability of observing the data if the null hypothesis (no difference between campaigns) is true.

- For both 'Click-Through Rate' and 'Conversion Rate', the p-values are greater than the typical alpha level of 0.05, suggesting that we do not have enough evidence to reject the null hypothesis at a 5% significance level.

- Therefore, based on this data, we cannot conclude that there are statistically significant differences between Campaign A and Campaign B in terms of 'Click-Through Rate' and 'Conversion Rate'.

This completes the statistical analysis part of the A/B testing exercise, showing how to use Python to compare the effectiveness of two marketing campaigns. The results suggest that, in this scenario, there might not be a significant difference in performance between the two campaigns.

CHAPTER **5**

Predictive Analytics and Machine Learning

5.1 INTRODUCTION

5.1.1 Overview of Predictive Analytics

Predictive analytics is a branch of advanced analytics that uses data, statistical algorithms, and machine learning techniques to predict future outcomes. Its aim is to go beyond knowing what has happened to provide the best estimation of what will happen in the future. This is achieved by leveraging a variety of techniques, including data mining, statistics, modeling, machine learning, and artificial intelligence.

Predictive analytics is predicated on the capture of relationships between explanatory variables and the predicted variables from past occurrences and using this to predict future outcomes (Provost & Fawcett, 2013). It exploits patterns found in historical and transactional data to identify risks and opportunities, thus providing insights that guide decision-making across various sectors.

In marketing, predictive analytics is used to analyze current data and historical facts in order to better understand customers, products, and partners, and to identify potential risks and opportunities. It can be used to forecast customer behavior, detect, and prevent fraud, optimize marketing campaigns, improve operations, reduce risk, meet customer's needs more effectively, and increase profitability (Sharda et al., 2018).

The ability of predictive analytics to provide actionable insights provides a competitive advantage and helps organizations make informed, forward-looking decisions. It gives businesses the power to predict what their customers will do or want in the future, enhancing business performance and driving strategic management decisions.

5.1.2 Machine Learning in Marketing

Machine learning, a subset of artificial intelligence, provides systems the ability to automatically learn and improve from experience without being explicitly programmed. It focuses on the development of computer programs that can access data and use it to learn for themselves (Goodfellow et al., 2016). Machine learning is a key enabler of predictive analytics, providing the algorithms that make predictions possible.

In the context of marketing, machine learning can be leveraged in numerous ways to drive more effective decision-making, enhance customer experience, and deliver increased value. Machine learning algorithms can be used to predict customer behavior, such as purchase patterns or likelihood of churn. They can help segment customers into meaningful groups, enabling more targeted and personalized marketing strategies. Machine learning can also be applied to optimize pricing, forecast demand, and enhance recommendations, among other applications.

For instance, supervised learning algorithms such as linear regression or support vector machines (SVMs) can be used to predict a specific outcome, such as customer lifetime value (CLV) or response to a marketing campaign. Unsupervised learning algorithms such as clustering can be used to identify segments or groups within your customer base. Reinforcement learning (RL), another branch of machine learning, can be applied to optimize dynamic pricing strategies or personalized recommendations (Sutton & Barto, 2018).

The advent of machine learning and the broader field of AI has opened up new opportunities for marketers to better understand their customers, anticipate their needs, and deliver more engaging and personalized experiences. However, successful application of machine learning in marketing requires a good understanding of both the business context and the technical aspects of machine learning.

5.1.3 Common Challenges in Predictive Analytics and Machine Learning in Marketing

In the landscape of marketing analytics, predictive analytics and machine learning have become indispensable tools. However, their effectiveness can be significantly hindered by myriad challenges. The following delineates the common hurdles encountered when leveraging these advanced techniques in marketing:

- **Data quality and preprocessing.** One of the most common challenges is obtaining high-quality data. Inaccurate, missing, or outdated data can adversely affect the performance of predictive models. Preprocessing steps such as data cleaning, normalization, and transformation are crucial to ensure the data feeds into the models are of optimal quality.
- **Model interpretability.** Especially with complex models such as deep neural networks or ensemble methods, understanding how the model is making decisions can be challenging. This can become an issue in marketing when stakeholders want to know the why behind a prediction.
- **Overfitting.** In the eagerness to capture every pattern from the data, there's a risk of creating models that are too complex and overfit the training data. Such models perform poorly in real-world scenarios because they've essentially memorized the training data rather than generalizing from it.
- **Handling imbalanced data.** In many marketing applications, such as churn prediction, the classes might be imbalanced with far fewer churners than non-churners. This can lead models to be biased toward the majority class, thereby missing out on valuable insights from the minority class.
- **Scalability issues.** As businesses grow, so does the volume of data. Models need to be robust and scalable to handle increased data loads without compromising on speed or accuracy.
- **Privacy and ethical concerns.** Using consumer data to train models raises ethical and privacy concerns. Ensuring data is anonymized and used ethically is paramount. This challenge is covered comprehensively in Chapter 13.
- **Constantly evolving consumer behavior.** Consumer behavior is not static. Especially in today's digital age, it can change rapidly. Models might become outdated if they don't adapt to these changing behaviors.

The effective management of these challenges is pivotal for businesses aiming to use predictive analytics and machine learning in crafting successful marketing strategies. The subsequent chapters will delve into strategies and best practices to mitigate these challenges and leverage predictive analytics to its fullest potential in marketing.

5.1.4　Misconceptions in Predictive Analytics and Machine Learning in Marketing

Unraveling the common misconceptions about predictive analytics and machine learning can help marketers set realistic expectations and use these tools more effectively. Here are some of the prevalent myths in the field:

- **Complex models are always better.** Although complex models such as deep learning can capture intricate patterns, they're not always necessary. Sometimes, simpler models such as linear regression can suffice and are more interpretable.
- **More data is always better.** Although having a larger dataset usually helps, it's the quality of data that matters most. Moreover, adding irrelevant data can reduce the model's performance.
- **Machine learning can solve everything.** Expectations for machine learning and predictive analytics can sometimes be unrealistic. They are tools, and similar to any other tool, their efficiency depends on how they're used.
- **A high accuracy means a good model.** Although accuracy is a critical metric, it's not the only one. Depending on the application, metrics such as precision, recall, or F1-score might be more relevant.
- **Models run on autopilot.** Once deployed, models need regular monitoring and updating. They can drift over time due to changing data patterns and might need retraining.
- **Every problem needs predictive analytics.** Although predictive analytics can offer valuable insights, not every marketing problem requires it. It's essential to determine if the costs and efforts of implementing predictive analytics outweigh the benefits.

By addressing these misconceptions, marketers can more judiciously apply predictive analytics and machine learning techniques, ensuring that these powerful tools deliver the best outcomes for their marketing objectives.

5.2　PREDICTIVE ANALYTICS TECHNIQUES

5.2.1　Linear and Logistic Regression

Linear and logistic regression are foundational techniques in predictive analytics and machine learning. They are both forms of predictive modeling that analyze the relationship between the outcome variable (also known as the *dependent variable*) and one or more predictors (also known as *independent variables*).

Linear regression is used when the outcome variable is continuous, meaning it can take on any value within a certain range. It models the relationship between the outcome and the predictors as a straight line, hence the term *linear* regression (Montgomery et al., 2021). For example, in marketing, a business might use linear regression to predict sales revenue based on advertising spend. Figure 5.1 provides a visual representation of this concept, specifically illustrating a scatterplot with a linear regression line. This figure demonstrates how linear regression is used to model the relationship between an outcome variable and predictors. The scatterplot shows individual data points, with the linear regression line representing the best fit through these points, depicting the trend and direction of the relationship.

Logistic regression, however, is used when the outcome variable is binary, meaning it can take on only two possible values, such as 0 or 1, yes or no, true or false. It models the log odds of the probability of the outcome as a linear combination of the predictors (Hosmer et al., 2013). For instance, a telecom company might use logistic regression to predict whether a customer will churn (1) or not (0) based on their use patterns and demographics.

Although linear and logistic regression are powerful tools, they also have limitations. For example, they assume a linear relationship between the outcome and the predictors, which may not always hold in real-world scenarios. Moreover, they may not perform well when dealing with complex, high-dimensional data or when the underlying relationship is nonlinear or involves interactions among predictors. In these cases, more sophisticated machine learning techniques, such as decision trees or neural networks, may be more appropriate (Goodfellow et al., 2016).

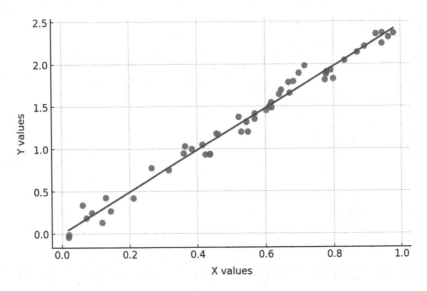

Figure 5.1 Scatterplot with Linear Regression Line.

5.2.2   Time Series Forecasting

Time series forecasting is a crucial component of predictive analytics and machine learning, particularly relevant in the field of marketing. A time series is a sequence of data points collected or recorded in time order at equally spaced time intervals. Forecasting involves predicting future values of the series based on historical data (Hyndman & Athanasopoulos, 2018).

Time series forecasting is used extensively in marketing for tasks such as predicting sales, web traffic, and customer demand. These forecasts can help businesses plan for the future, manage resources more efficiently, and make better strategic decisions. For example, a retail business might use time series forecasting to predict future sales and adjust inventory levels accordingly.

There are numerous methods for time series forecasting, each with its strengths and weaknesses. Some of the most common methods include autoregressive integrated moving average (ARIMA) models, exponential smoothing models, and state space models. More recently, machine learning methods such as recurrent neural networks have also been applied to time series forecasting (Goodfellow et al., 2016).

Despite its utility, time series forecasting is not without challenges. It requires dealing with components such as trend, seasonality, and noise, which can complicate the modeling process. It also assumes that the future will follow the same patterns as the past, which may not always hold true, especially in the presence of disruptive events or changes in market conditions. Therefore, successful time series forecasting requires not only technical expertise but also a good understanding of the business context and market dynamics. As we consider the importance of time series forecasting in the domain of marketing analytics, visualizing the application of these models to historical data is immensely valuable. Figure 5.2 offers a clear depiction of this, with a time series data plot

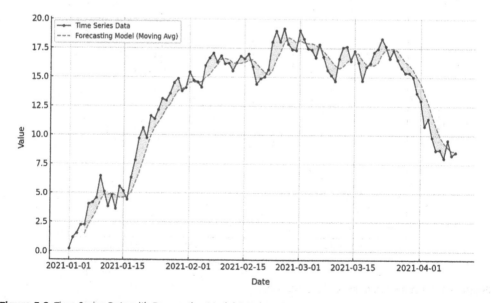

Figure 5.2 Time Series Data with Forecasting Model Overlay.

and an overlay of a forecasting model. The figure illustrates how historical data points are used to project future trends, providing a tangible representation of the forecasting process. This overlay enables marketers to compare the model's predictions against actual historical values, highlighting the model's capability to capture underlying patterns and trends. Such visual tools are not only essential for understanding the dynamics of time series data but also for communicating forecast results to stakeholders, assisting in strategic planning and decision-making.

5.3 MACHINE LEARNING TECHNIQUES

5.3.1 Supervised Learning for Marketing

Supervised learning is one of the main categories of machine learning. It involves using a set of labeled examples (input-output pairs) to train a model that can make predictions for new, unseen examples. The "supervision" comes in the form of the output labels provided for the training data (Goodfellow et al., 2016).

In the context of marketing, supervised learning can be applied to a wide array of tasks. For instance, it can be used to predict CLV, forecast sales, segment customers, or estimate the probability of customer churn. Each of these tasks can be framed as a supervised learning problem where the goal is to predict an output (e.g., CLV, sales, churn probability) based on a set of inputs (e.g., customer demographics, transaction history, engagement metrics).

There are many supervised learning algorithms available, each with its strengths and weaknesses. Some of the most common ones include linear regression, logistic regression, decision trees, random forests, gradient boosting, SVMs, and neural networks. The choice of algorithm depends on various factors, such as the nature of the task, the type of data, and the business constraints (Kelleher et al., 2020).

For instance, linear regression might be used for sales forecasting, where the goal is to predict a continuous outcome (sales) based on a set of predictors (e.g., advertising spend, seasonality, economic indicators). Logistic regression or decision trees, however, might be used for churn prediction, where the goal is to predict a binary outcome (churn or no churn) based on a set of predictors (e.g., use patterns, customer satisfaction, billing history).

Although supervised learning can provide valuable insights and drive effective decision-making in marketing, it also requires careful consideration of issues such as overfitting, underfitting, model interpretability, and data privacy (Dhar, 2013).

5.3.1.1 Decision Trees in Supervised Learning

Decision trees are a popular machine learning algorithm used primarily for classification and regression tasks. At their core, decision trees split data into subsets based on the value of input features. This process results in a tree-like model of decisions, where each node represents a feature, each branch represents a decision rule, and each leaf represents an outcome or class.

The formation of a decision tree involves the following steps:

1. **Selection of attribute.** Choose the best attribute to split the data. This decision often involves a metric like 'Information Gain', 'Gini Impurity', or 'Variance Reduction'.

2. **Splitting.** Divide the dataset into subsets based on the chosen attribute's value. This results in a node in the tree.

3. **Recursive splitting.** For each subset, repeat steps 1 and 2 until one of the stopping conditions is met, such as achieving a maximum depth of the tree or the nodes having less than a minimum number of samples.

4. **Assignment of leaf node.** Once the tree is built, assign an output class to each leaf node, which can be used to make predictions for new data.

Imagine a telecommunications company wants to predict customer churn based on various customer attributes. A decision tree could be structured as follows:

- The root node might split the data based on the feature 'Contract Length' (e.g., month-to-month vs. one year).
  - For customers with month-to-month contracts:
    - The next node might further split based on 'Monthly Charges', with a threshold of, say, $50.
      - Customers paying more than $50 might have a higher churn rate, leading to a leaf node labeled 'Churn.'
      - Customers paying less than or equal to $50 might be split further based on another feature, such as 'Customer Support Calls'.
  - For customers with one-year contracts:
    - The tree might split based on a different attribute, such as 'Internet Service Type'.

Following the branches of the tree from the root to a leaf provides decision rules that lead to the prediction outcome (in this case, whether a customer is likely to churn or not). See Figure 5.3 for an example.

Decision trees are favored in many business applications because of their interpretability. Each path in the tree represents a decision rule, and thus, they provide a clear rationale for each prediction. However, they can be prone to overfitting, especially when they are very deep. To mitigate this, techniques such as pruning or ensemble methods such as random forests can be used.

5.3.1.2 Random Forests in Supervised Learning

Random forests are an ensemble learning method predominantly used for classification and regression tasks. They operate by constructing multiple decision trees during training

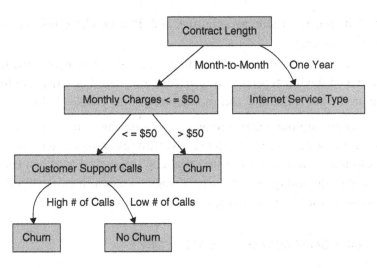

Figure 5.3 Decision Tree Structure.

and outputting the mode of the classes (for classification) or the mean prediction (for regression) of the individual trees for unseen data. Essentially, it's a "forest" of trees, where each tree casts a "vote" for a class, and the majority class is chosen as the final prediction.

The formation of a random forest involves the following steps:

1. **Bootstrap sampling.** Randomly select samples from the dataset with replacement, creating multiple subsets.

2. **Tree building.** For each subset, grow a decision tree. However, instead of using all features for splitting at each node, a random subset of features is chosen. This randomness ensures the trees are diverse.

3. **Aggregation.** For classification tasks, each tree in the forest predicts a class (votes for a class). The class that gets the most votes is the forest's prediction. For regression tasks, the forest's prediction is the average of the predictions of all the trees.

4. **Output.** Produce the prediction based on the majority (classification) or average (regression) outcome of all the trees in the forest.

Consider an e-commerce platform aiming to predict whether a user will buy a product based on features such as browsing history, time spent on site, past purchase history, and so on.

Using random forests, the platform would do the following:

- Create multiple subsets of the data using bootstrap sampling.
- For each subset, a decision tree is constructed, but each node in the tree uses only a random subset of features to make decisions (e.g., just 'Browsing History'

and 'Time Spent on Site' for one tree, and 'Past Purchase History' and 'Time of Day' for another).

■ Once the forest of trees is built, a prediction for a new user is made by having each tree in the forest predict 'buy' or 'not buy' based on the user's features. The final prediction is the one that the majority of the trees vote for.

Random forests are particularly powerful because they can capture complex non-linear patterns in the data, are less prone to overfitting compared to individual decision trees, and can handle a mixture of numerical and categorical features. However, they may lose some of the interpretability that a single decision tree offers. Still, their high accuracy in many tasks often outweighs this trade-off in practice.

5.3.1.3 Gradient Boosting in Supervised Learning

Gradient boosting is an ensemble machine learning technique used for regression and classification problems. It builds a model in a stage-wise fashion, and it generalizes them by allowing optimization of an arbitrary differentiable loss function. At its core, gradient boosting involves building and combining a sequence of weak models (typically decision trees) to create a strong predictive model.

The process of gradient boosting involves the following stages:

1. **Initialization.** Begin with an initial model, which makes a prediction, often just a simple average or another basic model.
2. **Compute residuals.** Calculate the difference (or residual) between the observed values and the predictions of the current model.
3. **Fit to residuals.** Construct a new model that predicts the residuals from the previous step.
4. **Update predictions.** Adjust the predictions of the main model using the predictions from the residual model. This is typically done by adding a fraction of the new model's predictions to the main model's predictions.
5. **Iterate.** Repeat steps 2–4 for a predetermined number of iterations or until the residuals are minimized below a threshold.
6. **Output.** The final prediction is the sum of the predictions from all models.

Suppose a company wants to predict the likelihood of a customer purchasing a new product based on features such as age, income, past purchase behavior, and engagement with past marketing campaigns.

Using gradient boosting you can accomplish the following:

■ The company starts with a basic model, perhaps predicting that every customer has the average likelihood of purchasing.
■ The difference between the actual purchasing behavior and the predictions of this initial model are calculated (these are the residuals).

- A new model is trained to predict these residuals based on customer features.
- The predictions of this new model are combined with the predictions of the initial model to produce a revised set of predictions.
- The process is repeated, each time refining the predictions by training a new model on the residuals of the previous combined model.
- After several iterations, the company has a powerful predictive model that effectively combines the insights from all the individual models.

Gradient boosting is known for its high accuracy and ability to handle a variety of data types and structures. One of its main strengths is its capacity to focus on instances that are hard to predict (those with large residuals) in successive iterations, leading to improved overall performance. However, careful tuning of parameters is required to prevent overfitting and ensure optimal performance. See Figure 5.4 for a visual representation of the gradient boosting structure, which illustrates how the model sequentially builds weaker learners to form a strong predictive model.

5.3.1.4 Support Vector Machines in Supervised Learning

An SVM is a supervised machine learning algorithm used primarily for classification tasks, but it can also be employed for regression. At its core, SVM tries to find the best hyperplane (or decision boundary) that separates data into different classes. The best hyperplane is the one that maximizes the margin between two classes. In higher-dimensional spaces, SVM looks for the hyperplane that best separates the data into classes.

The mechanics of SVM can be broken down into several stages:

1. **Maximize margin.** Find the hyperplane that has the maximum distance to the nearest training data point of any class. The data points that lie closest to the decision surface are called *support vectors*.
2. **Handle nonlinearity with kernel trick.** In cases where data is not linearly separable, SVM uses a function called the *kernel trick* to transform the input data into a higher-dimensional space where a hyperplane can be used to separate the data. Common kernels include polynomial, radial basis function (RBF), and sigmoid.
3. **Soft margin and regularization.** To handle noisy data where complete separation might not be optimal, SVM introduces a concept known as the *soft margin*, allowing some misclassifications in exchange for a broader and more generalizable margin. The regularization parameter, often referred to as 'C', determines the trade-off between maximizing the margin and minimizing misclassification.
4. **Prediction.** For a new input, determine which side of the hyperplane it falls on to classify it into a category.

Imagine an electronics company that has data on customer interactions with its email campaigns. Features might include the time taken to open the email, whether

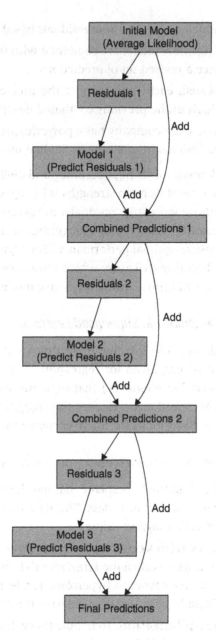

Figure 5.4 Gradient Boosting Structure.

links inside were clicked, previous purchase behavior, and so on. The company wants to classify customers into two groups: those likely to buy a new product and those who aren't.

Using SVM, the following can occur:

- The algorithm will attempt to find the best hyperplane that separates customers who made a purchase from those who did not, based on their email interaction features.

- If the decision boundary between these two groups isn't linear, an RBF kernel might transform the features into a space where the groups can be separated by a hyperplane.
- Once the SVM model is trained, when a new email campaign is sent, the company can use the model to predict, based on early interaction metrics, which customers are likely to make a purchase.

SVMs are recognized for their high accuracy, ability to handle high-dimensional data, and flexibility in modeling diverse sources of data. However, they can be computationally intensive, especially with a large number of features, and might require significant tuning and validation to optimize for specific applications.

5.3.1.5 Neural Networks in Supervised Learning

Neural networks are computational models inspired by the structure and functionality of biological neural systems. They are composed of interconnected nodes or "neurons" that process and transmit information. Deep learning, a subfield of machine learning, often uses neural networks with many layers (known as *deep neural networks*) to perform tasks such as image recognition, natural language processing, and more. These networks can learn intricate patterns from vast amounts of data.

The operation of a neural network can be broken down into the following stages:

1. **Architecture.** A neural network comprises an input layer, one or more hidden layers, and an output layer. Each neuron is connected to others via weights, which get adjusted during training.
2. **Activation functions.** When a neuron receives input, it processes it using an activation function. Common activation functions include the sigmoid, ReLU (rectified linear unit), and tanh functions.
3. **Forward propagation.** Input data travels through the network, undergoing weighted summation and activation. This process results in a prediction at the output layer.
4. **Cost calculation.** After obtaining the prediction, the network calculates the error or cost by comparing the prediction with the actual label. The goal is to minimize this error.
5. **Back propagation.** The error is propagated backward through the network, adjusting the weights using optimization algorithms such as gradient descent.
6. **Training iterations.** Steps 3 to 5 are repeated iteratively until the model achieves satisfactory performance or a set number of iterations (epochs) is reached.

Consider a fashion e-commerce platform aiming to provide personalized clothing recommendations to its users. The platform collects various user data, such as browsing behavior, previous purchases, search queries, and feedback ratings.

Using neural networks, the following can occur:

- Input features might include user activity patterns, like how often they visit the site, which categories they browse most, the average time they spend on product pages, and so on.
- The neural network, after being trained on historical data, can predict products or styles a particular user is likely to buy.
- As users continue to interact with the platform, feedback loops can further refine the recommendations, ensuring they are increasingly accurate and tailored over time.

Neural networks offer the ability to capture intricate patterns and relationships in data, making them especially powerful for tasks with high complexity. However, they often require larger amounts of data, considerable computational power, and careful tuning to avoid issues such as overfitting. Their "black box" nature can also pose challenges for interpretability and transparency in decision-making.

5.3.2 Unsupervised Learning for Marketing

Unsupervised learning is another primary branch of machine learning. Unlike supervised learning, which learns from labeled examples, unsupervised learning discovers patterns and structures within unlabeled data. It seeks to model the underlying distribution of the data or to find groups of similar examples within the data (Goodfellow et al., 2016).

In the marketing sphere, unsupervised learning has a wide range of applications. It is used in customer segmentation, anomaly detection, market basket analysis, and more. Each of these tasks can be framed as an unsupervised learning problem where the aim is to find patterns or structures in the data without a specific prediction target.

One of the most common uses of unsupervised learning in marketing is customer segmentation, where customers are grouped based on their similarities across various dimensions such as demographics, purchasing behavior, or engagement patterns. K-means clustering (see Section 4.6.1) and hierarchical clustering (see Section 4.6.2) are popular methods for this task (Hastie et al., 2009).

Market basket analysis (MBA), another key application of unsupervised learning in marketing, aims to discover associations between products based on transaction data. This is often achieved using association rule learning methods such as the a priori algorithm or FP-growth algorithm (Agrawal & Srikant, 1994). We will discuss MBA and recommendation systems in Section 5.6.

Although unsupervised learning can uncover valuable insights that might be missed with supervised methods, it comes with its own set of challenges. These include determining the optimal number of clusters in clustering analysis, dealing with noisy or high-dimensional data, and interpreting the results in a meaningful way (Hastie et al., 2009).

5.3.3 Reinforcement Learning for Marketing

RL is a type of machine learning in which an agent learns to make decisions by interacting with an environment. The agent takes actions, receives feedback in the form of rewards or penalties, and adjusts its behavior to maximize the cumulative reward over time. The goal of RL is to find the optimal policy, which is a strategy that prescribes the best action to take in each state of the environment (Sutton & Barto, 2018).

In the marketing context, RL can be used to personalize customer interactions, optimize marketing campaigns, and make real-time bidding decisions in online advertising, among other applications. Each of these tasks can be framed as an RL problem in which the goal is to make a sequence of decisions that maximize a long-term objective, such as CLV, campaign ROI, or advertising revenue.

For example, in personalized marketing, the environment could be the customer, the states could be the customer's behavior and attributes, the actions could be the marketing interventions (e.g., sending an email, offering a discount), and the reward could be the customer's response to the interventions (e.g., making a purchase, clicking on a link). The RL agent would then learn to personalize the marketing interventions based on the customer's behavior and attributes to maximize the customer's response over time (Li et al., 2010).

RL has several advantages over traditional marketing methods. It can handle dynamic environments, consider long-term effects, and continuously learn and adapt to new information. However, it also presents challenges, such as the exploration-exploitation trade-off, the credit assignment problem, and the need for large amounts of interaction data (Sutton & Barto, 2018).

Table 5.1 lays out the tabulated differences among supervised, unsupervised, and reinforcement learning, comparing them across various dimensions such as data requirements, applications, and outcomes. This comparative framework helps clarify the unique role of RL in marketing, especially in terms of its data-driven learning process and its potential for developing strategies that maximize long-term rewards.

Table 5.1 Differences Among Supervised, Unsupervised, and Reinforcement Learning in Terms of Data Requirements, Applications, and Outcomes.

Aspect	Supervised Learning	Unsupervised Learning	Reinforcement Learning
Data prerequisites	Labeled data (input-output pairs)	Unlabeled data	Environment, agent, rewards
Applications	Classification Regression	Clustering Dimensionality Reduction	Robotics Game playing Real-time decisions
Expected Outcomes	Predictive model based on past data	Patterns, structures in data	Strategy to maximize rewards

The table also contrasts the data prerequisites and typical applications of each learning paradigm, providing a clear distinction of where and how each method can be applied within the field of marketing.

5.4 MODEL EVALUATION AND SELECTION

Once a predictive model has been trained, it is crucial to evaluate its performance to ensure its reliability and effectiveness in making predictions. Choosing the appropriate evaluation metrics and techniques not only helps in assessing a model's performance but also aids in the selection of the most suitable model for a specific problem. In this section, we will explore various model evaluation metrics and techniques.

5.4.1 Model Accuracy, Precision, and Recall

5.4.1.1 Confusion Matrix

Before diving further into accuracy, precision, and recall, it's beneficial to understand the concept of a confusion matrix. A confusion matrix is a table used to describe the performance of a classification model on a set of data for which the true values are known (see Figure 5.5). It comprises four values:

- **True positives (TP).** The number of positives that were correctly classified.
- **True negatives (TN).** The number of negatives that were correctly classified.
- **False positives (FP).** The number of negatives that were incorrectly classified as positives.
- **False negatives (FN).** The number of positives that were incorrectly classified as negatives.

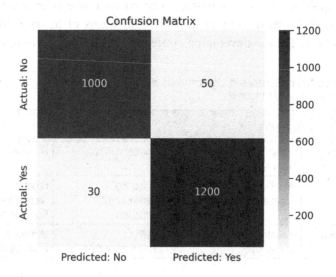

Figure 5.5 Confusion Matrix and Its Components.

5.4.1.2 Practical Example: Email Marketing Campaign

Imagine a company has just run an email marketing campaign targeting 1,000 of its customers, promoting a new product. The primary goal of this campaign is to make customers buy the product, so the company has tagged the campaign recipients based on their actions: 'Purchased' (if they bought the product) or 'Not Purchased' (if they didn't buy the product).

Now, the marketing team used a machine learning model to predict beforehand which of these customers would buy the product based on past purchase behavior, interaction with previous emails, and so on. So, for each customer, the model predicted 'Will Purchase' or 'Will Not Purchase'.

After the campaign has ended, we can create a confusion matrix to understand how well the model's predictions matched with the actual outcomes (see Table 5.2).

From this matrix we discern the following:

- **True positives (TP).** Three hundred customers were correctly predicted to purchase the product, and they did.
- **True negatives (TN).** Six hundred and thirty customers were correctly predicted not to purchase the product, and they didn't.
- **False positives (FP).** Fifty customers were predicted to purchase the product, but they didn't. This means the model was overly optimistic for these customers.
- **False negatives (FN).** Twenty customers were predicted not to purchase the product, but they ended up buying it. These are missed opportunities because the model didn't expect them to convert, but they did.

By understanding these numbers, the marketing team can refine their strategies. For instance, they might want to further investigate the profiles of the 50 FP customers: Why did the model think they would purchase? Were there any common characteristics or behaviors among them? This kind of insight can help in optimizing future campaigns and improving the prediction model.

Now, let's proceed with the metrics.

5.4.1.3 Accuracy

Accuracy is one of the most straightforward metrics in the realm of predictive modeling. It quantifies the proportion of correct predictions in the total predictions made:

$$Accuracy = \frac{Number\ of\ Correct\ Predictions}{Total\ Number\ of\ Predictions}$$

Table 5.2 Email Marketing Campaign Confusion Matrix.

	Actual: Purchased	Actual: Not Purchased
Predicted: Will Purchase	300 (TP)	50 (FP)
Predicted: Will Not Purchase	20 (FN)	630 (TN)

Although accuracy is a commonly used metric, it might not always be the best choice, especially when dealing with imbalanced datasets where one class significantly outnumbers the other.

5.4.1.4 Precision

Precision is the ratio of correctly predicted positive observations to the total predicted positives. It answers the question: Of all the positive labels we predicted, how many of those were correct?

$$Precision = \frac{True\ Positives}{True\ Positives + False\ Positives}$$

5.4.1.5 Recall (Sensitivity)

Recall calculates the ratio of correctly predicted positive observations to all the actual positives. It poses the question: Of all the actual positive labels, how many did we correctly predict?

$$Recall = \frac{True\ Positives}{True\ Positives + False\ Negatives}$$

In many scenarios, there's a trade-off between precision and recall. High precision indicates a low false positive rate, whereas high recall indicates that the classifier captured most of the positive instances.

5.4.1.6 Challenges with Accuracy in Imbalanced Datasets

Imagine a dataset in which 95% of the samples belong to Class A, and only 5% belong to Class B. Even a naive model that always predicts Class A would achieve an accuracy of 95%. Yet, this model would be entirely ineffective at predicting Class B, which might be of high interest (e.g., predicting disease onset where most samples are "healthy").

Introducing F1-Score. To address the shortcomings of accuracy in such scenarios, we introduce the F1-score. F1-score is the harmonic mean of precision and recall, and it offers a more balanced measure when classes are imbalanced.

$$F1\text{-}Score = 2 \times \frac{Precision \times Recall}{Precision + Recall}$$

where

- Precision is the number of correct positive results divided by the number of all positive results (including those wrongly classified).
- Recall (or sensitivity) is the number of correct positive results divided by the number of positive results that should have been returned.

The F1-score values range from 0 to 1, where 1 denotes perfect precision and recall, and 0 indicates neither precision nor recall. An F1-score gives a more holistic view of model performance, especially when data is skewed.

Synthetic minority over-sampling technique (SMOTE). Another approach to addressing imbalanced datasets is to balance them out by creating synthetic samples. SMOTE is one such technique.

Here's a brief overview on how SMOTE works:

1. For every instance in the minority class, a set of its nearest neighbors is chosen.

2. Based on these neighbors, synthetic samples are created by choosing a difference between the features of the instance under consideration and its neighbors, multiplying this difference by a random number between 0 and 1, and then adding it to the instance.

3. This effectively creates a synthetic instance slightly different from the original.

By repeating this method, SMOTE creates a balanced dataset where the minority class has been oversampled. Post this, any model can be trained on this new dataset.

Generative adversarial networks (GANs) for imbalanced datasets. In addressing the challenges associated with imbalanced datasets, GANs have emerged as a powerful tool. GANs are composed of two neural networks—the generator and the discriminator—that are trained simultaneously in a competitive setting where the generator aims to create data instances that are indistinguishable from real ones, and the discriminator strives to distinguish between the two.

Here's an outline of how GANs can be used for handling imbalanced datasets:

1. The generator network takes in random noise and outputs synthetic data points, aiming to replicate the distribution of the minority class.

2. The discriminator network is trained to differentiate between the real instances from the minority class and the synthetic instances created by the generator.

3. Through iterative training, the generator learns to produce more and more realistic data, while the discriminator becomes better at discerning the synthetic data from the real data.

4. Eventually, the generator produces high-quality synthetic data that can be added to the minority class, thus augmenting the dataset and helping to balance the classes.

5. The augmented dataset can then be used to train predictive models that are less biased toward the majority class and have a better generalization performance on unseen data.

The use of GANs for generating synthetic instances of the minority class can lead to improved model sensitivity to the minority class without losing specificity. This technique has shown promise in a variety of applications where class imbalance is a significant issue (Douzas & Bacao, 2018).

Although accuracy is a valuable metric, it's essential to be wary of its limitations, especially in the context of imbalanced datasets. Leveraging other metrics such as the F1-score and techniques such as SMOTE can provide a more comprehensive understanding of model performance and improve prediction capabilities on such datasets (Brown & Mues, 2012). Additionally, GANs present an innovative approach to generating synthetic data for the minority class, enhancing balance in datasets. The applications and methodologies of GANs in the context of marketing are discussed in further detail in Chapter 12.

5.4.2 ROC Curves and AUC

Receiver operating characteristic (ROC) curve. The ROC curve is a graphical representation of the performance of a binary classifier. It plots the true positive rate (recall) against the false positive rate across various threshold values.

Area under the curve (AUC). AUC measures the entire two-dimensional area underneath the entire ROC curve. AUC provides an aggregate measure of performance across all possible classification thresholds. A model with a perfect predictive capacity will have an AUC of 1, and a model that predicts purely by chance will have an AUC of 0.5.

See Figure 5.6 for an illustrative ROC curve with its corresponding AUC value, showcasing how different threshold settings affect the trade-off between true positive and false positive rates.

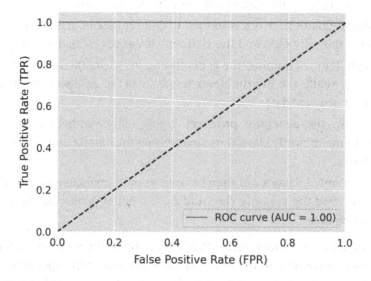

Figure 5.6 ROC Curve and AUC.

5.4.3 Cross-Validation Techniques

5.4.3.1 Holdout Method

The holdout method involves splitting the dataset into two distinct sets: a training set and a testing set. The model is trained on the training set and evaluated on the testing set. This method is simple and fast, but its evaluation can have high variance because the assessment depends heavily on which data points end up in the testing set. To mitigate this, often the splitting is done multiple times and results are averaged, or alternatively, more advanced methods like cross-validation are employed.

5.4.3.2 K-Fold Cross-Validation

In K-fold cross-validation, the dataset is randomly partitioned into k equal-sized subsets. Of the k subsets, one is retained for testing the model, and the remaining $k-1$ subsets are used for training. This process is repeated k times, with each subset serving as a test set once. The k results are then averaged to produce a single estimation.

5.4.3.3 Leave-One-Out Cross-Validation

In leave-one-out cross-validation (LOOCV), a single data point is used as the test set while the remaining data points constitute the training set. This process is iteratively repeated such that each data point serves as a test point once. Although LOOCV can be computationally expensive, it makes efficient use of the data because every data point is used for training and testing.

5.4.3.4 Stratified Cross-Validation

For datasets where the outcome variable is imbalanced, stratified cross-validation ensures that each fold is a good representative of the whole by having the same proportion of samples of each target class as the complete set.

5.4.3.5 Time Series Split

In time series split, data is ordered chronologically and split into training and test sets multiple times. The initial split might have the first 70% of the data as training and the next 30% as testing. For the next iteration, the training set might slide forward in time, including the next chunk of data, and so forth. This method is crucial for time series data where the assumption is that past information is used to predict future events. Unlike standard cross-validation methods, it ensures that the training set always precedes the test set in time, respecting the temporal order of the data.

See Table 5.3 for a comprehensive comparison of the benefits and drawbacks of various cross-validation techniques, including the time series split method and how it is uniquely adapted to handle data with temporal dependencies.

Table 5.3 Benefits and Drawbacks of Different Cross-Validation Techniques.

Technique	Advantages	Disadvantages
Holdout	Simple and fast	High variance if dataset is not large
K-fold	Reduces overfitting More reliable estimate than holdout	Computationally expensive for large k
Leave-one-out	Makes use of all data points Good for small datasets	Very computationally expensive for large datasets
Stratified K-fold	Maintains class distribution, reduces bias	Computationally expensive
Time series split	Considers time order Ideal for time series data	Does not shuffle data Might not capture all patterns

5.4.4 Model Complexity and Overfitting

Model complexity refers to the number of parameters in a model and the intricacy of its structure. A more complex model will have more parameters and can fit a wider range of functions. However, too much complexity might not always be beneficial. Overfitting occurs when a model is excessively complex and starts to capture noise in the data rather than the underlying pattern. An overfitted model will have very low training error but will perform poorly on unseen data because it has tailored itself too closely to the training dataset. To mitigate overfitting, techniques such as regularization, pruning, and using simpler models can be employed.

In summary, model evaluation and selection are pivotal steps in the machine learning pipeline. Using the right metrics and techniques ensures that the models developed are robust, reliable, and apt for their intended tasks, paving the way for effective predictions and insightful results.

5.5 CHURN PREDICTION, CUSTOMER LIFETIME VALUE, AND PROPENSITY MODELING

The role of data science in marketing has augmented traditional techniques, allowing for more precise and actionable insights into customer behavior. Among these, churn prediction, CLV assessment, and propensity modeling stand out for their value in understanding, retaining, and maximizing the potential of a customer base. Let's delve into these concepts and their significance in today's data-driven marketing landscape.

5.5.1 Understanding Churn and Its Importance

Churn, in the context of customer behavior, refers to when a customer stops doing business or ends the relationship with a company. Churn rate, a vital metric, denotes the percentage of customers who churn during a given time period.

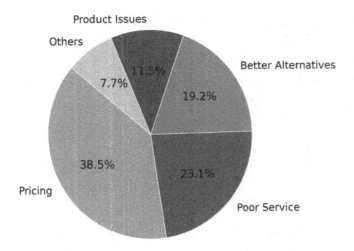

Figure 5.7 Common Reasons for Customer Churn.

Understanding and mitigating churn is critical for several reasons:

- **Cost efficiency.** Acquiring a new customer is often more expensive than retaining an existing one. Hence, reducing churn can lead to significant cost savings.
- **Revenue impact.** Regular customers often contribute more to a company's revenue. They might purchase more and can even act as brand advocates, bringing in new customers.
- **Feedback loop.** Analyzing the reasons behind churn can provide valuable insights into areas of improvement, be it in product offerings, customer service, or other operational facets.

By predicting which customers are most likely to churn, businesses can proactively address concerns and deploy retention strategies tailored to individual customer needs (see Figure 5.7).

5.5.2 CLV Computation and Applications

CLV signifies the total net profit a company anticipates earning from any specific customer over the course of their relationship. It provides a monetary estimation of the worth a customer brings throughout their life span as a patron of a particular business.

Simple CLV Computation

A basic way to compute CLV is using the formula:

$$CLV = (AverageOrderValue) \times (NumberofRepeatSales) \times (AverageRetentionTimeinMonthsorYears)$$

Although this formula provides a straightforward way to estimate CLV, it's worth noting that many businesses often employ more intricate models to get a nuanced understanding (see Figure 5.8).

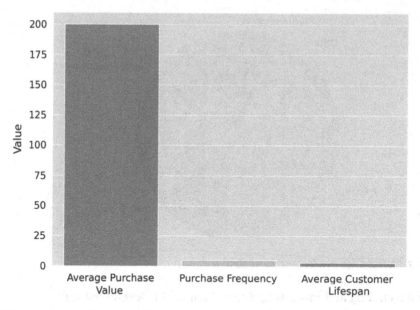

Figure 5.8 Components of Customer Lifetime Value.

Advanced CLV Models

- **Historical CLV.** Uses the gross profit from all past purchases of a customer to predict future behavior.

- **Predictive CLV.** Uses advanced statistical techniques and machine learning to forecast the potential future value of a customer based on their past and current behavior.

- **Traditional RFM (recency, frequency, monetary) model.** Focuses on three factors: how recently a customer made a purchase, how often they make a purchase, and how much they spend on average.

- **Gamma-gamma model of monetary value.** Applied when there are repeat transactions with varying monetary values.

Understanding CLV can be transformative for businesses:

- **Segmentation and personalization.** Customers with a higher CLV can be identified and treated with specialized marketing strategies, ensuring their continued engagement and loyalty.

- **Resource allocation.** Companies can decide where to allocate their resources more efficiently, focusing more on high CLV customers.

- **Product development.** Insights derived from CLV can guide product development, tailoring offerings to the most valuable customer segments.

- **Risk management.** Companies can anticipate revenue fluctuations based on projected changes in CLV.

Although the simple formula provides a foundational understanding of CLV, diving deeper into advanced models can offer businesses a more refined, comprehensive perspective, enabling them to better cater to their customers and optimize their operations.

5.5.3 Propensity Scoring and Its Marketing Applications

A propensity score gauges the probability that a customer will take a specific action. For marketers, this typically translates to the likelihood of a customer making a purchase, responding to an advertisement or campaign, or deciding to leave (churn).

Computing a propensity score. The process of computing a propensity score often begins with collecting relevant customer data, such as their purchase history, demographics, interactions with the brand, and other behavioral signals.

One commonly used methodology for determining the propensity score is logistic regression. Here's a brief overview:

- **Logistic regression in propensity scoring.** Logistic regression is a statistical method that predicts the probability of a binary outcome. When applied in marketing, the outcome could be 'Will Buy' versus 'Will Not Buy', 'Will Respond' versus 'Will Not Respond', or 'Will Churn' versus 'Will Stay', among others.

The outcome (or dependent variable) is binary, and the predictors (or independent variables) can be continuous, categorical, or a mix of both. The model provides coefficients for each predictor, indicating the strength and direction of the relationship with the outcome. The computed probabilities from the logistic regression model form the propensity scores (see Table 5.4).

Applications of Propensity Scores

- **Targeted marketing campaigns.** By identifying customers with a high propensity to respond positively to a campaign, businesses can optimize their marketing spend and efforts.
- **Cross-selling and upselling.** Understanding a customer's propensity to buy related products can inform cross-selling and upselling strategies, maximizing revenue.
- **Retention strategies.** Customers identified with a high propensity to churn can be targeted with specialized retention campaigns or offers.

Table 5.4 Use Cases and Benefits of Propensity Scoring in Marketing.

Applications	Advantages
Targeted marketing campaigns	Helps target customers more likely to respond, increasing ROI
Resource allocation	Ensures resources are directed toward high-value customers
Customer retention strategies	Identifies at-risk customers and informs retention strategies
Product recommendations	Personalizes shopping experience based on likelihood to purchase
Pricing strategies	Optimizes pricing based on a customer's likelihood to buy

- **Product recommendations.** E-commerce platforms often use propensity scores to recommend products that a customer is likely to purchase based on their browsing and buying behavior.

In summary, tools such as churn prediction, CLV evaluation, and propensity modeling are quintessential components of a marketer's toolkit. Interwoven with other data-centric methodologies, they afford a holistic grasp of consumer dynamics, empowering businesses to predict requirements, fine-tune approaches, and bolster both customer gratification and financial outcomes.

5.6 MARKET BASKET ANALYSIS AND RECOMMENDER SYSTEMS

The commercial landscape has witnessed an unprecedented surge in product variety and choice over the last few decades. Historically, the concept of market analysis traces its roots back to traditional brick-and-mortar stores. Retailers, keen on maximizing sales, would often observe buying habits of consumers to discern patterns. For example, they might notice that people who bought bread also tended to buy butter. Such observations influenced store layouts, with complementary products being placed together to encourage impulse buying.

Enter the digital age, and this traditional observation transformed into sophisticated data-driven analyses. With online shopping platforms recording every click, view, and purchase, there was a treasure trove of data waiting to be mined for patterns.

Why association rules are essential. Association rules, which form the core of market basket analysis, serve as bridges between products, revealing hidden relationships and patterns in large datasets. The importance of these rules can be summarized as follows:

- **Improved product placement.** Much like the bread and butter example, online stores can bundle products together or suggest them as 'Frequently Bought Together' based on association rules.
- **Tailored promotions.** If a strong association is found between products A and B, customers buying A can be given discounts or promotional offers on B, thereby increasing the likelihood of additional sales.
- **Inventory management.** By understanding which products are often bought together, businesses can manage their inventory more efficiently, ensuring that if one product is in stock, its complementary product is too.
- **Enhanced user experience.** Customers appreciate a seamless shopping experience where they can easily find related products. Association rules can power such recommendations, making the shopping journey intuitive and efficient.

Historical context. The birth of association rule mining is largely attributed to the work done by Rakesh Agrawal, Tomasz Imieliński, and Arun Swami in the early 1990s. They introduced an algorithm to determine regularities between products in large-scale transaction data recorded by point-of-sale systems in supermarkets. Their work laid the foundation for many of the recommendation engines and market basket analysis tools in use today.

In conclusion, as the digital marketplace continues to evolve and expand, the importance of market basket analysis and recommender systems only grows. By understanding and implementing the principles of association rules, businesses can not only drive sales but also offer an unparalleled shopping experience to their customers.

5.6.1 Principles of Association Rules

At its core, an association rule is an "If-Then" relationship between two sets of items. For instance, the rule {Onions, Potatoes} -> {Burger} indicates that if someone buys onions and potatoes, they are likely to buy a burger, too.

Key Metrics

- **Support.** Represents the proportion of transactions in the dataset that contain a particular item or combination of items. It helps filter out items or item combinations that are infrequent.
- **Confidence.** Denotes the likelihood that an item Y is purchased when item X is purchased. It measures the reliability of the inference.
- **Lift.** It indicates the increase in the ratio of the sale of item Y when item X is sold. A lift value greater than 1 suggests that item Y is likely to be bought with item X, whereas a value less than 1 suggests the items are unlikely to be bought together.

5.6.2 Apriori Algorithm and Market Basket Analysis

This is a popular algorithm used to identify frequently occurring item sets in a database and is foundational to market basket analysis. Its principle is simple: if an item set is frequent, then all its subsets must also be frequent.

Steps

1. Determine the support of item sets in the transactional database, and select the minimum support threshold.
2. Generate larger item sets using the frequent item sets identified in the previous step.
3. Repeat the process until no larger item sets can be formed.

Using principles such as the Apriori algorithm, market basket analysis aims to discover relationships between products purchased together. This is used extensively in retail to inform a range of strategies, from store layout design to promotional bundling. Table 5.5 provides a snapshot of sample market basket data, detailing items purchased in individual transactions. This forms the basis for applying the Apriori algorithm to determine frequently occurring item sets. Following this, Table 5.6 illustrates the resulting association rules derived from the data, complete with metrics such as

Table 5.5 Sample Market Basket Data.

Transaction ID	Items Purchased
1	Bread, Milk
2	Bread, Diaper, Beer, Eggs
3	Milk, Diaper, Beer, Coke
4	Bread, Milk, Diaper, Beer
5	Bread, Milk, Diaper, Coke

Table 5.6 Resulting Association Rules.

Association Rule	Support	Confidence	Lift
Bread -> Milk	0.6	0.75	1.25
Beer, Diaper -> Milk	0.2	0.5	1.5
Milk, Bread -> Diaper	0.4	0.67	1.2
Diaper -> Beer	0.5	0.62	1.4

support, confidence, and lift. These tables demonstrate the practical application of the Apriori algorithm from initial data exploration to the extraction of meaningful association rules, which are invaluable for informing retail strategies.

5.6.3 Collaborative Filtering in Recommender Systems

Collaborative filtering (CF) is based on the idea that users who have agreed in the past tend to agree in the future about the preference for certain items. It involves predicting a user's interests by collecting preferences or taste information from many users (collaborating). Figure 5.9 provides a visual representation of a user item rating matrix, a fundamental component of collaborative filtering.

Types of CF
- **User-based.** It finds users similar to the target user and recommends items based on what those similar users have liked.
- **Item-based.** It recommends items by comparing the content of the items and a user profile, with content being described in several descriptors that are inherent to the item (e.g., a book might be described by its author, its publisher, etc.).

Challenges in Collaborative Filtering
- **Scalability.** As the number of users and items grow, the computational complexity of finding similar users or items also increases.
- **Sparsity.** In many real-world scenarios, the user item matrix used in CF is sparse, meaning most users have interacted with only a small subset of the overall items, making it challenging to find reliable commonalities.

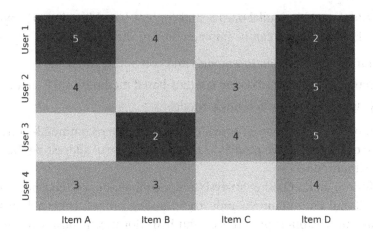

Figure 5.9 User Item Rating Matrix for Collaborative Filtering.

- ▦ **Cold start.** New users or items that just entered the system won't have suffi-cient data for the system to provide reliable recommendations. This lack of data is called the *cold start* problem.

Advantages of Collaborative Filtering

- ▦ **Personalization.** Recommendations are tailored to individual users based on their past behaviors and preferences.
- ▦ **No need for item metadata.** Unlike content-based filtering, CF doesn't rely on item attributes; it purely operates based on user behavior, making it versatile across different types of items.
- ▦ **Diversity.** Because CF considers the behaviors of similar users, it has the poten-tial to suggest items that the target user hasn't explicitly shown interest in but might still find appealing.

Concept of cold start. The cold start problem arises when new users or items join the system. For new users, because the system doesn't have prior knowledge about their preferences, making reliable recommendations is challenging. This is called the *user cold start*. Similarly, for new items that haven't been interacted with by users, the system finds it tough to suggest them to relevant users, known as the *item cold start*. Solutions to the cold start problem often involve hybrid models or leveraging content-based filtering until enough interaction data is accumulated.

5.6.4 Content-Based and Hybrid Recommendation Systems

These systems use item features to recommend additional items similar to what the user likes, based on their previous actions or explicit feedback. For example, if a user has liked a movie that belongs to the action genre, the system will recommend other movies from the same genre.

These systems combine collaborative and content-based filtering to provide recommendations. Hybrid systems can be implemented in various ways:

- Separating recommendation models and combining them
- Incorporating collaborative and content-based methods into a single model
- Unifying the models into a single model

Hybrid models, in many cases, provide more accurate recommendations than pure collaborative or content-based models as they are capable of addressing the limitations inherent in either model.

In conclusion, market basket analysis and recommender systems have revolutionized the retail and entertainment industries, among others. Their ability to provide deep insights into customer preferences and behavior means businesses can cater to individual needs more effectively, driving both satisfaction and revenue. As data continues to grow and algorithms become more sophisticated, these tools will play an even more central role in shaping the consumer landscape.

5.7 PRACTICAL EXAMPLES: PREDICTIVE ANALYTICS AND MACHINE LEARNING IN MARKETING

5.7.1 Predicting Customer Churn with Logistic Regression

Customer churn, also known as *customer attrition*, refers to the phenomenon of customers leaving a service or stopping the use of a product. In a competitive market, predicting and preventing customer churn is a key focus for many businesses. Accurately identifying customers who are likely to churn can enable businesses to proactively engage with these customers and implement retention strategies (Miglautsch, 2000).

Logistic regression is a statistical method that is commonly used for churn prediction due to its ability to handle binary outcomes, interpretability, and computational efficiency (see Figure 5.10). It models the relationship between a binary dependent variable (churn or no churn) and one or more independent variables (e.g., customer demographics, use patterns, satisfaction scores), and outputs a probability that the dependent variable is true (i.e., the customer will churn) (Hosmer et al., 2013).

A typical process for building a logistic regression model for churn prediction might involve the following steps:

1. **Data collection and preprocessing.** Collect historical data on customer behavior, interactions, and churn events. Clean the data, handle missing values, and create relevant features.
2. **Model training.** Split the data into a training set and a test set. Use the training set to fit the logistic regression model, that is, estimate the model parameters that maximize the likelihood of the observed data.

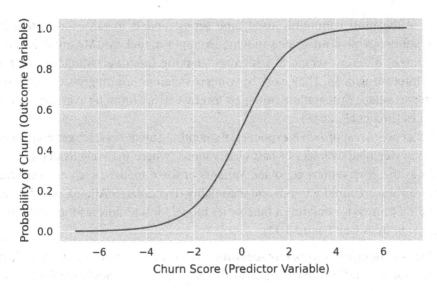

Figure 5.10 Churn Prediction.

3. **Model evaluation.** Evaluate the model's performance on the test set using appropriate metrics, such as accuracy, precision, recall, or the area under the receiver operating characteristic curve (AUC-ROC).

4. **Model deployment and monitoring.** Deploy the model, use it to score customers based on their churn risk, and monitor its performance over time. Update the model as needed when new data becomes available or when the business context changes.

Although logistic regression can be an effective tool for churn prediction, it has its limitations. It assumes a linear relationship between the logit of the outcome and the predictors, and it may not perform well when this assumption is violated or when there are complex interactions between predictors (Hosmer et al., 2013).

5.7.2 Sales Forecasting with Time Series Models

Sales forecasting is a critical business operation that guides a multitude of strategic and operational decisions, including inventory management, budget planning, and resource allocation. Accurate sales forecasts can lead to cost savings, improved customer satisfaction, and overall better business performance (Makridakis et al., 2020).

Time series models are commonly used for sales forecasting due to their ability to capture temporal patterns and trends in sales data. These models analyze historical data to identify patterns such as seasonality (repeating patterns over fixed periods), trends (upward or downward movements over time), and cyclicality (fluctuations around a long-term trend), and use these patterns to forecast future sales (Hyndman & Athanasopoulos, 2018).

One of the most commonly used time series models in sales forecasting is the ARIMA (autoregressive integrated moving average) model. ARIMA models can capture a suite of different temporal structures, making them versatile tools for a wide range of forecasting tasks. They work by using past values (autoregression), differences between past values (integration), and past forecast errors (moving averages) to predict future sales (Box et al., 2016).

Another popular approach is exponential smoothing models, which generate forecasts by applying weighted averages of past observations, where the weights decrease exponentially as the observations get older. Variants of these models, such as Holt-Winters' method, can also account for trends and seasonality (Hyndman & Athanasopoulos, 2018).

A typical process for building a time series model for sales forecasting might include the following steps (see Figure 5.11):

1. **Data collection and preprocessing.** Collect historical sales data, handle missing values, and possibly transform the data (e.g., log transformation) to stabilize variance.
2. **Model identification.** Analyze the data, identify potential trends and seasonality, and choose an appropriate model (e.g., ARIMA, exponential smoothing).
3. **Model fitting and diagnostics.** Estimate the model parameters and check the model fit and assumptions using diagnostic plots and tests.
4. **Forecasting and evaluation.** Generate forecasts for future sales and evaluate the model's predictive performance using out-of-sample validation techniques and appropriate accuracy measures (e.g., mean absolute percentage error, root mean squared error).

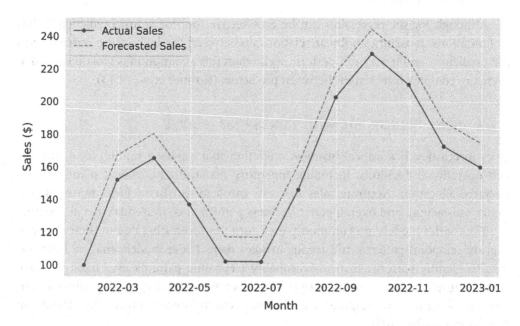

Figure 5.11 Sales Forecasting Using Time Series Analysis.

Although time series models can provide accurate forecasts, they have limitations. They assume that the underlying process generating the data remains stable over time, which may not hold in a rapidly changing market environment. Moreover, these models generally do not incorporate external factors that could influence sales, such as economic indicators or marketing activities (Makridakis et al., 2020).

5.7.3 Customer Segmentation with Clustering

In the realm of marketing, understanding customer behavior is crucial for making informed decisions. One way to gain such understanding is through customer segmentation, which involves grouping customers based on shared characteristics. These characteristics can be demographic (such as age, income, or location), behavioral (such as purchasing patterns or product use), psychographic (such as lifestyle or personality traits), or any combination of these (Smith, 1956).

Clustering is a form of unsupervised machine learning that is often used for customer segmentation. It groups data points (in this case, customers) so that points in the same group (or cluster) are more similar to each other than to those in other clusters. This similarity is typically measured based on distance in a multidimensional space (Kaufman & Rousseeuw, 2009).

Popular clustering algorithms include K-means, hierarchical clustering, and DBSCAN (density-based spatial clustering of applications with noise). K-means and hierarchical clustering work well with spherical clusters and are sensitive to the scale of variables, whereas DBSCAN can detect clusters of arbitrary shapes and is less sensitive to the scale of variables (Ester et al., 1996).

The process of customer segmentation using clustering might involve the following steps (see Figure 5.12):

1. **Data collection and preprocessing.** Gather data about customers, clean and preprocess the data, standardize variables if necessary, and create relevant features.
2. **Choosing a clustering method.** Choose a clustering method based on the data and business context. For example, if the number of clusters is known a priori, K-means might be a good choice.
3. **Model training.** Apply the chosen clustering method to the data to form clusters.
4. **Interpretation and application.** Interpret the clusters by analyzing the characteristics of customers within each cluster. Use the results to guide marketing strategies, such as personalized marketing, targeted promotions, and product development.

Although clustering can be a powerful tool for customer segmentation, it has its limitations. The quality of clustering results heavily depends on the choice of the clustering algorithm and its parameters, the feature representation, and the distance measure. Also, clustering does not provide explicit labels for the clusters, so interpreting

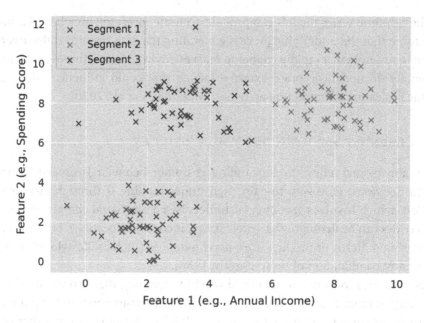

Figure 5.12 Customer Segmentation Through Clustering.

the clusters and deriving actionable insights require domain knowledge and careful analysis (Kaufman & Rousseeuw, 2009).

5.7.4 Personalized Recommendation with Collaborative Filtering

In the era of information overload, personalized recommendation systems have become an essential tool for many businesses to improve customer engagement, satisfaction, and conversion rates. These systems suggest items that a user might be interested in, based on their past behavior or the behavior of other similar users. Such systems are widely used in various domains, including e-commerce (Amazon), multimedia content (Netflix, Spotify), and social media (Facebook, LinkedIn) (Ricci et al., 2010).

Collaborative filtering is one of the most popular techniques used in recommendation systems. It predicts a user's interest by collecting preferences from many users. The underlying assumption is that if two users agree on one issue, they are likely to agree on others as well (Resnick & Varian, 1997).

There are two primary types of collaborative filtering: user-based and item-based. User-based collaborative filtering finds users similar to the target user and recommends items that these similar users have liked in the past. However, item-based collaborative filtering determines the similarity between items based on the ratings they have received from users. For a given user, it recommends items that are similar to the items the user has rated highly in the past (Sarwar et al., 2001).

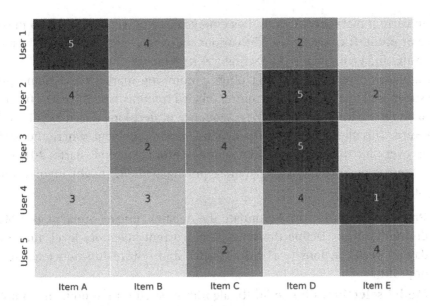

Figure 5.13 User Item Rating Matrix for Collaborative Filtering.

The process of generating personalized recommendations using collaborative filtering might involve the following steps (see Figure 5.13):

1. **Data collection and preprocessing.** Collect user item interaction data, preprocess the data to handle missing values, and transform the data into a user item matrix.
2. **Similarity computation.** Compute the similarity between users or items. Commonly used similarity measures include cosine similarity, Pearson correlation coefficient, and Jaccard similarity coefficient.
3. **Recommendation generation.** For a target user, identify similar users or items, compute predicted ratings for the items not yet seen by the user, and recommend the items with the highest predicted ratings.

Although collaborative filtering can provide personalized recommendations, it has its challenges. For example, it suffers from the cold start problem, that is, it cannot make recommendations for new users or new items that have little interaction data. Moreover, it tends to recommend popular items and might not capture the long-tail items that fewer people know about but might be interesting to some users (Ricci et al., 2010).

5.7.5 Dynamic Pricing with Reinforcement Learning

In today's fast-paced and competitive business environment, setting the right price for a product or service can be challenging. Traditional static pricing strategies are often inadequate because they fail to take into account the dynamic nature of market demand, supply, and competition. Dynamic pricing, which involves adjusting prices based on current market conditions, has emerged as a powerful strategy to maximize revenue or profit. It is widely used in various industries, such as airlines, hospitality, ride-sharing, and e-commerce (Elmaghraby & Keskinocak, 2003).

RL, a branch of machine learning, offers a promising approach to dynamic pricing. Unlike supervised learning, which requires labeled training data, RL learns from interaction with an environment to make a sequence of decisions that maximize a long-term reward. This aligns well with the dynamic pricing problem, where the goal is to set prices over time to maximize total revenue or profit (Sutton & Barto, 2018).

The process of implementing dynamic pricing with RL might involve the following steps:

1. **Problem formulation.** Formulate the dynamic pricing problem as a Markov decision process. Define the states (e.g., current inventory level, time of day, day of week), actions (e.g., price levels), and reward function (e.g., revenue or profit).

2. **Model selection.** Choose an RL algorithm based on the problem complexity and available data. Commonly used RL algorithms include Q-learning, deep Q-network, and proximal policy optimization.

3. **Model training.** Train the RL model using historical sales data, simulate interactions with the environment, or a combination of both. The model learns a policy that determines what action to take (i.e., what price to set) given the current state.

4. **Policy implementation.** Implement the learned policy in the real-world system. Continuously monitor the performance and retrain the model as needed to adapt to changing market conditions.

Despite its potential, RL-based dynamic pricing has its challenges. For example, it requires sufficient and quality data for training. The RL model might perform poorly if the data is noisy, sparse, or nonstationary. Moreover, RL typically involves a trial-and-error learning process, which might lead to suboptimal decisions during the learning phase (Sutton & Barto, 2018).

5.8 CONCLUSION

Predictive analytics and machine learning represent transformative technologies in the marketing domain, bridging the historical and future aspects of business operations. This chapter elucidated how these methodologies empower businesses to venture beyond mere understanding of what has happened and venture into predicting future occurrences.

We commenced our journey by demystifying the concept of predictive analytics, showcasing its prowess in analyzing data to forecast the future. Grounded in its principles, machine learning amplifies these capabilities by facilitating computers to learn from data without explicit programming, offering algorithms crucial for predictions. When applied in marketing, these methods have the potential to refine customer experiences, optimize marketing strategies, and predict customer behaviors with significant accuracy.

We delved deep into a gamut of techniques within predictive analytics and machine learning. These range from foundational techniques such as linear and logistic regression, often the starting point of many marketing analyses, to the intricacies of time series forecasting, which is pivotal in areas such as sales projections. As we ventured into the terrain of machine learning, the distinctions among supervised, unsupervised, and reinforcement learning became evident. Each serves a distinct purpose, whether it's predicting specific outcomes, detecting patterns in data, or learning optimal sequences of decisions from interactive environments.

Furthermore, through practical examples, the applicability of these techniques in real-world marketing scenarios was exemplified. The ability to predict customer churn using logistic regression, forecast sales via time series models, segment customers through clustering, and even the dynamic adaptation of prices using reinforcement learning, demonstrates the expansive applicability and transformative potential of predictive analytics and machine learning.

However, as with all tools and techniques, predictive analytics and machine learning come with their own set of challenges. Ensuring data quality, understanding underlying assumptions, addressing the cold-start problem in recommendation systems, and navigating the complexities of dynamic environments in reinforcement learning can present obstacles. Yet, with a nuanced understanding and careful application, they offer invaluable insights, making them indispensable in the modern marketer's toolkit.

In closing, as the marketing landscape evolves, being armed with the knowledge of predictive analytics and machine learning is not just beneficial—it's imperative. They offer a competitive advantage, enabling businesses to be proactive rather than reactive, and position themselves strategically in a dynamic marketplace. As we transition into the subsequent chapters, we'll explore more intricate facets of this interplay among data, marketing, and prediction, continuing our journey toward mastering marketing data science.

5.9 REFERENCES

Agrawal, R., & Srikant, R. (1994). Fast algorithms for mining association rules. *Proceedings of the 20th International Conference on Very Large Data Bases (VLDB)* (pp. 487–499).

Box, G.E.P., Jenkins, G. M., Reinsel, G. C., & Ljung, G. M. (2016). *Time series analysis: Forecasting and control.* Wiley.

Brown, I., & Mues, C. (2012). An experimental comparison of classification algorithms for imbalanced credit scoring data sets. *Expert Systems with Applications, 39*(3), 3446–3453.

Dhar, V. (2013). Data science and prediction. *Communications of the ACM, 56*(12), 64–73.

Douzas, G., & Bacao, F. (2018). Effective data generation for imbalanced learning using conditional generative adversarial networks. *Expert Systems with Applications, 91*, 464–471.

Elmaghraby, W., & Keskinocak, P. (2003). Dynamic pricing in the presence of inventory considerations: Research overview, current practices, and future directions. *Management Science, 49*(10), 1287–1309.

Ester, M., Kriegel, H. P., Sander, J., & Xu, X. (1996, August). A density-based algorithm for discovering clusters in large spatial databases with noise. *Proceedings of 2nd International Conference on Knowledge Discovery and Data Mining* (Vol. 96, No. 34, pp. 226–231).

Goodfellow, I., Bengio, Y., & Courville, A. (2016). *Deep learning.* MIT Press.

Hastie, T., Tibshirani, R., & Friedman, J. (2009). *The elements of statistical learning: Data mining, inference, and prediction* (2nd ed.). Springer.

Hosmer Jr., D. W., Lemeshow, S., & Sturdivant, R. X. (2013). *Applied logistic regression* (3rd ed.). Wiley.

Hyndman, R. J., & Athanasopoulos, G. (2018). *Forecasting: Principles and practice* (2nd ed.). OTexts.

Kaufman, L., & Rousseeuw, P. J. (2009). *Finding groups in data: An introduction to cluster analysis.* Wiley.

Kelleher, J. D., Mac Namee, B., & D'arcy, A. (2020). *Fundamentals of machine learning for predictive data analytics: Algorithms, worked examples, and case studies.* MIT Press.

Li, L., Chu, W., Langford, J., & Schapire, R. E. (2010). A contextual-bandit approach to personalized news article recommendation. *Proceedings of the 19th International Conference on World Wide Web* (pp. 661–670).

Makridakis, S., Spiliotis, E., & Assimakopoulos, V. (2020). The M4 Competition: 100,000 time series and 61 forecasting methods. *International Journal of Forecasting, 36*(1), 54–74.

Miglautsch, J. (2000). Thoughts on RFM scoring. *Journal of Database Marketing & Customer Strategy Management, 8*(1), 67–72.

Montgomery, D. C., Peck, E. A., & Vining, G. G. (2021). *Introduction to linear regression analysis.* Wiley.

Provost, F., & Fawcett, T. (2013). *Data science for business: What you need to know about data mining and data-analytic thinking.* O'Reilly Media.

Resnick, P., & Varian, H. R. (1997). Recommender systems. *Communications of the ACM, 40*(3), 56–58.

Ricci, F., Rokach, L., & Shapira, B. (2010). Introduction to recommender systems handbook. *Recommender systems handbook* (pp. 1–35). Springer US.

Sarwar, B., Karypis, G., Konstan, J., & Riedl, J. (2001, April). Item-based collaborative filtering recommendation algorithms. *Proceedings of the 10th international conference on World Wide Web* (pp. 285–295).

Sharda, R., Delen, D., & Turban, E. (2018). *Business intelligence, analytics, and data science: A managerial perspective.* Pearson.

Smith, W. R. (1956). Product differentiation and market segmentation as alternative marketing strategies. *Journal of Marketing, 21*(1), 3–8.

Sutton, R. S., & Barto, A. G. (2018). *Reinforcement learning: An introduction* (2nd ed.). MIT Press.

EXERCISE 5.1: CHURN PREDICTION MODEL

Objective: Use the **churn_data** to train a logistic regression model that predicts customer churn.

Tasks:

1. Split the **"churn_data.csv"** dataset into training and validation sets.

2. Train a logistic regression model to predict the binary dependent variable churn.

3. Make predictions and evaluate the model.

Steps:

1. **Importing Required Libraries:**

```
1. import pandas as pd
2. from sklearn.model_selection import train_test_split
3. from sklearn.linear_model import LogisticRegression
4. from sklearn.metrics import classification_report
```

- **pandas** is used for data manipulation and analysis.
- **train_test_split** from **sklearn.model_selection** is a utility to split datasets into training and test sets.
- **LogisticRegression** from **sklearn.linear_model** is a machine learning model for classification tasks.
- **classification_report** from **sklearn.metrics** provides a way to evaluate the quality of predictions from a classification algorithm.

2. **Loading the Dataset:**

```
5. churn_data = pd.read_csv('/data/churn_data.csv')
```

- We load the churn dataset from a CSV file into a pandas DataFrame. The dataset contains features that describe customer behavior and a target variable that indicates whether the customer has churned.

3. **Defining Features and Target:**

```
6. X = churn_data.drop('churn', axis=1)
7. y = churn_data['churn']
```

- We separate the features (**X**) and the target (**y**). The features include all columns except the target column 'churn', which we want to predict. The target is the 'churn' column, which is what our model will learn to predict.

4. Splitting the Data:

```
8. X_train, X_test, y_train, y_test = train_test_split(X, y,
test_size=0.2, random_state=42)
```

- The dataset is split into a training set (80%) and a test set (20%) using **train_test_split**. The **test_size** parameter dictates the proportion of the dataset to include in the test split. The **random_state** parameter ensures that the split is reproducible; the same random seed means the split will be the same each time the code is run.

5. Initializing the 'LogisticRegression' Model:

```
9. logreg = LogisticRegression()
```

- An instance of the 'LogisticRegression' model is created. 'LogisticRegression' is chosen because it is a common model for binary classification tasks, similar to predicting churn (yes or no).

6. Training the Model:

```
10. logreg.fit(X_train, y_train)
```

- The 'LogisticRegression' model is trained on the training data (**X_train** and **y_train**). The **fit** method adjusts the weights of the model to find the best linear boundary that separates the classes.

7. Making Predictions:

```
11. y_pred = logreg.predict(X_test)
```

- The trained model is used to make predictions on the test data (**X_test**). The **predict** method applies the weights learned during training to the test data to predict the churn outcome.

8. Evaluating the Model:

```
12. classification_report_output = classification_report(y_
test, y_pred)
13. print(classification_report_output)
```

- Finally, the **classification_report** function is used to evaluate the predictions. It compares the predicted churn outcomes (**y_pred**) with the actual outcomes from the test set (**y_test**).
- The report provides metrics such as precision, recall, and F1-score that help to understand the performance of the model across the different classes (churned or not churned).

■ The output is printed to provide a clear view of the model's performance.

This entire process constitutes a basic workflow for training and evaluating a binary classification model in machine learning. Each step is crucial for understanding how the model is built and how well it performs on unseen data.

EXERCISE 5.1: OUTPUT

The 'LogisticRegression' model was trained on the churn data and evaluated on the test set. The classification report provides several metrics to assess the model's performance:

STDOUT/STDERR

	precision	recall	f1-score	support
0	0.8	0.91	0.85	93
1	0.91	0.8	0.86	107
accuracy			0.85	200
macro avg	0.86	0.86	0.85	200
weighted avg	0.86	0.85	0.86	200

■ **Precision:** This is the ratio of correctly predicted positive observations to the total predicted positives. High precision relates to a low false positive rate. We have precision values of 0.80 for class 0 (non-churn) and 0.91 for class 1 (churn), which indicates the model is more precise in predicting customers who will churn than those who will not.

■ **Recall (Sensitivity):** This is the ratio of correctly predicted positive observations to all observations in the actual class. The recall is 0.91 for class 0 and 0.80 for class 1, indicating the model is more sensitive in predicting the non-churners correctly than churners.

■ **F1-score:** This is the weighted harmonic mean of precision and recall. The F1-score is 0.85 for class 0 and 0.86 for class 1, suggesting that the model is robust in its predictive performance for both classes.

■ **Support:** This is the number of actual occurrences of the class in the specified dataset. For non-churners (class 0), there are 93 instances, and for churners (class 1), there are 107 instances.

■ **Accuracy:** The model has an overall accuracy of 0.85, which means it correctly predicts the churn status 85% of the time on the test set.

■ **Macro Average:** This is the average precision, recall, and F1-score between classes. The macro average does not take class imbalance into account, which is appropriate here because the classes are balanced.

■ **Weighted Average:** This is the average precision, recall, and F1-score between classes weighted by the number of instances in each class. This gives us a better measure of the true quality of the classifier, particularly when there is class imbalance, which is not a significant issue in this dataset.

Overall, with an F1-score of approximately 0.85 for both classes, the model appears to perform well on this dataset, which suggests it could be a good starting point for making predictions in a real-world scenario.

EXERCISE 5.2: PREDICT WEEKLY SALES

Objective: Build a linear regression model to predict weekly sales based on marketing spend and other store features.

Tasks:

1. Split the **"regression_data.csv"** dataset into training and validation sets.
2. Train a linear regression model to predict the dependent variable **weekly_sales**.
3. Make predictions and evaluate the model.

Steps:

1. **Importing Libraries:**

```
1. import pandas as pd
2. from sklearn.model_selection import train_test_split
3. from sklearn.linear_model import LinearRegression
4. from sklearn.metrics import mean_squared_error
```

■ **pandas** is for data manipulation.

■ **train_test_split** will help divide the data into training and testing sets.

■ **LinearRegression** is the model we will use for prediction.

■ **mean_squared_error** will be used to evaluate the model's performance.

2. **Loading the Dataset:**

```
5. regression_data = pd.read_csv('/data/regression_data.csv')
```

■ The regression data is loaded into a pandas DataFrame from a CSV file.

3. **Defining Features and Target:**

```
6. X = regression_data.drop('weekly_sales', axis=1)
7. y = regression_data['weekly_sales']
```

- **X** contains the independent variables (features), which are all columns except 'weekly_sales'.
- **y** is the dependent variable (target), which we aim to predict—in this case, 'weekly_sales'.

4. **Splitting the Data:**

```
8. X_train, X_test, y_train, y_test = train_test_split(X, y,
test_size=0.2, random_state=42)
```

- The dataset is split into training (80%) and testing (20%) sets, with **random_state** set for reproducibility.

5. **Initializing and Training the Model:**

```
9. linreg = LinearRegression()
10. linreg.fit(X_train, y_train)
```

- A **LinearRegression** model instance is created and then fitted (trained) using the training data.

6. **Making Predictions:**

```
11. y_pred = linreg.predict(X_test)
```

- The model makes predictions (**y_pred**) on the test data (**X_test**).

7. **Evaluating the Model:**

```
12. mse = mean_squared_error(y_test, y_pred)
```

- The mean squared error (MSE) is calculated between the actual values (**y_test**) and the predicted values (**y_pred**).

EXERCISE 5.2: OUTPUT

The computed mean squared error is 0.01064, which is a measure of the model's accuracy. A lower MSE indicates a better fit of the model to the data. Given the low MSE, we can infer that our model has performed well on this dataset.

This exercise demonstrates the process of creating and evaluating a predictive model, which is a fundamental aspect of data science in marketing and many other fields. The small MSE suggests that the model's predictions are very close to the actual sales figures, making it a potentially useful tool in a real-world marketing context.

CHAPTER 6

Natural Language Processing in Marketing

6.0 BEGINNER-FRIENDLY INTRODUCTION TO NATURAL LANGUAGE PROCESSING IN MARKETING

Before diving deep into the world of natural language processing (NLP) in marketing, let's take a moment to understand some basic concepts. If you're already familiar with NLP and artificial intelligence (AI), feel free to skip this section.

6.0.1 What Is Natural Language Processing, and Why Should Marketers Care?

Imagine teaching a robot to understand human language—how we chat, argue, joke, and even make purchases. NLP is a technology that helps computers grasp, respond to, and process our language. For marketers, this means better understanding customer feedback, tailoring ads, or even having chatbots assist customers 24/7.

6.0.2 Simple Analogy: The Recipe of Language

Consider language as a recipe. Each ingredient (word) has its role, and when mixed in the right way, they create a delicious dish (meaningful sentence). NLP is like a master chef who knows each ingredient well and can even tweak the recipe to suit different tastes (contexts).

6.0.3 Natural Language Processing in Everyday Marketing

- **Social media.** Ever wondered how some tools can tell if tweets about a product are positive or negative? That's NLP in action, analyzing sentiment.
- **Chatbots.** When you visit a website and a chat window pops up offering assistance, NLP powers that interaction, helping the bot understand and respond to your queries.
- **Voice assistants.** Devices such as Amazon's Alexa or Google Home use NLP to understand and carry out voice commands, changing how we search for products or information.

6.0.4 Let's Dive Deeper

Now that we've skimmed the surface, let's dive into the ocean of NLP and explore how it's reshaping the world of marketing. From understanding its components to seeing it in action, this chapter will provide both foundational knowledge and practical insights.

6.1 INTRODUCTION TO NATURAL LANGUAGE PROCESSING

6.1.1 Overview of Natural Language Processing

NLP, a discipline that falls under the broader umbrella of AI, is dedicated to the interaction between computers and human language. The primary aim of NLP is to enable computers to understand, interpret, and generate human language in a way that is meaningful and valuable (Jurafsky & Martin, 2023). This involves teaching machines to understand the complexities of human language, including its semantics, syntax, and context, among other things.

In its early years, NLP was heavily rule-based, and linguists manually wrote complex sets of rules for language processing. However, with the advent of machine learning and especially deep learning, the approach shifted toward statistical and data-driven methods. These methods rely on large amounts of language data, or corpora, and learn to process language by identifying patterns in the data (Goodfellow et al., 2016).

NLP has a wide range of applications, including machine translation, speech recognition, sentiment analysis, information extraction, and text summarization, to name just a few. Within the context of marketing, NLP can be used to analyze customer sentiment, personalize advertising content, automate customer service, and gain insights from large volumes of unstructured text data. By harnessing the power of NLP, marketers can better understand their customers, enhance their marketing strategies, and ultimately drive business growth.

6.1.2 Importance of Natural Language Processing in Marketing

The rapid growth of digital platforms has resulted in an exponential increase in unstructured text data, such as customer reviews, social media comments, and online discussions. It is estimated that about 80% of the world's data is unstructured, and a significant portion of this is text data (Sumathy & Chidambaram, 2013). However, traditional data analysis methods are not well suited to handle this type of data. This is where NLP comes in.

NLP enables businesses to analyze large volumes of unstructured text data, derive meaningful insights, and make data-driven marketing decisions (Liu, 2012). For instance, NLP can be used to analyze customer sentiment from online reviews or social media posts, helping businesses to understand how their customers perceive their products, services, or brand. This information can be invaluable for guiding marketing strategies and improving customer satisfaction.

Moreover, NLP can enhance the effectiveness of marketing communications. By analyzing the language used by customers, NLP can help businesses to tailor their marketing messages to the preferences and sentiments of individual customers, leading to more personalized and engaging marketing communications.

NLP can also improve customer service, another critical aspect of marketing. NLP-powered chatbots, for instance, can provide instant, 24/7 customer service, answering customer queries, and providing product recommendations in natural language. This not only enhances the customer experience but also reduces the load on customer service representatives and cuts costs.

In summary, NLP plays a crucial role in modern marketing, helping businesses to understand their customers better, enhance their marketing communications, and improve customer service. By harnessing the power of NLP, businesses can gain a competitive edge in the increasingly digital and data-driven business landscape (see Table 6.1).

Table 6.1 Various Marketing Problems and How Natural Language Processing Provides Solutions.

Marketing Challenges	NLP Solutions
Understanding customer sentiments	Sentiment analysis
Automating customer support	Chatbots and virtual assistants
Targeted advertising	Ad content optimization using NLP
Content recommendation	Content-based filtering using NLP
Brand monitoring on social media	Social media scraping and sentiment analysis

6.1.3 Components of Natural Language Processing: Syntax, Semantics, and Pragmatics

6.1.3.1 Syntax

At its core, syntax refers to the rules that dictate the structure of sentences in a given language. In other words, it is concerned with how words come together to form phrases, clauses, and sentences. For NLP, syntactic analysis often involves tasks such as parsing (breaking down a sentence into its constituent parts and understanding their relationships) and part-of-speech tagging (identifying the grammatical categories of individual words, such as nouns, verbs, adjectives, etc.). Understanding syntax is crucial because even slight changes in word order or structure can drastically alter the meaning of a sentence.

6.1.3.2 Semantics

Moving beyond the structure, semantics dives into meaning. It deals with the interpretation of signs or symbols in a communication system, be it words, signs, symbols, or gestures. Within NLP, semantic analysis is used to understand the meaning of individual words in context, resolve ambiguities (e.g., determining the meaning of *bank* in *riverbank* versus *savings bank*), and extract structured information from unstructured text. Ontologies and knowledge graphs, which capture structured information about the world and relationships between entities, play a significant role in semantic understanding.

6.1.3.3 Pragmatics

Pragmatics delves into the context in which communication occurs, addressing questions such as: Who is speaking? To whom? Under what circumstances? And with what intent? It's about understanding language in context, capturing implied meanings, understanding indirect communication, and grasping the social norms and rules that guide communication. In the realm of NLP, pragmatics can aid in tasks such as sentiment analysis (where the same word can have different connotations based on context) or dialogue systems (where understanding the user's intent and the context of the conversation is paramount) (see Figure 6.1).

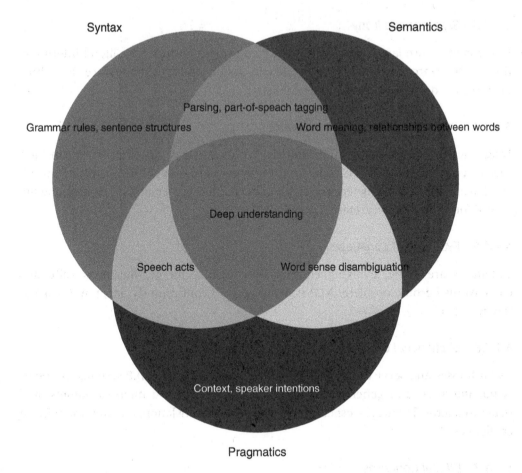

Figure 6.1 Overlap and Distinctions Among Syntax, Semantics and Pragmatics in Natural Language Processing.

6.1.4 Challenges in Natural Language Processing

6.1.4.1 Ambiguity

A primary challenge in NLP is ambiguity, which arises when a word or sentence can have multiple interpretations. For instance, "I saw her duck" can mean observing a bird or a person ducking. Resolving such ambiguities requires contextual understanding, which can be complex for computational systems.

6.1.4.2 Idioms and Phrasal Verbs

Languages are peppered with idiomatic expressions and phrasal verbs that don't directly translate word-for-word. For example, "kick the bucket" isn't about kicking or buckets but denotes someone's death. Recognizing and interpreting such expressions is challenging for NLP systems.

6.1.4.3 Sarcasm and Irony

Humans often use language in ways that mean the opposite of the literal interpretation, such as sarcasm or irony. Detecting and understanding such nuances in written or spoken text can be a considerable challenge.

6.1.4.4 Cultural and Contextual Nuances

Languages evolve within cultural contexts. Words, phrases, or constructs might have specific cultural connotations or historical references that might be opaque to outsiders. Ensuring NLP systems recognize and understand these nuances is challenging but crucial for accurate interpretation.

6.1.4.5 Evolution of Language

Languages are living, evolving entities. New words emerge, meanings shift, and older words become obsolete. NLP systems need to continuously adapt and learn to stay relevant.

6.1.4.6 Multilingual Challenges

As businesses and services operate globally, there's a need for NLP systems to understand, interpret, and generate multiple languages. Handling nuances, idioms, and structures across languages, especially in tasks such as translation, remains a significant challenge.

6.1.4.7 Ethical Concerns

As NLP models are trained on vast amounts of data, they can sometimes reflect and perpetuate biases present in the data. Addressing these biases and ensuring fairness in NLP applications is a challenge and a responsibility.

In summary, although NLP offers transformative potential for myriad applications, it comes with its set of challenges. Addressing these challenges requires a blend of linguistic expertise, advanced computational techniques, and a deep understanding of the ever-evolving nature of human language.

6.2 TEXT PREPROCESSING AND FEATURE EXTRACTION IN MARKETING NATURAL LANGUAGE PROCESSING

In the vast ocean of marketing data, textual information stands as a goldmine of insights. However, before any meaningful analysis can take place, this raw text must undergo a series of transformations to become both understandable and actionable. This section delves into the core techniques of text preprocessing and feature extraction, pivotal steps in transforming unstructured textual data into a structured format suitable for advanced analysis. From tokenization and stemming to the intricacies of vectorization and word embeddings, we'll explore how these techniques lay the foundation for effective NLP applications in marketing, ensuring that the insights gleaned are both accurate and relevant.

6.2.1 Tokenization and Stemming

Tokenization is the fundamental process of converting a text into tokens, which are smaller chunks or words. This process helps simplify the subsequent types of parsing and allows for easier mapping of meaning from human language (Schütze et al., 2008).

Stemming, however, is the process of reducing inflected (or sometimes derived) words to their word stem, base or root form—generally a written word form. For instance, the stem of the word *jumps* might be *jump*. Stemming is widely used in search engines and information retrieval systems to ensure different forms of a word match during a search, such as when a user searches for *marketing*, results with *marketed* or *marketer* also appear.

6.2.2 Stop Word Removal

Stop words are commonly used words in a language such as *and*, *the*, *is*, and so on, which might not contain significant information when analyzing text data. In NLP and text mining, these words are often filtered out before or after the process of text processing (Willett, 2006). The rationale behind removing these words is to focus on meaningful words, which can enhance the efficiency of subsequent processes such as text classification or sentiment analysis.

6.2.3 Vectorization: Bag of Words and TF–IDF

Once text data is tokenized and cleaned, it is converted into a format that can be easily understood by machine learning algorithms. One such method is the bag of words (BoW) model. BoW represents each document or text as a numerical vector, where the presence or absence of a word is denoted by 1 or 0, respectively (Harris, 1954).

Let's consider the following sample text documents:

1. **Document 0.** "AI with natural language processing are changing the world."
2. **Document 1.** "AI and robotics are the future of technology."
3. **Document 2.** "Marketing with AI and data are the key to success."

From these sample documents, we derive the BoW and TF-IDF representations (see Table 6.2).

TF–IDF (term frequency-inverse document frequency) is another method that not only considers the frequency of a word in a particular document but also how often it appears across all documents. The idea behind this is to give higher importance to words that are unique to a specific document. This method helps in suppressing

Table 6.2 BoW Representation.

	ai	and	are	changing	data	future	key	language	marketing	...
Doc 0	1	0	1	1	0	0	0	1	0	...
Doc 1	1	1	1	0	0	1	0	0	0	...
Doc 2	1	1	1	0	1	0	1	0	1	...

	natural	processing	robotics	success	technology	the	to	with	world
Doc 0	1	1	0	0	0	0	0	1	1
Doc 1	0	0	1	0	1	1	0	0	0
Doc 2	0	0	0	1	0	1	1	1	0

frequent words that occur across all documents that might not carry much information (Ramos, 2003).

To determine the TF–IDF representation, we compute the term frequency for each term in each document and then adjust this by the inverse document frequency for the term across all documents. Given our three sample documents, let's break down the computation of TF–IDF for the sample documents:

Step 1. Compute term frequency (TF).

The term frequency (TF) of a word is the frequency of a word in a document divided by the total number of words in that document. For instance, for the word 'AI' in Document 0: TF('AI', Document 0) = 1 / 9 = 0.111.

Step 2. Compute inverse document frequency (IDF).

The inverse document frequency (IDF) of a word is the log of the total number of documents divided by the number of documents containing the word. For instance, for the word 'AI': IDF('AI') = log(3 / 3) = 0 (because 'AI' appears in all three documents).

Step 3. Compute TF–IDF.

TF–IDF is the product of TF and IDF. For instance, for the word 'AI' in Document 0: TF-IDF('AI', Document 0) = TF('AI', Document 0) * IDF('AI') = 0.111 * 0 = 0.

Using this process, we can compute the TF–IDF values for all words across all documents. Table 6.3 shows the illustrative TF–IDF values. (Note: For simplicity, we've rounded the values to three decimal places and considered the natural logarithm.)

Keep in mind that these values are based on the simplistic computation for illustrative purposes. In actual implementations, additional preprocessing steps and adjustments might be applied.

6.2.4 Word Embeddings: Word2Vec, GloVe

Word embeddings are modern ways to represent words as vectors in a dense space where the semantics of the word are captured by the position in the space. Two of the most famous models for creating such embeddings are Word2Vec and GloVe.

Table 6.3 Term Frequency-Inverse Document Frequency (TF–IDF) Representation.

	ai	and	are	changing	data	future	key	language	marketing	...
Doc 0	0	0	0	0.356	0	0	0	0.356	0	...
Doc 1	0	0	0	0	0	0.356	0	0	0	...
Doc 2	0	0	0	0	0.356	0	0.356	0	0.356	...

	natural	processing	robotics	success	technology	the	to	with	world
Doc 0	0.356	0.356	0	0	0	0	0	0	0.356
Doc 1	0	0	0.356	0	0.356	0	0	0	0
Doc 2	0	0	0	0.356	0	0	0.356	0	0

Word2Vec, introduced by Mikolov et al. in 2013, captures semantic meanings of words based on their context in the data. There are two main training algorithms for Word2Vec: continuous bag of words (CBOW) and Skip-Gram.

GloVe (global vectors for word representation), introduced by Pennington et al. in 2014, is another method for obtaining vector representations for words. It combines the benefits of two major methods in the field: count-based methods and predictive methods. It does so by factorizing the word co-occurrence matrix.

Word2Vec and GloVe have been extensively used in various NLP applications, including sentiment analysis, machine translation, and more (see Figure 6.2).

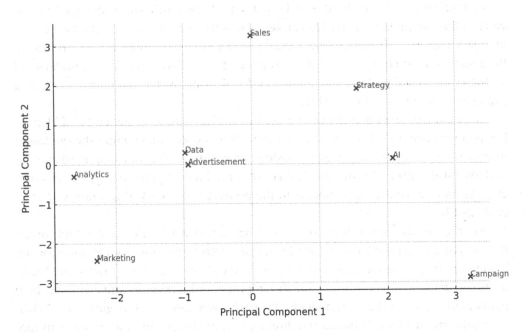

Figure 6.2 Word Embeddings in a 2D Space.

6.3 KEY NATURAL LANGUAGE PROCESSING TECHNIQUES FOR MARKETING

As we delve deeper into the practical applications of NLP within the marketing sector, it's imperative to grasp the core techniques that make these applications possible. In this section, we will explore some of these key NLP techniques and how they can be leveraged to optimize marketing efforts. These techniques include sentiment analysis, topic modeling, named entity recognition (NER), and text classification, each of which has a distinct role in transforming unstructured text data into actionable insights.

With the evolution of machine learning algorithms and the continual advancements in computational capabilities, these techniques have become more efficient and accurate. They now provide marketers with a robust framework to understand customer opinions, detect emerging trends, personalize communication, and much more. The subsequent sections will delve into each of these techniques, providing a comprehensive overview of their operation, importance, and practical applications in marketing.

6.3.1 Text Analytics

Text analytics, also known as *text mining*, is a process of deriving high-quality information from text data using various NLP, information retrieval, and machine learning techniques (Feldman & Sanger, 2007). It involves structuring the input text, deriving patterns within the structured data, and finally, evaluating and interpreting the output.

In marketing, text analytics can be particularly beneficial in understanding the voice of the customer, as it enables marketers to analyze vast amounts of unstructured text data such as customer reviews, social media posts, and customer support tickets. By doing so, marketers can identify common themes, detect sentiment, understand customer needs and preferences, and gain valuable insights that can inform marketing strategies (Cambria & White, 2014).

For example, text analytics can be used to analyze customer reviews and identify key product attributes that customers frequently mention, and whether the sentiment toward these attributes is generally positive or negative. This can help marketers to understand the strengths and weaknesses of a product, as perceived by the customers, and make necessary adjustments to the product or its marketing strategy (Netzer et al., 2012).

Another application of text analytics in marketing is in social media monitoring. By analyzing social media posts, marketers can detect emerging trends, monitor the brand's online reputation, and gain insights into customer attitudes toward the brand or its competitors. This can guide the development of marketing campaigns and help marketers to react quickly to changes in the market environment (Stieglitz et al., 2018).

In the realm of social media monitoring, text analytics serves as a powerful tool for extracting valuable insights from vast amounts of unstructured data. Figure 6.3

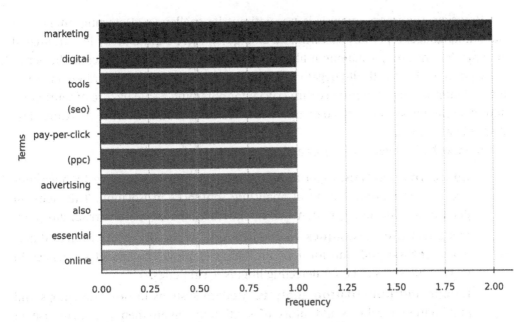

Figure 6.3 The Most Frequent Terms in a Sample Text Using Text Analytics.

illustrates this application vividly, presenting a bar chart that displays the most frequent terms appearing in a sample of social media text. This visualization encapsulates the core of text analytics in marketing, showing how common phrases and keywords can signal trends, brand reputation, and customer sentiment.

In summary, text analytics provides a powerful tool for marketers to make sense of vast amounts of unstructured text data and gain valuable customer insights, thereby enabling data-driven decision-making in marketing.

6.3.2 Sentiment Analysis

Sentiment analysis, sometimes also referred to as *opinion mining*, is a subfield of NLP that involves the use of natural language processing, text analysis, and computational linguistics to identify, extract, quantify, and study affective states and subjective information from source materials (Pang & Lee, 2008). In the context of marketing, it is commonly used to understand customer sentiment toward products, services, or brands based on written (or spoken) reviews, feedback, or social media conversations.

One of the primary uses of sentiment analysis in marketing is in social media monitoring. Marketers can analyze tweets, Facebook posts, or other social media content to gauge public sentiment toward their brand, products, or specific marketing campaigns (Cambria et al., 2017). The insights derived from such analysis can help marketers to quickly respond to positive or negative trends, tailor their communication to address customer concerns or capitalize on positive feedback, and generally make data-informed decisions that can enhance brand perception and customer satisfaction.

However, sentiment analysis is not without its challenges. Detecting nuances in human language, especially sarcasm and ambiguity, can be quite tricky for automated systems. For instance, a statement like "Oh great, just what I needed!" could be genuinely positive or sarcastically negative, depending on the context. Accurately identifying and interpreting such nuances are crucial for obtaining a true picture of sentiment, and this remains an ongoing challenge in the realm of sentiment analysis (González-Ibáñez et al., 2011).

To tackle this, several advances and solutions are being explored:

- **Contextual analysis.** Algorithms are being designed to consider broader contextual information instead of analyzing sentences in isolation. This helps in determining the mood or intent behind statements based on the surrounding text.

- **Deep learning techniques.** Neural networks, especially recurrent neural networks (RNNs) and transformers, are being employed to model sequences in texts, which aids in better detecting linguistic subtleties.

- **Emojis and punctuation analysis.** Modern systems incorporate emojis and punctuation marks as indicators of sentiment, given their prevalent use in expressing emotions online.

- **Human-in-the-loop (HITL).** Some companies integrate human reviewers into their sentiment analysis processes. These reviewers help train the model by correcting its mistakes, thereby refining its accuracy over time.

Sentiment analysis can also be employed to assess customer reviews and ratings on e-commerce platforms or review sites. By automatically analyzing the sentiment expressed in written reviews, marketers can gain insights into customer experiences, product or service quality, and potential areas for improvement, often in real time. This can help companies to address issues proactively and enhance their product or service offerings based on customer feedback (Liu, 2012).

Moreover, sentiment analysis can also be used in competitive analysis. By analyzing the sentiment toward competitors' brands or products, companies can identify opportunities and threats in the market and strategize accordingly (Cambria et al., 2017).

Through sentiment analysis, marketers gain a robust method to comprehend and address customer attitudes and opinions, subsequently improving their capacity to fulfil customer needs and forge deeper brand connections.

6.3.3 Topic Modeling

Topic modeling is a type of statistical model used for discovering the abstract topics that occur in a collection of documents, such as customer reviews or social media posts. Latent dirichlet allocation is one of the most commonly used methods for topic modeling (Blei et al., 2003).

In marketing, topic modeling can be used to automatically identify common themes or topics in large amounts of unstructured text data. For example, by applying topic modeling to customer reviews, marketers can identify the key topics that customers frequently

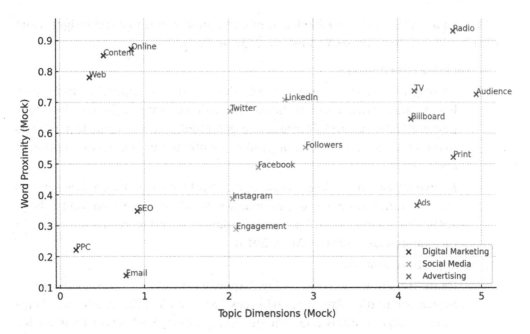

Figure 6.4 Topic Modeling Results Showing Word Clusters for Different Topics.

discuss, such as product features, customer service, pricing, and so on. This can provide valuable insights into what aspects of the product or service are most important to customers, which can inform product development and marketing strategies (Jacobi et al., 2016).

Topic modeling can also be used in social media analysis. For instance, by applying topic modeling to tweets mentioning a brand, marketers can identify the key topics of conversation around the brand. This can help marketers to understand the brand's perception, identify emerging trends, and monitor the impact of marketing campaigns (Röder et al., 2015).

Furthermore, topic modeling can be used for content analysis in content marketing. By applying topic modeling to a collection of blog posts or articles, marketers can identify the key topics covered and how these topics relate to each other. This can inform the development of future content and help marketers to create content that resonates with their target audience (Blei & Lafferty, 2009; see Figure 6.4).

Through topic modeling, marketers have an effective instrument to automatically discern principal topics in vast amounts of text data, offering invaluable insights that can shape marketing strategies.

6.3.4 Named Entity Recognition

Named entity recognition (NER) is an information extraction subtask that identifies and classifies named entities in text into predefined categories such as person names, organizations, locations, medical codes, time expressions, quantities, monetary values, percentages, and so on (Nadeau & Sekine, 2007).

In the marketing sphere, NER offers numerous applications to distill insights from unstructured text. Here are some illustrative applications:

1. **Social media analysis:**

   ▪ **Example.** Consider a tweet, "Just tried the new Frappuccino from Starbucks, and it's heavenly! #coffeeLover." NER can extract the entities 'Frappuccino' (product) and 'Starbucks' (organization). This can enable marketers to monitor and analyze specific product mentions and understand sentiment about them.

   ▪ By extracting entities from social media, marketers can discern key subjects such as brands, products, or personalities. It aids in brand mention tracking, sentiment analysis toward particular products, or influencer identification in the brand's digital sphere (Marr, 2015).

2. **Competitive analysis:**

   ▪ **Example.** From an article stating, "Apple is set to launch its new iPhone in September, putting Samsung on its toes," NER can identify 'Apple' and 'Samsung' as organizations and 'iPhone' as a product. Such extractions enable businesses to monitor competitor activities and strategize accordingly.

   ▪ Through NER in industry reports, news, or competitors' social media, companies can get insights into competitors, market trends, and potential opportunities or threats (Chiticariu et al., 2013).

3. **Content marketing:**

   ▪ **Example.** In a blog post titled "Top European Destinations in Summer," NER can automatically tag entities such as 'Paris', 'Rome', or 'Amsterdam'. When a user reads about 'Paris' and interacts positively, the system could recommend other content associated with 'Paris' for subsequent readings.

   ▪ NER aids in automatically spotting and tagging entities in content, improving content discoverability and personalization. This ensures users can easily locate content or receive recommendations based on prior entity interactions (Marr, 2015).

By leveraging NER, marketers can adeptly extract and analyze indispensable information from vast unstructured text data, garnering insights pivotal for refining marketing strategies.

6.3.5 Text Classification

Text classification, also termed text *categorization*, assigns predefined categories or labels to textual documents grounded in their content (Sebastiani, 2002). This process underpins numerous NLP and information retrieval operations such as spam detection, sentiment analysis, and document organization.

Technologically, text classification is facilitated by machine learning models that are trained on labeled datasets. Here's a brief overview of the algorithms and techniques involved:

- **Preprocessing.** Prior to classification, the text must be processed. Common steps include tokenization, stemming or lemmatization, and removal of stop words. This transforms the raw text into a structured format suitable for machine learning.

- **Feature extraction.** Techniques such as BoW, TF–IDF, and word embeddings (like Word2Vec or GloVe) convert textual data into numerical vectors that capture the essence of the content.

- **Model training.** Various algorithms can be employed for text classification:

  - **Naive Bayes.** A probabilistic algorithm, this algorithm is popular for its simplicity and efficiency in text classification tasks, especially spam detection.

  - **Support vector machines (SVM).** These can create hyperplanes that separate data into distinct classes, making them suitable for high-dimensional text data.

  - **Neural networks:** Deep learning models, particularly RNNs and transformers, have been achieving state-of-the-art results in text classification by capturing sequential dependencies in text.

- **Evaluation and optimization.** Once trained, models are evaluated using metrics such as accuracy, precision, recall, and F1-score. They can then be optimized using techniques like hyperparameter tuning.

In the realm of marketing, text classification can have various applications. It can be used for sentiment analysis, where customer reviews, comments, or social media posts are classified into positive, negative, or neutral sentiments. This enables marketers to gain insights into customer opinions and feelings toward their products or services (Pang & Lee, 2008).

Text classification can also be used for spam detection in email marketing. By classifying emails into spam or not spam, marketers can ensure their marketing emails are not mistakenly marked as spam and reach their intended recipients (Sahami et al., 1998).

In content marketing, text classification can be used for automatic tagging or categorization of articles or blog posts. By assigning relevant tags or categories to each piece of content, marketers can improve content discoverability and recommendation, leading to a better user experience (Kotsiantis et al., 2007).

Moreover, text classification can be employed for customer service automation. By classifying customer inquiries or complaints into different categories, companies can automatically route each inquiry to the appropriate department or generate automatic responses, leading to more efficient customer service (Apté et al., 1994).

Text classification equips marketers with a robust mechanism to analyze and categorize vast volumes of text data, yielding valuable insights and efficiencies that shape marketing strategies.

6.4 CHATBOTS AND VOICE ASSISTANTS IN MARKETING

In the contemporary digital landscape, instant communication and user-centric interactions have become the norm. Companies and brands are increasingly turning to technology-driven solutions, such as chatbots and voice assistants, to foster real-time interactions and improve customer experience. These technologies not only facilitate seamless customer journeys but also provide marketers with invaluable data and insights to tailor their strategies. In this section, we will explore the evolution, best practices, and implications of chatbots and voice assistants in marketing.

6.4.1 Evolution and Importance of Chatbots

Evolution. Chatbots, although now ubiquitous, have humble origins. Beginning as rule-based systems in which interactions were limited to predefined inputs and outputs, modern chatbots now employ sophisticated NLP algorithms that allow for more fluid, human-like conversations. With the rise of platforms such as Facebook Messenger and WhatsApp, the integration of chatbots into these platforms has driven an exponential growth in their adoption.

Importance. Chatbots are revolutionizing customer service and engagement in several ways. They provide 24/7 customer support, handle multiple queries simultaneously, and offer instant responses, leading to increased customer satisfaction. Furthermore, the data they capture aids marketers in understanding user behavior, preferences, and pain points, enabling more targeted and personalized marketing campaigns.

6.4.2 Designing Effective Chatbots: Best Practices

- **User-centric design.** The design should reflect the primary needs of your audience. Chatbots should be designed with user intent in mind, ensuring that the most common queries are addressed efficiently.
- **Seamless handoff to humans.** Chatbots should recognize when a user's query is too complex and seamlessly transition the conversation to a human representative.
- **Iterative feedback loop.** Regularly gather user feedback and use this data to refine and improve the chatbot's responses and functionalities.
- **Natural language understanding.** Incorporate advanced NLP techniques to ensure chatbots understand user inputs more accurately and provide relevant outputs.

- **Multimodal interactions.** In addition to text, consider integrating multimedia content, such as images or videos, to enrich user interactions.

To further elucidate the best practices of chatbot design, Table 6.4 provides concrete examples for each principle, illustrating how they can be effectively implemented to enhance user interaction and satisfaction.

6.4.3 Voice Assistants and Voice Search

Voice assistants, such as Amazon's Alexa, Google Assistant, and Apple's Siri, have heralded a paradigm shift in user behavior and brand interactions. These digital helpers are increasingly becoming a primary interface for users to gather information, perform tasks, and connect with brands.

The adoption of smart speakers, in-car voice systems, and voice-enabled wearables has fueled the ascendancy of voice search. As more households integrate these devices into their daily routines, voice searches are poised to outpace traditional text queries. For marketers, this not only signifies a change in the medium but also a fundamental alteration in the way consumers articulate their needs and expectations.

6.4.3.1 Characteristics of Voice Search

- **Conversational tone.** Voice queries are inherently more conversational and natural, often formulated as questions. For example, "Where can I find a blue summer dress?" instead of "blue summer dress store near me."
- **Long-tail keywords.** Due to their conversational nature, voice searches tend to be longer and more specific, emphasizing the importance of long-tail keyword optimization in content.
- **Locally oriented.** Many voice searches are local in intent, such as "Where's the nearest clothes retailer?" This underscores the importance of local SEO for businesses.

Table 6.4 Best Practices for Chatbot Design with Examples.

Best Practices	Examples
Set clear objectives for the chatbot	A chatbot designed to assist with product inquiries on an e-commerce site
Design for the target audience	A chatbot for a gaming website using gaming jargon
Ensure smooth handoff to human agents	When a chatbot cannot answer a query, it directs the user to a customer service representative.
Opt for a conversational tone	Instead of "Query not understood," the chatbot says "Oops, I didn't catch that. Can you rephrase?"
Implement feedback mechanisms	After a chat session, the bot asks, "Did I help answer your question?"

6.4.3.2 Challenges and Considerations for Marketers

- **Changing SEO dynamics.** Traditional SEO practices focus on typed search patterns. Voice searches demand an overhaul of these strategies, prioritizing natural language, question-based queries, and featured snippets that voice assistants might read out.

- **Ensuring quick, relevant responses.** Voice search users expect quick and accurate answers. Content must be structured to provide direct responses to potential voice queries.

- **Adaptation to different platforms.** Each voice assistant has its unique algorithm and preferences. Marketers need to understand the nuances of each platform to optimize effectively.

- **Loss of screen real estate.** Unlike text-based searches that display multiple results, voice assistants typically provide one answer, making the competition for the coveted top spot even fiercer.

- **Privacy concerns.** The always-listening nature of some devices has raised privacy concerns among users. Marketers must tread carefully, ensuring transparent data collection and use practices.

- **Monetizing voice search.** Traditional online advertising doesn't seamlessly translate to voice interactions. Brands must find innovative ways to integrate themselves into voice search results without disrupting the user experience.

6.4.3.3 Innovative Approaches in Voice Search Marketing

- **Creating voice apps or skills.** Brands can develop specific applications for voice assistants, such as Alexa Skills or Google Actions, offering users a more interactive and branded experience.

- **FAQs and rich content.** Creating FAQ sections and providing detailed answers to commonly asked questions can position a brand as an authority and increase the chances of being the featured answer in voice search.

- **Engage in conversational marketing.** Embracing chatbots and voice-activated assistants for direct consumer engagement, answering queries, offering suggestions, and even facilitating purchases can transform the shopping experience.

In the evolving landscape of voice-first interactions, marketers need to stay agile, continuously adapting to the changing norms and expectations of consumers. The brands that can effectively integrate voice search into their digital strategy stand to gain a significant edge in this burgeoning arena. As marketers navigate the voice-first landscape, recognizing the distribution of market share among different voice assistants is critical. Figure 6.5 provides a bar graph illustrating the estimated market share, offering a visual benchmark of the competitive field in which brands are vying to establish their voice search presence.

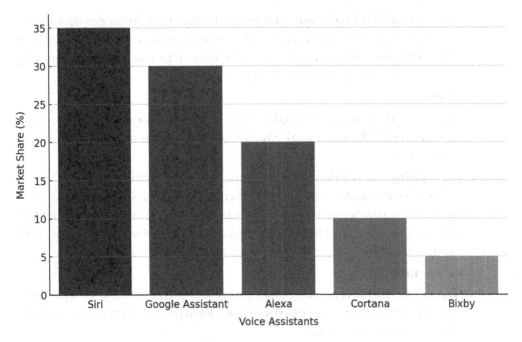

Figure 6.5 Estimated Market Share for Different Voice Assistants.

6.4.4.4 Implications and Challenges of Voice-Activated Marketing

Implications

- **Shift in SEO strategies.** As voice searches lean toward a conversational tone, marketers need to prioritize long-tail phrases and full sentences over traditional keywords. This means optimizing for natural language queries such as "What's the best sunscreen for sensitive skin?" rather than "best sunscreen."

- **Instant gratification.** Voice search users don't have the patience to sift through multiple search results. They expect direct and accurate answers. This mandates brands to craft content that's not only relevant but also concise and to the point.

- **Increased personalization.** Voice assistants, having access to user data and previous interactions, can offer tailored responses or product suggestions. This paves the way for highly personalized marketing strategies, where offers and recommendations are adapted to individual user behaviors and preferences.

Challenges

- **Data privacy:**
  - **Concern.** Voice assistants gather extensive user data, from daily routines to personal preferences. This accumulation of data has intensified concerns about user privacy and the potential misuse of personal information.

- **Navigating the challenge.** Brands must prioritize transparent data collection and use policies. They should also provide users with control over their data, allowing them to opt in or out of data collection processes, ensuring trust and compliance with privacy regulations.

- **Monetization:**

  - **Concern.** Many voice-activated devices, such as smart speakers, lack screens. This means traditional visual advertising, such as banners or video ads, is not feasible.

  - **Navigating the challenge.** Marketers must think outside the box. Potential strategies include sponsored content or branded voice apps. Another approach is partnering with voice platform providers to be the "preferred" solution, ensuring their brand is the first recommended option when relevant queries are made.

- **Interoperability:**

  - **Concern.** With several voice platforms in the market (Alexa, Google Assistant, Siri, etc.), there's no one-size-fits-all. Each platform has its unique algorithms and user behaviors.

  - **Navigating the challenge.** Brands should aim for platform-agnostic content and solutions when possible. This ensures consistent brand experiences across devices. Additionally, understanding the nuances and strengths of each platform can help brands tailor their strategies to get the best results on each one.

In summary, the ascent of chatbots and voice assistants in our daily lives is reshaping the marketing landscape. These technologies, although offering avenues for deeper engagement and personalization, bring with them a new set of challenges. Marketers who can effectively harness the potential of voice while skillfully navigating its challenges will position themselves at the forefront of this voice-first revolution.

6.5 PRACTICAL EXAMPLES OF NATURAL LANGUAGE PROCESSING IN MARKETING

6.5.1 Social Media Sentiment Analysis

Social media sentiment analysis is the use of NLP, text analysis, and computational linguistics to identify and extract subjective information from source materials in social media platforms (Liu, 2012). It helps to determine the attitude of the speaker or the writer with respect to some topic or the overall contextual polarity of a document.

In the marketing context, social media sentiment analysis enables businesses to identify consumer sentiment toward products, brands, or services in online conversations and feedback (Jiang et al., 2011). The analysis results can be leveraged to understand the customer's emotions toward a brand, to measure the effectiveness of marketing campaigns, and to identify potential crises before they escalate.

For example, a company could monitor tweets about their brand, categorizing them as positive, negative, or neutral. This would enable the company to identify customer dissatisfaction immediately and handle the situation before it harms their brand image (Thelwall et al., 2012).

Furthermore, sentiment analysis can guide the content creation process. By understanding what customers appreciate or dislike about a product or service, businesses can craft messages that address these issues and resonate with their audience (Cambria et al., 2017).

Finally, sentiment analysis can also help in competitive analysis. By comparing the sentiment toward their brand with that of their competitors, businesses can identify areas where they need to improve and discover opportunities for differentiation (Cambria et al., 2017).

To illustrate the practical application of social media sentiment analysis in marketing, Figure 6.6 provides a dashboard screenshot showing the results of such an analysis derived from social media content, offering a clear visualization of customer sentiments categorized as positive, negative, or neutral.

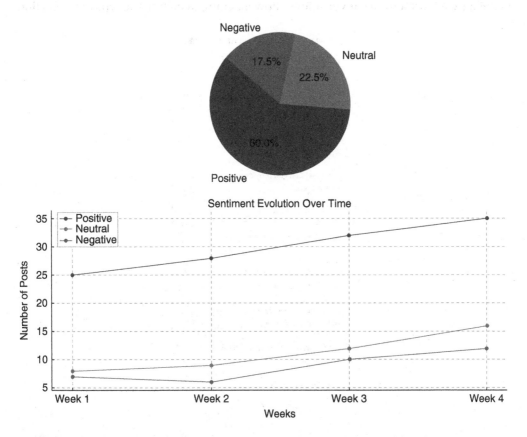

Figure 6.6 A Dashboard Screenshot Showing a Sentiment Analysis Result from Social Media.

In conclusion, social media sentiment analysis provides a powerful tool for marketers to understand and react to customer sentiment in real time, providing valuable insights that can inform marketing strategies.

6.5.2 Chatbots for Customer Service

As discussed in Section 6.4, in marketing, chatbots serve as an innovative tool to engage customers, answer queries, and provide personalized recommendations in real time, at any hour of the day (Dale, 2016). NLP is a key component in the design and functioning of chatbots, enabling them to understand and respond to user input in a human-like manner (McTear et al., 2016).

For instance, a customer might interact with a clothes retailer's chatbot to check the availability of a particular item or find information on the latest fashion collections. The chatbot, using NLP, can understand the user's intent and provide a suitable response or action. This helps to reduce waiting times and improve the customer experience, which can lead to increased customer retention and loyalty (Jain et al., 2018).

To provide a tangible example of how chatbots enhance customer service in marketing, Figure 6.7 presents a conversational flow diagram, depicting the typical interaction

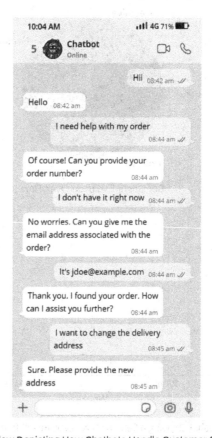

Figure 6.7 A Conversational Flow Depicting How Chatbots Handle Customer Service Interactions.

between a customer and a chatbot. This visual illustrates the chatbot's ability to understand and respond to customer inquiries, showcasing the efficiency and effectiveness of these digital assistants in real-time customer engagement.

Moreover, chatbots can gather and analyze customer data in real time, providing businesses with valuable insights into customer behavior and preferences. This data can then be used to personalize marketing campaigns and improve product offerings.

However, it is essential for companies to handle the implementation of chatbots wisely, ensuring a balance between automation and human touch. Although chatbots can handle routine queries effectively, human intervention may still be required for complex or sensitive issues (McTear et al., 2016).

With the assistance of NLP, chatbots are revolutionizing customer service in marketing, providing businesses an valuable instrument to elevate customer engagement and derive insights.

6.5.3 Personalized Marketing Communications

Personalization in marketing communications has gained considerable attention in recent years as a powerful tool for enhancing customer relationships and driving sales (Kumar et al., 2017). It involves tailoring messages to individual customers based on their preferences, behavior, and demographic information. This level of customization is made possible by advanced data analytics techniques, including NLP.

NLP provides a means to understand and generate human language in a way that is meaningful and personalized. This technology can be used to analyze customer interactions, such as emails, social media posts, and customer reviews, to gain insights into individual customer preferences and sentiment (Casillas & López, 2010).

For example, an e-commerce company might use NLP to analyze customer reviews and identify common themes or sentiments. This information could then be used to personalize email marketing campaigns, suggesting products based on the customer's expressed interests and sentiments (Casillas & López, 2010).

Furthermore, NLP can assist in generating personalized content for each customer. For example, dynamic content generation can create unique product descriptions or promotional messages that appeal specifically to the recipient based on their prior interactions and preferences (Casillas & López, 2010).

To visually demonstrate the impact of personalization in marketing communications, Figure 6.8 provides a before-and-after comparison, illustrating the transformation from generic messaging to communications that are personalized based on customer data and insights.

However, it's essential to note that although personalization can improve customer engagement and conversion rates, it must be executed with a keen understanding of the customer and respect for their privacy (Kumar et al., 2017). Overly intrusive or irrelevant personalized messages can have the opposite effect, alienating customers and damaging the brand-customer relationship.

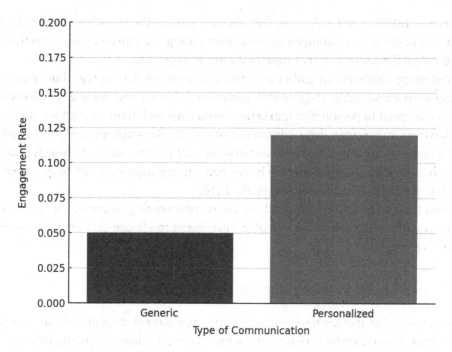

Figure 6.8 A Before-and-After Comparison of Generic Versus Personalized Marketing Communications.

In conclusion, NLP offers significant opportunities for personalizing marketing communications, thereby enhancing customer relationships and improving marketing effectiveness. Yet, its application must be balanced with a deep understanding of the customer and respect for their privacy.

6.6 CONCLUSION

In this chapter, we journeyed through the transformative realm of NLP and its profound implications for modern marketing. As we stand at the nexus of technology and human communication, the opportunities NLP offers to marketers are vast and revolutionary.

From understanding the foundational aspects of NLP to diving deep into specific techniques such as sentiment analysis and the use of chatbots, it's evident that the bridge between human language and computational processing is strengthening. This bridge not only enables businesses to navigate the vast sea of unstructured data but also to decode the sentiments, desires, and needs of their audience.

The rise of chatbots and voice assistants exemplifies the convergence of utility and experience. These tools, powered by NLP, provide real-time, personalized interactions, reshaping the expectations of digital-native consumers and setting new benchmarks for customer experience. Yet, as with all technologies, it's imperative to use them judiciously, recognizing their strengths and limitations. The challenges of sarcasm, ambiguity, and cultural nuances in language underscore the complexity of human communication and remind us that although technology can augment our efforts, it's the human touch that often makes the difference.

The applications of NLP in marketing—whether in social media sentiment analysis, content personalization, or customer service automation—are not just tools for efficiency but also are instruments of insight. They enable brands to listen closely, respond aptly, and anticipate needs, weaving a tapestry of trust and loyalty with their audience.

As we conclude this chapter, it's essential to remember that the landscape of marketing and technology is ever-evolving. Although NLP provides an arsenal of capabilities today, the future will undoubtedly bring new advancements, challenges, and opportunities. For marketers, the call-to-action is clear: stay curious, stay adaptable, and always strive to enhance the dialogue with your audience. In the symphony of business and technology, may your brand always strike the right chord.

6.7 REFERENCES

Apté, C., Damerau, F., & Weiss, S. M. (1994). Automated learning of decision rules for text categorization. *ACM Transactions on Information Systems (TOIS), 12*(3), 233–251.

Blei, D. M., & Lafferty, J. D. (2009). Topic models. *Text mining: Classification, Clustering, and Applications, 10*(71), 34.

Blei, D. M., Ng, A. Y., & Jordan, M. I. (2003). Latent dirichlet allocation. *Journal of Machine Learning Research, 3*(Jan.), 993–1022.

Cambria, E., Das, D., Bandyopadhyay, S., & Feraco, A. (2017). Affective computing and sentiment analysis. *A practical guide to sentiment analysis* (pp. 1–10). Springer.

Cambria, E., & White, B. (2014). Jumping NLP curves: A review of natural language processing research. *IEEE Computational Intelligence Magazine, 9*(2), 48–57.

Casillas, J., & López, F.J.M. (Eds.). (2010). *Marketing intelligent systems using soft computing: Managerial and research applications*. Springer.

Chiticariu, L., Li, Y., & Reiss, F. (2013, October). Rule-based information extraction is dead! Long live rule-based information extraction systems! *Proceedings of the 2013 Conference on Empirical Methods in Natural Language Processing* (pp. 827–832).

Dale, R. (2016). The return of the chatbots. *Natural Language Engineering, 22*(5), 811–817.

Feldman, R., & Sanger, J. (2007). *The text mining handbook: Advanced approaches in analyzing unstructured data*. Cambridge University Press.

Goodfellow, I., Bengio, Y., & Courville, A. (2016). *Deep learning*. MIT Press.

González-Ibáñez, R., Muresan, S., & Wacholder, N. (2011). Identifying sarcasm in Twitter: A closer look. *Proceedings of the 49th Annual Meeting of the Association for Computational Linguistics: Human Language Technologies*: (Vol. 2, pp. 581–586).

Harris, Z. S. (1954). Distributional structure. *Word, 10*(2–3), 146–162.

Jacobi, C., Van Atteveldt, W., & Welbers, K. (2016). Quantitative analysis of large amounts of journalistic texts using topic modelling. *Digital Journalism, 4*(1), 89–106.

Jain, M., Kumar, P., Kota, R., & Patel, S. N. (2018). Evaluating and informing the design of chatbots. *Proceedings of the 2018 Designing Interactive Systems Conference (DIS '18)* (pp. 895–906).

Jiang, L., Yu, M., Zhou, M., Liu, X., & Zhao, T. (2011). Target-dependent Twitter sentiment classification. *Proceedings of the 49th Annual Meeting of the Association for Computational Linguistics*.

Jurafsky, D., & Martin, J. H. (2023). *Speech and language processing* (3rd ed. draft). https://web
.stanford.edu/~jurafsky/slp3/ed3book.pdf

Kotsiantis, S. B., Zaharakis, I., & Pintelas, P. (2007). Supervised machine learning: A review of
classification techniques. *Emerging Artificial Intelligence Applications in Computer Engineering,
160*, 3–24.

Kumar, V., Anand, A., & Song, H. (2017). Future of retailer profitability: An organizing framework. *Journal of Retailing, 93*(1), 96–119.

Liu, B. (2012). Sentiment analysis and opinion mining. *Synthesis Lectures on Human Language
Technologies, 5*(1), 1–167.

Marr, B. (2015). *Big data: Using SMART big data, analytics and metrics to make better decisions and
improve performance*. Wiley.

McTear, M. F., Callejas, Z., & Griol, D. (2016). *The conversational interface* (Vol. 6, No. 94, p.
102). Springer.

Mikolov, T., Chen, K., Corrado, G., & Dean, J. (2013). Efficient estimation of word representations in vector space. *arXiv*:1301.3781.

Nadeau, D., & Sekine, S. (2007). A survey of named entity recognition and classification. *Ling-
visticae Investigationes, 30*(1), 3–26.

Netzer, O., Feldman, R., Goldenberg, J., & Fresko, M. (2012). Mine your own business: Market-
structure surveillance through text mining. *Marketing Science, 31*(3), 521–543.

Pang, B., & Lee, L. (2008). Opinion mining and sentiment analysis. *Foundations and Trends® in
Information Retrieval, 2*(1–2), 1–135.

Pennington, J., Socher, R., & Manning, C. D. (2014, October). Glove: Global vectors for word
representation. *Proceedings of the 2014 Conference on Empirical Methods in Natural Language Processing (EMNLP)* (pp. 1532–1543).

Ramos, J. (2003, December). Using TF–IDF to determine word relevance in document queries.
Proceedings of the First Instructional Conference on Machine Learning (Vol. 242, No. 1, pp. 29–48).

Röder, M., Both, A., & Hinneburg, A. (2015, February). Exploring the space of topic coherence
measures. *Proceedings of the Eighth ACM International Conference on Web Search and Data Mining*
(pp. 399–408).

Sahami, M., Dumais, S., Heckerman, D., & Horvitz, E. (1998, July). A Bayesian approach to
filtering junk e-mail. *Learning for Text Categorization: Papers from the 1998 Workshop* (Vol. 62,
pp. 98–105).

Schütze, H., Manning, C. D., & Raghavan, P. (2008). *Introduction to information retrieval* (Vol. 39,
pp. 234–265). Cambridge University Press.

Sebastiani, F. (2002). Machine learning in automated text categorization. *ACM Computing Surveys
(CSUR), 34*(1), 1–47.

Stieglitz, S., Mirbabaie, M., Ross, B., & Neuberger, C. (2018). Social media analytics–
Challenges in topic discovery, data collection, and data preparation. *International Journal of
Information Management, 39*, 156–168.

Sumathy, K. L., & Chidambaram, M. (2013). Text mining: Concepts, applications, tools and
issues—an overview. *International Journal of Computer Applications, 80*(4).

Thelwall, M., Buckley, K., & Paltoglou, G. (2012). Sentiment strength detection for the social
web. *Journal of the American Society for Information Science and Technology, 63*(1), 163–173.

Willett, P. (2006). The Porter stemming algorithm: Then and now. *Program, 40*(3), 219–223.

EXERCISE 6.1: SENTIMENT ANALYSIS

Objective: Write a Python script to perform sentiment analysis on the provided social media posts.

Tasks:

1. Load the "**sentiment_analysis_data.csv**" into a Python program.
2. Use a sentiment analysis library **TextBlob** to analyze the sentiment of each post.
3. Categorize each post as 'Positive', 'Negative', or 'Neutral' based on the sentiment score.
4. Output the sentiment analysis results in a readable format.

Steps:

1. **Load the Data:**

   ▪ First, import necessary libraries and read the CSV file containing the sentiment data.

```
1. import pandas as pd
2. sentiment_df = pd.read_csv('path_to_csv_file')
```

2. **Install and Import TextBlob:**

   ▪ Install TextBlob, if not already installed, using **!pip install textblob**.
   ▪ Import TextBlob for sentiment analysis.

```
3. !pip install textblob
4. from textblob import TextBlob
```

3. **Perform Sentiment Analysis:**

   ▪ Define a function to analyze sentiment using TextBlob.
   ▪ Apply this function to each post in the dataset.

```
5. def analyze_sentiment(post):
6. analysis = TextBlob(post)
7. return 'Positive' if analysis.sentiment.polarity > 0 else
'Negative' if analysis.sentiment.polarity < 0 else 'Neutral'
8. sentiment_df['Analyzed_Sentiment'] = sentiment_df['Post'].
apply(analyze_sentiment)
```

4. **Display the Results:**

   ▪ Show the first few rows of the DataFrame with the original posts and their analyzed sentiments.

```
9. sentiment_df.head()
```

This code provides a step-by-step approach to performing sentiment analysis on text data using Python and the TextBlob library. Each post's sentiment is analyzed and categorized as 'Positive', 'Negative', or 'Neutral' based on its content.

EXERCISE 6.1: OUTPUT

Here's the output after running the sentiment analysis on these new posts:

Post	Analyzed Sentiment
I love this new smartphone. It has an amazing camera!	Positive
Really unhappy with the customer service. Very disappointing experience.	Negative
This is just an average product. Nothing special about it.	Positive
Absolutely fantastic! Could not have asked for anything better.	Positive
Worst purchase ever. Totally regret buying it.	Negative

As you can see, each post has been analyzed by **TextBlob**, and a sentiment ('Positive', 'Negative', or 'Neutral') has been assigned based on the content of the post. For instance, posts expressing satisfaction or happiness are labeled as 'Positive', whereas those expressing dissatisfaction or disappointment are labeled as 'Negative'. This demonstrates how sentiment analysis can be used to categorize text data based on the sentiment expressed in it.

EXERCISE 6.2: TEXT CLASSIFICATION

Objective: Develop a Python program to classify customer reviews into categories such as electronics, clothing, or food.

Tasks:

1. Load the "**text_classification_data.csv**" data.
2. Implement a text classification model using the machine learning library **scikit-learn**.
3. Train the model on a portion of the data and test it on the remaining data.
4. Evaluate the model's performance using metrics such as accuracy and confusion matrix.

Steps:

1. **Load the Data:**

   ▪ Import pandas to read the CSV file.
   ▪ Load the text classification data.

```
1. import pandas as pd
2. classification_df = pd.read_csv('path_to_classification_csv_
file')
```

2. **Prepare the Data:**

   ▪ Split the data into features (reviews) and labels (categories).

```
3. X = classification_df['Review']
4. y = classification_df['Category']
```

3. **Text Preprocessing and Feature Extraction:**

   ▪ Use **TfidfVectorizer** to convert text data into numerical vectors.

```
5. from sklearn.feature_extraction.text import TfidfVectorizer
6. vectorizer = TfidfVectorizer()
7. X = vectorizer.fit_transform(X)
```

4. **Split the Dataset:**

   ▪ Divide the dataset into training and testing sets.

```
8. from sklearn.model_selection import train_test_split
9. X_train, X_test, y_train, y_test = train_test_split(X, y,
test_size=0.2)
```

5. **Model Training:**

   ▪ Choose a classification model (e.g., multinomial naive Bayes).
   ▪ Train the model on the training set.

```
10. from sklearn.naive_bayes import MultinomialNB
11. model = MultinomialNB()
12. model.fit(X_train, y_train)
```

6. **Model Evaluation:**

   ▪ Predict the categories on the test set.
   ▪ Evaluate the model's performance using metrics such as accuracy, precision, recall.

```
13. from sklearn.metrics import classification_report
14. y_pred = model.predict(X_test)
15. print(classification_report(y_test, y_pred))
```

This process involves typical steps in a machine learning workflow: data preparation, feature extraction, model training, and evaluation.

EXERCISE 6.2: OUTPUT

Here's the output from the model evaluation:

Category	Precision	Recall	F1-Score	Support
Clothing	0.00	0.00	0.00	55
Electronics	0.00	0.00	0.00	63
Food	0.41	1.00	0.58	82
Accuracy			0.41	200
Macro Avg	0.14	0.333	0.19	200
Weighted Avg	0.17	0.310	0.24	200

Analysis of the Results:

■ The model's performance varies significantly across different categories.

■ For the categories 'Clothing' and 'Electronics', the model shows a precision and recall of 0.00, indicating it failed to correctly classify any reviews in these categories.

■ For the 'Food' category, the model demonstrates a recall of 1.00 but a lower precision. This means it classified most of the reviews as 'Food', likely including many that belong to other categories.

■ The overall accuracy of the model is 0.41, indicating that only about 41% of the classifications are correct.

Interpretation:

■ The model's tendency to classify most reviews as 'Food' suggests a potential bias. This might be due to imbalanced training data or the limitations of the naive Bayes model for this particular task.

■ The warnings about precision and *F1-score* being ill-defined stem from the model's failure to make correct predictions for the 'Clothing' and 'Electronics' categories.

■ This example highlights a basic application of text classification. Potential improvements could involve enhanced data preprocessing, employing a more sophisticated model, or fine-tuning the parameters of the current model for more balanced and accurate results.

This exercise purposely demonstrates a basic application of text classification. Improvements might include better data preprocessing, using a more sophisticated model, or tuning the parameters of the current model to achieve more balanced and accurate results.

CHAPTER **7**

Social Media Analytics and Web Analytics

7.1 INTRODUCTION

The digital revolution has profoundly affected the marketing landscape. As businesses and consumers alike have moved online, social media platforms and websites have become critical touchpoints for brands. These platforms generate an abundance of data, providing unique insights into consumer behavior, preferences, and sentiment (Tiago & Veríssimo, 2014). The ability to understand and use this data is crucial for marketers in today's digital-first environment.

Social media analytics and web analytics are two key methodologies for harnessing this data. Social media analytics involves the collection and analysis of data from social media platforms to inform marketing decisions (Stieglitz et al., 2014). It can help marketers understand their audience, gauge sentiment for their brand, and track the effectiveness of their social media campaigns.

Web analytics, however, focuses on the analysis of data generated by visitor activity on a website. This can include metrics such as page views, bounce rate, session duration, and conversion rates. Web analytics can provide insights into user behavior, enabling marketers to optimize their website for better user experience (UX) and increased conversions (Chaffey & Patron, 2012).

In this chapter, we will provide a comprehensive overview of social media analytics and web analytics, exploring key concepts, techniques, and practical applications. We will also delve into specific methodologies within these domains, including social network analysis, social media listening and tracking, and conversion rate optimization. As we navigate through this chapter, we will understand how these techniques can be effectively employed to drive marketing success in the digital age.

7.2 SOCIAL NETWORK ANALYSIS

Before diving deep into analytics tools, it's essential to grasp the underlying frameworks guiding our examination. The world of social media is intrinsically connected, resembling vast webs of interlinked nodes.

7.2.1 Overview of Social Network Analysis

Social network analysis (SNA) is a research technique that is used to visualize and analyze relationships between different entities (Borgatti et al., 2009). In the context of marketing, these entities are often individuals or organizations that interact on social media platforms. SNA provides a way to map and measure complex, and sometimes hidden, relationships that are often difficult to visualize or understand in traditional ways.

SNA encompasses a variety of metrics and concepts, including nodes (individual actors within the network), ties (the relationships between the actors), centrality (a measure of the importance of a node within the network), and density (the general level of connectivity within a network) (Hansen et al., 2010). Through these metrics, SNA can help marketers understand the structure and dynamics of their social media audience. For example, centrality metrics can identify influencers or key opinion leaders within a network, whereas density metrics can provide insights into the overall engagement of the audience.

Figure 7.1 presents a pentagon-shaped graph with nodes labeled A, B, C, D, and E, each representing an individual actor within the network. These nodes are connected by edges that denote the relationships between them. The geometric arrangement in a pentagon suggests that each node is connected to two other nodes, illustrating a closed loop where information or influence can flow in a circular manner. This visualization serves as a foundational example of how individuals or entities are interconnected in a social network.

The placement of the nodes and their connecting lines (edges) provide insights into the network's structure. For example, the absence of direct lines between nonadjacent nodes, such as A and C or B and D, highlights the lack of immediate communication paths between certain actors. This structure may indicate a level of hierarchy or gatekeeping, where information must pass through adjacent nodes to reach others in the network.

The symmetrical shape of the pentagon suggests a network with equal distribution of relationships among the nodes. Each node has the same number of connections, indicating a uniform level of influence or accessibility within this particular network model. In a marketing context, this might imply that messages have an equal chance of being disseminated through the network from any starting point, assuming that the strength and influence of each connection are equal.

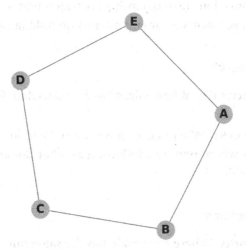

Figure 7.1 A Simple Social Network, Illustrating Nodes and Edges.

However, it's crucial to note that real-world social networks are often more complex, with varying levels of connectivity and centrality. Thus, although Figure 7.1 provides a simplified view, it forms a basis for understanding the potential paths through which information and influence can travel in a social network. By analyzing such structures, marketers can devise strategies to optimize communication and influence within their target audiences.

By providing a more nuanced understanding of social media interactions, SNA can inform a wide range of marketing decisions. It can help brands identify potential influencers for marketing campaigns, understand the spread of information or sentiment within a network, or even predict future trends based on network dynamics (Stephen & Toubia, 2010).

7.2.2 Basics of Network Theory

To comprehend these patterns, we first need to establish a foundational understanding of the network theory, encompassing its components, types, and structures. Network theory is a multidisciplinary field that delves into the study of networks to understand their structure, behavior, evolution, and the interconnections of their constituent elements. From biology to sociology and computer science, networks appear everywhere. In the context of social media analytics, network theory provides a lens to view and understand the intricate web of relationships and interactions on platforms.

7.2.2.1 *Components of a Network*

- **Nodes.** The individual entities of the network, which can represent users, web pages, or any other entity.
- **Edges.** The connections or relationships between nodes. For social media, this can be friendships, followers, or any interaction linking two nodes.

7.2.2.2 *Types of Networks*

- **Undirected networks.** Where edges have no direction, for example, Facebook friendships.
- **Directed networks.** Where edges have a direction; for instance, X (formerly Twitter) follows where one user following another doesn't necessarily mean a mutual relationship.

7.2.2.3 *Network Structures*

- **Regular networks.** Where each node has the same number of connections.
- **Random networks.** Where connections are formed randomly.
- **Scale-free networks.** Where some nodes (often called *hubs*) have significantly more connections than others.

■ **Star networks.** A network structure where a central node is connected to all other nodes, but the peripheral nodes are not connected to each other. This forms a pattern resembling a star.

■ **Bridge networks.** A structure where two or more groups of nodes are connected by a few intermediary nodes or links. These intermediary nodes or links act as bridges between the groups.

■ **Fully connected networks.** Every node is directly connected to every other node in the network. This type of network ensures maximum redundancy and fault tolerance because there are multiple paths for data to travel, but it's complex and costly to implement as the network grows.

To better illustrate the diverse types of network structures, Figure 7.2 presents a diagram that visually depicts basic network configurations, including star, bridge, and fully connected networks, thereby providing a clear understanding of their distinct patterns and connections.

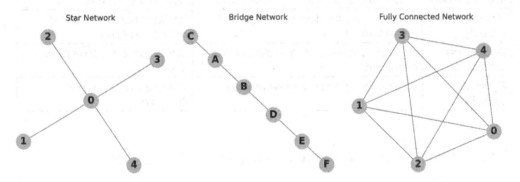

Figure 7.2 Basic Network Structures (Star, Bridge, and Fully Connected).

7.2.3 Metrics: Centrality, Density, and Clusters

Moving beyond the basics, specific metrics help us quantify the nature and strength of connections within a network, guiding our marketing strategies.

Centrality measures the importance of individual nodes within the network:

■ **Degree centrality.** Counts the number of edges a node has. A user with many friends or followers will have higher degree centrality.

■ **Closeness centrality.** Measures how close a node is to all other nodes in the network. It's calculated as the inverse of the sum of the shortest paths from the node to all other nodes. A high closeness centrality indicates that a node can spread information quickly to all other nodes.

■ **Betweenness centrality.** Measures how often a node appears on the shortest paths between nodes in the network. High betweenness indicates influence over information flow.

■ **Eigenvector centrality.** Considers the quality of connections. Being connected to other high-centrality nodes increases a node's eigenvector centrality.

Density is the proportion of direct ties in a network relative to the total number possible. High-density indicates a closely-knit community.

Clusters are subsets of interconnected nodes within a larger network. Clustering coefficient measures the extent to which the neighbors of a particular node are also neighbors of each other.

To offer a comprehensive understanding of different centrality measures and their relevance in network analysis, Table 7.1 presents a comparison that includes brief definitions and potential applications for each measure, elucidating how they can be applied in various contexts to identify influential nodes and patterns within a network.

Table 7.1 Different Centrality Measures with Brief Definitions and Potential Applications.

Measure	Definition	Application
Degree centrality	Measures the number of edges connected to a node	Identifying popular nodes
Closeness centrality	Measures the average shortest path length from a node to all other nodes	Identifying nodes that can spread information efficiently
Betweenness centrality	Measures the number of shortest paths that pass through a node	Identifying nodes that act as bridges or gatekeepers
Eigenvector centrality	Considers the importance of a node's neighbors	Identifying influential nodes in the network

7.2.4   Influencer Identification and Engagement Strategies

By harnessing the power of these metrics, marketers can then pinpoint key influencers and craft targeted engagement approaches. Given the vastness of social networks, identifying key players or influencers becomes paramount. High centrality scores (degree, betweenness, eigenvector) often indicate influential nodes.

Strategies

■ **Engagement.** Engage directly with influencers through collaborations or partnerships.

■ **Content amplification.** Use influencers to amplify content reach and engagement.

■ **Feedback loop.** Influencers can be a gold mine of feedback, given their deep connection with communities.

■ **Network expansion.** Partnering with influencers can help brands penetrate deeper or into newer networks.

To visually underscore the distinction between influencer nodes and regular nodes within a network, Figure 7.3 presents a graph that compares these two types of nodes (represented in dark gray for influencers and light gray for regular nodes) in terms

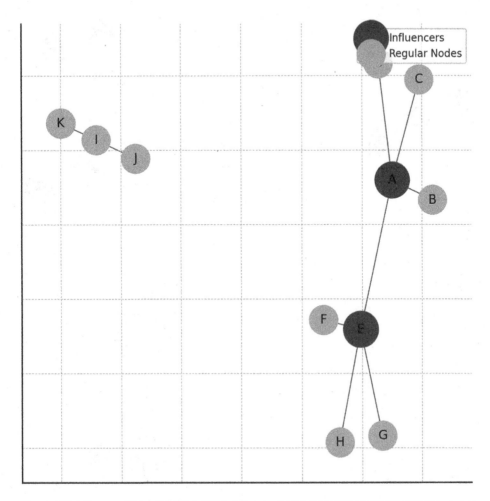

Figure 7.3 Influencer Nodes (Dark Gray) Versus Regular Nodes (Light Gray) in Terms of Their Centrality Measures.

of their respective centrality measures, highlighting how influencers typically exhibit higher centrality scores in a social network.

7.2.5 Community Detection in Social Networks

Within these vast networks, there lie subgroups or communities. Detecting these groups can offer additional layers of strategic insights. Communities are tightly knit groups within larger networks. Identifying these communities can provide insights into user behaviors, preferences, and potential marketing segments.

To illuminate the concept of community detection within social networks, Figure 7.4 provides a visual representation, clearly delineating different communities within a larger network. This visualization aids in understanding how these communities are formed and interconnected, offering valuable insights for targeted marketing strategies.

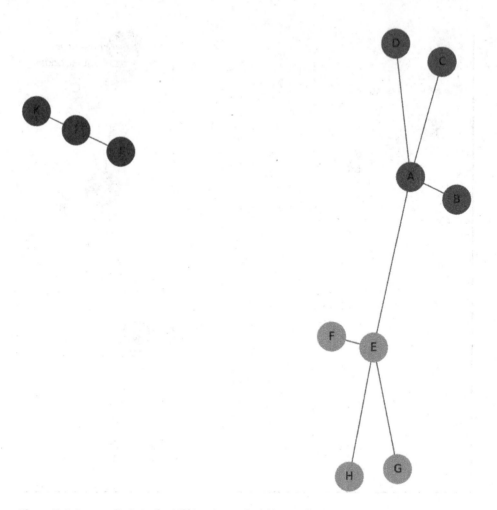

Figure 7.4 Community Detection Within a Larger Social Network.

7.2.5.1 Modularity

Modularity is a metric that measures the strength of division of a network into clusters. High modularity indicates dense connections between nodes within clusters and sparse connections between nodes in different clusters.

7.2.5.2 Algorithms

- **Girvan-Newman algorithm.** This algorithm iteratively removes the network's most central edge (highest betweenness) to detect communities.
- **Louvain method.** This method maximizes modularity to detect communities at different scales.

Community detection aids in targeted marketing campaigns, understanding user dynamics, and creating more resonating content based on community preferences and behaviors.

7.2.6 Key Concepts in Social Network Analysis

Now that we've navigated the realm of social networks, it's pertinent to distil the core concepts that will be instrumental in real-world applications. SNA employs various key concepts that are critical to understanding the complex dynamics of social interactions. Let's delve deeper into some of these concepts:

- **Nodes and ties.** In SNA, nodes represent entities within the network, such as individuals, groups, or even companies, and ties represent the relationships or interactions between these entities (Wasserman & Faust, 1994). The nature of these ties can vary, ranging from friendship, following, or liking on social media platforms to more complex interactions such as retweeting or sharing content.
- **Centrality.** Centrality measures help identify the most influential nodes within a network. They determine which entities are central or influential based on their position within the network structure. There are several centrality measures, such as degree centrality (number of direct ties a node has), betweenness centrality (number of times a node acts as a bridge along the shortest path between two other nodes), and eigenvector centrality (measure of the influence of a node in a network) (Bonacich, 2007).
- **Density.** Density is a measure of the network's interconnectedness. It's calculated as the proportion of the total possible ties that are actual ties. High-density networks suggest that members of the network are well connected, which can affect the speed and breadth of information or influence dissemination (Scott, 2017).
- **Clustering coefficient.** This is a measure of the degree to which nodes in a network tend to cluster together. In the context of social media, a high clustering coefficient may suggest that users tend to form tightly knit groups characterized by relatively high interaction levels (Opsahl & Panzarasa, 2009).

Understanding these concepts can provide marketing professionals with deeper insights into their audience's behavior, enabling more targeted and effective marketing strategies.

7.2.7 Practical Example: Social Network Analysis in Influencer Marketing

SNA has become a vital tool in influencer marketing, enabling marketers to identify and target key influencers in their respective industries. To bridge theory and practice, let's examine a tangible example of how SNA aids in influencer marketing.

Imagine a fashion brand looking to launch a new product line. The marketing team decides to leverage influencer marketing to create buzz for the product. But with millions of fashion influencers on social media, how do they decide whom to partner with?

This is where SNA comes into play. By creating a network graph of influencers and their followers, the team can identify key influencers who sit at the center of the network (high degree centrality), influencers who act as bridges between different communities (high betweenness centrality), and influencers whose followers are also influential (high eigenvector centrality).

For example, an influencer with high betweenness centrality might not have the largest follower count but can reach different communities or demographics, making them a valuable partner for the campaign. However, an influencer with high degree centrality is well connected and can disseminate information quickly through their numerous connections.

Moreover, by analyzing the density and clustering coefficient of the network, the team can understand how closely knit the fashion influencer community is and how quickly information can spread within the network.

To visually demonstrate the effectiveness of influencer marketing in altering network dynamics, Figure 7.5 presents a before-and-after network graph, illustrating the impact of influencer involvement on the connectivity and structure of the social network.

This strategic, data-driven approach enables the brand to maximize its marketing efforts, ensuring the right message reaches the right audience at the right time. It also provides insights into the social dynamics of the influencer community, which can be invaluable in planning future campaigns (Chaffey & Ellis-Chadwick, 2022).

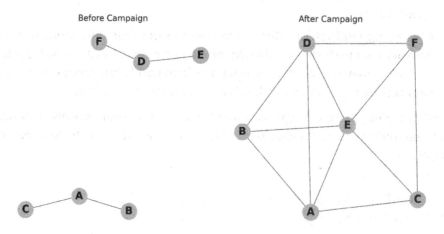

Figure 7.5 The Before-and-After Impact of Influencer Marketing on Network Connectivity.

7.3 WEB ANALYTICS TOOLS AND METRICS

Shifting our gaze from social networks to the broader web, we plunge into the domain of web analytics, arming ourselves with tools and metrics that decipher user interactions on websites.

7.3.1 Overview of Web Analytics Tools and Metrics

Web analytics, in essence, is the measurement, collection, analysis, and reporting of web data for the purpose of understanding and optimizing web use. It provides tools and metrics that enable marketers to measure the effectiveness of their marketing strategies, identify potential improvements, and make informed decisions about their online presence (Clifton, 2012).

Web analytics tools can be broadly classified into two categories:

- **On-site web analytics.** These tools measure a visitor's behavior once they are on your website. This includes metrics such as page views, unique visitors, bounce rate, conversion rate, and average time spent on the site. These metrics provide insight into how well your website is performing and how users are interacting with it.
- **Off-site web analytics.** These tools measure your website's potential audience (opportunity), share of voice (visibility), and buzz (comments) happening on the internet as a whole.

Some of the popular web analytics tools include Google Analytics, Adobe Analytics, and IBM Digital Analytics. These tools provide a plethora of data that can be analyzed to gain insights into user behavior, website performance, and marketing effectiveness.

To provide a clear perspective on the competitive landscape of web analytics tools, Figure 7.6 presents a pie chart illustrating the estimated market share of popular web analytics tools.

For example, Google Analytics provides data on where your visitors are coming from (referrers), which pages are the most popular, how long visitors stay on your site, and what keywords are leading people to your site. It also provides demographic information about your visitors, such as their location, age, and interests, which can be incredibly useful for targeted marketing campaigns (Kaushik, 2009).

7.3.2 Key Metrics: Page Views, Bounce Rate, and Conversion Rate

7.3.2.1 Page Views

A page view represents a single view of a web page by a user. It indicates the total number of times a page has been loaded or reloaded. Although it provides a basic measure of web page activity, it doesn't differentiate between unique users or the quality of interaction.

- **Applications.** Page views enable monitoring traffic trends, understanding popular content, and tracking advertising effectiveness.

7.3.2.2 Bounce Rate

Bounce rate is the percentage of sessions where a user loads the website and then leaves without taking any other action, such as clicking on a link or filling out a form.

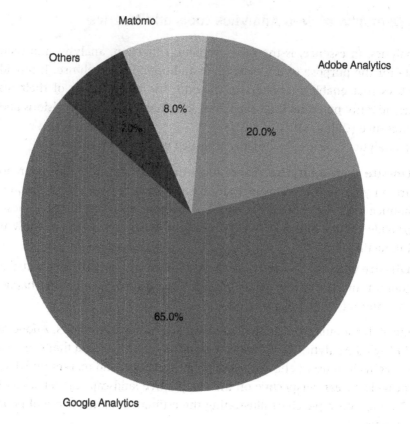

Figure 7.6 Estimated Market Share of Popular Web Analytics Tools.

A high bounce rate might indicate unengaging content or that users didn't find what they were looking for.

- **Applications.** Bounce rates enable evaluating landing page effectiveness, gauging user engagement, and identifying potential site issues.

7.3.2.3 Conversion Rate

This is the percentage of website visitors who take a desired action, such as making a purchase, signing up for a newsletter, or filling out a contact form. It is a critical metric for measuring the effectiveness of a website in guiding users toward its goals.

- **Applications.** Conversion rates enable assessing the efficacy of sales funnels, optimizing landing pages, and measuring marketing campaign success.

To offer a comprehensive understanding of the various metrics used in web analytics, Table 7.2 lists key metrics such as page views, bounce rate, and conversion rate, accompanied by brief descriptions and their significance in measuring and optimizing website performance.

Table 7.2 Key Metrics with Brief Descriptions and Their Importance.

Metric	Description	Significance
Page views	Total number of pages viewed	Assess content popularity
Sessions	Group of interactions within a given time frame	Measure site engagement
Users	Individuals who have visited a site at least once	Estimate audience size and potential reach
Bounce rate	Percentage of single-page visits	Evaluate user engagement and content relevancy
Average session duration	Average time a user spends on the site per session	Analyze user engagement depth
Conversion rate	Percentage of visits that result in a conversion	Gauge effectiveness in driving desired actions
Exit rate	Percentage of exits from a page	Identify potential problem areas in the user journey
Page value	Average value of a page visited	Determine the contribution of a page to site revenue
Click-through rate	Percentage of users who click on a specific link	Evaluate the effectiveness of online advertising or call-to-action

7.3.3 Advanced Metrics: Funnel Analysis and Cohort Analysis

Beyond the basic metrics lies a more nuanced analysis, offering a granular view of user behavior through advanced analytical methods.

7.3.3.1 Funnel Analysis

Funnels represent the journey a user takes to complete a specific action on a website, such as making a purchase. Funnel analysis breaks down this journey into individual steps and shows where users drop off at each stage. By identifying these drop-off points, marketers can optimize the user journey to increase conversions.

- **Optimization strategies for funnel analysis:**
  - **Segmentation.** Divide users into distinct segments based on criteria such as traffic source, device type, or demographic info. This enables businesses to identify specific segments that may be facing issues and target optimizations accordingly.
  - **A/B testing.** If drop-offs are observed at a particular stage, test variations of that step to see which version retains more users. This could be different calls-to-action (CTAs), page designs, or content.
  - **User feedback.** Combine funnel data with user feedback to understand why users might be dropping off. Surveys or quick feedback prompts can provide context to observed data.

- **Performance optimization.** Slow-loading pages or technical glitches can be reasons for drop-offs. Ensuring pages load quickly and are free of errors can aid in smoother user progression through the funnel.
- **Applications.** In addition to optimizing checkout processes, improving onboarding flows for software products, and refining lead generation funnels, funnel analysis can guide content strategy, shape UX design, and more.

To visually demonstrate the effectiveness of funnel analysis in identifying areas for improvement, Figure 7.7 presents a bar chart showing user flow and drop-off rates at each stage of a website's funnel, providing clear insights into where potential optimizations can be made.

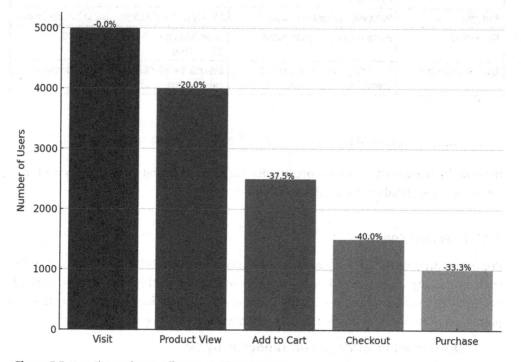

Figure 7.7 User Flow and Drop-Off Rates at Different Stages.

7.3.3.2 Cohort Analysis

Cohort analysis is a type of time-lapse analytics that divides a user base into related groups over time. These groups, or cohorts, share common characteristics or experiences within a defined period. By studying how specific cohorts behave over time, businesses can glean deeper insights into life cycle patterns and trends.

- **Key aspects of cohort analysis:**
  - **Time-based cohorts.** This type of cohort groups users based on specific time frames, such as monthly or weekly cohorts of new users. This can help in

understanding how product changes or specific marketing campaigns affect user behavior over time.

- **Behavior-based cohorts.** This cohort segments users based on a specific action they took, such as making a first purchase, upgrading a product, or engaging with a particular feature.
- **Size and duration.** Cohorts can vary in size and duration. For instance, daily cohorts might be smaller and more specific, whereas monthly or quarterly cohorts offer a broader view.
- **Optimization strategies for cohort analysis:**
  - **Tailored marketing.** By understanding the behavior of specific cohorts, businesses can design marketing campaigns that cater to each group's unique needs and preferences.
  - **Product development.** Product developments identifies features or aspects of a product that resonate most with specific cohorts, guiding future development or refinement.
  - **Retention strategies.** Retention strategies recognize patterns in when and why certain cohorts disengage, enabling businesses to address these issues and improve retention.
  - **Life cycle prediction.** Life cycle prediction helps to understand the average life cycle of a user or customer, augmenting forecasting and long-term planning.
- **Applications.** Cohort analysis goes beyond tracking the success of marketing campaigns. It's also pivotal in understanding customer loyalty, predicting churn, evaluating product changes, and shaping long-term business strategies.

7.3.4 Integration with Other Data Sources

To achieve a holistic understanding of user behavior, it's often beneficial to integrate web analytics data with other data sources.

7.3.4.1 Customer Relationship Management Systems

By integrating with customer relationship management (CRM) systems, businesses can bridge the gap between online behavior and actual sales or customer interactions. This integration allows for a more detailed user segmentation and personalized marketing campaigns.

7.3.4.2 Social Media Analytics

Merging web analytics with social media metrics can provide insights into how social interactions drive website behavior. For instance, it can show how a viral tweet impacts website traffic or conversions.

7.3.4.3 Offline Sales Data

For businesses with both online and offline sales channels, integrating offline sales data can provide a comprehensive view of the customer journey. It can show how online marketing campaigns impact offline sales or vice versa.

7.3.4.4 Surveys and Feedback Forms

Merging qualitative data from surveys with quantitative web analytics can provide context to user behavior. For instance, if users are leaving a website at a specific stage, survey data might reveal why they're doing so.

To illustrate how web analytics data can be effectively integrated with a CRM system for a more comprehensive understanding of user behavior, Table 7.3 provides an example that combines metrics such as sessions and page views with customer-specific information such as total purchases and lifetime value.

7.3.4.5 Complications and Pitfalls in Integrating Data Sources

Although integrating various data sources promises a richer, more comprehensive perspective, it isn't devoid of challenges. It's crucial to be aware of these potential pitfalls to ensure that data integration yields actionable insights without compromising accuracy or privacy.

- **Data consistency issues.** Different systems often have varying ways of capturing and storing data. Mismatches in data formats, units, or time zones can lead to skewed interpretations.
- **Privacy concerns.** Integrating personal data from different sources might breach privacy regulations such as GDPR or CCPA. Businesses must be cautious about how they handle, store, and process integrated data.
- **Data overlap.** If the same data is captured in multiple systems, there's a risk of double-counting. This can artificially inflate metrics and lead to misguided decisions.
- **System integration complexities.** Not all systems are designed to integrate seamlessly. Integration might require custom solutions or middleware, adding to costs and potential points of failure.

Table 7.3 Example Showing Integration of Web Analytics Data with a CRM System.

User_ID	Sessions	Page Views	Conversions	Name	Total Purchases	Lifetime Value
1	5	25	2	Alice	5	300
2	3	15	1	Bob	3	200
...	...	...	...	...	...	...

- **Incomplete data sync.** In real-time integrations, there's a risk of data not syncing correctly or completely between systems, leading to gaps in data.
- **Misinterpretation.** More data doesn't always equate to better insights. Without proper context or understanding, the integrated data might lead to erroneous conclusions.
- **Increased data management overhead.** Merging data from different sources can exponentially increase the amount of data to be managed, stored, and processed, necessitating more robust systems and possibly incurring higher costs.

Although incorporating multiple data sources offers businesses a more nuanced understanding of their users and augments the efficacy of their digital strategies, it's essential to navigate the complexities and pitfalls of integration. By doing so, organizations can ensure that their decision-making is not only more informed but also accurate and compliant with best practices and regulations.

7.3.5 Key Concepts in Web Analytics

There are several key concepts and metrics that are central to understanding the data provided by web analytics tools. Here's an overview of some of these crucial concepts:

- **Page views.** This is the total number of pages viewed by all visitors. Repeated views of a single page are also counted.
- **Unique visitors.** These are individuals who have visited a website at least once within a specific period.
- **Bounce rate.** This is the percentage of visitors who navigate away from the site after viewing only one page.
- **Exit rate.** This is the percentage of visitors who leave your site from a specific page based on the number of visits to that page.
- **Average session duration.** This is the average length of time that visitors spend on your site during a single visit.
- **Conversion rate.** This is the percentage of visitors who complete a desired action on a website, such as filling out a form, signing up for a newsletter, or making a purchase.
- **Click path.** This is the sequence of pages viewed by a visitor during a website visit.
- **Traffic sources.** This indicates where your visitors are coming from—direct visits, search engines, or referrals from other websites.
- **Cost per click.** This is the amount of money an advertiser pays a publisher for each click in a pay-per-click ad campaign.
- **Return on investment (ROI).** This is a measure of the profitability of an investment. In the context of web analytics, it refers to the revenue generated from a digital marketing campaign compared to the cost of that campaign.

Understanding these concepts can help marketers make informed decisions about their online strategies, identify areas of improvement, and maximize the return on their marketing investments (Clifton, 2012; Kaushik, 2009).

7.3.6 Challenges in Interpreting Web Analytics Data

As enlightening as web analytics can be, it is not without its complexities. Often, businesses find themselves ensnared in a web of misconceptions or errors while trying to derive meaning from the data. Let's unpack some of the most common challenges faced and provide solutions for overcoming them:

- **Data overload.** With an abundance of metrics available, marketers can feel overwhelmed, unsure which metrics align best with their business objectives. The key is to focus on KPIs that directly tie back to goals, rather than trying to analyze everything.

- **Misinterpretation of metrics.** Without a clear understanding, metrics such as bounce rate or time on site can be misleading. For instance, a high bounce rate might not always indicate dissatisfaction; it could mean the user found what they needed quickly.

- **Inconsistent data across platforms.** Different analytics tools might yield slightly varying results due to unique tracking methodologies. It's vital to understand the nuances of each tool and, when possible, rely on a primary source for decision-making.

- **Not accounting for external factors.** Seasonal trends, offline marketing campaigns, or even global events can influence web traffic and user behavior. Marketers need to contextualize their data within the bigger picture.

- **Reliance on vanity metrics.** Although metrics such as page views or total followers can boost egos, they might not contribute to business goals. Marketers should differentiate between vanity metrics and actionable metrics.

- **Lack of clear goals.** Without established goals for a website or campaign, interpreting data becomes aimless. It's like having a map without a destination. Ensure goals are defined, measurable, and aligned with business objectives.

7.3.7 Practical Example: Using Google Analytics for Customer Behavior Insights

Google Analytics is a widely used web analytics tool that provides insightful data about website users, enabling businesses to understand customer behavior better. Let's navigate the practical realms of web analytics by analyzing how Google Analytics illuminates customer behavior patterns.

Let's consider a hypothetical example of an online fashion retailer. The primary goal of the retailer is to increase its sales and reduce the number of cart abandonments.

Using Google Analytics, the marketing team can track various metrics such as page views, bounce rates, average session duration, and conversion rates. They can also identify the pages with the highest exit rates, potentially indicating issues with these pages that prompt customers to leave.

For instance, the team finds that many users are dropping off at the checkout page. Digging deeper, they discover that the shipping costs, revealed only at the final step, are causing these abandonments. Based on these insights, the retailer might decide to offer free shipping for orders above a certain amount or be more transparent about shipping costs earlier in the process to reduce surprises at checkout.

Furthermore, the retailer can use Google Analytics to segment its audience and understand different user behaviors. For instance, they might find that mobile users have a higher bounce rate compared to desktop users. This could indicate issues with the mobile version of the site, prompting a review of the mobile UX.

They can also track the effectiveness of their marketing campaigns by monitoring traffic sources. Suppose the majority of their traffic comes from an organic search, but a paid social media campaign generates the most conversions. In that case, the retailer might decide to allocate more budget toward social media advertising.

In summary, Google Analytics can provide a wealth of customer behavior insights, guiding the retailer's decision-making and strategy. It enables the retailer to focus its efforts on areas that will likely yield the most significant benefits, improving the overall effectiveness of their marketing efforts (Clifton, 2012; Kaushik, 2009).

7.4 SOCIAL MEDIA LISTENING AND TRACKING

Listening is as vital as speaking in the digital world. By tuning into social media conversations, marketers can glean a wealth of information.

7.4.1 Overview of Social Media Listening and Tracking

Social media listening, also known as *social media monitoring*, involves tracking mentions of your brand, competitors, products, or relevant keywords across social media platforms and the web. This process enables companies to gain insights into customer opinions, emerging trends, and the overall perception of their brand (Zafarani et al., 2014).

One major aspect of social media listening is sentiment analysis, which involves interpreting and categorizing the emotions expressed in social media posts. This can help companies understand the general sentiment toward their brand or a specific product and identify any potential issues early (Cambria et al., 2013).

Social media tracking, however, involves measuring the performance of your social media campaigns and content. Key performance indicators (KPIs) might include likes, shares, comments, click-through rates (CTRs), and the overall reach of your posts. Monitoring these metrics over time can help companies understand what type

Table 7.4 Comparative Overview of Popular Social Media Listening and Tracking Tools.

Tool	Strengths	Weaknesses	Use Cases
Brandwatch	Offers a powerful AI-driven analysis, real-time data tracking, and a vast data pool; highly customizable queries allow for very specific searches	Might be overwhelming for beginners due to its extensive features	Best for large enterprises or industries that require in-depth analysis, competitor benchmarking, and trend prediction
Hootsuite Insights	User-friendly interface, integration with multiple social platforms, and provides real-time data	More limited in-depth analytical capabilities compared to specialized tools	Suitable for small to medium businesses or agencies that manage multiple social accounts and want a combined platform for posting and analysis
Sprout Social	Comprehensive analytics dashboard, built-in CRM features, and team collaboration tools	More expensive for smaller businesses and can have a steeper learning curve	Ideal for businesses focusing on community management, customer service, and team collaboration alongside social listening
Mention	Real-time monitoring, competitive analysis, and integration with influencers, making it easy to reach out and collaborate	Some limitations in historical data access and depth of sentiment analysis	Great for businesses that want a quick overview of their brand's mentions, competitor benchmarking, and influencer outreach

of content resonates most with their audience and informs future content strategies (Shareef et al., 2019; see Table 7.4).

In essence, social media listening and tracking are crucial aspects of a company's online presence. They provide valuable insights into customer preferences and behaviors, enabling companies to optimize their marketing strategies, improve customer service, and build stronger relationships with their customers.

7.4.2 The Importance of Social Listening in Modern Marketing

In today's hyper-connected digital age, where consumer conversations and interactions are constantly taking place on various platforms, understanding these dialogues becomes imperative.

Here's why social listening is quintessential for modern marketing:

- **Real-time feedback.** Social listening offers immediate feedback. Whether it's a product launch, marketing campaign, or any brand activity, marketers can gauge real-time reactions and adjust strategies accordingly.
- **Reputation management.** Negative comments or reviews can spread like wildfire in the digital domain. Social listening enables brands to monitor sentiment,

detect potential PR crises in their infancy, and strategize on damage control or response mechanisms swiftly.

- **Understanding the audience.** Beyond monitoring brand mentions, listening tools can provide deeper insights into what the target audience is talking about and their pain points, desires, or trends they're following, leading to better audience profiling and segmentation.

- **Competitor analysis.** Marketers can use social listening to keep a tab on competitors. Understanding how competitors are perceived, their successful campaigns, or areas where they falter can offer invaluable strategic insights.

- **Innovation and product development.** Real-time feedback from actual users provides a gold mine of information for product development. Brands can identify features users want, issues they face, and accordingly iterate on their offerings.

- **Engagement and community building.** Social listening isn't just about monitoring; it's about engagement. By responding to user mentions—be it queries, grievances, or praises—brands can foster community, loyalty, and enhance their brand image.

- **Data-driven decisions.** With concrete data on how certain campaigns or content types perform among audiences, brands can make more informed decisions about where to invest their resources and how to strategize their future marketing initiatives.

- **Discovering influencers and brand advocates.** Often, social listening tools can help identify not just the volume of mentions but also the sources that have a considerable influence in their communities. Partnering with such influencers can amplify brand reach and credibility.

- **Seizing real-time marketing opportunities.** Tapping into current discussions and trends can make brands part of larger conversations. For instance, if a topic relevant to a brand starts trending, they can chime into the dialogue, making their marketing efforts more contemporary and relatable.

- **Refining SEO and content strategies.** Understanding the language, phrases, and topics that the audience discusses can inform SEO strategies and content creation, ensuring that brands resonate with what the audience is actively seeking.

To exemplify the effectiveness of social listening, particularly in tracking the influence of marketing efforts, Figure 7.8 displays a graph showing the increase in brand mentions over time as a result of a specific campaign, highlighting how strategic initiatives can significantly amplify a brand's presence in digital conversations.

In essence, social listening is not just a passive monitoring tool; it's an active strategy enabler. It bridges the gap between brands and their audiences, allowing for a more authentic, responsive, and data-driven approach to modern marketing.

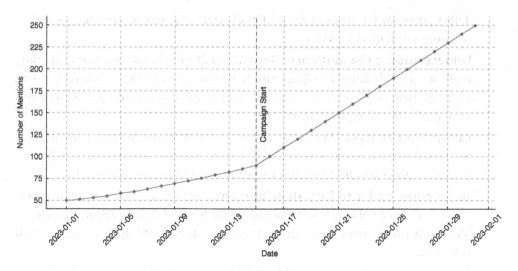

Figure 7.8 Increase in Brand Mentions over Time Due to a Particular Campaign.

7.4.3   Analyzing Social Mentions and Share of Voice

7.4.3.1   Analyzing Social Mentions

Every day, consumers take to social media platforms to discuss brands, share their experiences, and offer feedback. These discussions, known as *social mentions*, are invaluable data sources for brands to understand public perception and adjust strategies.

When analyzing social mentions, it's vital to dig deeper than just the volume of mentions. Although it's encouraging to see high numbers of brand mentions, understanding the context is crucial. Mentions can be positive, negative, or neutral. Brands must categorize these mentions by sentiment to gauge the overall brand health.

For instance, if a new product is launched and there's a surge in negative mentions, brands can quickly identify potential issues with the product and rectify them. Conversely, a spike in positive mentions can indicate successful campaigns or well-received products, guiding future endeavors.

7.4.3.2   Share of Voice

Share of voice (SOV) is a metric that showcases a brand's presence in its industry's conversation. In simpler terms, it answers the question, "Out of all the chatter in our industry, how much is about us?"

SOV is determined by comparing the number of mentions a brand receives relative to the total mentions of its industry or its key competitors. Analyzing SOV helps brands understand their position in the marketplace (see Figure 7.9).

If a brand's SOV is increasing, it suggests growing brand awareness and a growing position in market conversations. Conversely, a declining SOV may signal that competitors are becoming more dominant in industry dialogues, and a reassessment of marketing strategies might be necessary.

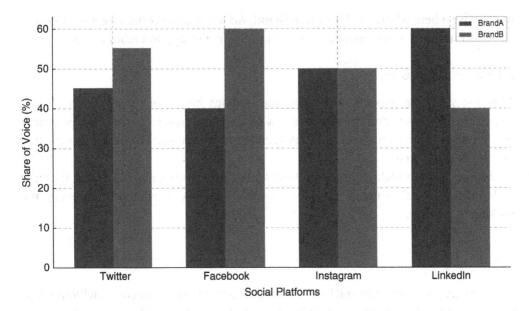

Figure 7.9 Comparing SOV for Two Competing Brands over Various Social Platforms.

7.4.4 Crisis Management Through Social Listening

In today's digital age, when news travels at lightning speed, managing brand reputation during crises becomes a paramount challenge. This is where social listening plays a crucial role.

7.4.4.1 Early Detection

Before a small issue turns into a full-blown crisis, there are usually warning signs on social platforms. A sudden spike in mentions or a growing number of negative sentiments can be early indicators. By monitoring these metrics in real time, brands can potentially identify and address issues before they spiral out of control.

7.4.4.2 Understanding the Nature of the Crisis

Once an issue is detected, social listening can help brands understand the root cause. Is it a product defect? Perhaps an inappropriate advertisement? Or maybe a statement made by a company representative? Pinpointing the exact nature of the problem is the first step in crafting an appropriate response.

7.4.4.3 Engaging and Communicating

During a crisis, communication is key. Social platforms become primary channels where consumers look for responses and updates from brands. By actively listening, brands can choose when, where, and how to respond. Addressing concerns, offering solutions, and communicating transparently can help mitigate damage and rebuild trust.

7.4.4.4 Post-Crisis Analysis

After the storm has passed, social listening remains invaluable. Brands can analyze discussions to understand the effectiveness of their response strategies. Did consumer sentiment improve after the brand's interventions? Were there lingering concerns that need to be addressed?

In essence, although no brand wishes to face a crisis, being equipped with the right tools, such as social listening, can mean the difference between a swift recovery and prolonged damage.

7.4.5 Key Concepts in Social Media Listening and Tracking

Social media listening and tracking encompass several key concepts, including sentiment analysis, brand mentions, influencer tracking, and social media KPIs, among others. Each of these concepts plays a vital role in monitoring the brand's presence and understanding customer perception online (Zafarani et al., 2014).

- **Sentiment analysis.** Also referred to as opinion mining, sentiment analysis involves determining the emotional tone behind a series of words to gain an understanding of the attitudes, opinions, and emotions expressed within an online mention. It's not only about monitoring positive, neutral, and negative comments but also about understanding the intensity of the sentiment (Cambria et al., 2013).

- **Brand mentions.** A brand mention refers to any time a company or its products are mentioned on social media. Monitoring these mentions can help a brand understand its market presence and gauge its reputation among customers and competitors (Zafarani et al., 2014).

- **Influencer tracking.** Influencer tracking is about identifying and monitoring key individuals who have a significant influence over potential customers or the industry as a whole. By monitoring these influencers, companies can identify opportunities for collaborations, endorsements, or partnerships (Freberg et al., 2011).

- **Social media KPIs.** KPIs are metrics used to evaluate the success of a social media campaign. Common KPIs include reach, engagement rate, conversion rate, and ROI. These KPIs help businesses understand how well their social media campaigns are performing and inform future strategies (Shareef et al., 2019).

In summary, these key concepts in social media listening and tracking provide the necessary tools to measure the effectiveness of social media strategies and actions, paving the way for data-driven decision-making processes in marketing.

7.4.6 Practical Example: Social Media Listening for Brand Reputation Management

One practical application of social media listening is in the management of a brand's reputation online. Join us on a journey through a real-world application, when social listening proves its mettle in managing brand reputation:

Consider a hypothetical scenario involving a global beverage company, SoftDrink Inc. This company has a presence on several social media platforms, including X (formerly Twitter), Facebook, Instagram, and LinkedIn, and they have recently launched a new product line of healthy, sugar-free beverages.

To gauge consumer reactions to the new product line, SoftDrink Inc. uses social media listening tools to monitor mentions of their brand and the new product line across various social media platforms. They are particularly interested in understanding the sentiment concerning these mentions, that is, whether the reactions are positive, negative, or neutral.

A systematic analysis of collected data reveals that although there's a generally positive sentiment toward the new product line, some consumers have voiced concerns about the taste. SoftDrink Inc. takes this feedback into account and initiates a dialog with concerned consumers to understand their preferences better.

Additionally, SoftDrink Inc. identifies a set of influencers who have positively reviewed their product. By reaching out to these influencers for potential collaboration, they can boost their product's visibility and reach in their target demographic.

Last, the company tracks KPIs such as the number of mentions, sentiment score, reach, and engagement rate. They use this data to assess the success of their product launch and use these insights to inform their future product development and marketing strategies.

Social media listening in this way helps SoftDrink Inc. stay ahead of potential reputation issues, engage with their audience in a meaningful way, and derive actionable insights to improve their product and marketing strategy (Felix et al., 2017).

7.5 CONVERSION RATE OPTIMIZATION

With insights in hand, the final step is to optimize. Conversion rate optimization becomes the key to unlocking a website's full potential.

7.5.1 Overview of Conversion Rate Optimization

Conversion rate optimization (CRO) is a systematic process that involves improving the percentage of website visitors who complete a website's desired action, known as a *conversion*. This could be anything from making a purchase, filling out a form, downloading a resource, signing up for a newsletter, or any other action that aligns with the organization's goals.

The primary aim of CRO is to make the most of the existing web traffic by optimizing the UX to guide visitors toward completing the desired action. The foundation of successful CRO lies in understanding how users move through your site, what actions they perform, and what's stopping them from completing your goals.

One of the first steps in CRO involves identifying KPIs that relate to the site's objectives. This could be the conversion rate for a specific page, the number of form completions, or the total number of new sign-ups.

Then, through a combination of quantitative and qualitative data gathering methods, such as web analytics, heat maps, visitor recordings, surveys, and user testing, hypotheses are developed about what changes to the site can improve performance.

These hypotheses are then tested, typically using A/B or multivariate testing. The results of these tests inform further optimization steps, making CRO a continuous, iterative process.

To provide a visual road map of the CRO process, Figure 7.10 presents a bar chart illustrating the various stages in CRO, from awareness to conversion.

Effective CRO can lead to increased ROI, improved UX, and insights about customers that can inform other areas of digital marketing and product development.

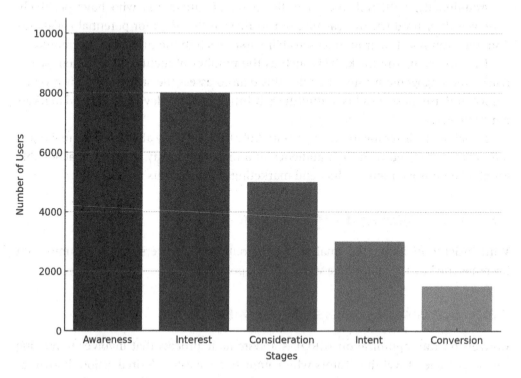

Figure 7.10 Stages in CRO.

7.5.2 A/B Testing for Landing Pages

A/B testing, at its core, is an experiment where two or more versions of a web page are shown to users at random, and statistical analysis is used to determine which version performs better for a given conversion goal. When applied to landing pages, A/B testing serves as a critical tool for marketers to optimize for conversions.

Landing pages are the digital entryways to a brand, product, or service. They're typically the page a visitor lands on after clicking a marketing CTA, such as an advertisement or an email link. Given their importance in the conversion funnel, ensuring they are optimized is crucial.

In A/B testing for landing pages, marketers might make variations in the headline, CTA buttons, images, testimonials, or any other element. The objective is to determine which version compels visitors more effectively to take the desired action, be it signing up for a newsletter, purchasing a product, or any other conversion goal.

For instance, if a company feels their sign-up rate is subpar, they might hypothesize that the CTA button's color or text is not compelling enough. They could then create two versions of the landing page: one with the original button and another with a different color or text. By directing half of the traffic to each version, they can collect data on which one achieves better conversion rates.

However, it's crucial to change only one element at a time during A/B testing. This ensures that any difference in performance can be attributed to that one change.

7.5.3 User Experience Best Practices for Conversions

UX is a holistic approach that encompasses all aspects of a user's interaction with a company, its services, and its products. When optimized, it ensures users find genuine value, leading to increased conversions.

For landing pages, an excellent UX means the visitor can quickly understand the value proposition and is effortlessly guided toward the conversion goal. To achieve this make sure to consider the following during your landing page creation:

- **Simplicity is key.** Landing pages should be clean, uncluttered, and free of any extraneous information. Every element should serve the purpose of guiding the visitor toward the conversion goal.
- **Clear value proposition.** Within seconds of landing on the page, a visitor should be able to grasp what is being offered and its benefits. This can be achieved through concise headlines, clear descriptions, and relevant visuals.
- **Relevant imagery.** Visuals play a critical role in capturing attention. Using high-quality, relevant images or videos can help illustrate the offering's benefits and resonate with the visitors' needs or desires.

- **Compelling CTA.** The CTA button should stand out and use action-oriented text. Instead of generic text such as 'Click here', using more specific prompts such as 'Get my free e-book' can be more effective.
- **Mobile optimization.** With a significant chunk of web traffic coming from mobile devices, ensuring the landing page is mobile-optimized can greatly influence conversions. This means fast load times, readable text sizes, and touch-friendly buttons.

To better understand the tangible impact of UX best practices on conversion rates, Table 7.5 presents a list of these practices, each accompanied by a brief explanation of its specific influence on enhancing user engagement and encouraging conversions.

7.5.4 Analyzing and Iterating Conversion Rate Optimization Strategies

CRO is not a one-off process but a continuous cycle of analysis and iteration. After implementing strategies, the next crucial step is to measure their effectiveness.

Analysis involves collecting data on the new conversion rates, user engagement metrics, and other relevant KPIs. Tools such as Google Analytics can offer in-depth insights, from bounce rates to time spent on the page. This data provides a clear picture of how well the implemented changes are driving conversions.

However, CRO doesn't stop at analysis. The insights derived should then inform further strategies. For instance, if a change resulted in higher conversions but increased the bounce rate, there might be an element that's driving away users after the initial conversion. This might prompt a new round of A/B testing to optimize that element.

Moreover, user feedback can be invaluable. Direct feedback tools or surveys can uncover user frustrations or desires that quantitative data might miss.

To illustrate the dynamic and evolving nature of CRO, Figure 7.11 presents a line graph showing improvements in the conversion rate after multiple iterations of CRO, highlighting the effectiveness of continuous analysis and strategy refinement.

Table 7.5 UX Best Practices with Brief Explanations.

Best Practice	Impact on Conversion Rates
Clear CTA	Directs users toward the desired action, increasing the likelihood of conversion.
Responsive design	Ensures consistent UX across devices, catering to a wider audience.
Fast load times	Reduces bounce rate by quickly presenting content to users.
Intuitive navigation	Helps users find what they are looking for with ease, leading to better engagement.
High-quality images	Offers a professional look and feel, enhancing perceived product value.
Trust signals	Enhances credibility, making users more comfortable taking action.
User reviews/testimonials	Provides social proof, increasing users' confidence in the product or service.
Minimal distractions	Keeps users focused on the main goal, increasing the chance of conversion.

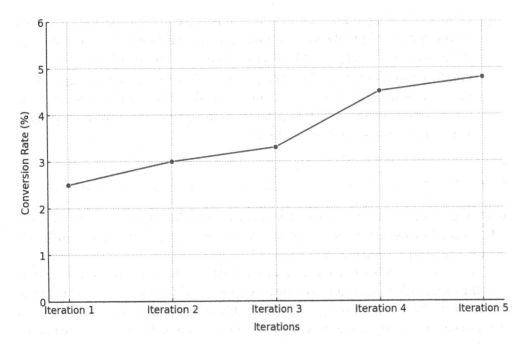

Figure 7.11 Improvements in Conversion Rate After Multiple Iterations of CRO.

In essence, the cycle of implementing, analyzing, and iterating is the heartbeat of CRO. It's a continuous journey toward perfecting the UX and maximizing conversions.

7.5.5 Key Concepts in Conversion Rate Optimization

There are several key concepts in CRO that are essential for understanding and executing effective CRO strategies:

- **Conversion funnel.** This is a representation of the customer journey from the initial visit to the website to the final conversion. Understanding the conversion funnel is crucial for identifying where potential customers are dropping out and what can be done to prevent this (Farris et al., 2010).

- **A/B testing.** This is a method used to test changes to web pages against the current design and determine which one produces superior results. It involves testing two versions (A and B) by showing them to similar visitors at the same time. The one that gives a better conversion rate wins (Kohavi et al., 2009).

- **Multivariate testing.** Similar to A/B testing, but instead of testing a single change, multiple variables are changed and tested to understand the interaction between different elements of the page.

- **UX.** This refers to the overall experience a user has while interacting with a website. A positive UX is crucial for CRO as it directly affects the user's likelihood to convert (Nielsen, 2012).

- **CTA.** A CTA is a prompt on a website that tells the user to take some specified action. A CTA is typically written as a command or action phrase, such as 'Sign Up' or 'Buy Now' and generally takes the form of a button or hyperlink.
- **Landing page optimization.** The process of improving elements on a website to increase conversions. Landing page optimization is a subset of CRO and involves using methods such as A/B testing to improve the conversion goals of a given landing page (Ash et al., 2012).

7.5.6   Practical Example: A/B Testing for Conversion Rate Optimization

As discussed A/B testing is a popular method used by businesses to optimize their websites and increase conversions. For this practical example, we will examine a hypothetical e-commerce store that sells shoes.

The e-commerce store has noticed that although they have a steady stream of traffic to their site, their conversion rate (the percentage of visitors who make a purchase) is lower than the industry average. To address this, they decide to run an A/B test on their product pages, which are the last step before a visitor adds an item to their cart.

They hypothesize that the 'Add to Cart' button is not prominent enough, and visitors may be missing it. In the current design (Version A), the 'Add to Cart' button is below the product description and is the same color as the rest of the website. They create a new design (Version B) where the 'Add to Cart' button is moved above the product description and changed to a contrasting color.

Half of the website visitors are shown Version A, and the other half are shown Version B. They then collect data on the number of visitors each version receives and how many of those visitors add a product to their cart.

After a month, they analyze the results. They find that Version B, with the more prominent 'Add to Cart' button, has a significantly higher conversion rate than Version A. Based on this, they decide to implement Version B for all visitors (see Figure 7.12).

This example illustrates the process and potential benefits of A/B testing. By making data-driven decisions, businesses can significantly improve their conversion rates and overall performance (Kohavi et al., 2007).

7.6   CONCLUSION

In the digital age, analytics has become crucial to marketing success. With social media platforms hosting billions of users worldwide, marketers have an unprecedented opportunity to reach their target audiences. SNA provides a way to understand the complex dynamics of these platforms and can guide strategies for influencer marketing, viral marketing, and more.

Web analytics, however, offer insights into how users interact with a brand's website. They can provide critical metrics such as bounce rate, session duration,

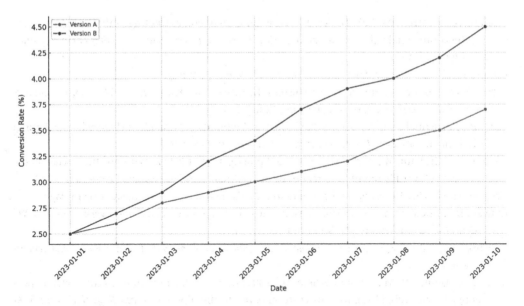

Figure 7.12 An A/B Testing Result Showcasing the Performance Difference Between Version A and Version B.

conversion rate, and more. Using these insights, marketers can optimize their websites to improve UX and increase conversions. A/B testing, as we've seen, can play a crucial role in this optimization process.

Last, social media listening and tracking help marketers understand the conversation about their brand on social media platforms. By tracking mentions, sentiment, and trends, brands can manage their reputation, respond to customer concerns, and identify opportunities for engagement.

In conclusion, social media analytics and web analytics are essential tools for modern marketers. They provide the insights needed to understand audiences, optimize digital properties, and engage with customers effectively. The techniques and examples discussed in this chapter only scratch the surface of what's possible in this exciting field (Chaffey & Ellis-Chadwick, 2022; Grigsby, 2015).

7.7 REFERENCES

Ash, T., Ginty, M., & Page, R. (2012). *Landing page optimization: The definitive guide to testing and tuning for conversions*. Wiley.

Bonacich, P. (2007). Some unique properties of eigenvector centrality. *Social Networks, 29*(4), 555–564.

Borgatti, S. P., Mehra, A., Brass, D. J., & Labianca, G. (2009). Network analysis in the social sciences. *Science, 323*(5916), 892–895.

Cambria, E., Schuller, B., Xia, Y., & Havasi, C. (2013). New avenues in opinion mining and sentiment analysis. *IEEE Intelligent Systems, 28*(2), 15–21.

Chaffey, D., & Ellis-Chadwick, F. (2022). *Digital marketing* (8th ed.). Pearson.

Chaffey, D., & Patron, M. (2012). From web analytics to digital marketing optimization: Increasing the commercial value of digital analytics. *Journal of Direct, Data and Digital Marketing Practice, 14*(1), 30–45.

Clifton, B. (2012). *Advanced web metrics with Google Analytics*. Wiley.

Farris, P. W., Bendle, N., Pfeifer, P., & Reibstein, D. (2010). *Marketing metrics: The definitive guide to measuring marketing performance*. Pearson Education.

Felix, R., Rauschnabel, P. A., & Hinsch, C. (2017). Elements of strategic social media marketing: A holistic framework. *Journal of Business Research, 70*, 118–126.

Freberg, K., Graham, K., McGaughey, K., & Freberg, L. A. (2011). Who are the social media influencers? A study of public perceptions of personality. *Public Relations Review, 37*(1), 90–92.

Grigsby, M. (2015). *Marketing analytics: A practical guide to real marketing science*. Kogan Page.

Hansen, D., Shneiderman, B., & Smith, M. A. (2010). *Analyzing social media networks with NodeXL: Insights from a connected world*. Morgan Kaufmann.

Kaushik, A. (2009). *Web analytics 2.0: The art of online accountability and science of customer centricity*. Wiley.

Kohavi, R., Henne, R. M., & Sommerfield, D. (2007, August). Practical guide to controlled experiments on the web: Listen to your customers not to the hippo. In *Proceedings of the 13th ACM SIGKDD International Conference on Knowledge Discovery and Data Mining* (pp. 959–967).

Kohavi, R., Longbotham, R., Sommerfield, D., & Henne, R. M. (2009). Controlled experiments on the web: Survey and practical guide. *Data Mining and Knowledge Discovery, 18*, 140–181.

Nielsen, J. (2012). *Usability 101: Introduction to usability*. Nielsen Norman Group.

Opsahl, T., & Panzarasa, P. (2009). Clustering in weighted networks. *Social Networks, 31*(2), 155–163.

Scott, J. (2017). *Social network analysis*. SAGE.

Shareef, M. A., Mukerji, B., Dwivedi, Y. K., Rana, N. P., & Islam, R. (2019). Social media marketing: Comparative effect of advertisement sources. *Journal of Retailing and Consumer Services, 46*, 58–69.

Stephen, A. T., & Toubia, O. (2010). Deriving value from social commerce networks. *Journal of Marketing Research, 47*(2), 215–228.

Stieglitz, S., Dang-Xuan, L., Bruns, A., & Neuberger, C. (2014). Social media analytics: An interdisciplinary approach and its implications for information systems. *Business & Information Systems Engineering, 6*, 89–96.

Tiago, M.T.P.M.B., & Veríssimo, J.M.C. (2014). Digital marketing and social media: Why bother? *Business Horizons, 57*(6), 703–708.

Wasserman, S., & Faust, K. (1994). *Social network analysis: Methods and applications*. Cambridge University Press.

Zafarani, R., Abbasi, M. A., & Liu, H. (2014). *Social media mining: An introduction*. Cambridge University Press.

EXERCISE 7.1: SOCIAL NETWORK ANALYSIS (SNA) IN MARKETING

Objective: To understand the application of social network analysis in identifying influential users in a marketing context.

Tasks:

1. **Visualize the Social Network:**
   - Use **networkx** to create a visual representation of the network.
   - Highlight key nodes that might represent influential users.

2. **Calculate Centrality Measures:**
   - Calculate degree, betweenness, and eigenvector centrality for each node.
   - Identify top five influential users based on these centrality measures.

3. **Discussion:**
   - Discuss how these measures can help in identifying potential influencers for marketing campaigns.
   - What are the limitations of this approach?

Steps:

1. **Load the Data and Import Libraries:**

```
1. import matplotlib.pyplot as plt
2. import networkx as nx
3. sna_data = pd.read_csv("/data/Social_Network_Analysis_
Data.csv")
```

This line imports the matplotlib and networkx library and loads the social network data from the CSV file into a pandas DataFrame.

2. **Create the Graph:**

```
4. G = nx.Graph()
5. for index, row in sna_data.iterrows():
6. G.add_node(row['User'], followers=row['Followers'], engage-
ment_rate=row['Engagement Rate'])
```

Here, we create an empty graph using networkx and then add nodes (users) from the DataFrame. Each node is added with attributes 'followers' and 'engagement_rate'. The graph currently has 25 nodes. Here are the attributes for the first five nodes:

- User 0: 2,832 followers, 5.93% engagement rate
- User 1: 3,364 followers, 6.03% engagement rate
- User 2: 9,325 followers, 6.24% engagement rate
- User 3: 5,974 followers, 4.38% engagement rate
- User 4: 6,844 followers, 2.73% engagement rate

3. Add Random Edges:

```
7. for _ in range(100):
8. G.add_edge(np.random.choice(sna_data['User']), np.random.
choice(sna_data['User']))
```

We simulate social connections by randomly creating edges between nodes.

4. Visualize the Social Network:

```
 9. plt.figure(figsize=(12, 8))
10. pos = nx.spring_layout(G)
11. nx.draw_networkx_nodes(G, pos, node_size=700)
12. nx.draw_networkx_edges(G, pos, width=1.0, alpha=0.5)
13. nx.draw_networkx_labels(G, pos, font_size=10)
14. plt.title("Social Network Graph")
15. plt.axis('off')
16. plt.show()
```

This block of code visualizes the social network. We use the **spring_layout** for positioning nodes and then draw nodes, edges, and labels.

5. Calculate Centrality Measures:

```
17. degree_centrality = nx.degree_centrality(G)
18. betweenness_centrality = nx.betweenness_centrality(G)
19. eigenvector_centrality = nx.eigenvector_centrality(G)
```

Here, we calculate three centrality measures for each node: degree centrality, betweenness centrality, and eigenvector centrality.

6. Identify Top Influential Users:

```
20. top_5_degree = sorted(degree_centrality.items(), key=lambda
x: x[1], reverse=True)[:5]
21. top_5_betweenness = sorted(betweenness_centrality.items(),
key=lambda x: x[1], reverse=True)[:5]
22. top_5_eigenvector = sorted(eigenvector_centrality.items(),
key=lambda x: x[1], reverse=True)[:5]
```

We identify the top five users based on each centrality measure by sorting the nodes and selecting the top five.

EXERCISE 7.1: OUTPUT

1. Social Network Graph Visualization:

- The social network graph was successfully created and visualized. This graph represents the social network with nodes (users) and edges (relationships).

N.B. As the edges between nodes were randomly generated, this graph will differ from future creations.

Synthetic Social Network Graph

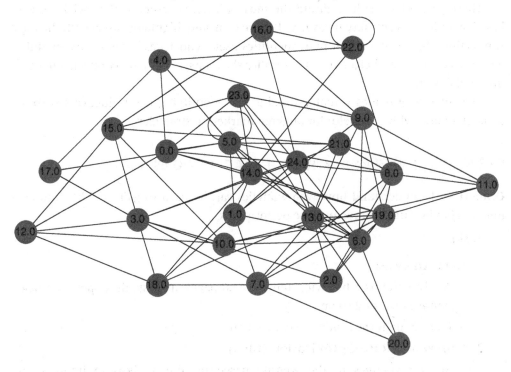

2. **Top Five Users Based on Different Centrality Measures:**
   - **Degree Centrality:**
     - User 5: 0.4583
     - User 6: 0.4167
     - User 13: 0.4167
     - User 19: 0.4167
     - User 3: 0.3333
   - **Betweenness Centrality:**
     - User 13: 0.0713
     - User 6: 0.0685
     - User 9: 0.0629
     - User 5: 0.0590
     - User 19: 0.0588
   - **Eigenvector Centrality:**
     - User 6: 0.3079
     - User 5: 0.3020

- User 19: 0.2995
- User 13: 0.2982
- User 14: 0.2483

These particular results indicate the most influential users in the social network based on different centrality measures. Degree centrality highlights users with the most connections, betweenness centrality identifies users who act as bridges between different network parts, and eigenvector centrality shows users who are connected to other influential users.

This analysis provides valuable insights into identifying key influencers within a social network, which is useful for targeted marketing strategies.

EXERCISE 7.2: WEB ANALYTICS FOR MARKETING INSIGHTS

Objective: To understand how web analytics can be used to gain insights into customer behavior and improve website performance.

Tasks:

1. **Data Analysis:**
   - Analyze the user behavior: most visited pages, average time spent per page, bounce rate, and so on.
   - Identify patterns leading to conversions.
2. **Conversion Rate Optimization (CRO):**
   - Suggest changes to the website based on the analysis to improve the conversion rate.
   - Discuss how A/B testing could be used to test these changes.
3. **Discussion:**
   - Discuss the role of web analytics in understanding customer behavior.
   - How can these insights be integrated with broader marketing strategies?

Steps:

1. **Import Necessary Libraries and Load the Web Analytics Data:**

```
1. import seaborn as sns
2. import pandas as pd
3. web_analytics_data = pd.read_csv("/data/Web_
Analytics_Data.csv")
```

This line imports necessary libraries for data analysis and loads the web analytics data from a CSV file into a pandas DataFrame.

2. Convert 'Session Timestamp':

```
4. web_analytics_data['Session_Timestamp'] =
pd.to_datetime(web_analytics_data['Session_Timestamp'])
```

Here, we convert the 'Session_Timestamp' column to datetime format for easier analysis.

3. Analyze User Behavior:

▪ Most Visited Pages:

```
5. most_visited_pages = web_analytics_data
['Page_Visited'].value_counts()
```

This line calculates the frequency of visits to each page.

▪ Average Time Spent on Pages:

```
6. web_analytics_data['Time_Spent'] = np.random.randint
(1, 300, size=len(web_analytics_data))
7. avg_time_spent = web_analytics_data.groupby
('Page_Visited')['Time_Spent'].mean()
```

Here, we simulate the average time spent on each page. We then calculate the average time spent per page.

▪ Bounce Rate Calculation:

```
8. bounce_rate = web_analytics_data[web_analytics_
data['Action'] == 'View'].groupby('User_ID').size()
9. bounce_rate = (bounce_rate == 1).sum() / len(bounce_rate)
```

We calculate the bounce rate by finding the percentage of sessions where only one page was viewed.

▪ Conversion Rate Calculation:

```
10. conversion_rate = web_analytics_data['Conversion'].mean()
```

The conversion rate is calculated as the mean of the 'Conversion' column.

4. Data Visualization:

▪ Page Visits Distribution:

```
11. sns.countplot(x='Page_Visited', data=web_analytics_data)
```

This line creates a count plot showing the distribution of page visits.

▪ Average Time Spent on Each Page:

```
12. sns.barplot(x=avg_time_spent.index, y=avg_time_
spent.values)
```

This line creates a bar plot showing the average time spent on each page.

The output consists of the following:

- The count of visits to each page (**most_visited_pages**)
- The average time spent on each page (**avg_time_spent**)
- The calculated bounce rate (**bounce_rate**)
- The overall conversion rate (**conversion_rate**)

These analyses and visualizations help in understanding user behavior on the website, identifying popular content, and gauging the website's effectiveness in keeping visitors engaged and driving conversions.

EXERCISE 7.2: OUTPUT

1. **Page Visits Distribution Visualization:**
   - The count plot shows the distribution of visits across different pages. The HomePage received the most visits, followed by the Confirmation page, ProductPage, and Checkout page.

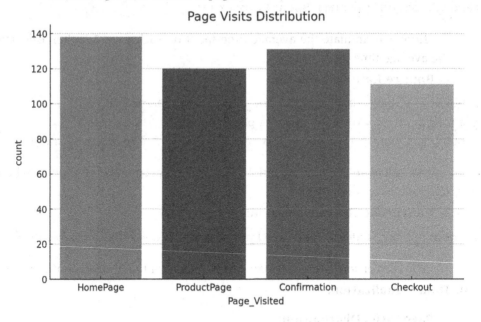

2. **Average Time Spent on Each Page Visualization:**
   - The bar plot indicates the average time spent on each page. The Confirmation page had the highest average time spent, followed by HomePage, Checkout, and ProductPage.

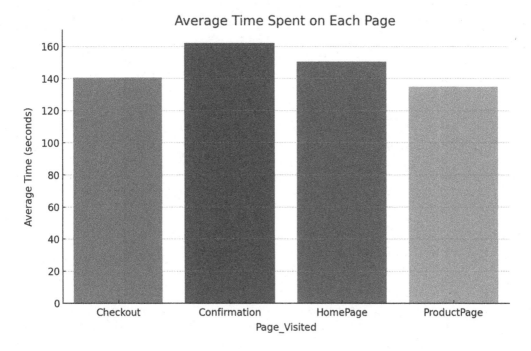

Average Time Spent on Each Page

3. **Most Visited Pages:**
   - HomePage: 138 visits
   - Confirmation: 131 visits
   - ProductPage: 120 visits
   - Checkout: 111 visits

4. **Average Time Spent on Pages:**
   - Checkout: 140.65 seconds
   - Confirmation: 162.15 seconds
   - HomePage: 150.54 seconds
   - ProductPage: 134.92 seconds

5. **Bounce Rate:**
   - The bounce rate is approximately 55.71%, indicating that more than half of the sessions are single-page sessions.

6. **Conversion Rate:**
   - The conversion rate is about 29.6%, representing the proportion of visits that result in a conversion.

These results provide insights into user behavior on the website, such as which pages are most and least engaging, and the overall effectiveness of the website in retaining visitors and driving conversions. This information can be used to optimize the website and improve user experience.

CHAPTER **8**

Marketing Mix Modeling and Attribution

8.1   INTRODUCTION

In the complex and multichannel world of modern marketing, understanding the impact of various marketing activities and accurately attributing outcomes to them is a challenging but essential task. This chapter will delve into the concepts of marketing mix modeling (MMM) and attribution, two powerful methodologies that help marketers measure the effectiveness of their efforts and allocate resources more efficiently.

MMM is a statistical technique that uses historical data to quantify the impact of various marketing components on sales or other key performance indicators (KPIs) (Ataman et al., 2010). However, attribution models help in assigning the proper credit to different marketing touchpoints in a customer's journey toward a conversion (Lemon & Verhoef, 2016).

Understanding and applying these methodologies can provide a competitive edge by informing strategic decisions, optimizing marketing spend, and, ultimately, maximizing the return on marketing investment (ROMI) (Lenskold, 2003).

As digital marketing continues to evolve and become more data-driven, the application of these techniques has become more sophisticated. This chapter aims to provide an in-depth understanding of these methodologies, their applications, and their significance in the current marketing landscape.

8.2   MARKETING MIX MODELING CONCEPTS

After laying down the foundational understanding of MMM and attribution, let's delve deeper into the key concepts of MMM, which has long been a cornerstone in the marketing analytics world.

8.2.1   Overview of Marketing Mix Modeling

As described in the introduction, MMM is a statistical approach used to gauge the impact of various marketing efforts on a company's sales or other KPIs. The technique emerged as a response to the increasing need for accountability in marketing activities and the drive toward data-driven decision-making (Ataman et al., 2010).

This approach incorporates multiple regression analysis to predict the outcome (typically sales or market share) based on different marketing inputs. These inputs, often referred to as *the marketing mix*, typically include the four Ps (product, price, promotion, and place), although it can extend to other factors such as macroeconomic indicators, seasonality, and competitor activities (Ataman et al., 2010).

One of the key strengths of MMM is its ability to disentangle the effect of different marketing activities on sales. By doing so, it enables marketers to understand the individual and combined effectiveness of different marketing channels and campaigns. It also helps in determining the optimal allocation of marketing budgets across different channels and activities (Pauwels et al., 2004).

However, MMM also has its limitations. For instance, it is primarily a historical analysis, which means it may not accurately predict future performance, especially in fast-changing markets. Also, it may not fully capture the intricacies of customer behavior or the indirect effects of marketing activities (Hanssens, 2015).

Despite these limitations, MMM remains a critical tool in a marketer's toolkit, providing valuable insights that can guide strategic decision-making and resource allocation.

8.2.2 Key Components: Advertising, Promotions, Distribution, and Pricing

Having understood the broader picture of MMM, let's break it down into its key components: advertising, promotions, distribution, and pricing, which form the pillars of this approach.

Understanding the components that constitute the marketing mix is essential to the application of MMM. The traditional four Ps framework encompasses the following (see Figure 8.1):

- **Advertising (product).** This is a paid form of nonpersonal communication used to promote or sell a product, service, or idea. Effective advertising can build brand awareness, drive product demand, and facilitate long-term market success. Tools include print ads, TV commercials, online ads, and outdoor billboards (Tellis, 2003).
- **Promotions.** Promotional activities aim to stimulate demand for a product or service. They often offer temporary advantages such as discounts, coupons, or

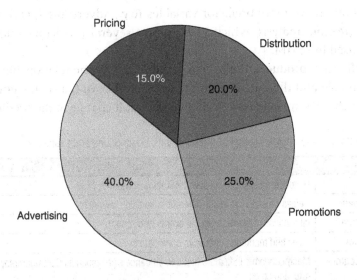

Figure 8.1 The Distribution of Budgets Across Various Components: Advertising, Promotions, Distribution, and Pricing.

free samples to entice purchase. Promotions can drive short-term sales spikes and can be particularly effective when launching a new product or entering a new market (Shankar et al., 2011).

- **Distribution (place).** This refers to how a product gets to the consumer. Effective distribution ensures that products are available in the right locations and at the right times. Channels can include brick-and-mortar retailers, e-commerce platforms, or direct-to-consumer methods. The distribution strategy can significantly influence sales performance and brand perception.

- **Pricing.** Pricing decisions determine how much a consumer pays for a product. It's a critical component, influencing profitability, demand, and brand positioning. Factors to consider include production costs, competitor pricing, perceived value, and demand elasticity. Dynamic pricing and psychological pricing are popular strategies in certain industries.

Each of these components can significantly influence sales and other KPIs. In MMM, understanding their individual and combined effects is essential for crafting effective marketing strategies (see Table 8.1).

8.2.3 Econometric Techniques and Regression Analysis in Marketing Mix Modeling

Although the components provide a structure, the heart of the modeling lies in the techniques employed. The application of econometric techniques, especially regression analysis, is foundational to MMM. Econometric models employ statistical methods to test hypotheses and estimate relationships among variables.

Regression analysis, specifically, is used to predict the outcome variable (e.g., sales) based on one or more predictor variables (e.g., advertising spend, promotions). Multiple regression analysis, which incorporates several predictor variables, is most commonly used in MMM.

The coefficients produced from the regression signify the relationship between the predictor variable and the outcome. In the context of MMM, a coefficient would indicate how much sales are expected to change for a unit change in the predictor variable,

Table 8.1 Key Components of Marketing Mix Modeling with Descriptions and Examples.

Component	Description
Sales data	Historical sales data, usually at a weekly or monthly level
Advertising spend	Details on expenditure for different advertising channels
Promotional data	Information about promotional events or discounts
Competitor data	Sales and marketing data from competitors
Economic indicators	Macroeconomic indicators that can influence sales, such as GDP, unemployment rate, and so on
Digital data	Data from digital channels such as website visits, clicks, and so on

Table 8.2 Econometric Techniques Used in Marketing Mix Modeling and Their Applications.

Technique	Application
Linear regression	Assess the impact of various marketing activities on sales
Time series analysis	Analyze and forecast sales data that is sequential over time
Generalized linear models	Model relationships with non-normal error distribution
ARIMA	Forecast sales using auto-regressive and moving average components
Multivariate regression	Analyze the impact of multiple predictors on a response variable

assuming other factors remain constant. Furthermore, the goodness-of-fit statistics (such as R-squared) provide insights into how well the model explains the variability in the outcome variable (Greene, 2003).

To provide a comprehensive overview of the range of econometric techniques employed in MMM and their respective applications, Table 8.2 details various methodologies such as linear regression and ARIMA, outlining how each is used to analyze and forecast the impact of marketing activities on sales and other key business outcomes.

8.2.4 Challenges and Limitations of Traditional Marketing Mix Modeling

Although regression offers a robust approach, similar to all models, MMM has its own challenges and limitations (see Figure 8.2). Let's dissect what these are and how they affect our analyses:

- ■ **Historical data dependence.** MMM relies on past data, which might not always be indicative of future outcomes, especially in rapidly evolving markets.

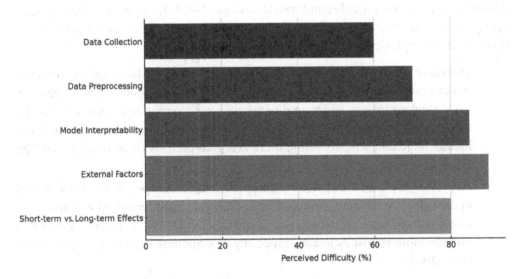

Figure 8.2 Challenges Faced in Traditional Marketing Mix Modeling.

- **Exclusion of non-quantifiable factors.** Certain influential factors, such as brand sentiment or word-of-mouth, might not be easily quantifiable and may be excluded from the model.

- **Causality versus correlation.** MMM might indicate correlations, but it doesn't necessarily establish causation.

- **Granularity.** Traditional MMM might not capture granular details of campaigns or customer segments. This lack of detail can mean that specific insights about individual campaigns or niche customer segments are missed. For modern MMM, this necessitates the integration of more advanced data analytics tools, as explained later in this chapter, that can capture and analyze data at a more detailed level. By leveraging more sophisticated models and tools, businesses can address this granularity issue, ensuring that their marketing strategies are tailored more precisely to specific audiences and campaigns, thus optimizing their marketing efforts.

- **Multiplatform challenges.** In today's digital world, consumers interact across multiple platforms, which can make data collection and interpretation more complex.

- **Model overfitting.** If too many variables are included, the model might fit the historical data too closely, reducing its predictive accuracy for future data.

As with all analytical models, it's crucial to understand these limitations when interpreting results and making strategic decisions (Hanssens, 2015; Kireyev et al., 2016).

8.2.5   Beyond Regression: Supplementary Analytical Techniques in Marketing Mix Modeling

Although regression is a widely employed technique in MMM, a well-rounded analytical approach should also consider integrating supplementary methods to account for nuances and complexities not captured by regression alone:

- **Machine learning and artificial intelligence.** With the surge in computational power and data availability, machine learning models such as decision trees, random forests, and neural networks offer alternative ways to analyze the data. These models can uncover nonlinear relationships, interactions, and can handle large datasets, providing more accurate predictions in certain scenarios (Provost & Fawcett, 2013).

- **Bayesian methods.** Bayesian techniques, which incorporate prior beliefs and update them with new data, can be useful, especially when data is sparse or when integrating expert opinions is crucial. For MMM, Bayesian models can provide more robust estimates, especially in situations with limited data (Rossi et al., 2003).

- **Segmentation analysis.** MMM can sometimes miss the nuances of different consumer segments. Cluster analysis and other segmentation techniques can identify and analyze these segments, offering a more granular understanding of consumer behaviors and responses to marketing stimuli (Wedel & Kamakura, 2000).

- **Endogeneity correction.** Issues such as simultaneity, where marketing spend might be influenced by sales (and vice versa), can lead to biased regression coefficients. Instruments, control functions, and other econometric techniques can help correct for endogeneity, providing more accurate estimates (Wooldridge, 2010).

- **Decomposition analysis.** Techniques such as Shapley value decomposition and can help in attributing the effect of a marketing action across different channels, especially in the digital space. This helps in understanding the interplay and combined impact of different marketing actions (Israeli, 2007).

Although regression remains a foundational tool in MMM, modern complexities require an integrated approach that taps into multiple analytical methods. By doing so, marketers can capture a more comprehensive and nuanced view of their efforts, leading to better-informed decisions and optimized marketing strategies.

8.2.6 Key Concepts in Marketing Mix Modeling

Despite its challenges, there are certain foundational concepts in MMM that are indispensable. Grasping these will enable a more nuanced understanding and application. The key concepts in MMM are as follows:

- **Dependent and independent variables.** The dependent variable is the outcome that the business is trying to predict or influence, often sales or market share. Independent variables are the marketing inputs or other factors that might influence the dependent variable, such as advertising spend across different channels, pricing, distribution, promotions, competitor activities, and economic factors (Leeflang et al., 2013).

- **Regression analysis.** Regression analysis is a statistical method used to understand the relationship between the dependent and independent variables. In the context of MMM, multiple regression analysis is typically used to understand the simultaneous effect of multiple marketing inputs on sales or other KPIs (Leeflang et al., 2013).

- **Coefficients.** The coefficients resulting from the regression analysis represent the estimated impact of each independent variable on the dependent variable. In the context of MMM, these coefficients tell marketers how much sales or market share is expected to change for a unit change in a given marketing input, holding all other factors constant (Hanssens, 2015).

- **Elasticity.** Elasticity measures the percentage change in the dependent variable (e.g., sales) for a 1% change in an independent variable (e.g., advertising spend). This concept helps marketers understand the responsiveness of sales to changes in various marketing inputs and is particularly helpful in making budget allocation decisions (Kotler & Keller, 2016).

- **Synergy effects.** In many cases, the impact of combined marketing activities is greater than the sum of their individual effects. These synergy effects can be captured in an MMM through the inclusion of interaction terms in the regression model (Hanssens, 2015).

8.2.7   Practical Example: Marketing Mix Modeling for a Consumer Goods Company

Theory and concepts are best understood when put into practice. Let's walk through a practical example of how MMM is implemented for a consumer goods company. MMM can be a valuable tool for a consumer goods company in understanding the effectiveness of their marketing efforts.

Imagine a company, Sunrise Soaps, that sells various home and personal care products. They invest in multiple marketing channels, including TV advertising, online advertising, print media, and in-store promotions. They also face varying degrees of competition and are influenced by seasonal factors.

They decide to use MMM to understand the impact of their marketing efforts on their quarterly sales. The dependent variable in their model is quarterly sales, and the independent variables include marketing spend in various channels, competitor marketing spend, and dummy variables to capture seasonal effects.

Using historical data, they fit a multiple regression model and find the following results (see Figure 8.3):

- TV advertising has the highest coefficient, suggesting it has the greatest impact on sales. This is consistent with the vast reach and exposure that TV advertising provides (Kotler & Keller, 2016).

- Online advertising has a smaller coefficient but a high elasticity. This suggests that although the current impact of online advertising on sales is less than TV advertising, sales are highly responsive to changes in online advertising spend. Given the increasing trend of digital consumption, this presents an opportunity to optimize the marketing budget (Hanssens, 2015).

- The dummy variables show significant seasonal effects, with sales increasing in the holiday quarter. This insight can be used to time marketing activities for maximum impact.

- The interaction term between TV and online advertising is positive and significant, suggesting a synergy effect. This means the combined effect of TV and online advertising is greater than the sum of their individual effects (Leeflang et al., 2013).

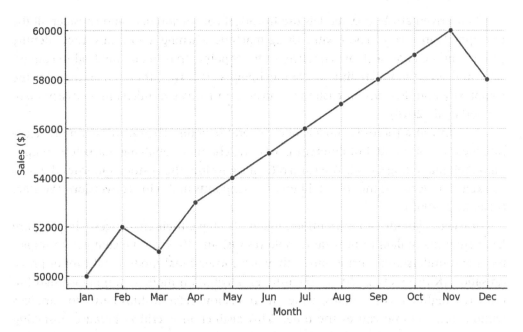

Figure 8.3 Results from the Practical Example for a Consumer Goods Company.

These insights can guide Sunrise Soaps in making data-driven decisions about their marketing budget allocation, timing of marketing activities, and coordination of marketing efforts across channels for maximum impact.

8.3 DATA-DRIVEN ATTRIBUTION MODELS

Pivoting from traditional models, the rise of digital channels necessitates a more nuanced approach: data-driven attribution models. These models shed light on the journey a customer takes with your brand.

8.3.1 Overview of Data-Driven Attribution Models

Data-driven attribution models are a type of attribution model that uses machine learning and statistical algorithms to assign credit to marketing touchpoints. Unlike rule-based attribution models, such as last-click or first-click, which assign credit based on predefined rules, data-driven attribution models learn from the data to understand the contribution of each touchpoint in the conversion path.

With the rise of digital marketing, customers often interact with a brand multiple times across various channels before making a purchase. These interactions can include seeing an online ad, visiting the company's website, clicking on a social media post, or receiving an email. Each of these touchpoints can influence the customer's decision to purchase, and data-driven attribution models aim to quantify this influence (Gupta et al., 2006).

Data-driven attribution models use historical conversion data and consider all the touchpoints in a conversion path. Using machine learning algorithms, they identify patterns in the data, such as sequences of touchpoints that frequently lead to conversions and assign more credit to these touchpoints. This way, they can account for the complexity and diversity of customer journeys in today's multichannel environment (Anderl et al., 2016).

Data-driven attribution models offer several benefits. They provide a more accurate measure of the ROI of different marketing channels, enabling marketers to optimize their marketing spend. They also offer insights into the customer journey, helping marketers understand the role of different touchpoints in driving conversions (Verhoef & Donkers, 2005).

However, data-driven attribution models also have their challenges. They require large amounts of data to provide reliable results, and they can be complex to implement and understand. Furthermore, they are correlational models and cannot prove causation (Kireyev et al., 2016). Data-driven attribution models, although insightful, primarily highlight correlations, which merely show relationships between variables without proving one causes the other. This distinction is critical because mistaking correlation for causation can lead to misguided marketing investments, overlooking key touchpoints, and misconstruing the real drivers behind conversions. The multifaceted nature of today's customer journeys, the presence of confounding variables, and feedback loops add complexity, making it challenging to isolate the true causal impact of individual touchpoints on conversions. As a result, marketers must interpret these models with caution, ensuring they don't confuse observed patterns with definitive causative actions (see Table 8.3).

8.3.2 Last-Touch, First-Touch, and Linear Attribution Models

There are several attribution models used in the industry. Some of the most popular ones include the last-touch, first-touch, and linear models. Let's dive into the intricacies of these models. Understanding the value that different touchpoints contribute to a conversion is essential. Different attribution models help to determine this, with each providing unique insights:

- **Last-touch attribution.** This is the most commonly used model and attributes 100% of the conversion value to the last touchpoint before the conversion.

Table 8.3 Advantage and Disadvantage of Traditional and Data-Driven Attribution Models.

Attribute	Traditional Attribution	Data-Driven Attribution
Basis	Assigns credit based on simple rules (e.g., last-touch, first-touch)	Uses algorithms and statistical models to assign credit
Advantage	Easy to understand and implement	More accurate as it considers all touchpoints
Disadvantage	Doesn't account for all interactions in the customer journey	Requires substantial data and can be complex to set up

It's straightforward but can overemphasize the final touchpoint, often at the expense of earlier marketing efforts.

■ **First-touch attribution.** This model gives 100% credit to the first touchpoint that led a customer to the conversion path. It's useful for understanding awareness-building campaigns but can overlook subsequent touchpoints that might have driven the final conversion.

■ **Linear attribution.** This distributes the conversion credit equally across all touchpoints. It recognizes every step in the customer's journey but can oversimplify by assuming each touchpoint has the same impact.

8.3.3 Algorithmic or Probabilistic Attribution Models

Algorithmic or probabilistic attribution models employ advanced statistics, machine learning, and big data to attribute the value of each touchpoint. Unlike rule-based models (such as last-touch or linear), algorithmic models analyze vast amounts of data to determine the most likely contribution of each touchpoint (see Table 8.4):

■ **Data analysis.** These models consider all interactions across a user's conversion path, analyzing patterns and sequences that lead to conversion (Kireyev et al., 2016).

■ **Flexibility.** Algorithmic models can adapt to changes in customer behavior and market dynamics, continually updating based on the latest data (Dalessandro et al., 2012).

8.3.4 Evaluating Model Performance

Once you've leveraged algorithmic models, the next critical step is evaluating their performance to ensure they align with business objectives:

■ **Accuracy.** Assess if the model correctly assigns value to touchpoints. Comparing model predictions against holdout sets or running A/B tests (see Section 4.4) can validate accuracy (Lewis & Rao, 2015).

■ **Granularity.** A good model should provide granular insights, capturing the nuances of different channels, campaigns, or customer segments (Anderl et al., 2016).

Table 8.4 Overview and Comparison of Last-Touch, First-Touch, Linear, and Algorithmic Attribution Models.

Model	Description
Last-touch	Assigns 100% credit to the last touchpoint before conversion
First-touch	Assigns 100% credit to the first touchpoint of the customer journey
Linear	Distributes credit equally across all touchpoints
Algorithmic	Uses data-driven techniques to distribute credit based on the influence of each touchpoint

- **Adaptability.** Marketing landscapes change. A model's performance might degrade over time, so it should be adaptable to shifts in customer behavior or market conditions (Kireyev et al., 2016).

8.3.5 Implementation Challenges and Pitfalls

Successful evaluation doesn't guarantee smooth implementation. There are various challenges and pitfalls we must be wary of when implementing data-driven attribution models:

- **Data silos.** Data might exist in silos across different platforms, making consolidation and analysis challenging (Kumar et al., 2016).
- **Over-complexity.** Overly complex models might be accurate but can become hard to interpret and act upon.
- **Ignoring external factors.** Focusing only on internal data can miss external influences, such as economic conditions or competitor actions, which can affect performance (Gupta et al., 2006).
- **Assuming static behavior.** Customers' behavior and preferences evolve. Assuming static behavior can lead to inaccurate attributions (Verhoef & Donkers, 2005).

Although attribution models offer valuable insights, it's vital to approach them judiciously, understanding their strengths, limitations, and the potential challenges in implementation.

8.3.6 Key Concepts in Data-Driven Attribution Models

To navigate these challenges, a grasp on the key concepts of data-driven attribution models is indispensable. Data-driven attribution models leverage key concepts that enable marketers to provide a more accurate representation of the value of different marketing touchpoints. Here are some of these concepts:

- **Conversion paths.** A conversion path refers to the sequence of touchpoints that a customer interacts with before completing a conversion, such as making a purchase or filling out a form. Data-driven attribution models analyze conversion paths to understand the patterns that lead to conversions (Anderl et al., 2016).
- **Touchpoints.** A touchpoint is any interaction a customer has with a brand. In a digital marketing context, touchpoints can include ad impressions, clicks, website visits, social media engagements, and more. Data-driven attribution models assign credit to different touchpoints based on their influence on conversions.

- **Credit assignment.** Credit assignment refers to the process of distributing credit for a conversion among the various touchpoints in the conversion path. Data-driven attribution models use algorithms to determine how much credit each touchpoint should receive (Gupta et al., 2006).

- **Machine learning.** Data-driven attribution models use machine learning algorithms to learn from conversion data and identify patterns. These algorithms can handle large amounts of data and account for complex, nonlinear relationships between variables (Kireyev et al., 2016).

- **Statistical significance.** Statistical significance is a measure of the likelihood that the results observed in the data occurred by chance. In the context of data-driven attribution, statistical significance can be used to determine whether the differences in credit assignment between different touchpoints are meaningful (Verhoef & Donkers, 2005).

8.3.7 Practical Example: Data-Driven Attribution for an E-Commerce Company

With concepts in hand, let's solidify our understanding with a practical example centered on an e-commerce company. Implementing data-driven attribution models for an e-commerce company involves various steps and practices. Let's consider a scenario in which an e-commerce company wants to better understand the value of its various marketing channels in driving conversions, and thus decides to implement a data-driven attribution model.

1. **Data collection.** The first step is to gather data about customer interactions across all marketing channels, including search ads, display ads, email marketing, social media, and organic search. This data would typically include the type of interaction (e.g., ad click, email open), the time of the interaction, and whether the interaction eventually led to a conversion.

2. **Conversion path analysis.** The company then analyzes the conversion paths—sequences of touchpoints leading up to a conversion—to identify patterns. For example, the company might find that customers who interact with a display ad are more likely to make a purchase if they later receive an email (Dalessandro et al., 2012).

3. **Model development.** The company uses machine learning algorithms to develop a model that predicts conversions based on the sequence of touchpoints. This model is trained on historical conversion data, enabling it to learn patterns and relationships between variables.

4. **Credit assignment.** The company applies the model to assign credit for conversions to different touchpoints. For example, if the model finds that display

ads play a crucial role in driving conversions, it might assign a higher percentage of credit to display ads.

5. **Implementation and iteration.** The company implements the attribution model and uses its results to inform its marketing strategy. For example, if the model assigns a high value to email marketing, the company might invest more in this channel. The model is regularly updated as new data becomes available (Kireyev et al., 2016).

8.4 MULTI-TOUCH ATTRIBUTION

Moving a step further from single touchpoints, multi-touch attribution (MTA) considers multiple touchpoints in a customer's journey, providing a more holistic view.

8.4.1 Overview of Multi-Touch Attribution

MTA is a sophisticated method of understanding and attributing the value that different marketing touchpoints contribute to a final conversion. This model acknowledges the complexity of modern customer journeys that often include multiple touchpoints across various channels before a purchase is made (Kumar et al., 2016).

In traditional single-touch models, all credit for a conversion is given to a single touchpoint, usually the last one before the conversion (last-click attribution) or the first one (first-click attribution). Although these models are simple and easy to implement, they do not accurately reflect the reality of the customer journey, which is typically much more complex (Anderl et al., 2016).

However, MTA models distribute the credit for a conversion across multiple touchpoints. This enables marketers to understand the impact of each touchpoint and optimize their marketing efforts accordingly. There are several types of MTA models, including linear, time decay, and *U*-shaped models. The choice of model depends on the specifics of the business and its marketing strategies.

However, implementing MTA is not without its challenges. It requires a significant amount of data, advanced analytics capabilities, and often the integration of data across multiple platforms and channels. A notable limitation of many MTA models is the underlying assumption of independence among touchpoints. This means the models often assume that each touchpoint's effect on a conversion is independent of the effects of other touchpoints. In reality, interactions between touchpoints can be synergistic or antagonistic. For instance, seeing a social media post might amplify the effect of a subsequent email campaign, or vice versa. When touchpoints aren't truly independent, attributing value based on this assumption can lead to misestimations of the real influence each touchpoint has on conversions. This can then misguide marketers when optimizing their strategies. It's crucial for marketers to be aware of this limitation when interpreting the results and making decisions based on MTA (see Figure 8.4).

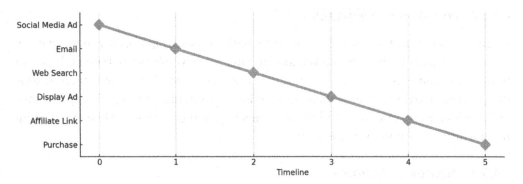

Figure 8.4 Multi-Touch Attribution Touchpoints Emphasizing the Importance of Multiple Interactions.

Despite these challenges, the insights provided by MTA can significantly improve the effectiveness and efficiency of marketing campaigns (Kumar et al., 2016).

8.4.2 Rationale for Multi-Touch Approaches

To fully appreciate MTA, it's essential to understand the rationale behind its development and increasing importance. In today's intricate digital landscape, customers interact with brands through myriad channels and touchpoints before making a purchase decision. From initial brand discovery to final conversion, a consumer might engage with a company's social media post, click on a search engine advertisement, open an email, and more. Given this complexity, it becomes clear that relying on a single point of contact—such as the last advertisement clicked or the first website visited—can provide a distorted view of what truly influences consumer decisions.

The essence of the MTA approach lies in its recognition of the multifaceted nature of the modern customer journey. Rather than oversimplifying this journey, multi-touch models aim to capture a more holistic view of the role and value of each touchpoint. By providing a nuanced understanding of how various touchpoints contribute to the end goal, marketers can more effectively allocate resources, refine strategies, and enhance customer engagement (Gupta et al., 2006). The interconnectedness of the digital ecosystem requires a method that mirrors its complexity, and MTA models rise to the occasion.

8.4.3 Time Decay, Position-Based, and Algorithmic Approaches

8.4.3.1 Time Decay Approach

This model values touchpoints based on their proximity to the final conversion, progressively assigning greater value to touchpoints as they get closer to the conversion moment. This recognizes that although early interactions play a role in raising awareness, the touchpoints closer to conversion are typically more influential in the final decision-making process.

8.4.3.2 Position-Based Approach

Often described as a *U*-shaped model, the position-based approach assigns specific value percentages to the first and last touchpoints, acknowledging their pivotal roles in introducing and sealing the consumer's decision. The remaining value is then distributed evenly across the intermediate touchpoints. This model captures the significance of the initial brand discovery and the final push toward conversion while still valuing the nurturing touchpoints in between.

8.4.3.3 Algorithmic Approach

Employing sophisticated machine learning and statistical techniques, the algorithmic model dives deep into historical data to ascertain the most probable influence of each touchpoint (Kireyev et al., 2016). Instead of predefined rules, this approach dynamically adjusts based on patterns and relationships found in the data, offering a highly adaptive and customized attribution model.

To elucidate the distinctions among various multi-touch attribution models, Table 8.5 presents a comparison of key features and best use cases for time decay, position-based, and algorithmic models, offering insights into how each model attributes credit to different touchpoints in a customer's journey.

Table 8.5 Key Features and Differences Among Time Decay, Position-Based, and Algorithmic Multi-Touch Attribution Models.

Model	Description	Best For
Time decay	Assigns more credit to touchpoints closer to the conversion	Short sales cycles where recent interactions matter more
Position-based	Gives more credit to the first and last touchpoints, and distributes the rest equally among middle touchpoints	Journeys where the introduction and conclusion are pivotal
Algorithmic	Uses algorithms and statistical techniques to assign credit based on the actual influence of touchpoints	Complex customer journeys with a lot of data available

8.4.4 Tools and Platforms for Multi-Touch Attribution

With an understanding of the various approaches, the tools and platforms available aid in effectively leveraging MTA (see Table 8.6).

Table 8.6 Tools and Platforms for Multi-Touch Attribution with Features.

Tool/Platform	Features
Google Analytics	User journey analysis, event tracking, segmentation
Adobe Analytics	Cross-channel attribution, real-time analytics, segmentation
Facebook Attribution	Cross-device tracking, ad performance, conversion paths
Visual IQ	Multichannel tracking, customer journey visualization, ROI analysis

The rise of the digital era has been accompanied by the development of myriad tools and platforms designed to help marketers navigate MTA. Solutions such as Google Analytics, Adobe Analytics, and Visual IQ provide comprehensive insights into the customer journey. These platforms harness vast amounts of data, processing them through sophisticated algorithms to map out the impact of various touchpoints.

Google Analytics, for instance, offers models that enable a comparative view of how different attribution approaches might paint the customer journey, facilitating informed decision-making (Kumar et al., 2016). However, platforms such as Visual IQ emphasize the importance of cross-channel interactions, shedding light on the synergies between various marketing activities.

8.4.5 Integrating Offline and Online Data for Holistic Attribution

In today's blended world, integrating offline and online data becomes paramount to achieve a 360-degree view of attribution. Although the digital realm offers a treasure trove of data points, it's crucial to remember that consumers still engage with brands offline. Integrating offline data—such as in-store purchases, call center interactions, or physical event attendances—into the attribution model is vital for a holistic understanding.

Modern tools have begun to bridge this gap. For instance, Google's Store Visits in Google Ads attempts to connect the dots between online ad clicks and offline store visits. Similarly, CRM systems can be integrated into digital analytics platforms, bringing data from offline sales and interactions into the digital attribution fold.

Incorporating offline data not only offers a complete picture of the customer journey but also helps in understanding the interplay between online and offline touchpoints. Recognizing the influence of a digital ad on an in-store purchase, or how an in-store experience drives online searches, can provide marketers with invaluable insights, guiding strategies that truly resonate with the consumer's journey (Lemon & Verhoef, 2016).

8.4.6 Key Concepts in Multi-Touch Attribution

Mastering MTA requires a solid foundation in its key concepts. MTA models distribute the credit for a conversion across multiple touchpoints, reflecting the contribution of each touchpoint in the customer's journey toward conversion. There are several key concepts involved in MTA that are critical to understanding and implementing these models effectively:

- **Touchpoint.** A touchpoint refers to any interaction a customer has with a brand, product, or service. This can include viewing an advertisement, visiting a website, reading an email newsletter, or interacting with a sales representative. Each touchpoint provides an opportunity for the brand to influence the customer's decision-making process (Kumar et al., 2016).

- **Customer journey.** The customer journey is the complete series of experiences that customers go through when interacting with a brand or product. In MTA, the customer journey is analyzed to identify the sequence and impact of touchpoints that lead to a conversion (Anderl et al., 2016).
- **Attribution model.** An attribution model is the rule or set of rules that determine how credit for conversions is assigned to touchpoints in the customer journey. Different models assign credit differently, depending on the specifics of the business and its marketing strategies (Kumar et al., 2016).
- **Linear, time decay, and *U*-shaped models.** These are examples of MTA models. The linear model assigns equal credit to all touchpoints, the time decay model assigns more credit to touchpoints closer to the conversion, and the *U*-shaped model assigns more credit to the first and last touchpoints.

Understanding and correctly applying these concepts can help marketers gain a more accurate picture of the effectiveness of their marketing efforts and make more informed decisions about where to invest their marketing resources.

8.4.7 Practical Example: Multi-Touch Attribution for an Online Retailer

Now, let's apply our knowledge through a practical example focusing on an online retailer. Consider an online retailer aiming to optimize its digital marketing strategy. The retailer uses several marketing channels: search engine optimization, pay-per-click (PPC) advertising, email marketing, social media, and display advertising. Each of these channels represents a potential touchpoint in the customer's journey, and the retailer wants to understand the contribution of each touchpoint to the final conversion: a purchase on their website.

To implement a MTA model, the retailer first collects data on customer touchpoints. These data include the sequence and timing of touchpoints and conversions, as well as details about the customer and the context of each touchpoint (Kumar et al., 2016).

The retailer then applies an MTA model to assign credit for each conversion to the contributing touchpoints. For example, they might use a U-shaped model, which assigns more credit to the first and last touchpoints in the sequence.

Analyzing the results of the MTA model, the retailer might find that although PPC advertising often initiates customer journeys, email marketing is most effective at closing sales. Armed with these insights, the retailer can make more informed decisions about where to invest its marketing budget and how to sequence its marketing messages for maximum effect.

However, it's important to note that MTA models have their limitations. They rely on the assumption that all touchpoints are independent and that their effects are additive, which may not always be the case. Additionally, they do not account for the influence of offline touchpoints, such as in-store experiences or word-of-mouth recommendations (Anderl et al., 2016).

8.5 RETURN ON MARKETING INVESTMENT

Transitioning from attribution, let's explore the ultimate measure of marketing success: ROMI.

8.5.1 Overview of Return on Marketing Investment

ROMI is a metric used to measure the efficacy of a company's marketing strategy. Unlike traditional return on investment (ROI) metrics, ROMI specifically focuses on the return attributable to marketing investments (Lenskold, 2003).

ROMI provides a way to quantify the impact of marketing activities on a firm's profitability. It's calculated by comparing the incremental financial value gained as a result of specific marketing spend to the cost of the marketing spend itself. This calculation helps marketers understand the effectiveness of their strategies in terms of generating revenue and contributing to the bottom line (Rust et al., 2004).

ROMI is an important tool for marketing decision-making (see Figure 8.5). As companies face increasing pressure to justify their marketing expenses, ROMI offers a

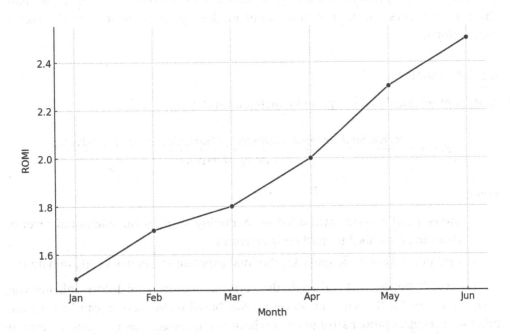

Figure 8.5 Return on Marketing Investment over Time.

means to demonstrate the value of marketing activities in financial terms. It helps in budget allocation by identifying the marketing activities that yield the highest return, thus allowing for more efficient use of marketing resources (Lenskold, 2003).

However, measuring ROMI is not without challenges. It requires accurate attribution of revenues to specific marketing activities, which can be difficult in practice, especially when multiple channels and touchpoints are involved in the customer journey. It also requires a clear understanding of the time lag between marketing activities and their impact on customer behavior, which can vary widely across different marketing activities and customer segments (Kumar & Gupta, 2016).

8.5.2 Calculating Return on Marketing Investment: Principles and Formulas

Before delving deeper, let's understand the principles and formulas behind calculating ROMI. ROMI stands as a foundational metric for marketers to determine the efficacy of their marketing activities. Essentially, it seeks to relate marketing expenditure to the financial benefits that these activities bring about (Lenskold, 2003).

8.5.2.1 Principle

The core principle behind ROMI is that marketing should not be viewed merely as an expense, but as an investment that generates a financial return. ROMI helps quantify this by expressing the net profit from marketing efforts relative to the cost of those efforts.

8.5.2.2 Formula

ROMI can be calculated using the following formula:

$$ROMI = \frac{Incremental\ Revenue\ Attributed\ to\ Marketing - Cost\ of\ Marketing,}{Cost\ of\ Marketing}$$

where

- Incremental revenue attributed to marketing signifies the additional revenue that can be ascribed to marketing activities.
- Cost of marketing encompasses the total expenditure on marketing initiatives.

It's worth noting that although the formula appears straightforward, deriving accurate values for 'Incremental Revenue Attributed to Marketing' can be intricate, because it requires proper attribution mechanisms to correctly assign sales or revenue to specific marketing activities (Rust et al., 2004).

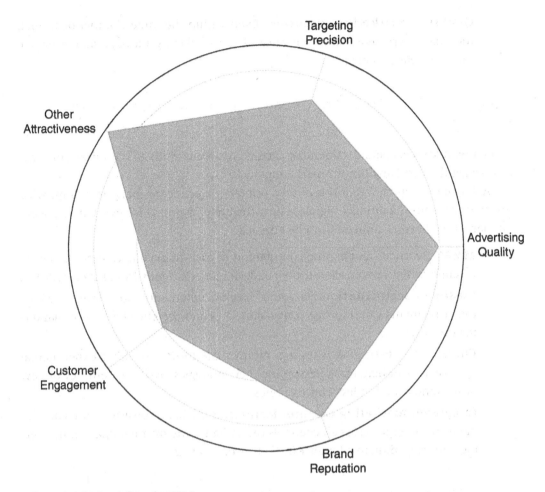

Figure 8.6 Factors Influencing ROMI.

8.5.3 Factors Influencing Return on Marketing Investment

ROMI, though a singular metric, is influenced by myriad factors (see Figure 8.6). Let's explore what factors drive this critical number:

- **Market maturity.** In mature markets, where brand awareness is already high, the incremental revenue from additional marketing might be lower than in emerging markets (Kotler & Keller, 2016).

- **Product life cycle.** New product launches often require significant marketing investments, but they may also bring higher incremental revenues as the market is introduced to the offering.

- **Marketing channels used.** Different channels have distinct cost structures and potential reach. Digital advertising might have lower upfront costs than a nationwide TV campaign but could also have different conversion rates.

- **Competitive actions.** Competitor marketing activities can dampen or enhance the effectiveness of a firm's marketing, affecting its ROMI (Kumar & Gupta, 2016).

- **Quality of marketing execution.** Even within the same channel or format, the quality, creativity, and relevance of the marketing message play a pivotal role in its effectiveness.

8.5.4 Optimizing Marketing Spend for Better Return on Marketing Investment

Armed with knowledge on influencing factors, the focus shifts to optimization—how can we get the best bang for our marketing buck?

Achieving an optimal ROMI is often a primary objective for marketers. Improving this metric means obtaining a higher return (revenue or profit) for every dollar spent on marketing. Several strategies can be pursued:

- **MMM.** By understanding the contribution of each marketing channel to overall revenue, businesses can allocate their budgets more efficiently (Ataman et al., 2010).
- **Customer segmentation.** Targeting specific, potentially more profitable customer segments can improve conversion rates and the effectiveness of marketing campaigns.
- **Continuous testing.** A/B testing, multivariate testing, or other experimental approaches can help marketers refine their strategies, assess the efficacy of new tactics, and abandon less effective ones.
- **Integrated marketing communications.** Ensuring a consistent and complementary message across all channels can enhance the overall impact of marketing efforts, leading to a better ROMI (Luxton et al., 2015).

8.5.5 Case Studies: Successful Return on Marketing Investment Optimization

Theories and principles come alive when seen in action. Let's review some real-world case studies showcasing successful ROMI optimization.

Company A. A leading e-commerce platform, despite having a significant online presence, was struggling with stagnating sales. By employing MMM, they identified underinvestment in email marketing. Shifting funds from other less effective channels to targeted email campaigns, the company saw a 20% increase in sales, significantly boosting their ROMI (Kireyev et al., 2016).

Company B. A multinational beauty brand decided to optimize its ROMI by integrating offline and online data. Through the use of unique QR codes in physical stores and unified customer profiles, they linked offline purchases to online advertising. By understanding this holistic customer journey, they optimized their digital ads, resulting in a 15% increase in overall sales and a marked improvement in ROMI (Lemon & Verhoef, 2016).

Such case studies underscore the importance of a data-driven, customer-centric approach in optimizing ROMI. By understanding the customer journey, leveraging the right channels, and ensuring consistent messaging, companies can significantly improve their ROMI.

8.5.6 Key Concepts in Return on Marketing Investment

From these practical applications, there are certain foundational concepts in ROMI that stand out and are worth highlighting:

- **Incremental sales.** This refers to the additional sales generated due to a specific marketing activity. It is the difference between the sales during a promotional period and a comparable period without the promotion. Incremental sales are often challenging to measure due to external factors and market fluctuations (Bendle & Bagga, 2016).
- **Marginal profit.** This is the profit generated by the incremental sales. It is calculated by multiplying the incremental sales by the profit margin per unit. Not all incremental sales lead to incremental profit, especially if they result from price promotions that reduce the profit margin.
- **Marketing investment.** This is the total cost of the marketing activity, including the cost of the products sold, the cost of the marketing campaign (e.g., advertising, public relations), and any other related expenses.
- **ROMI calculation.** ROMI is usually expressed as a ratio or percentage, calculated as (Incremental Sales Revenue − Marketing Cost)/Marketing Cost. A ROMI of 0.2, for instance, means that for every dollar spent on marketing, the company made a profit of 20 cents (Lenskold, 2003).

It's important to note that although ROMI provides a useful measure of marketing effectiveness, it has its limitations. It doesn't account for the long-term effects of marketing activities, such as brand awareness and customer loyalty. Also, it might not fully capture the impact of digital marketing activities, which often influence the customer journey in nonlinear and complex ways (Rust et al., 2004).

8.5.7 Practical Example: Calculating Return on Marketing Investment for a Digital Marketing Campaign

Drawing from our theoretical and case-based exploration, let's dive into a hands-on example, calculating ROMI for a digital marketing campaign. Consider a hypothetical example where a company named E-Fashions launched a digital marketing campaign for its new line of clothing. The total cost of the campaign, which includes expenses for content creation, ad placements, and agency fees, amounted to $50,000.

After the campaign, E-Fashions saw an increase in their online sales. They were able to trace $120,000 in revenue directly back to customers who clicked on their digital ads, through their web analytics platform. The profit margin on these sales was 60%.

To calculate the ROMI, we first need to find the incremental profit. This would be the revenue from the campaign multiplied by the profit margin, that is, $120,000 × 0.60 = $72,000.

The ROMI is then calculated as follows:

ROMI = (Incremental Profit − Marketing Investment)/Marketing Investment

ROMI = ($72,000 − $50,000)/$50,000

ROMI = 0.44 or 44%

This means that for every dollar spent on the campaign, E-Fashions made a profit of 44 cents. This result would suggest that the digital marketing campaign was quite effective (Lenskold, 2003).

Remember that although this is a simplified example, in reality, the calculation could be more complex. For instance, it could be challenging to accurately track all sales that resulted from the campaign. Also, the campaign could have benefits that are not captured in the ROMI, such as improved brand awareness or customer loyalty (Rust et al., 2004).

8.6 CONCLUSION

Chapter 8 provides a comprehensive review of MMM and attribution, two critical components in the modern marketing landscape. MMM offers a holistic perspective of the effectiveness of various marketing channels and initiatives, enabling organizations to optimize their marketing strategies and budgets. However, attribution models, particularly data-driven and multi-touch models, offer granular insights into the customer journey, highlighting the role of individual touchpoints in leading to a conversion.

Both these methods, when used effectively, can significantly improve the ROMI, a key metric that quantifies the profitability of marketing activities. By measuring ROMI, organizations can ensure that their marketing expenditures are generating a positive return and contributing to the bottom line.

As the marketing landscape becomes increasingly digital and data-driven, the importance of these concepts is expected to grow. Marketers who can effectively leverage these techniques will have a competitive advantage in driving customer engagement and achieving business.

8.7 REFERENCES

Anderl, E., Becker, I., Von Wangenheim, F., & Schumann, J. H. (2016). Mapping the customer journey: Lessons learned from graph-based online attribution modeling. *International Journal of Research in Marketing, 33*(3), 457–474.

Ataman, M. B., Van Heerde, H. J., & Mela, C. F. (2010). The long-term effect of marketing strategy on brand sales. *Journal of Marketing Research, 47*(5), 866–882.

Bendle, N. T., & Bagga, C. K. (2016). The metrics that marketers muddle. *MIT Sloan Management Review.*

Dalessandro, B., Perlich, C., Stitelman, O., & Provost, F. (2012, August). Causally motivated attribution for online advertising. *Proceedings of the Sixth International Workshop on Data Mining for Online Advertising and Internet Economy* (pp. 1–9).

Greene, W. H. (2003). *Econometric analysis*. Pearson Education India.

Gupta, S., Hanssens, D. M., Hardie, B. G., Kahn, W., Kumar, V., Lin, N., Ravishanker, N., & Sriram, S. (2006). Modelling customer lifetime value. *Journal of Service Research, 9*(2), 139–155.

Hanssens, D. M. (2015). *Empirical generalizations about marketing impact* (2nd ed.). Marketing Science Institute.

Israeli, O. (2007). A Shapley-based decomposition of the R-square of a linear regression. *The Journal of Economic Inequality, 5*, 199–212.

Kireyev, P., Pauwels, K., & Gupta, S. (2016). Do display ads influence search? Attribution and dynamics in online advertising. *International Journal of Research in Marketing, 33*(3), 475–490.

Kotler, P., & Keller, K. L. (2016). *Marketing management*. Pearson Education.

Kumar, V., Dixit, A., Javalgi, R. G., & Dass, M. (2016). Research framework, strategies, and applications of intelligent agent technologies (IATs) in marketing. *Journal of the Academy of Marketing Science, 44*, 24–45.

Kumar, V., & Gupta, S. (2016). Conceptualizing the evolution and future of advertising. *Journal of Advertising, 45*(3), 302–317.

Leeflang, P. S., Wittink, D. R., Wedel, M., & Naert, P. A. (2013). *Building models for marketing decisions* (Vol. 9). Springer Science & Business Media.

Lemon, K. N., & Verhoef, P. C. (2016). Understanding customer experience throughout the customer journey. *Journal of Marketing, 80*(6), 69–96.

Lenskold, J. D. (2003). *Marketing ROI: The path to campaign, customer, and corporate profitability*. McGraw Hill.

Lewis, R. A., & Rao, J. M. (2015). The unfavorable economics of measuring the returns to advertising. *The Quarterly Journal of Economics, 130*(4), 1941–1973.

Luxton, S., Reid, M., & Mavondo, F. (2015). Integrated marketing communication capability and brand performance. *Journal of Advertising, 44*(1), 37–46.

Pauwels, K., Silva-Risso, J., Srinivasan, S., & Hanssens, D. M. (2004). New products, sales promotions, and firm value: The case of the automobile industry. *Journal of Marketing, 68*(4), 142–156.

Provost, F., & Fawcett, T. (2013). *Data science for business: What you need to know about data mining and data-analytic thinking*. O'Reilly Media.

Rossi, P. E., & Allenby, G. M. (2003). Bayesian statistics and marketing. *Marketing Science, 22*(3), 304–328.

Rust, R. T., Lemon, K. N., & Zeithaml, V. A. (2004). Return on marketing: Using customer equity to focus marketing strategy. *Journal of Marketing, 68*(1), 109–127.

Shankar, V., Inman, J. J., Mantrala, M., Kelley, E., & Rizley, R. (2011). Innovations in shopper marketing: Current insights and future research issues. *Journal of Retailing, 87*, S29–S42.

Tellis, G. J. (2003). *Effective advertising: Understanding when, how, and why advertising works*. SAGE Publications.

Verhoef, P. C., & Donkers, B. (2005). The effect of acquisition channels on customer loyalty and cross-buying. *Journal of Interactive Marketing, 19*(2), 31–43.

Wedel, M., & Kamakura, W. A. (2000). *Market segmentation: Conceptual and methodological foundations*. Springer Science & Business Media.

Wooldridge, J. M. (2010). *Econometric analysis of cross section and panel data*. MIT Press.

EXERCISE 8.1: MARKETING MIX MODELING (MMM)

Objective: Develop a multiple regression model to understand the impact of various marketing efforts on a hypothetical company's sales.

Tasks:

1. Load the generated data into a DataFrame.
2. Perform exploratory data analysis (EDA) to understand data distributions and correlations.
3. Build a multiple regression model to analyze the influence of each marketing channel on sales.
4. Interpret the coefficients and evaluate the model's performance.

Steps:

1. **Loading Libraries:**

   First, we need to import the necessary libraries for data manipulation and statistical analysis.

```
1. import pandas as pd
2. import numpy as np
3. import statsmodels.api as sm
```

   - **pandas** is used for data manipulation and analysis.
   - **numpy** is for numerical operations.
   - **statsmodels** is for estimating and interpreting models for statistical analysis.

2. **Loading the Data:**

   Next, we load the generated CSV file into a DataFrame. This is where our MMM data resides.

```
4. df = pd.read_csv('/mnt/data/marketing_mix_modeling_
data.csv')
```

   - We use "**pd.read_csv**" to read the CSV file and load it into a Data-Frame named **df**.

3. **Exploratory Data Analysis (EDA):**

   Before modeling, it's crucial to understand the data. Let's get a quick overview and check for any anomalies or patterns.

```
5. print(df.describe())
6. print(df.corr())
```

- **df.describe()** provides a statistical summary of the DataFrame, including mean, standard deviation, and quartiles.

- **df.corr()** calculates the correlation matrix, helping us understand the relationships between different variables.

4. **Preparing the Data for Regression:**

    We separate the dependent variable ('Sales') and independent variables (marketing spends and discount).

```
7. X = df[['TV_Ad_Spend', 'Online_Ad_Spend', 'Radio_Ad_Spend',
'Promotional_Discount']] # Independent variables
8. y = df['Sales'] # Dependent variable
```

5. **Adding a Constant to the Model:**

    For our regression model, we add a constant to the independent variables. This is a typical step in linear regression to include an intercept in the model.

```
9. X = sm.add_constant(X)
```

6. **Building the Regression Model:**

    Now, we use ordinary least squares (OLS) regression to model the relationship between the independent and dependent variables.

```
10. model = sm.OLS(y, X).fit()
```

- **sm.OLS** is used to create an OLS regression model. **fit()** is then called on this model to fit it to the data.

7. **Viewing the Regression Results:**

    Finally, we print the summary of our regression model to see the coefficients and other statistical measures.

```
11. print(model.summary())
```

- **model.summary()** provides a detailed summary of the regression results, including coefficients, R-squared value, p-values, and so on.

EXERCISE 8.1: OUTPUT

1. **Exploratory Data Analysis (EDA):**

- **Statistical Summary:**

    - **Sales**: Ranged from about 22,195 to 99,835 with an average of approximately 62,417.

- **TV_Ad_Spend, Online_Ad_Spend, Radio_Ad_Spend:** Showed varying degrees of expenditure, with TV ads generally having the highest spending.
- **Promotional_Discount:** Varied between 5% to about 20%.
- **Correlation Matrix:**
  - The correlations between the marketing spends (**TV_Ad_Spend, Online_Ad_Spend, Radio_Ad_Spend**) and **Sales** were relatively low. This suggests that these variables may not have a strong linear relationship with sales in this dataset.
  - **Radio_Ad_Spend** had a negative correlation with **Sales,** which is an interesting aspect that merits further investigation.

2. **Regression Model Results:**
- **Coefficients:**
  - **TV_Ad_Spend, Online_Ad_Spend, Radio_Ad_Spend,** and **Promotional_Discount** had coefficients of 0.1358, 0.1138, −2.1305, and −390.0831 respectively.
  - It's notable that **Radio_Ad_Spend** had a negative coefficient, indicating a potential negative impact on sales for each unit increase in radio ad spending.
- **Model Fit:**
  - The R-squared value of the model was 0.018, which is quite low. This suggests that the model explains only a small portion of the variability in the sales data.
  - The F-statistic and its associated p-value indicate that the model is not statistically significant at a conventional significance level.
- **Interpretation:**
  - The model's low explanatory power (R-squared) and the lack of statistical significance (p-value of the F-statistic) suggest that the model may not be the best fit for this data. It could be due to the nature of the synthetic data or the possibility that the relationship between these variables and sales is not linear.
  - The negative coefficient for **Radio_Ad_Spend** might imply that radio advertising is not effective for this particular dataset or there are other confounding factors not accounted for in the model.

In real-world scenarios, such findings would lead to further investigations, perhaps considering additional variables, exploring nonlinear models, or refining data collection methods. This exercise is valuable for understanding the process of building and interpreting a marketing mix model, even though the synthetic nature of the data may limit the real-world applicability of these specific findings.

EXERCISE 8.2: DATA-DRIVEN ATTRIBUTION

Objective: Analyze customer journey data to attribute conversions to different marketing touchpoints using a probabilistic model.

Tasks:

1. Load the generated data into a DataFrame.
2. Perform data preprocessing to structure the touchpoints data.
3. Apply a probabilistic model to assign conversion credit to each touchpoint.
4. Analyze the results to identify which touchpoints have the most significant influence on conversions.

Steps:

1. **Loading Libraries:**

   As with the previous exercise, we begin by importing necessary libraries.

```
1. import pandas as pd
2. from sklearn.preprocessing import MultiLabelBinarizer
3. from sklearn.linear_model import LogisticRegression
```

- **pandas** is for data manipulation.
- **MultiLabelBinarizer** from **sklearn.preprocessing** is used to transform the touchpoint data into a binary format suitable for modeling.
- **LogisticRegression** from **sklearn.linear_model** is for performing the 'LogisticRegression' model.

2. **Loading the Data:**

   Next, load the synthetic data for data-driven attribution.

```
4. df_attribution = pd.read_csv('/mnt/data/data_driven_
attribution_data.csv')
```

3. **Preprocessing the Data:**

   The 'Touchpoints' column contains lists of touchpoints, which need to be transformed into a format that can be used for modeling.

```
5. # Splitting the touchpoint strings into lists
6. df_attribution['Touchpoints'] = df_attribution
['Touchpoints'].apply(lambda x: x.split(', '))
7. # Using MultiLabelBinarizer to transform the touchpoint
lists into binary format
8. mlb = MultiLabelBinarizer()
9. touchpoints_binary = mlb.fit_transform(df_attribution
['Touchpoints'])
```

```
10. # Creating a DataFrame for the binary touchpoints
11. df_touchpoints = pd.DataFrame(touchpoints_binary,
columns=mlb.classes_)
```

4. **Preparing the Model:**

Now, prepare the data for logistic regression analysis, which we will use for attribution.

```
12. X = df_touchpoints # Independent variables (binary
touchpoints)
13. y = df_attribution['Conversion'] # Dependent variable
(conversion)
```

5. **Building and Fitting the 'LogisticRegression' Model:**

With the data prepared, we can build and fit the 'LogisticRegression' model.

```
14. model = LogisticRegression()
15. model.fit(X, y)
```

6. **Interpreting the Model Coefficients:**

The coefficients from the logistic regression will help us understand the impact of each touchpoint on the likelihood of conversion.

```
16. coefficients = pd.DataFrame({"Touchpoint": mlb.classes_,
"Coefficient": model.coef_[0]})
```

7. **Sorting the Coefficients:**

To better interpret the results, we sort the touchpoints by their coefficients. Higher coefficients suggest a greater positive impact on conversion.

```
17. sorted_coefficients = coefficients.sort_
values(by="Coefficient", ascending=False)
```

Let's execute this code to analyze the touchpoints and their influence on conversion in our synthetic dataset.

EXERCISE 8.2: OUTPUT

The sorted coefficients represent the impact of each touchpoint on the likelihood of conversion. A positive coefficient suggests a positive influence on conversion, and a negative coefficient suggests a negative influence.

1. **Touchpoints and Their Coefficients:**
   - **Online Ad:** Coefficient of 0.210482. This indicates the strongest positive influence on conversion among the touchpoints.

- **Social Media:** Coefficient of 0.082429. This also positively influences conversion but to a lesser extent than online ads.
- **Email:** Coefficient of −0.079067. This touchpoint seems to have a slight negative influence on conversion.
- **Direct Visit:** Coefficient of −0.290814. This indicates a negative influence on conversion, more so than email.
- **Search Ad:** Coefficient of −0.381058. This has the most significant negative impact on conversion among the touchpoints.

2. **Interpretation:**
   - **Positive Influence:** The positive coefficients for 'Online Ad' and 'Social Media' suggest that these touchpoints are effective in driving conversions in the synthetic dataset.
   - **Negative Influence:** 'Email', 'Direct Visit', and 'Search Ad' showing negative coefficients indicate that these touchpoints may be less effective or even counterproductive in leading to conversions in this specific dataset.

This analysis provides a hypothetical insight into how different touchpoints might influence customer conversion. In a real-world scenario, these insights could be instrumental in guiding marketing strategies, though the results would be contingent on the quality and nature of the actual data.

This exercise, with its focus on logistic regression for attribution, highlights the potential of data-driven methods in understanding customer journeys and optimizing marketing touchpoints for better conversion outcomes.

CHAPTER **9**

Customer Journey
Analytics

9.1 INTRODUCTION

The modern customer journey is complex and multifaceted, cutting across multiple channels and touchpoints over time. It starts from the moment a customer becomes aware of a brand or product, and continues through consideration, evaluation, purchase, and post-purchase experiences (Lemon & Verhoef, 2016). This evolving consumer behavior has made it imperative for marketers to understand and analyze the customer journey in order to optimize marketing strategies and deliver superior customer experiences (Rawson et al., 2013).

Customer journey analytics is the process of tracking and analyzing how customers use combinations of channels to interact with a company and then using those insights to enable customer engagement in the most optimized way (Verhoef et al., 2015). It encompasses a variety of techniques, including customer journey mapping, touchpoint analysis, cross-channel marketing optimization, and path to purchase and attribution analysis. By leveraging these techniques, businesses can gain a holistic view of the customer journey, uncover hidden customer insights, and identify opportunities to streamline the journey and enhance the overall customer experience (Klaus & Maklan, 2013).

This chapter will delve into these concepts and provide practical examples of how businesses can leverage customer journey analytics to drive marketing success.

9.2 CUSTOMER JOURNEY MAPPING

9.2.1 Overview of Customer Journey Mapping

Customer journey mapping is a technique used by marketers to visually depict the customer's interactions with a brand across various touchpoints and channels (Lemon & Verhoef, 2016). This method helps to illustrate the customer's path from initial contact through the process of engagement, purchase, and beyond.

Journey maps are typically created from the customer's perspective and are designed to depict the customer's experiences, emotions, and expectations at each touchpoint (Rawson et al., 2013). They can be used to uncover moments of friction or pain points in the customer's journey, as well as opportunities for enhancing the customer experience (Zomerdijk & Voss, 2010).

Customer journey mapping is a powerful tool for driving customer-centricity within an organization. It helps to break down silos by encouraging cross-functional collaboration and fostering a shared understanding of the customer's journey across the organization (Stein & Ramaseshan, 2016). Furthermore, it provides valuable insights that can guide strategic decision-making and inform the design of more effective and personalized marketing interventions (Verhoef et al., 2015).

9.2.2 Stages of the Customer Journey: Awareness to Advocacy

Every interaction a customer has with a brand adds to their journey. This journey can be broadly divided into distinct stages:

1. **Awareness.** This is the stage where a potential customer first learns about a brand or product. They might come across an advertisement, a social media post, or hear about it through word-of-mouth. The focus for brands in this stage is to capture attention and generate interest (Edelman, 2015).

2. **Consideration.** Having gained some knowledge about the brand, the potential customer is now actively researching and comparing options. They might visit the brand's website, read reviews, or seek recommendations. Brands should offer valuable and easily accessible information at this stage to sway the customer's decision.

3. **Purchase/decision.** The customer has decided to make a purchase. The experience at this stage, including the ease of the purchasing process and the quality of customer service, can heavily influence their overall perception of the brand (Lemon & Verhoef, 2016).

4. **Retention/post-purchase.** After the purchase, the journey doesn't end. How the brand supports the customer, whether it's through after-sales service, warranty support, or simply through thank-you messages, plays a crucial role in determining if the customer will return.

5. **Advocacy.** The ultimate goal for many brands is to turn customers into advocates. Satisfied customers may share their positive experiences, recommend the brand to others, or even write favorable reviews. This stage of advocacy can provide significant organic growth and brand trustworthiness (Klaus & Maklan, 2013).

9.2.3 Tools and Techniques for Journey Mapping

To create an effective customer journey map, businesses often employ a mix of tools and techniques, including the following:

- **Interviews and surveys.** Direct feedback from customers can provide a wealth of information. Brands can conduct interviews or distribute surveys to gather insights on customer experiences at various touchpoints (Zomerdijk & Voss, 2010).

- **Web and app analytics.** Tools such as Google Analytics can provide data on how customers interact with a brand's digital platforms, revealing potential pain points or stages where customers might drop off (Verhoef et al., 2015).

- **Heat maps.** These tools visually represent where users click, move, and scroll on a web page, giving insights into their behavior and preferences.

- **Customer feedback platforms.** Platforms such as Uservoice or GetSatisfaction enable customers to provide direct feedback, report issues, or suggest features.
- **Workshops.** Organizing internal workshops with sales, marketing, and support teams can help gather insights from different departmental perspectives, ensuring a comprehensive journey map.

9.2.4 Leveraging Journey Maps for Strategy Development

Journey maps, once created, can be instrumental in formulating a brand's strategy:

1. **Identify gaps.** By visually representing the customer's journey, brands can quickly identify areas that might be lacking in terms of engagement or support (Rawson et al., 2013).
2. **Optimize touchpoints.** With a clear view of all touchpoints, brands can allocate resources more effectively, ensuring that every interaction adds value to the customer's experience.
3. **Enhance personalization.** By understanding customer behavior, preferences, and pain points, brands can craft more personalized and effective marketing campaigns.
4. **Foster collaboration.** A shared understanding of the customer journey can promote cross-departmental collaboration, ensuring that teams are aligned in their efforts to enhance the customer experience (Stein & Ramaseshan, 2016).
5. **Measure impact.** By comparing journey maps from different periods, brands can measure the impact of any changes or improvements made.

In conclusion, understanding the stages of the customer journey, using tools for journey mapping, and leveraging these maps for strategy development are integral to optimizing the customer experience. The insights gained can guide brands in delivering more personalized, efficient, and impactful interactions at every touchpoint.

9.2.5 Key Concepts in Customer Journey Mapping

Customer journey mapping is a strategic process of capturing the total customer experience across all touchpoints with a brand. The process involves the identification of different stages a customer goes through in their interaction with the brand, from the initial contact to the final purchase or interaction. Key concepts involved in this process include the following:

- **Customer persona.** A customer persona is a semifictional character that represents a segment of a company's target audience. The persona is based on real data about customer demographics and behaviors, along with educated speculation about their motivations, challenges, and concerns (Cooper et al., 2014).

- **Touchpoints.** These are the points of interaction between the customer and the brand. They can occur across different channels (such as website, social media, in-store) and at various stages of the customer journey (Lemon & Verhoef, 2016).

- **Moments of truth.** Introduced by Procter & Gamble, these are critical interactions where customers invest a high amount of emotional energy in the outcome. They significantly influence the customer's perception of the brand (Lemon & Verhoef, 2016).

- **Pain points.** These are obstacles or frustrations experienced by the customer at different stages of their journey. Identifying these points can help brands improve their customer experience (Rawson et al., 2013).

- **Emotion mapping.** This involves capturing the emotional journey of the customer alongside their physical journey. It helps in understanding how customers feel at different stages, which can greatly affect their overall experience (Stein & Ramaseshan, 2016).

9.2.6 Practical Example: Customer Journey Mapping for a Retail Company

Customer journey mapping can be a crucial tool for retail companies in understanding their customers' experiences and identifying areas for improvement. Here is a practical example of how a retail company might use customer journey mapping:

1. **Customer persona creation.** The company first creates customer personas based on its target audience. This could include a busy working parent, a price-conscious student, or an older retiree. These personas are created using a combination of demographic data, customer behavior analytics, market research, and customer feedback (Cooper et al., 2014).

2. **Identifying touchpoints.** The company then identifies all potential touchpoints a customer might have with the brand. This could include seeing an ad online, visiting the website, receiving an email newsletter, visiting a physical store, contacting customer service, or making a purchase.

3. **Mapping the customer journey.** The company maps out the journey for each persona, from initial awareness through to purchase and post-purchase interactions. They identify key moments of truth—instances that have a significant impact on the customer's overall experience (Lemon & Verhoef, 2016).

4. **Identifying pain points.** The company uses customer feedback, social media listening, and data analysis to identify pain points in the customer journey. For example, they might find that customers are frustrated by the length of time it takes to receive an online order or the difficulty in finding products in-store (Rawson et al., 2013).

5. **Developing solutions.** The company uses the insights gained from the customer journey map to develop solutions to the identified pain points. This could include introducing express shipping options, improving in-store signage, or introducing a more user-friendly website design (Stein & Ramaseshan, 2016).

By using customer journey mapping, retail companies can gain a better understanding of their customers' experiences, identify areas for improvement, and take action to enhance the overall customer journey.

9.3 TOUCHPOINT ANALYSIS

9.3.1 Overview of Touchpoint Analysis

Touchpoint analysis is a crucial component of customer journey analytics. It focuses on identifying and evaluating all the points of interaction between a customer and a brand, from the initial discovery phase through the purchasing process, and even into post-purchase interactions (Lemon & Verhoef, 2016).

These touchpoints can occur across multiple channels and include a wide range of interactions, such as browsing a company's website, speaking with a sales representative, receiving marketing emails, engaging with the brand on social media, or visiting a physical store. Each of these touchpoints can significantly affect a customer's perception of a brand, their decision-making process, and their overall customer experience (Gentile et al., 2007).

Effective touchpoint analysis involves mapping out all potential touchpoints, understanding how customers interact with these touchpoints, and assessing the quality of these interactions. This requires a combination of data collection methods, including customer surveys, social media monitoring, website analytics, and sales data (Verhoef et al., 2009).

Touchpoint analysis is particularly valuable for identifying pain points, which can then be addressed to improve customer satisfaction and loyalty. It also helps brands understand which touchpoints have the most significant impact on customer decisions, enabling them to focus their resources effectively (Stein & Ramaseshan, 2016).

9.3.2 Identifying Key Touchpoints in the Customer Journey

Recognizing key touchpoints in the customer journey is central to providing an optimized customer experience (see Table 9.1). The inception of digital evolution has amplified these touchpoints, requiring brands to meticulously map out each interaction to ensure a holistic understanding. Employing methods such as customer surveys, feedback forms, and digital analytics tools can offer brands insights into when and where these interactions occur, thereby enabling them to allocate resources effectively (Rawson et al., 2013).

Although the digital landscape has vastly expanded the array of touchpoints, it's crucial to recognize the continued significance of offline interactions in shaping the

Table 9.1 Potential Key Touchpoints in a Customer's Journey.

Touchpoint	Description
Website visit	Initial landing on the e-commerce website
Product search	Using search to find specific products
Product details	Viewing detailed specifications and reviews of a product
Adding to cart	Selecting items and adding them to the shopping cart
Checkout	Process of finalizing the purchase, including selecting delivery options
Payment	Completing the financial transaction
Post-purchase email	Emails received post-purchase, including receipts and shipping notifications
Product delivery	Moment the customer receives and unpacks the ordered products
Returns or support	Engaging with customer service for post-purchase support or processing returns

Table 9.2 Potential Offline Key Touchpoints in a Customer's Journey.

Touchpoint	Description
In-store experience	The ambiance, layout, and navigation ease within a physical store; includes interactions with products and sales representatives
Phone inquiry	Calls made to inquire about products, services, or any other information
Physical catalogues	Printed catalogs or brochures provided to customers
In-store promotions	Special events or promotions held within the physical premises of the store
Direct mail	Physical mailers or promotional offers sent to customers' homes
Product demonstrations	In-person demonstrations or trial sessions of a product
Face-to-face customer support	Direct interactions with customer service representatives or help desks
Word of mouth	Personal recommendations or feedback from friends, family, or acquaintances
Events and workshops	Brand-held events or workshops customers may attend

customer experience. Offline touchpoints, often termed as *traditional touchpoints*, hold immense value as they frequently offer direct, human-centric interactions that can deeply influence perceptions and emotions. For instance, the physical ambiance of a store, the demeanor of sales staff, or the ease of a phone call inquiry can leave lasting impressions on customers. Table 9.2 is a continuation of Table 9.1, highlighting some potential offline touchpoints.

Incorporating online and offline touchpoints offers a comprehensive view of the multifaceted journey customers embark on. To truly master the customer journey, brands need to ensure cohesion between these touchpoints, fostering a seamless transition and consistent experience.

9.3.3 Quantifying Touchpoint Impact and Effectiveness

Given myriad touchpoints in a customer's journey, it is pivotal for businesses to ascertain the impact and effectiveness of each one. Touchpoint effectiveness can be gauged by analyzing metrics such as customer satisfaction scores, conversion rates, and the frequency of engagement (Gentile et al., 2007). For instance, a brand might observe higher conversion rates on their website following interactions via a particular social media campaign, suggesting its efficacy. Advanced analytics tools, combined with attribution models, enable businesses to measure the direct and indirect impact of touchpoints, granting them the ability to discern which ones most strongly influence purchase decisions or heighten brand loyalty (Dalessandro et al., 2012). Such insights are crucial, not only for quantifying touchpoint effectiveness but also for identifying potential areas for refinement (see Figure 9.1).

The key lies in identifying the right metrics that can accurately capture this impact:

- **Customer lifetime value (CLV).** This metric estimates the total value a customer brings to a business over the duration of their relationship. CLV provides a lens into the long-term value of a customer, accounting for all touchpoints they've interacted with. By comparing the CLV of customers who have experienced different touchpoints, marketers can ascertain which interactions contribute most significantly to long-term profitability.

- **Churn rate.** This metric reveals the percentage of customers who cease their relationship with a company over a specific period. High churn rates may indicate problems with specific touchpoints or the overall customer journey. By studying the churn rate in tandem with touchpoint interactions, businesses can identify which channels may be contributing to customer attrition and rectify them.

- **Net promoter score (NPS).** NPS measures customers' likelihood to recommend a brand to others. By correlating NPS scores with specific touchpoints, brands can discern which interactions lead to higher brand advocacy. A decline in NPS after an interaction at a particular touchpoint can be a red flag, signaling a need for further investigation and possible refinement.

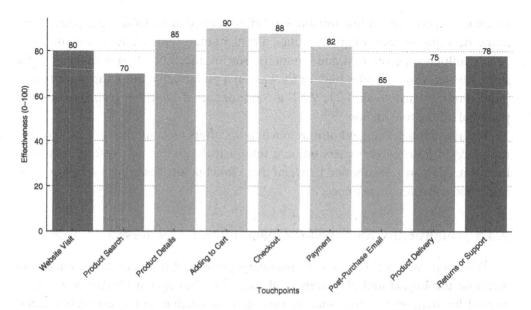

Figure 9.1 Impact and Effectiveness of Each Touchpoint.

- **Customer effort score (CES).** CES gauges the ease with which customers can achieve their goals with a brand, be it purchasing a product or resolving an issue. A high CES post-interaction can suggest friction in that touchpoint, necessitating optimization.
- **Average order value (AOV).** Tracking AOV alongside touchpoint data can offer insights into which channels drive higher-value transactions. For example, if a specific email campaign results in a spike in AOV, it suggests that campaign's strong influence on purchasing behavior.
- **Engagement rate.** Typically used for digital channels such as social media or email campaigns, engagement rate measures the percentage of the audience that interacts with content. High engagement rates often signify the effectiveness of a touchpoint in capturing customer interest and prompting action.

In summary, by using these metrics, businesses can gain a comprehensive view of the effectiveness of their touchpoints. By regularly assessing these figures, they can continuously optimize the customer journey, ensuring sustained growth and brand loyalty. Remember, in the fast-paced world of marketing, what gets measured gets improved.

9.3.4 Improving and Refining Touchpoints

With a clear understanding of touchpoint impact and effectiveness, businesses can begin the process of refinement. Continuous enhancement is vital in the dynamic landscape of customer interactions. A touchpoint that proves effective today might evolve or become obsolete tomorrow. Feedback mechanisms, such as customer reviews or NPSs, provide direct insights into areas of improvement (Stein & Ramaseshan, 2016). Additionally, A/B testing, especially in digital channels, enables businesses to compare the performance of different touchpoint strategies, thus aiding in refining the most impactful ones. For instance, if customers frequently abandon online shopping carts, improving the checkout process's simplicity and speed could reduce dropout rates (Edelman, 2015).

9.3.5 Integrating Touchpoints for Seamless Experiences

Because customers often interact with brands across various touchpoints, a disjointed experience can result in confusion or dissatisfaction. Thus, it's essential to integrate touchpoints to deliver a consistent and seamless customer journey. Centralized data repositories or integrated customer relationship management (CRM) systems can offer businesses a holistic view of customer interactions across touchpoints (Verhoef et al., 2015). This integration ensures that if a customer inquires about a product on social media and later visits the brand's website, their experience remains consistent. Furthermore, advanced technologies such as AI can harness this integrated data to predict future customer interactions, enabling brands to proactively tailor touchpoints, thereby enhancing the overall customer experience (Klaus & Maklan, 2013).

9.3.6   Key Concepts in Touchpoint Analysis

Key concepts in touchpoint analysis are based on understanding how customers interact with a brand across different stages of their journey:

- **Touchpoint.** A touchpoint is any point of interaction between a customer and a brand (Baxendale et al., 2015). This includes advertising, social media interactions, customer service encounters, in-store experiences, and any other medium through which the customer engages with the brand.

- **Customer journey.** The customer journey is the complete set of experiences that customers go through when interacting with a company or brand (Lemon & Verhoef, 2016). It includes all stages from initial awareness and consideration, through the purchase, and onto post-purchase interactions.

- **Pain points.** Pain points are any aspects of the customer's interaction with a brand that cause frustration or dissatisfaction (Rawson et al., 2013). Identifying and addressing these is a key part of touchpoint analysis.

- **Moments of truth.** These are crucial touchpoints that significantly influence the customer's perception of a brand (Schmitt, 2010). These can be make-or-break moments for customer satisfaction and loyalty.

- **Omnichannel experience.** In today's digital age, customers often interact with brands across multiple channels (e.g., online, in-store, social media). An effective touchpoint analysis should consider all these channels and how they contribute to the overall customer experience (Verhoef et al., 2015).

9.3.7   Practical Example: Touchpoint Analysis for an E-Commerce Company

In this section, we'll explore how an e-commerce company, E-shop, uses touchpoint analysis to better understand their customer interactions and experiences. To start, E-shop maps out all the different touchpoints where customers interact with their brand. These include the website, email communications, social media channels, customer service interactions, and other digital platforms such as mobile apps. Each touchpoint is analyzed in detail, taking into account factors such as the user interface, ease of navigation, response times, and personalized engagement.

E-shop then gathers data from various sources, such as website analytics, customer surveys, social media listening tools, and customer service records, to understand customer behaviors and perceptions at each touchpoint (Verhoef et al., 2015). They pay particular attention to pain points—areas where customers express dissatisfaction or frustration. For instance, if customers complain about the checkout process being too complicated, this becomes a focus area for improvement.

Next, E-shop identifies the moments of truth—crucial stages in the customer journey that significantly affect the customer's decision to purchase or repurchase (Schmitt, 2010). This could be the product selection process, the ease of finding information, or the quality of customer service interactions.

Based on this analysis, E-shop implements changes to enhance the customer experience at each touchpoint. They may redesign parts of the website for easier navigation, refine their email communication strategy to provide more personalized content, or invest in better customer service training. They continually monitor customer feedback and metrics to assess the effectiveness of these changes and make further improvements as necessary.

E-shop's touchpoint analysis (see Figure 9.2) demonstrates how a systematic review of customer interactions across all touchpoints can provide valuable insights for enhancing the customer experience and improving business performance.

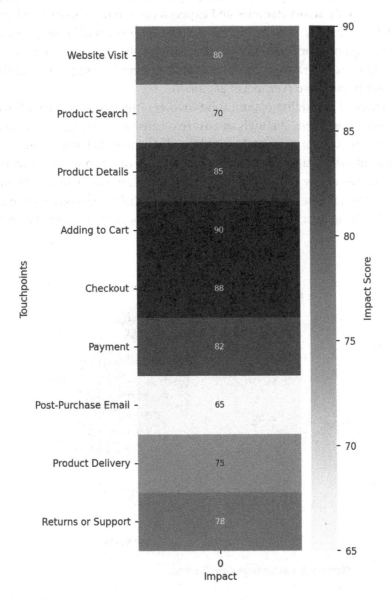

Figure 9.2 Touchpoint Analysis for an E-Commerce Company, Marking High- and Low-Impact Touchpoints.

9.4 CROSS-CHANNEL MARKETING OPTIMIZATION

9.4.1 Overview of Cross-Channel Marketing Optimization

Cross-channel marketing optimization is an advanced marketing strategy that involves creating a consistent and seamless customer experience across multiple channels. Today's customers engage with brands across a variety of touchpoints: websites, mobile apps, social media, email, physical stores, and more. Each of these channels offers a unique opportunity to connect with customers and influence their purchasing decisions (Neslin & Shankar, 2009).

At the heart of cross-channel marketing optimization is the understanding that customers move fluidly across channels and expect a consistent experience wherever they interact with the brand. They might browse products on a mobile app, seek advice on social media, compare prices on the website, and finally make a purchase in a physical store. Each of these interactions contributes to their overall perception of the brand and their decision to purchase (Verhoef et al., 2015).

Cross-channel marketing optimization involves integrating and coordinating marketing efforts across these channels to ensure a consistent and personalized customer experience. It requires a deep understanding of customer behaviors and preferences, robust data analytics capabilities to track and analyze customer interactions across channels, and the agility to respond to customer needs in real time (see Figure 9.3).

By optimizing marketing efforts across channels, companies can engage customers more effectively, deliver more personalized experiences, and ultimately drive better

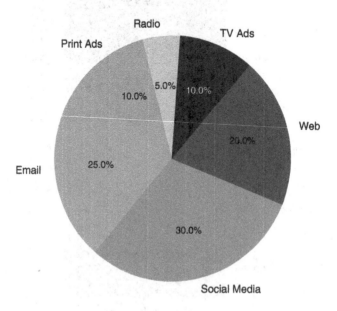

Figure 9.3 Various Marketing Channels.

business outcomes. A successful cross-channel marketing strategy can lead to increased customer engagement, higher conversion rates, and improved customer loyalty.

9.4.2 Need for a Unified Cross-Channel Strategy

In today's connected age, consumers interact with brands through multiple channels such as websites, mobile apps, social media, and brick-and-mortar stores. Each of these interactions can shape a consumer's perception, loyalty, and purchasing decisions. A fragmented approach, where each channel operates in isolation, can lead to inconsistent messaging, potential missed opportunities, and customer confusion (Neslin & Shankar, 2009). A unified cross-channel strategy, however, ensures consistent and synchronized messaging, creating a cohesive brand narrative irrespective of the medium. Such a holistic strategy is crucial for brands to maintain relevance, because customers expect seamless experiences that resonate regardless of their interaction point. Moreover, a harmonized strategy can optimize marketing spend, enhance customer satisfaction, and offer better ROI by leveraging the strengths of each channel in concert rather than in isolation (Verhoef et al., 2015).

To provide a clear comparative perspective, Table 9.3 outlines the advantages and disadvantages of employing singular versus integrated cross-channel strategies, highlighting the potential impacts of each on customer experience and marketing effectiveness.

9.4.3 Analyzing Cross-Channel Behavior and Patterns

Understanding customer behavior across different channels is essential for an effective unified strategy. This involves tracking and analyzing how consumers move between channels, their preferences within each channel, and the sequence of their interactions (Edelman, 2015). For instance, a consumer might discover a product on social media, research it on a company website, but finalize their purchase in a physical store. Recognizing such patterns helps in predicting customer behaviors, enabling marketers to tailor their strategies to facilitate and optimize these cross-channel journeys. Advanced

Table 9.3 Advantages and Disadvantages of Singular Versus Cross-Channel Strategies.

Strategy	Pros	Cons
Singular channel	Easier to manage and optimize Focused approach can yield deeper insights for that specific channel	Misses out on insights from other channels May not provide a comprehensive view of customer behavior
Integrated cross-channel	Provides a holistic view of the customer journey Allows for more personalized and timely engagement	Requires more sophisticated tools and expertise Risk of information overload if not managed properly

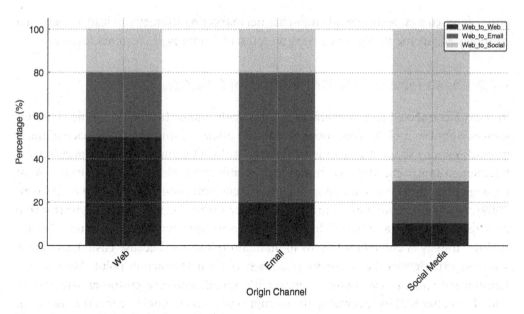

Figure 9.4 Cross-Channel Behavior and Patterns.

analytical tools can provide granular insights into these behaviors, showcasing where consumers drop off, where they engage the most, and the potential reasons for such behaviors (Ghose & Todri-Adamopoulos, 2016; see Figure 9.4).

Actionable insights derived from cross-channel behavior analysis are the linchpin in shifting from mere observation to strategic optimization. These insights, when translated effectively, can serve as a road map, directing marketers about where to allocate resources, which touchpoints to bolster, and how to remedy potential pitfalls in the customer journey. For example, using a technique such as sequence analysis can help marketers identify common paths customers take, highlighting optimal sequences that lead to conversions and sequences where customers often drop off. Another methodology is cluster analysis, which segments customers based on similar cross-channel behaviors, empowering marketers to craft personalized strategies for each segment. Furthermore, multi-touch attribution models can pinpoint which channels have the most significant influence on a customer's decision-making process. With such actionable insights, businesses can proactively refine their strategies, ensuring they not only meet but also anticipate and exceed customer expectations. By embedding these methodologies into their analytical processes, brands can turn data into a strategic weapon, always staying one step ahead in the ever-evolving game of customer engagement.

9.4.4 Tools for Cross-Channel Analytics

To effectively analyze cross-channel behavior, robust tools and platforms are indispensable. Many modern analytics platforms offer multichannel tracking capabilities.

Table 9.4 Comparison of Tools Available for Cross-Channel Analytics.

Tool	Features	Pricing	Ease of Use
ChannelMaster	Real-time analytics Segmentation ROI tracking	$$$	Medium
OptiFlow	Automated reports Customer journey mapping Segmentation	$$	Easy
JourneyScope	Advanced visualization Real-time analytics Conversion tracking	$$$$	Hard
TrackPulse	ROI tracking Automated reports Advanced visualization	$$	Easy

Google Analytics, for instance, provides insights into how users navigate between various channels before completing a desired action (Chaffey, 2018). More specialized platforms such as Adobe's Experience Cloud offer a suite of solutions designed to measure and optimize customer interactions across channels. Additionally, CRM systems such as Salesforce or HubSpot can integrate data from various touchpoints, giving brands a comprehensive view of customer journeys. Employing these tools can provide businesses with actionable insights, from pinpointing successful touchpoints to identifying areas that need refinement (Rust & Huang, 2014; see Table 9.4).

9.4.5 Case Studies: Successful Cross-Channel Campaigns

Nike's "The Ten" campaign. Nike collaborated with designer Virgil Abloh to create a unique blend of online and offline engagements. They used their SNKRS app for exclusive content and early releases, coupled with pop-up workshops in major cities worldwide. This multipronged approach made consumers feel involved and engaged across digital and physical spaces, leading to heightened brand loyalty and substantial sales (Berman, 2018).

Sephora's digital store experience. Sephora seamlessly integrated online and in-store experiences. In-store, they introduced Sephora + Pantone Color IQ, a service that scans the surface of your skin and matches a foundation shade available in the store. Customers can then save this shade to their online profile, facilitating online purchases in the future. This synergy between the physical and digital experience resulted in increased customer satisfaction and streamlined shopping experiences (Lemon & Verhoef, 2016).

These case studies underscore the importance and efficacy of unified cross-channel strategies. Brands that succeed in weaving together online and offline experiences stand to gain in customer trust, loyalty, and revenue.

9.4.6   Key Concepts in Cross-Channel Marketing Optimization

Cross-channel marketing optimization involves several key concepts:

- **Omnichannel experience.** The term *omnichannel* refers to a type of retail that integrates the different methods of shopping available to consumers (online, in a physical store, or by phone). The customer's experience is at the center of this approach, in which the goal is to deliver a seamless and consistent experience across all channels (Verhoef et al., 2015).

- **Customer data integration.** For successful cross-channel optimization, brands need to integrate customer data from all channels. This includes online behavior, transaction data, and even offline interactions. The unified view of the customer helps brands deliver personalized experiences across channels (Kumar & Reinartz, 2018).

- **Personalization.** Personalization is the process of delivering individualized content through data analysis and digital technology. This is an essential aspect of cross-channel marketing optimization because it enables businesses to tailor their messages and offers based on a customer's past behavior and preferences (Li & Kannan, 2014).

- **Real-time interaction management.** In the era of digital marketing, real-time interaction management has become crucial. Brands need to respond to customer actions immediately, whether it's a comment on social media, a product search on the website, or a purchase in the store (Rust & Huang, 2014).

- **Attribution modeling.** Attribution modeling involves determining which marketing touchpoints contribute to conversion and to what extent. Understanding this helps marketers optimize their marketing efforts across channels (Dalessandro et al., 2012).

9.4.7   Practical Example: Cross-Channel Marketing Optimization for a Travel Company

The travel industry is one where the customer journey is often complex and multifaceted, involving various touchpoints across multiple channels, making it a prime example for understanding cross-channel marketing optimization.

Suppose we consider a hypothetical company, TravelCo. TravelCo is a well-established company offering a range of services from flight bookings and hotel reservations to holiday packages. They have a significant online presence with a user-friendly website, a mobile application, and active social media profiles. They also have an offline presence through local travel agents and direct mail.

TravelCo decides to implement cross-channel marketing optimization. Their first step is to integrate customer data from all channels to create a unified view of their customers. This includes tracking online behavior on their website and mobile app, interaction data from social media, and offline data from travel agents (Kumar & Reinartz, 2018).

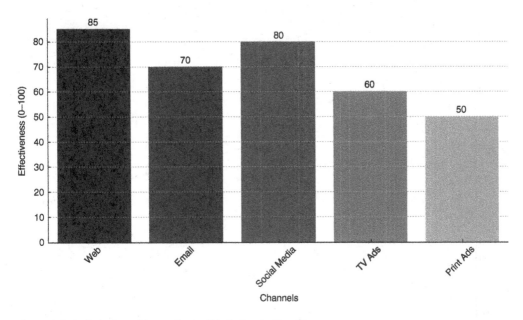

Figure 9.5 Optimization of Cross-Channel Marketing for TravelCo.

With this data, they leverage machine learning algorithms to predict customer preferences and personalize their offers. For instance, if a customer is frequently searching for beach destinations on their website, TravelCo can personalize their email campaigns to include more beach holiday packages (Li & Kannan, 2014).

TravelCo also implements real-time interaction management. If a customer comments on their social media post asking about a particular holiday package, they immediately respond with the required information. Moreover, they provide personalized recommendations based on the customer's interaction history (Rust & Huang, 2014).

Finally, TravelCo uses attribution modeling to understand which channels are contributing more to their conversions. They notice that customers who interact with their email campaigns are more likely to book a holiday package. Therefore, they decide to invest more in optimizing their email marketing efforts (Dalessandro et al., 2012; see Figure 9.5).

In this way, by implementing cross-channel marketing optimization, TravelCo can enhance their customer experience and boost their conversions.

9.5 PATH TO PURCHASE AND ATTRIBUTION ANALYSIS

9.5.1 Overview of Path to Purchase and Attribution Analysis

The path to purchase, often referred to as the *customer journey*, represents the series of steps a consumer takes from the initial awareness of a need or desire through to the eventual purchase. The complexity of this journey has grown with the proliferation of digital channels and touchpoints, making it essential for businesses to understand and map these journeys to optimize their marketing strategies (Lemon & Verhoef, 2016).

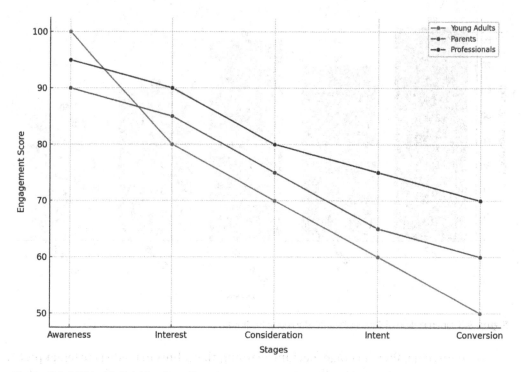

Figure 9.6 A Typical Path-to-Purchase Funnel.

Attribution analysis plays a critical role in understanding the path to purchase. Attribution is the process of identifying a set of user actions, or events, that contribute in some manner to a desired outcome, and then assigning a value to each of these events (Kireyev et al., 2016). In the context of marketing, it is the practice of determining the role that different channels play in informing, persuading, and converting consumers.

For example, a customer might first become aware of a product through a social media ad, research the product on a company's website, read reviews on a third-party site, and finally make a purchase through a targeted email promotion. Attribution analysis in this context would aim to understand the influence each of these touchpoints had on the final purchase decision (Dalessandro et al., 2012; see Figure 9.6).

Understanding the path to purchase and conducting attribution analysis are vital for optimizing marketing spend, personalizing customer interactions, and ultimately driving conversions and customer loyalty.

9.5.2 Understanding Path to Purchase: Variations and Complexities

In the digital age, the path to purchase isn't linear. A blend of digital and physical touchpoints makes the consumer journey more intricate than ever before. Traditionally, the journey from awareness to purchase was viewed as a straight progression through a funnel. Today, however, consumers might oscillate between stages, influenced by myriad touchpoints, ranging from online reviews to in-store experiences (Edelman, 2015). These variations arise from differences in consumer preferences, external influences, and the nature of the purchase itself. For instance, buying a home would involve a more convoluted path than purchasing a book. This understanding of myriad variations and complexities is essential for marketers to create tailored strategies that resonate with individual consumer behaviors and preferences (Lemon & Verhoef, 2016).

9.5.3 Quantitative Techniques for Path Analysis

Quantitative techniques provide a data-driven approach to understanding and mapping the path to purchase (see Table 9.5). Machine learning algorithms, for instance, can be employed to trace digital footprints, identifying patterns in consumer behavior (Kireyev et al., 2016). Sequence analysis can be used to determine the order in which consumers engage with touchpoints, offering insights into their preferences and habits. Additionally, clustering techniques can segment consumers based on similarities in their paths to purchase, enabling more personalized marketing strategies. By using these advanced analytical techniques, businesses can derive actionable insights, predict future behaviors, and streamline the path to purchase (Rust & Huang, 2014).

9.5.4 Implications for Attribution Modeling

With an intricate path to purchase, determining which touchpoints significantly influence consumer decisions becomes paramount. This is where attribution modeling comes into play. As paths become more complex, traditional models, such as first-click or last-click attribution, might offer an oversimplified view of the journey (Dalessandro et al., 2012). Modern scenarios demand more intricate models that consider the entire journey. Data-driven attribution models, for instance, analyze large datasets to determine the precise impact of each touchpoint. Understanding the path's intricacies and nuances ensures that the attribution model chosen

Table 9.5 Overview of Quantitative Techniques Used for Path Analysis.

Technique	Description
Sequence analysis	Analysis of sequences of events or stages in customer journeys
Markov chains	Statistical model to represent transitions between stages
Probabilistic models	Models to predict the likelihood of certain paths or outcomes
Survival analysis	Analysis to estimate the time until one or more events occur
Cluster analysis	Grouping customer journeys into clusters based on similarities

resonates with the actual consumer experience, leading to more accurate and actionable insights (Bendle & Bagga, 2016).

9.5.5 Strategies for Shortening and Optimizing the Path to Purchase

Optimizing the path to purchase can lead to quicker conversions and enhanced customer satisfaction. Several strategies can be employed to this end:

- **Frictionless experience.** Streamlining the digital experience by ensuring quick loading times, intuitive navigation, and straightforward checkout processes can significantly reduce drop-offs (Chaffey, 2018).
- **Personalization.** Tailoring content to individual consumer preferences, using data-driven insights, can make the purchase journey more engaging and efficient (Li & Kannan, 2014).
- **Omnichannel consistency.** Ensuring consistency across all touchpoints, be it in-store, on a website, or a mobile app, can prevent confusion and foster trust (Verhoef et al., 2015).
- **Educative content.** Providing consumers with comprehensive product details, reviews, and comparisons can expedite the decision-making process (Edelman, 2015).

By adopting these strategies, businesses can create a more streamlined and efficient path to purchase, leading to heightened conversions and enhanced customer loyalty.

9.5.6 Key Concepts in Path to Purchase and Attribution Analysis

Understanding the key concepts in path to purchase and attribution analysis can empower businesses to optimize their marketing strategies and improve customer experience. The path to purchase is often visualized as a funnel, beginning with awareness and interest at the top, followed by consideration, intent, evaluation, and ultimately purchase at the bottom. Each stage represents different touchpoints where a consumer interacts with a brand or product (Court et al., 2009).

Attribution analysis is used to assign credit to these different touchpoints based on their impact on the final purchase decision. There are several models for attribution analysis:

- **Last click attribution.** Credits the final touchpoint before purchase. This model is simple, but it can overemphasize the role of the last touchpoint and neglect the influence of earlier interactions (Berman, 2018).
- **First click attribution.** Credits the first touchpoint that led a customer to the product or service. Similar to the last-click model, it can oversimplify the purchase journey.

- **Linear attribution.** Credits each touchpoint equally. This model acknowledges that each interaction plays a role but doesn't account for the varying impact of different touchpoints.
- **Time decay attribution.** Gives more credit to touchpoints that occur closer to the time of purchase. This model recognizes that later interactions are likely more influential in the final decision (Berman, 2018).
- **Data-driven attribution.** Uses algorithms to assign credit to touchpoints based on how they contribute to the likelihood of purchase. This model requires significant data and analytical capabilities but provides a more nuanced view of the customer journey (Kireyev et al., 2016).

Understanding these key concepts is crucial for businesses to accurately measure the effectiveness of their marketing efforts and to make informed decisions about where to invest their resources.

9.5.7 Practical Example: Path to Purchase and Attribution Analysis for a Software Company

In the competitive field of software companies, understanding the path to purchase and implementing effective attribution analysis is vital to success. For instance, a B2B software company might have a complex sales process involving multiple touchpoints, including digital ads, email campaigns, webinars, product demos, and sales calls.

Suppose the company uses a data-driven attribution model to analyze the impact of these touchpoints on the final purchase decision. After collecting data over several months, they might find that their digital ads are effectively driving awareness and interest, but their webinars and product demos are more influential in driving final purchase decisions.

As a result, they might decide to allocate more resources to developing high-quality webinars and demos, while maintaining their digital ad spend to ensure continued awareness and interest. This could involve creating more targeted webinar content or investing in better demo software to provide a more interactive and engaging experience for potential customers (Ghose & Todri-Adamopoulos, 2016).

Furthermore, they could use this information to optimize their sales funnel, ensuring that potential customers are smoothly transitioned from awareness and interest to consideration and intent, ultimately leading to more successful conversions (see Figure 9.7).

In this way, understanding the path to purchase and attribution analysis can enable a software company to optimize its marketing strategy, improve the customer experience, and increase sales (Bendle & Bagga, 2016).

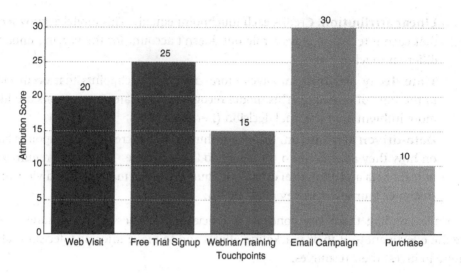

Figure 9.7 A Breakdown of the Path to Purchase and Attribution Analysis for a Software Company, Showing Influential Touchpoints.

9.6 CONCLUSION

Understanding the customer journey is an integral aspect of modern marketing strategies. By leveraging advanced analytics, marketers can gain valuable insights into how consumers interact with their brands across various touchpoints and channels, and how these interactions influence their purchasing decisions.

Customer journey analytics can provide a holistic view of the customer experience, enabling marketers to identify key moments of engagement and potential areas of friction. This can lead to more effective and personalized marketing strategies, ultimately resulting in increased customer satisfaction and loyalty (Lemon & Verhoef, 2016).

Furthermore, cross-channel marketing optimization and attribution analysis can enable marketers to allocate their resources more effectively, ensuring that each touchpoint and channel contributes to the overall marketing objectives. This can lead to improved marketing ROI and business performance (Barwitz & Maas, 2018).

As technology continues to evolve, customer journey analytics will likely become an even more critical tool for marketers, enabling them to navigate the increasingly complex and interconnected digital landscape (Edelman, 2015).

In conclusion, the concepts and examples presented in this chapter highlight the immense value of customer journey analytics in marketing. By understanding and applying these concepts, marketers can create more effective and customer-centric strategies, driving short-term results and long-term business success.

9.7 REFERENCES

Barwitz, N., & Maas, P. (2018). Understanding the omnichannel customer journey: Determinants of interaction choice. *Journal of Interactive Marketing*, *43*, 116–133.

Baxendale, S., Macdonald, E. K., & Wilson, H. N. (2015). The impact of different touchpoints on brand consideration. *Journal of Retailing*, *91*(2), 235–253.

Bendle, N. T., & Bagga, C. K. (2016). The metrics that marketers muddle. *MIT Sloan Management Review* (Spring).

Berman, R. (2018). Beyond the last touch: Attribution in online advertising. *Marketing Science, 37*(5), 771–792.

Chaffey, D. (2018). *Digital marketing: Strategy, implementation and practice*. Pearson.

Cooper, A., Reimann, R., Cronin, D., & Noessel, C. (2014). *About face: The essentials of interaction design*. Wiley.

Court, D., Elzinga, D., Mulder, S., & Vetvik, O. J. (2009). The consumer decision journey. *McKinsey Quarterly, 3*(3), 96–107.

Dalessandro, B., Perlich, C., Stitelman, O., & Provost, F. (2012, August). Causally motivated attribution for online advertising. *Proceedings of the Sixth International Workshop on Data Mining for Online Advertising and Internet Economy* (pp. 1–9).

Edelman, D. C. (2015). Competing on customer journeys. *Harvard Business Review, 93*(11), 88.

Gentile, C., Spiller, N., & Noci, G. (2007). How to sustain the customer experience: An overview of experience components that co-create value with the customer. *European Management Journal, 25*(5), 395–410.

Ghose, A., & Todri-Adamopoulos, V. (2016). Toward a digital attribution model. *MIS Quarterly, 40*(4), 889–910.

Kireyev, P., Pauwels, K., & Gupta, S. (2016). Do display ads influence search? Attribution and dynamics in online advertising. *International Journal of Research in Marketing, 33*(3), 475–490.

Klaus, P. P., & Maklan, S. (2013). Towards a better measure of customer experience. *International Journal of Market Research, 55*(2), 227–246.

Kumar, V., & Reinartz, W. (2018). *Customer relationship management*. Springer-Verlag GmbH Germany.

Lemon, K. N., & Verhoef, P. C. (2016). Understanding customer experience throughout the customer journey. *Journal of Marketing, 80*(6), 69–96.

Li, H., & Kannan, P. K. (2014). Attributing conversions in a multichannel online marketing environment: An empirical model and a field experiment. *Journal of Marketing Research, 51*(1), 40–56.

Neslin, S. A., & Shankar, V. (2009). Key issues in multichannel customer management: Current knowledge and future directions. *Journal of Interactive Marketing, 23*(1), 70–81.

Rawson, A., Duncan, E., & Jones, C. (2013). The truth about customer experience. *Harvard Business Review, 91*(9), 90–98.

Rust, R. T., & Huang, M. H. (2014). The service revolution and the transformation of marketing science. *Marketing Science, 33*(2), 206–221.

Schmitt, B. H. (2010). *Customer experience management: A revolutionary approach to connecting with your customers*. Wiley.

Stein, A., & Ramaseshan, B. (2016). Towards the identification of customer experience touch point elements. *Journal of Retailing and Consumer Services, 30*, 8–19.

Verhoef, P. C., Kannan, P. K., & Inman, J. J. (2015). From multi-channel retailing to omni-channel retailing: Introduction to the special issue on multi-channel retailing. *Journal of Retailing, 91*(2), 174–181.

Verhoef, P. C., Lemon, K. N., Parasuraman, A., Roggeveen, A., Tsiros, M., & Schlesinger, L. A. (2009). Customer experience creation: Determinants, dynamics and management strategies. *Journal of Retailing, 85*(1), 31–41.

Zomerdijk, L. G., & Voss, C. A. (2010). Service design for experience-centric services. *Journal of Service Research, 13*(1), 67–82.

EXERCISE 9.1: CREATING A CUSTOMER JOURNEY MAP

Objective: Understand the process of customer journey mapping by creating a synthetic map for a fictitious company (ZaraTech).

Tasks:

1. **Persona Development:** Create detailed profiles for each customer persona, including their goals, challenges, and preferences.

2. **Touchpoint Identification:** List all possible interactions these personas might have with ZaraTech across different channels.

3. **Journey Mapping:** Create a journey map for each persona. Include stages such as 'Awareness', 'Consideration', 'Purchase', and 'Loyalty.' Plot touchpoints and potential emotions or pain points at each stage.

4. **Analysis:** Identify key moments of truth and pain points for each persona.

Steps:

1. **Import Necessary Libraries:**

```
1. import pandas as pd
2. import matplotlib.pyplot as plt
3. import seaborn as sns
```

- **pandas:** Used for data manipulation and analysis.
- **matplotlib.pyplot** and **seaborn:** Used for data visualization.

2. **Load the Data**

```
4. file_path = 'Customer_Journey_Map_Data.csv'   # Replace with
the correct file path
5. journey_map_df = pd.read_csv(file_path)
```

- We load the CSV file into a DataFrame using **pandas**. Ensure the file path is correct.

3. **Exploratory Data Analysis:**

```
6. # Display the first few rows of the DataFrame
7. print(journey_map_df.head())
8. # Get a summary of the dataset
9. print(journey_map_df.describe(include='all'))
```

- **journey_map_df.head():** Shows the first few rows of the data for a quick overview.
- **journey_map_df.describe(include='all'):** Provides a statistical summary of the data, including count, unique values, and frequency for categorical data.

4. **Analyze Emotions and Pain Points:**

```
10. # Count of emotions per persona
11. emotion_count = journey_map_df.groupby(['Persona',
'Emotion']).size().unstack() print(emotion_count)
12. # Count of pain points per persona
13. pain_point_count = journey_map_df.groupby(['Persona', 'Pain
Point']).size().unstack() print(pain_point_count)
```

- Grouping data by 'Persona' and 'Emotion' to see the distribution of emotions for each persona.
- Similarly, grouping by 'Persona' and 'Pain Point' to understand common pain points.

5. **Visualize the Data:**

```
14. # Plotting emotion count
15. sns.barplot(data=emotion_count)
16. plt.title("Emotion Count per Persona")
17. plt.ylabel("Count")
18. plt.show()
19. # Plotting pain point count sns.barplot(data=pain_point_
count)
20. plt.title("Pain Point Count per Persona")
21. plt.ylabel("Count")
22. plt.show()
```

- Using **seaborn** to create bar plots for emotion and pain point counts.
- These plots will help visualize which emotions and pain points are most common for each persona.

This code provides a basic framework for analyzing the customer journey map data. It helps in understanding the distribution of emotions and pain points across different personas, which can be invaluable for tailoring marketing strategies and improving the customer experience. Remember to adjust the file path and possibly modify the code to suit the specific format and requirements of your data and analysis goals.

EXERCISE 9.1: OUTPUT

1. **Emotion and Pain Point Analysis:**

   The emotion count per persona shows a uniform distribution across the different personas for each emotion. Similarly, the pain point count also displays a uniform distribution across personas.

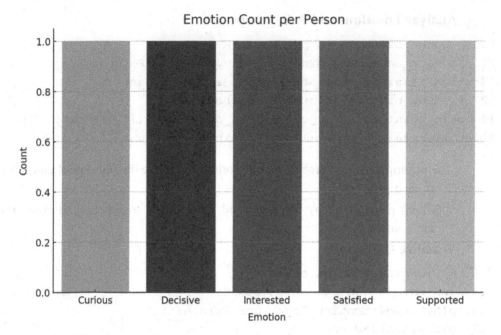

2. Visualizations:

▪ **Emotion Count per Persona:** The bar plot visualizes the count of different emotions for each persona. Each persona experiences each emotion once, indicating a balanced representation in the data.

▪ **Pain Point Count per Persona:** This bar plot shows the count of different pain points for each persona. Similar to emotions, each pain point is also uniformly represented across personas.

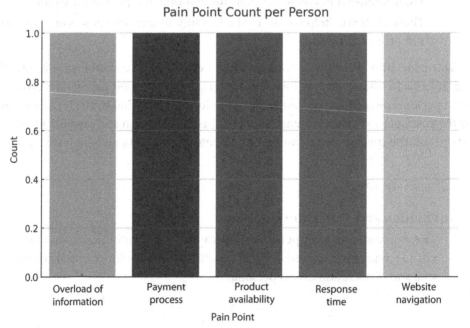

These analyses and visualizations provide insights into how different personas interact with various touchpoints, along with their emotional responses and pain points. This information is crucial for tailoring customer experience strategies.

EXERCISE 9.2: TOUCHPOINT EFFECTIVENESS ANALYSIS

Objective: Analyze the effectiveness of different touchpoints in a customer journey.

Tasks:

1. **Data Collection:** Use the synthetic data to simulate customer interactions across different touchpoints.

2. **Metric Analysis:** Calculate the effectiveness of each touchpoint. For example, determine conversion rates for website visits and email campaigns.

3. **Insight Generation:** Identify which touchpoints are most effective in driving customer satisfaction and conversions.

4. **Strategy Formulation:** Based on the analysis, suggest improvements or strategic shifts for ZaraTech to enhance customer experience.

Steps:

1. **Import Necessary Libraries:**

```
1. import pandas as pd
2. import matplotlib.pyplot as plt
3. import seaborn as sns
```

- **pandas** is used for data manipulation and analysis.
- **matplotlib.pyplot** and **seaborn** are used for data visualization.

2. **Create Synthetic Data:**

```
4. file_path = 'Touchpoint_Effectiveness_Analysis_Data.csv'  #
Replace with the correct file path
5. touchpoint_df = pd.DataFrame(touchpoint_data)
```

- We load the CSV file into a DataFrame using **pandas**. Ensure the file path is correct.

3. **Data Overview:**

```
6. print(touchpoint_df.head())
```

- **touchpoint_df.head()**: Shows the first few rows of the DataFrame.

4. **Analyze the Data:**

```
7. # Descriptive statistics of the dataset
8. print(touchpoint_df.describe())
```

- **touchpoint_df.describe()**: Provides a statistical summary of the dataset.

5. **Visualize the Data:**

We'll create visualizations for each metric to better understand their distribution and effectiveness:

```
9. # Visualizing Customer Satisfaction Scores
10. plt.figure(figsize=(10, 6))
11. sns.barplot(x='Touchpoint', y='Customer Satisfaction
Scores', data=touchpoint_df)
12. plt.title('Customer Satisfaction Scores by Touchpoint')
13. plt.show()
14. # Visualizing Conversion Rates
15. plt.figure(figsize=(10, 6))
16. sns.barplot(x='Touchpoint', y='Conversion Rates',
data=touchpoint_df)
17. plt.title('Conversion Rates by Touchpoint')
18. plt.show()
19. # Visualizing Repeat Visits/Purchases
20. plt.figure(figsize=(10, 6))
21. sns.barplot(x='Touchpoint', y='Repeat Visits/Purchases',
data=touchpoint_df)
22. plt.title('Repeat Visits/Purchases by Touchpoint')
23. plt.show()
```

■ These plots will visually represent the effectiveness of each touchpoint in terms of customer satisfaction, conversion rates, and repeat visits or purchases.

This exercise will help in understanding how different touchpoints contribute to customer satisfaction and business outcomes. The visualizations will provide a clear and immediate way to identify which touchpoints are performing well and which may need improvement.

EXERCISE 9.2: OUTPUT

Here are the results of the analysis and visualization for Exercise 9.2:

1. **Data Overview:**

The first few rows of the dataset provide a quick look at the structure, with each row representing a touchpoint and associated metrics like customer satisfaction scores, conversion rates, and repeat visits/purchases.

2. **Dataset Summary:**

The summary of the dataset gives us a statistical overview. It shows that the average customer satisfaction score is about 82.6, with a mean conversion rate of 6.22% and an average of 33% for repeat visits/purchases.

3. **Visualizations:**

  ▪ **Customer Satisfaction Scores by Touchpoint:** The bar plot shows the customer satisfaction scores for each touchpoint. 'In-store Visits' have the highest satisfaction score, indicating a strong performance in this area.

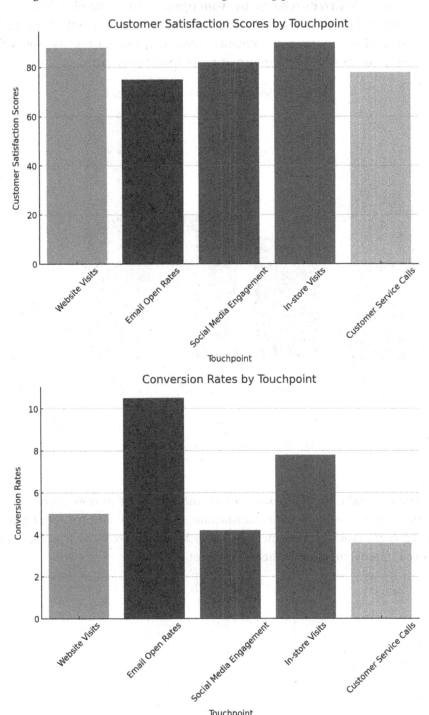

- **Conversion Rates by Touchpoint:** This plot visualizes the conversion rates associated with each touchpoint. 'Email Open Rates' stand out with the highest conversion rate, suggesting that email marketing is particularly effective for this synthetic dataset.
- **Repeat Visits/Purchases by Touchpoint:** The final plot shows the percentage of repeat visits or purchases for each touchpoint. 'In-store Visits' again show a strong performance, indicating that customers who visit the store are more likely to return or make repeat purchases.

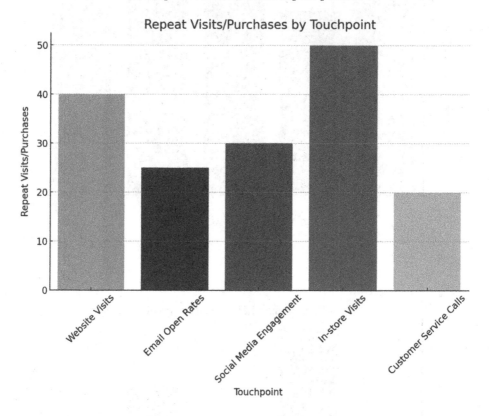

These visualizations provide a clear understanding of how each touchpoint is performing in terms of customer satisfaction, conversion, and customer retention. Such insights are crucial for businesses to identify which areas are working well and which need improvement or further investment.

CHAPTER **10**

Experimental Design in Marketing

10.1 INTRODUCTION

Experimental design in marketing is an essential tool for businesses aiming to optimize their marketing strategies. It refers to the methodical procedure of devising, implementing, analyzing, and interpreting regulated tests to evaluate marketing strategies or tactics. The goal is to discern the actual impact of various marketing inputs on outcomes such as sales, customer engagement, or brand awareness.

This scientific method enables marketers to establish causal relationships rather than mere correlations, offering a higher degree of confidence in the outcomes. For example, if a business alters its advertising strategy and subsequently observes an increase in sales, an experimental design can help determine whether the increase in sales was indeed due to the altered advertising strategy or if it was influenced by external factors (Armstrong & Green, 2007).

Experimental design can be applied in various marketing contexts, including product pricing, promotional strategies, digital marketing, and more. The robustness of this approach stems from its ability to control for potential confounding factors, thereby providing more accurate results (Gerber & Green, 2012).

But, as we proceed further into this chapter, prepare to unravel deeper layers of experimental design. Fractional factorial designs offer a nuanced yet efficient way to study multiple factors simultaneously without needing to test all possible combinations—a real boon when resources are limited. Meanwhile, multi-armed bandits (MABs) are an intriguing approach, balancing exploration and exploitation in real-time marketing experiments, proving invaluable in scenarios demanding rapid decisions with limited data.

Stay with us as we embark on a journey through these advanced tools and methodologies, enhancing your expertise in experimental design and its profound implications in marketing (Kohavi et al., 2009).

10.2 DESIGN OF EXPERIMENTS

10.2.1 Overview of Design of Experiments

Design of experiments (DoE) is a statistical methodology that enables structured, scientific exploration of a problem space. It involves a systematic method to determine the relationship between factors affecting a process and the output of that process (Montgomery, 2017). In marketing, these factors could be various elements of a marketing strategy such as advertising spend, pricing, product features, and the output could be sales, customer engagement, or brand awareness.

The DoE approach is especially beneficial when dealing with multiple input variables, as it allows for the assessment of the impact of individual factors and their interactions on the output. It aims to provide a statistical model that identifies factors that may influence the variables of interest, and also the interactions among those factors (Box et al., 2005).

In essence, DoE is a strategic approach to conducting experiments that enables multiple input factors to be manipulated determining their effect on a desired output (response) while using a minimum of experimental runs. This efficiency is critical in marketing where resource and time constraints are common (Anderson & Whitcomb, 2017).

One of the main benefits of DoE is its ability to minimize the risk of reaching incorrect conclusions. By simultaneously varying multiple factors, it is possible to avoid confounding effects where the impact of multiple factors is combined, making it difficult to attribute changes in the response to individual factors (Myers et al., 2016).

10.2.2 Factors, Levels, and Responses in Experiments

Experimental design is a structured approach used to determine the cause-and-effect relationship between variables. A proper understanding of the terminology is essential for effective implementation and interpretation of experiments. In this context, three fundamental concepts are factors, levels, and responses.

Factors in an experiment refer to the controlled independent variables that are manipulated to ascertain their effect on the dependent variable. For example, in a marketing experiment, factors could be advertising methods, product pricing, or promotional strategies (see Table 10.1). It's essential to differentiate between a factor and an external variable that isn't deliberately changed or controlled by the experimenter (Montgomery, 2017).

Levels represent the different values or settings that a factor can assume. For instance, if we're examining the factor 'advertising method', the levels might be 'social media', 'print media', and 'television'. The choice of levels can profoundly influence the results and conclusions drawn from the experiment. Experimenters must carefully select levels that are practically and theoretically relevant (Box et al., 2005).

The response is the dependent variable in the experiment, representing the outcome or result that we measure. Using the previous example, if we are looking at the effect of different advertising methods on product sales, then the 'number of units sold' would be the response. Responses are crucial because they help us quantify the impact of our manipulated factors, thereby enabling objective analysis and decision-making (Wu & Hamada, 2011).

Table 10.1 Factors, Their Levels, and Potential Responses in a Hypothetical Marketing Experiment.

Factor	Levels	Potential Responses
Price	High, low	Sales volume
Ad placement	Top, middle, bottom	Click-through rate
Ad color	Red, blue, green	Engagement rate

10.2.3 Randomization, Replication, and Blocking in Experimental Design

Effective experimental design is not just about selecting factors and levels; it's also about how we run the experiments. Three core principles are fundamental to the integrity and validity of experiments: randomization, replication, and blocking.

Randomization involves randomly assigning experimental units to different factor-level combinations. By doing this, we ensure that the effects of extraneous factors are evenly spread across all experimental conditions, helping mitigate potential biases. This approach ensures that the conclusions drawn are valid and attributable to the factors being studied, not to external influences (Montgomery, 2017).

Replication refers to the repetition of the entire experiment or specific treatments within the experiment. By replicating, we can understand the inherent variability in our measurements. It provides a more precise estimate of factor effects, improving the reliability and robustness of our conclusions (Box et al., 2005).

Blocking is a technique used to account for variability that can be attributed to external sources that are not of primary interest in the experiment. By grouping experimental units into blocks based on these external sources, we can control or remove the variability caused by these sources, leading to a clearer assessment of the primary factors of interest (Wu & Hamada, 2011; see Figure 10.1).

10.2.4 Case Studies: Effective Use of Experimental Design in Marketing

Effective experimental design has driven numerous successful marketing initiatives. Here are a few case studies that showcase its utility:

- **Pricing strategy experiment for an e-commerce site.** An online retailer suspected that its pricing strategy was not optimal. They set up an experiment where they randomly assigned visitors to one of three pricing levels for a product. By analyzing sales, they identified the optimal price point that maximized revenue (Kohavi et al., 2009).

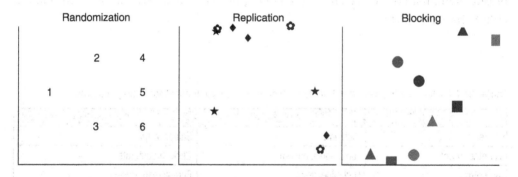

Figure 10.1 The Importance of Randomization, Replication, and Blocking with Simple Diagrams.

- **Ad placement on a social media platform.** A social media company wanted to determine the best placement for its ads to maximize clicks without alienating users. They created multiple ad placements (factors) with varying degrees of prominence (levels) and measured click-through rates (CTRs) (response). Through this experimental design, the company pinpointed an optimal ad placement that balanced visibility with user experience (Lewis & Rao, 2015).
- **Packaging design for a consumer product.** A consumer goods company hypothesized that product packaging influenced purchase decisions. They designed an experiment with two packaging designs and placed them in select stores. Sales data indicated a clear preference for one design over the other, leading to a company-wide rollout of the preferred packaging (Gelman & Hill, 2006).

Each of these case studies underscores the power of experimental design in driving marketing decisions. By systematically testing hypotheses in controlled settings, businesses can glean actionable insights that directly affect the bottom line.

10.2.5 Key Concepts in Design of Experiments

DoE involves several key concepts that are critical to understanding and applying this technique in marketing or other fields (Box et al., 2005):

- **Factor.** A factor is a controlled independent variable whose levels are set by the experimenter. For instance, in a marketing experiment, factors could be the price, promotional strategies, or product features.
- **Level.** A level is a specific value of the factor. If the factor was the price, for instance, different levels could be $5, $10, $15, and so on.
- **Response.** The response is the dependent variable or outcome measurement.
- **Treatment.** A treatment is a specific combination of factor levels.
- **Randomization.** Randomization is the random assignment of treatments to experimental units in order to mitigate the effects of extraneous factors (Montgomery, 2017).
- **Replication.** Replication involves repeating the experiment several times to get a more accurate estimate of the variability in the data.
- **Blocking.** Blocking is a technique used to remove the effects of identifiable sources of variation.
- **Interaction.** Interaction between factors occurs when the effect of one factor depends on the level of another factor.

Understanding these concepts is crucial in order to design and execute effective experiments, interpret the results accurately, and make informed decisions based on these results (Anderson & Whitcomb, 2017).

10.2.6 Practical Example: Design of Experiments in Email Marketing

DoE can be practically applied in various aspects of marketing, including email marketing (see Table 10.2). Here's an example. Suppose a company wishes to optimize its email marketing strategy to increase the CTR. The company identifies four factors that could potentially influence this rate: subject line, email length, time of sending, and presence of an offer. Each factor is set at two levels:

- **Subject line:** 'Product-focused' versus 'Customer-focused'
- **Email length:** 'Short' versus 'Long'
- **Time of sending:** 'Morning' versus 'Evening'
- **Presence of an offer:** 'Yes' versus 'No'

The company uses a 2^4 factorial design, resulting in 16 different combinations of these factors. Each combination (treatment) is randomly assigned to a group of customers, and the CTR (response) is observed. Statistical analysis of the resulting data enables the company to determine the individual and interactive effects of these factors on the CTR.

For instance, the company might find that emails with a customer-focused subject line, sent in the evening, with an offer included, lead to the highest CTRs, regardless of email length. This would enable the company to optimize its email marketing strategy based on the results of the experiment (Kohavi et al., 2009).

10.3 FRACTIONAL FACTORIAL DESIGNS

10.3.1 Overview of Fractional Factorial Designs

Fractional factorial designs represent a subset of full factorial experimental designs. Although full factorial designs consider every possible combination of factors and their levels, fractional factorial designs only include a "fraction" of these combinations, making them more efficient and cost-effective, especially when dealing with a large number of factors (Montgomery, 2017).

In a fractional factorial design, not all possible combinations of levels for every factor are tested. Instead, a carefully chosen subset of combinations is used. This results in fewer total experiments, which can save significant time and resources. However, the trade-off is that some information about interactions between factors may be lost or confounded.

Table 10.2 Comparing Outcomes from Different Experimental Designs in Email Marketing.

Experimental Design	Email Subject	Open Rate (%)	CTR (%)	Conversion Rate (%)
Control group	Standard Offer	20	5	2
Treatment group 1	10% Discount	30	10	3
Treatment group 2	Buy 1 Get 1 Free	25	7	2.5

For example, consider a company interested in testing the effectiveness of four different marketing strategies, each with two levels. A full factorial design would involve $2^4 = 16$ experiments. However, a half-fraction design would only include $2^{(4-1)} = 8$ experiments, saving the company time and resources while still providing valuable insights into the effects of the strategies (see Figure 10.2).

It's important to note that the selection of combinations in a fractional factorial design should be done carefully, ideally with the assistance of statistical software or a statistician, to ensure that the design is balanced and allows for meaningful analysis.

10.3.2 Benefits of Fractional Designs: Efficiency and Cost-Effectiveness

Fractional factorial designs, as a subset of the broader spectrum of experimental designs, bring a unique value proposition. Their primary benefit, as the name suggests, lies in their ability to use only a fraction of the full set of experimental conditions, thereby proving to be efficient and cost-effective.

10.3.2.1 Efficiency

Traditional full factorial experimental designs, which study all possible combinations of the factors, can become impractical when the number of factors increases because the number of required experimental conditions grows exponentially with the number of factors and their levels. Fractional factorial designs address this challenge by intelligently selecting a subset of the possible conditions, allowing for the study of primary factor effects and select interactions without the need for a full-scale experiment. This makes the process more manageable, particularly in contexts where there are constraints on time or resources (Montgomery, 2017).

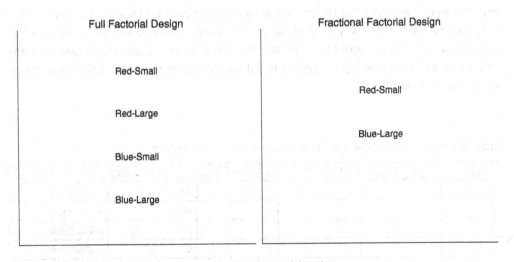

Figure 10.2 A Full Factorial Design Versus a Fractional Factorial Design.

10.3.2.2 Cost-Effectiveness

Running full-scale experiments, especially in real-world contexts such as market testing or industrial settings, can be costly. By reducing the number of experimental runs, fractional factorial designs can significantly lower costs. This is especially important for small and medium enterprises or startups with limited budgets because it enables them to obtain valuable insights without heavy financial investment (Box et al., 2005).

10.3.3 Generating and Analyzing Fractional Designs

The creation and subsequent analysis of fractional factorial designs require a structured approach.

10.3.3.1 Generation

Fractional designs are constructed using a series of generators that define the relationship between factors. Generators help in producing the fraction of the full factorial design by determining which factor combinations are to be included. Typically, specific statistical software or expert guidance is sought to generate these designs, ensuring they're statistically valid and effectively balanced. The resolution of the design, which dictates the degree of confounding between factors, is an essential consideration in this generation process (Montgomery, 2017).

10.3.3.2 Analysis

Once the experiments have been conducted, the collected data is analyzed using statistical techniques to estimate factor effects and their significance (see Table 10.3). This involves determining whether the observed changes in the response variable are statistically significant and can be attributed to the manipulated factors. It's vital to note that, due to the fractional nature of the design, there might be certain factor interactions for which effects cannot be distinctly separated, known as *aliasing*. Understanding and interpreting these effects require careful consideration to ensure valid conclusions (Box et al., 2005).

Table 10.3 How Fractional Designs Are Generated and How to Analyze Them.

Run	Factor A	Factor B	Factor C	Generator	Analyzed as
1	+	+	+	ABC	Main effect A
2	-	+	-	ABC	Main effect B
3	+	-	-	A	Interaction AB
4	-	-	+	B	Interaction AC

10.3.4 Applications in Marketing: Testing Multiple Campaign Elements

In the dynamic world of marketing, where multiple elements combine to dictate campaign success, fractional factorial designs find critical application. For instance, consider a digital marketing campaign in which an organization wants to test the combined effect of advertisement design, call-to-action text, placement of the ad on a web page, and time of day the ad is displayed. Conducting a full factorial experiment would involve testing every possible combination of these factors, a process that could be time-consuming and expensive.

By applying a fractional factorial design, the organization can efficiently test a subset of these combinations, enabling them to discern the most impactful elements of their campaign. This approach would provide insights into the main effects of each factor and some critical interactions without the need for exhaustive testing.

In another example, a company launching a new product might want to determine the best combination of pricing, packaging, and promotional strategy. Instead of testing every possible combination in the market, a fractional design could help identify the optimal mix by testing only a subset of combinations, saving both time and money while still providing valuable market insights (Wu & Hamada, 2011; see Figure 10.3).

In essence, fractional factorial designs offer marketers a powerful tool to optimize campaigns by making the experimental process more efficient and cost-effective.

10.3.5 Key Concepts in Fractional Factorial Designs

Fractional factorial designs are a powerful tool in experimental design, particularly when dealing with multiple factors and limited resources. To ensure a proper understanding of these designs, it is essential to be familiar with several key concepts:

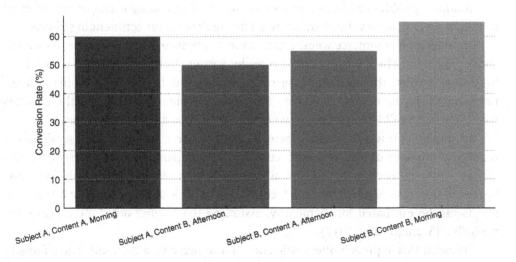

Figure 10.3 Results from Using Fractional Designs in Marketing Campaign Tests.

- **Resolution.** The resolution of a fractional factorial design refers to the level of confounding or aliasing between main effects and interactions (Montgomery, 2017). Higher-resolution designs have less confounding, but they also require more experiments. Lower-resolution designs are more efficient in terms of the number of experiments but may have more confounding.

- **Confounding or aliasing.** In fractional factorial designs, certain factor effects can be confounded or aliased with others, meaning that their individual effects cannot be separated (Box et al., 2005). This occurs when only a fraction of the full factorial design is used, leading to the loss of some information. Careful planning is needed to minimize confounding and ensure meaningful results.

- **Orthogonality.** Orthogonal designs ensure that the factors are independent of each other, enabling the separate estimation of main effects and interactions without interference (Box et al., 2005). Orthogonality is a desirable property in fractional factorial designs because it helps minimize the impact of confounding.

- **Generators and defining relations.** Generators are used to define a fractional factorial design by specifying the confounding structure (Montgomery, 2017). Defining relations are algebraic expressions that relate the factors in the design and can be used to identify aliases and construct the design matrix.

- **Blocking.** Blocking is a technique used to account for variability in the experimental units, ensuring that the results are not affected by these nuisance factors (Montgomery, 2017). In fractional factorial designs, blocking can be used to control for variability while maintaining the efficiency of the design.

10.3.6 Practical Example: Fractional Factorial Designs in A/B Testing

Fractional factorial designs are extensively used in A/B testing, especially when there are multiple variables to test and limited resources. These designs enable the efficient testing of several factors simultaneously while controlling for confounding effects.

Consider an e-commerce website that wants to optimize its landing page to increase conversion rates. The company might consider various factors such as the color of the 'Buy Now' button, the position of customer reviews, the font size of product descriptions, and the layout of product images. Testing all possible combinations of these factors would require a full factorial design, which could be time and resource-intensive.

By implementing a fractional factorial design, the company could significantly reduce the number of tests required. Let's say the company chooses to test three factors at two levels each; a 2^{3-1} fractional factorial design would require only four tests instead of the eight required by a full factorial design. This design ensures that the main effects can be estimated independently, assuming that higher-order interactions are negligible (Montgomery, 2017).

Although this approach offers efficiency, it also presents a trade-off. The company will not be able to distinguish between the effects of certain combinations of factors (known as *confounding*). However, with careful planning, important interactions can be estimated, and this limitation can be addressed. Table 10.4 compares these two testing approaches across various factors such as the number of variations tested, experiment duration, complexity, and resolution, providing a clear overview of their respective advantages and limitations.

A fractional factorial design offers an efficient way to explore the most influential factors and their interactions on the conversion rate. By applying statistical analysis to the results, the company can identify the optimal combination of these factors to maximize conversions.

10.4 MULTI-ARMED BANDITS

10.4.1 Overview of Multi-Armed Bandits

MABs are a significant tool used in experimental design and decision-making, particularly when there is a need for balancing exploration (trying out all options to gather more data) and exploitation (sticking to the best-known option). It originates from the field of reinforcement learning, which is an area of machine learning in which an agent learns to make decisions by interacting with its environment (Sutton & Barto, 2018).

The term *multi-armed bandit* is derived from a hypothetical scenario involving a gambler at a row of slot machines (often referred to as *one-armed bandits* due to their lever mechanism and the propensity to empty players' pockets), who must decide which machines to play, how many times to play each machine, and in what order to play them to maximize the total reward. In marketing, this scenario can be seen as a metaphor for various decision-making problems, such as choosing among different marketing strategies, designs, advertisements, or pricing models, when it is unclear which one will yield the best results (Scott, 2015).

MAB algorithms are designed to minimize regret, which is the difference between the total reward that could have been achieved by always selecting the best option and the total reward that was actually achieved by the algorithm. They provide a more sophisticated alternative to traditional A/B testing in many situations because they continuously update their knowledge about each option and adjust the allocation of resources accordingly (Bubeck & Cesa-Bianchi, 2012).

Table 10.4 Comparing Outcomes from Standard A/B Tests to Fractional Factorial A/B Tests.

Comparison Factor	Standard A/B Tests	Fractional Factorial A/B Tests
Number of variations tested	Two (A and B)	Multiple
Experiment duration	Short to medium	Medium to long
Complexity	Low	Medium to high
Resolution	High for two variations	High for multiple variations

10.4.2 Exploration Versus Exploitation Dilemma

One of the primary challenges in decision-making processes, especially within the context of MABs and reinforcement learning, is the tension between exploration and exploitation. This dilemma is a central theme in many machine learning and optimization scenarios.

Exploration involves investigating the unknown. In practical scenarios, this means allocating resources to areas with uncertain outcomes in the hope of discovering new or better solutions. Although exploration carries potential rewards, it also comes with risks because there's no guarantee of a positive return (Sutton & Barto, 2018).

However, **exploitation** involves leveraging known information to make decisions. When exploiting, an entity relies on acquired knowledge to maximize immediate reward, selecting options that have previously demonstrated positive outcomes. However, excessive reliance on exploitation might mean missed opportunities that arise from novel solutions or changing environments (Bubeck & Cesa-Bianchi, 2012).

Balancing the two is challenging: leaning too heavily toward exploration might mean wasted resources on less optimal choices, and a focus on exploitation could prevent the discovery of more efficient or beneficial options (see Figure 10.4).

10.4.3 Algorithms: ε-Greedy, Upper Confidence Bound, and Thompson Sampling

Various algorithms have been devised to address the exploration versus exploitation challenge, aiming to strike an effective balance between the two.

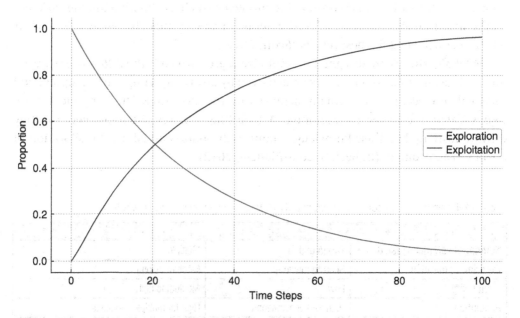

Figure 10.4 The Trade-Off Between Exploration and Exploitation over Time.

10.4.3.1 ε-Greedy (Epsilon-Greedy)

This is one of the simplest methods. It works by selecting the best-known option most of the time (exploitation) but occasionally (with a small probability ε) choosing a random option (exploration). The parameter ε dictates the balance, and a larger ε increases exploration at the cost of exploitation (Tokic, 2010).

10.4.3.2 Upper Confidence Bound

The UCB (upper confidence bound) approach takes into account the uncertainty in the estimated value of each option. The algorithm selects options based on upper confidence bounds of their estimated values. This ensures that options are chosen based not just on their observed average rewards but also on the uncertainty or variance in their rewards. Over time, as more data is collected, the uncertainty diminishes, and the UCB strategy tends to favor options with higher observed average rewards (Auer et al., 2002).

10.4.3.3 Thompson Sampling

This is a probabilistic method that selects options based on the Bayesian posterior distribution of their rewards. The algorithm models the uncertainty in the reward distribution of each option and samples from these distributions to determine which option to select next. Over time, as more data is gathered, the posterior distributions become more refined, guiding the algorithm to increasingly optimal choices (Chapelle & Li, 2011).

To provide a comprehensive comparison of key algorithms used in decision-making, including ε-Greedy, UCB, and Thompson Sampling, Table 10.5 details their advantages, disadvantages, and ideal use case scenarios, offering insights into the selection of the most appropriate algorithm based on specific requirements and contexts.

Table 10.5 Key Algorithms (ε-Greedy, Upper Confidence Bound, Thompson Sampling) with Their Pros, Cons, and Best-Use Scenarios.

Algorithm	Pros	Cons	Best Used For
ε-Greedy	Simple Allows for fine-tuning exploration	Requires manual tuning of ε	Scenarios in which exploration rate can be predefined
UCB	Balances exploration-exploitation based on confidence intervals	Can be computationally intensive	When there's sufficient computational resources
Thompson Sampling	Probabilistic approach Adapts based on prior data	Requires prior knowledge or beliefs about rewards	When prior beliefs about rewards are available

10.4.4 Practical Use Cases in Marketing Optimization

The exploration versus exploitation algorithms have found significant utility in marketing optimization scenarios:

- **Ad campaign optimization.** An online platform could use the ε-greedy algorithm to serve users with the highest performing ad (exploitation) but occasionally show a new or less-performing ad (exploration) to gauge its potential effectiveness or gather more data on its performance.

- **Product recommendations.** E-commerce platforms can employ the UCB or Thompson sampling algorithm to recommend products. Although the platform might have a set of products known to be popular (exploitation), it can also introduce newer products or those with fewer user interactions to understand their potential appeal to customers (exploration).

- **Email marketing.** When introducing a new newsletter format or content strategy, companies can leverage these algorithms to send the new version to a subset of their subscribers (exploration) while continuing to send the traditional format to the majority (exploitation). This enables real-time feedback without risking engagement rates for the entire subscriber base.

To visually depict the effectiveness of MABs in enhancing marketing optimization, Figure 10.5 presents a bar graph showcasing conversion rates, before and after

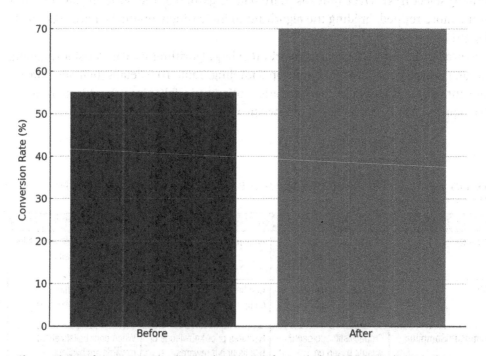

Figure 10.5 Performance Metrics (Conversion Rates) Before and After Using MABs in Marketing Optimization.

the application of MAB algorithms, illustrating the tangible benefits of this strategic approach in real-world scenarios.

In all these scenarios, the key lies in the continual refinement of strategies, ensuring that as more data becomes available, marketing decisions evolve to become more effective and customer-centric.

10.4.5 Key Concepts in Multi-Armed Bandits

The fundamental problem in MABs is deciding which arm to pull (i.e., which action to take), given that each action's reward is unknown until it is chosen. This problem is also known as the *explore-exploit dilemma* (Sutton & Barto, 2018).

Here are some of the key concepts in MABs:

- **Arm.** In the context of MABs, an arm represents an option or decision to be made. The term originates from the lever (arm) of a slot machine (one-armed bandit). In marketing, an arm could represent a specific advertising campaign, a pricing strategy, or a product design.
- **Reward.** This is the payoff received after an arm is pulled. The reward can vary each time the same arm is pulled. In marketing, this could be the revenue generated, customer engagement, or any other desired outcome.
- **Regret.** Regret is a key concept in MABs. It represents the opportunity cost of not having pulled the best arm. The goal of MAB algorithms is to minimize regret over time.
- **Exploration versus exploitation.** This is the fundamental trade-off in MABs. Exploration is about gathering more information by pulling different arms, whereas exploitation is about pulling the arm with the highest expected reward based on the information currently available.
- **ε-greedy strategy.** This is a simple yet effective strategy in MABs. With a probability of ε, an arm is chosen at random (exploration), and with a probability of 1−ε, the arm with the highest estimated reward is chosen (exploitation) (Tokic, 2010).
- **UCB strategy.** This is a more sophisticated MAB strategy. It involves pulling the arm with the highest upper confidence bound on the expected reward. This strategy achieves a better balance between exploration and exploitation (Auer et al., 2002).

10.4.6 Practical Example: Multi-Armed Bandits in Website Optimization

MABs have found various applications in the field of marketing. One such application is in website optimization. Let's consider the case of an e-commerce company that wishes to optimize the layout of its home page to maximize customer engagement.

Suppose the company has designed three different layouts (A, B, and C) for its home page. Each layout is an arm in the MAB context. The company wants to identify the most effective layout, that is, the one that results in the highest CTR. However, the company doesn't know the true CTRs of the layouts. Therefore, it faces the explore-exploit dilemma: should it gather more information about the layouts (explore) or choose the layout that currently seems best (exploit)?

The company can use a MAB algorithm, such as ε-greedy or UCB, to address this dilemma. The algorithm will balance between exploring all layouts and exploiting the currently best-performing layout. Over time, the algorithm will converge to the best layout, minimizing the regret (i.e., the opportunity cost of not having chosen the best layout).

An example of such an application is provided by Chapelle and Li (2011). They reported that a contextual bandit algorithm (a variant of MABs) resulted in a 12.5% improvement in CTR for news article recommendation at Yahoo!

10.5 ONLINE AND OFFLINE EXPERIMENTS

10.5.1 Overview of Online and Offline Experiments

Experimental design is a critical part of marketing analytics, and it involves testing different strategies or tactics to understand their impact on key performance indicators. Experiments can be broadly classified into two categories: online and offline.

Online experiments, also known as *A/B testing* or *split testing*, are conducted in a live digital environment such as a website, app, or email marketing campaign. Here, the performance of different versions of a web page, app interface, or marketing message (such as emails or ads) is tested on different groups of users. This approach enables real-time data collection and rapid insights. Online experiments have been popularized by digital-first companies such as Google and Amazon, and they have been instrumental in shaping user experience design and digital marketing strategies (Kohavi et al., 2012).

However, offline experiments are conducted in a controlled environment, often physically. These could involve focus groups, in-person interviews, surveys, or field trials. For example, a company might test a new product by releasing it in a select number of stores and measuring its performance compared to a control group of stores. Offline experiments are particularly useful when the experiment involves factors that cannot be digitized, such as physical product attributes or in-store experiences.

Online and offline experiments have their strengths and weaknesses. The choice between them depends on factors such as the nature of the product/service, target audience, the hypothesis being tested, and available resources.

10.5.2 Challenges and Benefits of Online A/B Testing

Online A/B testing, when two or more variations of a digital strategy are compared, has emerged as a fundamental tool in digital marketing and user experience optimization (see Table 10.6).

Benefits

- **Real-time feedback.** Online tests offer immediate insights, enabling marketers to swiftly adjust strategies based on user behavior (Kohavi et al., 2012).
- **Scalability.** With digital platforms, it's possible to test variations on a large scale, spanning diverse geographies and demographics.
- **Flexibility.** Online environments enable easy adjustments. If a particular strategy isn't working, it can be replaced or tweaked without significant costs.

Challenges

- **Overreliance on quantitative data.** Online tests provide abundant quantitative data, but the information might lack qualitative insights that help explain user behaviors (Gerber & Green, 2012).
- **Multiplicity of variables.** Digital environments are dynamic, with numerous concurrent variables. This can sometimes make it difficult to ascertain causality.
- **Privacy concerns.** Collecting and analyzing online user data come with privacy implications, necessitating strict adherence to data protection regulations (Armstrong & Green, 2007).

10.5.3 Designing and Implementing Offline Experiments

Although online experiments have the luxury of automated tools and vast data streams, offline experiments in physical settings often pose distinct challenges, intertwined with complex variables and the unpredictability of human behaviors.

Table 10.6 A Comparison of the Challenges and Benefits of Online A/B Testing Versus Offline Methods.

Comparison Factor	Online A/B Testing	Offline Methods
Speed	Fast	Slower
Cost	Variable (can be low)	Can be high
Scalability	High	Lower
Flexibility	High	Variable
Real-time analysis	Possible	Not always possible
Depth of insights	Depends on tracking	Can be deeper with qualitative data

10.5.3.1 Design

The bedrock of any offline experiment lies in its meticulous design. It's not just about listing out variables but understanding the intricate web of interactions in real-world settings.

Consider a retail scenario. A brand wants to discern the influence of a new store layout on sales. Beyond hypothesizing the potential impact, they'd need to delve deep and consider these factors:

- **Hypothesis.** Whether the new layout increases sales
- **Variables.** Store layout, product placement, signage visibility, staff-customer interactions, and even factors such as store lighting or ambient music
- **Measurement criteria.** Sales volume, customer footfall, average customer dwell time, and perhaps even metrics such as customer satisfaction or repeat visits

But here's a real-world anecdotal twist: In 2018, a global coffee chain decided to experiment with a "no-seating" design in select outlets to promote take-away orders and reduce in-store crowding. By measuring not just sales but also order processing time and customer feedback, they gained insights leading to the expansion of this design to more urban outlets.

10.5.3.2 Implementation

The magic lies in turning theory into tangible action. In our retail example, the store would initiate changes in select outlets, acting as the treatment group, while others remain unchanged, serving as the control group.

However, here's where complexities creep in:

- **Time frame.** How long should the experiment run to account for initial novelty effects?
- **Seasonal effects.** What if a holiday season skews sales data?
- **Unanticipated factors.** A local event could suddenly increase footfall.

To summarize, offline experiments are akin to orchestrating a symphony with numerous moving parts. Although the challenges are manifold, so are the rewards: offering marketers a lens into real-world consumer behaviors and preferences.

10.5.4 Bridging Online and Offline Data for Comprehensive Insights

In today's interconnected world, it's imperative to integrate insights from online and offline channels for a holistic understanding of consumer behavior. Combining data from both realms can provide a more comprehensive picture of the customer journey. For instance, a consumer might first encounter a brand online through a social media ad but make a purchase in a physical store. By integrating online data (such as CTRs or website visits) with offline data (such as in-store purchases or feedback), brands can gain deeper insights into touchpoints that influence purchasing decisions.

The challenge, however, lies in integrating these diverse datasets cohesively. Advanced data analytics tools and customer relationship management systems play a pivotal role in this integration, enabling marketers to trace customer interactions across multiple channels and touchpoints (Kohavi et al., 2009).

10.5.5 Key Concepts in Online and Offline Experiments

There are several key concepts that are essential to understanding and implementing online and offline experiments in marketing:

- **Randomization.** This involves randomly assigning subjects (users, customers, etc.) to different groups, such as a control group and one or more treatment groups. Randomization is crucial to minimize the effects of confounding variables and bias, thus ensuring the results of the experiment are valid and reliable (Box et al., 2005).
- **Control group.** The control group receives the "standard" or "default" treatment, which is typically the current strategy or offering. This group serves as a benchmark against which the treatment groups are compared.
- **Treatment group.** The treatment groups receive the new or different treatments being tested. For example, in an A/B test, one group might see the current web page (control group), and the other sees a version with a modified layout (treatment group).
- **Hypothesis testing.** The purpose of an experiment is often to test a specific hypothesis. For instance, 'Changing the color of the "Buy Now" button from green to red will increase CTRs'. The results of the experiment are used to either reject or fail to reject the hypothesis.
- **Statistical significance.** This concept relates to the likelihood that the results of the experiment occurred by chance. If an experiment's results are statistically significant, it means that we can be reasonably confident that the observed effect is real and not due to randomness or chance (Fisher, 1925).
- **Power analysis.** Power analysis is used to determine the sample size required to detect an effect of a given size with a certain degree of confidence. It helps ensure that an experiment is neither too small (risking a Type II error, or failing to detect a real effect) nor too large (wasting resources) (Cohen, 2013).

In the realm of online experiments, these concepts are applied on a large scale and often in real time. Offline experiments, however, may involve smaller sample sizes and longer time frames but still adhere to the same principles.

10.5.6 Practical Example: Online and Offline Experiments in Multichannel Marketing

Online and offline experiments can be effectively used in multichannel marketing to optimize customer experience and maximize business results. Here is a practical example:

Consider a large retail company that operates brick-and-mortar stores and an e-commerce website. The company wants to determine the most effective marketing strategy for promoting a new product line. To do this, they decide to conduct online and offline experiments:

- **Online experiment.** The company could run an A/B test on their website, where half of the website visitors are shown a pop-up ad for the new product line (treatment group), and the other half sees the website as usual without the pop-up (control group). The company then measures the CTR on the pop-up and the subsequent conversion rate among those who clicked.
- **Offline experiment.** In physical stores, the company could conduct a similar experiment by setting up a promotional display for the new product line in some stores (treatment group), and in others, the product is placed in the regular shelves (control group). The company then compares the sales of the new product line in the treatment stores against those in the control stores.

In both experiments, the company uses hypothesis testing to determine if the treatment (pop-up ad or promotional display) led to a statistically significant increase in interest or sales for the new product line. By comparing the results of the online and offline experiments, the company can gain insights into the effectiveness of different marketing strategies across multiple channels (see Table 10.7).

The integration of online and offline experiments in this way enables a more comprehensive understanding of customer behavior and marketing effectiveness. It also underscores the value of a multichannel approach to marketing, which aims to reach customers wherever they are, online or offline.

10.6 CONCLUSION

In conclusion, experimental design in marketing is a powerful tool that enables marketers to systematically test hypotheses, measure the effectiveness of various marketing

Table 10.7 Outcomes of a Multichannel Marketing Strategy Using Both Online and Offline Experimental Insights.

Metric	Before Combined Insights (%)	After Combined Insights (%)
Engagement rate	60	75
Conversion rate	20	30
ROI	150	190

strategies, and generate actionable insights. The methodologies discussed in this chapter, including DoE, fractional factorial designs, MABs, and online and offline experiments, offer different approaches to understand and optimize marketing strategies based on empirical evidence.

DoE and fractional factorial designs, for instance, can help marketers understand the effect of various factors on marketing outcomes and optimize their strategies based on these insights. MABs, however, provide an effective way of balancing the exploration-exploitation trade-off in situations when resources are limited and decisions need to be made in real time. Last, online and offline experiments provide a way to integrate digital and traditional marketing channels to provide a holistic view of customer behavior and marketing effectiveness.

The use of these methods has been shown to result in improved marketing performance, such as higher CTRs, increased conversion rates, and improved customer retention. However, as with any method, the success of experimental design in marketing depends on the careful design and execution of the experiments, as well as a proper understanding of the underlying statistical principles.

By understanding and applying these concepts, marketers can make data-driven decisions, optimize their marketing strategies, and ultimately drive better business outcomes.

10.7 REFERENCES

Anderson, M. J., & Whitcomb, P. J. (2017). *DOE simplified: Practical tools for effective experimentation.* CRC Press.

Armstrong, J. S., & Green, K. C. (2007). Competitor-oriented objectives: Myth of market share. *International Journal of Business, 12,* 117–136.

Auer, P., Cesa-Bianchi, N., & Fischer, P. (2002). Finite-time analysis of the multiarmed bandit problem. *Machine Learning, 47,* 235–256.

Box, G. E., Hunter, J. S., & Hunter, W. G. (2005). *Statistics for experimenters: Design, innovation, and discovery.* Wiley.

Bubeck, S., & Cesa-Bianchi, N. (2012). Regret analysis of stochastic and nonstochastic multiarmed bandit problems. *Foundations and Trends® in Machine Learning, 5*(1), 1–122.

Chapelle, O., & Li, L. (2011). An empirical evaluation of Thompson sampling. Advances in Neural Information Processing Systems, p. 24.

Cohen, J. (2013). *Statistical power analysis for the behavioral sciences.* Academic Press.

Fisher, R. A. (1925). *Statistical methods for research workers.* Oliver and Boyd.

Gelman, A., & Hill, J. (2006). *Data analysis using regression and multilevel/hierarchical models.* Cambridge University Press.

Gerber, A. S., & Green, D. P. (2012). *Field experiments: Design, analysis, and interpretation.* W. W. Norton.

Kohavi, R., Deng, A., Frasca, B., Longbotham, R., Walker, T., & Xu, Y. (2012, August). Trustworthy online controlled experiments: Five puzzling outcomes explained. In *Proceedings of the 18th ACM SIGKDD International Conference on Knowledge Discovery and Data Mining* (pp. 786–794).

Kohavi, R., Longbotham, R., Sommerfield, D., & Henne, R. M. (2009). Controlled experiments on the web: Survey and practical guide. *Data Mining and Knowledge Discovery, 18*, 140–181.

Lewis, R. A., & Rao, J. M. (2015). The unfavorable economics of measuring the returns to advertising. *The Quarterly Journal of Economics, 130*(4), 1941–1973.

Montgomery, D. C. (2017). *Design and analysis of experiments*. Wiley.

Myers, R. H., Montgomery, D. C., & Anderson-Cook, C. M. (2016). *Response surface methodology: Process and product optimization using designed experiments*. Wiley.

Scott, S. L. (2015). Multi-armed bandit experiments in the online service economy. *Applied Stochastic Models in Business and Industry, 31*(1), 37–45.

Sutton, R. S., & Barto, A. G. (2018). *Reinforcement learning: An introduction*. MIT press.

Tokic, M. (2010, September). Adaptive ε-Greedy exploration in reinforcement learning based on value differences. *Annual Conference on Artificial Intelligence* (pp. 203–210). Springer Berlin Heidelberg.

Wu, C. J., & Hamada, M. S. (2011). *Experiments: Planning, analysis, and optimization*. Wiley.

EXERCISE 10.1: ANALYZING A SIMPLE A/B TEST

Objective: To demonstrate the basic principles of experimental design using an A/B test scenario in email marketing.

Tasks:
You are provided with data from an email marketing campaign where two different subject lines were tested to see which one yields a higher open rate. Your task is to analyze the data to determine which subject line performed better.

1. **Statistical Test:** Perform a *t*-test to see if the difference in open rates between the two groups is statistically significant.
2. **Interpret Results:** Based on the *p*-value from the *t*-test, conclude which subject line performed better.

Steps:

1. **Import Libraries:**

```
1. import scipy.stats as stats
2. import pandas as pd
```

We import two libraries: **scipy.stats** for statistical tests and **pandas** for handling data in a structured form (DataFrames).

2. **Load the Data:**

```
3. email_marketing_data = pd.read_csv('/data/Email_Marketing_
AB_Test_Data.csv')
```

We load the data into a pandas DataFrame. This data simulates the open rates of emails for two different subject lines (Group A and Group B).

3. **Separate the Data into Two Groups:**

```
4. group_A = email_marketing_data[email_marketing_data['Group']
== 'A']['OpenRate']
5. group_B = email_marketing_data[email_marketing_data['Group']
== 'B']['OpenRate']
```

Here, we filter the DataFrame to create two separate series: one for each group. **group_A** contains the open rates for subject line A, and **group_B** for subject line B.

4. **Perform a *t*-Test:**

```
6. t_stat, p_value = stats.ttest_ind(group_A, group_B)
```

We perform an independent *t*-test (**ttest_ind**) to compare the mean open rates of the two groups. This test will help us determine if there is a statistically significant difference between the two subject lines' open rates.

EXERCISE 10.1: OUTPUT

1. **Results:**
   - **t_stat**: −7.041427369013264
   - **p_value**: 3.059820094514218e-11

The **t_stat** is the calculated *t*-statistic value, and the **p_value** is the probability of observing a value as extreme as the *t*-statistic under the null hypothesis. In this case, the *p*-value is extremely low (way below the typical threshold of 0.05), suggesting that there is a statistically significant difference between the open rates of Group A and Group B.

In conclusion, based on this analysis, we can confidently say that the open rates of the two subject lines are significantly different. If Group B's mean open rate is higher, it implies that subject line B was more effective in this email marketing campaign.

EXERCISE 10.2: FRACTIONAL FACTORIAL DESIGN IN AD OPTIMIZATION

Objective: To illustrate the application of fractional factorial designs in optimizing an advertising campaign.

Tasks:

You are given a dataset from an online advertising experiment with several factors (such as ad color, placement, and size) and their levels. Your task is to analyze the data to determine the optimal combination of these factors for maximum click-through rate.

1. **Factorial Analysis:** Use regression analysis to understand the impact of each factor and their interactions on the click-through rate.
2. **Optimization:** Identify the combination of factors that leads to the highest predicted click-through rate.

Steps:

1. **Import Libraries and Load Data:**

```
1. import statsmodels.api as sm
2. import pandas as pd
3. file_path = 'Ad_Optimization_Fractional_Factorial_Design_
Data.csv'  # Replace with the correct file path
4. ad_optimization_data = pd.read_csv(file_path)
```

We import **statsmodels** for regression analysis and **pandas** for data manipulation. Then, we load the data into a pandas DataFrame.

2. **Create Dummy Variables:**

```
5. ad_data_dummies = pd.get_dummies(ad_optimization_data,
drop_first=True)
```

Because our data contains categorical variables (AdColor, Placement, Size), we convert them into dummy variables for regression analysis. The **drop_first=True** argument is used to avoid multicollinearity by dropping the first level of each categorical variable.

3. **Prepare Data for Regression:**

```
6. X = ad_data_dummies.drop('ClickThroughRate', axis=1)
7. y = ad_data_dummies['ClickThroughRate']
8. X = sm.add_constant(X)
```

We separate the independent variables (X) and the dependent variable ('ClickThroughRate', y). We also add a constant to the model, which acts as the intercept in the regression equation.

4. **Fit the Regression Model:**

```
9. model = sm.OLS(y, X).fit()
```

We use ordinary least squares (OLS) regression to fit the model. This method finds the best-fitting line through the data by minimizing the sum of the squares of the vertical deviations from each data point to the line.

EXERCISE 10.2: OUTPUT

Model Summary: The summary of the regression model provides various statistics, including coefficients for each independent variable, standard errors, t-values, and p-values. These values help us understand the impact of each factor on the click-through rate.

- **Coefficients:** Indicate the change in the dependent variable for a one-unit change in the independent variable.
- **P-values:** Help determine the statistical significance of each coefficient. A low p-value (typically < 0.05) indicates that the factor is likely to have a significant impact on the click-through rate.
- **R-squared and Adjusted R-squared:** Measure the proportion of the variance in the dependent variable that is predictable from the independent variables.

OLS Regression Results

- **Dependent Variable:** ClickThroughRate

- **R-squared:** 0.015, suggesting that only about 1.5% of the variability in 'Click-ThroughRate' is explained by the model.
- **Adjusted R-squared:** −0.026, which is negative, indicating that the model might not be well suited for the data.
- **F-statistic:** 0.3724 with a p-value of 0.828, suggesting that the model may not be statistically significant as a whole.
- **Coefficients:**
  - **const:** 0.2808 (Intercept)
  - **AdColor_Green:** 0.0188
  - **AdColor_Red:** 0.0134
  - **Placement_Top:** 0.0137
  - **Size_Small:** 0.0174
- **p-values:** The p-values for individual coefficients are high, indicating that none of the advertising factors (AdColor_Green, AdColor_Red, Placement_Top, Size_Small) have a statistically significant impact on the 'ClickThroughRate' at the 5% significance level.

In this specific analysis, the R-squared value is quite low, indicating that the model does not explain a large portion of the variance in the click-through rates. This might suggest that other factors not included in the model or inherent randomness play a significant role in the click-through rates. The individual factors (ad color, placement, size) do not show strong statistical significance in this model, as indicated by their high p-values.

CHAPTER **11**

Big Data Technologies and Real-Time Analytics

11.1 INTRODUCTION

As the digital landscape continues to evolve, so does the amount of data that businesses generate and collect. This data, often characterized by its volume, velocity, and variety, is commonly referred to as *big data* (Gandomi & Haider, 2015). The rise of big data has drastically transformed the way businesses operate and make decisions. By leveraging it, businesses can gain deeper insights into their operations, understand customer behavior, predict future trends, and make data-driven decisions.

For marketing professionals, big data presents an opportunity to gain a 360-degree view of the customer. By analyzing the vast amounts of data generated through customer interactions across various touchpoints, marketers can develop more personalized and effective marketing strategies (Wedel & Kannan, 2016).

However, harnessing the power of big data is not without its challenges. The sheer size and complexity of big data require robust and scalable technologies for storage, processing, and analysis. This is when distributed computing frameworks, such as Hadoop and Spark, come into play. These technologies enable businesses to process and analyze big data efficiently and effectively (Zaharia et al., 2016).

In addition to processing and analyzing big data, there is also a growing need for real-time analytics. As the name suggests, real-time analytics involves analyzing data as it is generated to provide insights in real time. Real-time analytics plays a crucial role in various marketing activities, such as real-time bidding in digital advertising and personalization in e-commerce (Lu et al., 2018).

In this chapter, we will delve into the world of big data, explore distributed computing frameworks, discuss real-time analytics tools and techniques, and understand how these elements enable personalization and real-time marketing.

11.2 BIG DATA

11.2.1 Overview of Big Data

Big data is a term that describes the large volume of data, structured and unstructured, that inundates businesses on a day-to-day basis. It is characterized by the four Vs—volume, variety, velocity, and veracity—to highlight the importance of data quality (Laney, 2001):

- **Volume** refers to the enormous scale of data. With the digitization of businesses and the proliferation of online activities, organizations now deal with data amounts ranging from terabytes to zettabytes (Chen et al., 2014).

- **Variety** pertains to the diverse forms of data, which can be classified as structured (e.g., relational databases), semi-structured (e.g., XML files), and unstructured (e.g., text files, video, audio) (Jagadish et al., 2014).

- **Velocity** refers to the speed at which data is created, stored, analyzed, and visualized. In many cases, real-time or near-real-time data processing is required to gain timely insights and make quick decisions (Chen & Zhang, 2014).

- **Veracity** highlights the reliability and trustworthiness of data. Given the vast amount of data and its various sources, ensuring data quality and accuracy becomes a critical concern (Wang, 1998).

Big data has significant implications for marketing because it enables businesses to gain a deeper understanding of customer behavior, enhance customer engagement, predict future trends, and optimize marketing strategies (Wedel & Kannan, 2016). However, to fully leverage the potential of big data, businesses need to employ robust and scalable technologies for data storage, processing, and analysis (see Table 11.1).

11.2.2 Historical Perspective: From Traditional Databases to Big Data

The journey from traditional databases to the era of big data is a testament to the rapid evolution of technology and the ever-growing thirst for information. In the early days, businesses relied on simple file systems and later, structured relational databases, to store, retrieve, and manage data (Stonebraker & Cetintemel, 2018). These systems were designed for specific tasks, with clear schemas and a fixed infrastructure.

However, the digital explosion of the late 20th and early 21st centuries, driven by the internet, e-commerce, and social media, brought forth an avalanche of data. This data differed from the traditional structured format, encompassing varied forms such as text, images, and videos (Zikopoulos & Eaton, 2011). The existing systems, no matter how advanced, were ill-equipped to handle this surge in terms of volume and variety.

The need to process this vast and diverse data gave birth to the concept of big data and the development of technologies specifically tailored for it. NoSQL databases emerged as alternatives to traditional relational databases, emphasizing flexibility, scalability, and the capability to manage unstructured data (Han et al., 2011).

Table 11.1 The Challenges and Opportunities in Handling Big Data Along with Potential Solutions and the Current State of the Industry.

Challenge	Opportunity	Solution	Current State
Data volume	Derive insights from massive datasets	Scalable storage solutions such as HDFS	Widely adopted in the industry
Data velocity	Real-time analytics and decision-making	Real-time processing tools such as Kafka and Storm	Growing adoption for real-time applications
Data variety	Harnessing diverse data sources	Data integration tools and flexible databases	Tools in development and adoption phase
Data security	Ensuring privacy and trustworthiness	Advanced encryption and data masking techniques	High concern Solutions being actively developed

In parallel, distributed computing frameworks such as Hadoop came into existence, specifically designed for storing and processing vast amounts of data. These frameworks leveraged the power of multiple machines working concurrently, transcending the limitations of single-machine systems (White, 2012).

The transition from traditional databases to big data wasn't just a technological shift. It represented a broader change in the understanding of data's potential. With big data, businesses and researchers were no longer confined to looking at samples. They could analyze entire datasets, leading to richer insights and more robust decision-making processes (McAfee et al, 2012; see Figure 11.1).

11.2.3 Challenges and Opportunities in Handling Big Data

Big data, despite its potential, comes with a set of challenges. The sheer volume of data can be overwhelming, and without the right tools and strategies, organizations can easily find themselves drowning in data but starved of insights (Davenport, 2014).

Data quality is another concern. With the variety and speed at which data is generated, ensuring its accuracy, consistency, and reliability becomes challenging (Redman, 2013). Without addressing these issues, the insights derived might be flawed or misleading.

Data security and privacy are pressing concerns, especially in an age when data breaches and unauthorized data access are frequent. Protecting massive datasets, especially those containing sensitive or personal information, is paramount (Romanosky et al., 2011).

On the brighter side, the opportunities offered by big data are immense. Businesses can derive deep insights about their operations and customer behavior, enabling

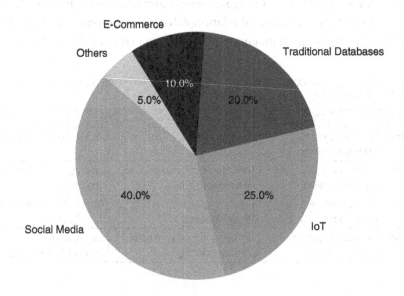

Figure 11.1 Distribution of Data Sources Contributing to Big Data

them to tailor their strategies with a precision that was previously unimaginable (Chen et al., 2012). Additionally, sectors such as health care, urban planning, and research have benefited immensely, harnessing big data for predictive analytics, simulations, and innovative solutions to long-standing problems (Lohr, 2015).

11.2.4 Relevance of Big Data in Modern Marketing

In today's hyper-connected digital world, marketing has transformed from a function that largely relied on intuition to one deeply rooted in data-driven decision-making. Big data plays a pivotal role in this transformation.

First, big data offers a comprehensive view of the customer. By analyzing data from various touchpoints, businesses can understand customer preferences, behaviors, and pain points with remarkable depth (Wedel & Kannan, 2016).

Segmentation and targeting have reached new levels of precision. Instead of broad-based campaigns, marketers can create highly tailored messages, optimizing them for micro-segments or even individual customers (Rust & Huang, 2014).

Predictive analytics, powered by big data, enables marketers to forecast trends, understand potential market shifts, and preemptively adjust strategies. This not only helps in resource optimization but also in gaining a competitive edge (Siegel, 2013).

Finally, big data has paved the way for real-time marketing. Brands can now respond instantly to emerging trends or events, creating marketing messages that resonate with the current mood or situation (Leppäniemi & Karjaluoto, 2008).

In essence, big data has fundamentally changed the way marketing functions, making it more agile, precise, and customer-centric than ever before.

11.2.5 Key Concepts in Big Data

The advent of big data has brought forth a set of new concepts that are critical for understanding its potential and challenges. These include data storage and management, data processing, data analytics, and data privacy and security:

- **Data storage and management.** Traditional data storage and management systems, such as relational databases, often fall short in dealing with the scale and complexity of big data. To address these challenges, NoSQL databases (e.g., MongoDB, Cassandra) have emerged and offer flexible schemas and horizontal scalability (Moniruzzaman & Hossain, 2013). Distributed file systems, such as Hadoop distributed file system (HDFS), are also employed to store large volumes of data across multiple machines (Shvachko et al., 2010).
- **Data processing.** To process big data, particularly in real time or near real time, distributed computing frameworks (e.g., Hadoop, Spark) are commonly used. These frameworks enable data processing tasks to be divided and run concurrently across multiple machines, significantly improving the processing speed (Zaharia et al., 2016).

- **Data analytics.** Big data analytics involves the application of advanced analytical techniques (e.g., machine learning, data mining) to large and complex datasets to discover patterns, generate insights, and support decision-making. It can be categorized into descriptive, diagnostic, predictive, and prescriptive analytics (Chen et al., 2012).

- **Data privacy and security.** With the increase in data volume and variety, issues related to data privacy and security have become more prominent. Businesses need to implement robust mechanisms to protect sensitive data and comply with relevant data protection regulations (Wang et al., 2011).

11.2.6   Practical Example: Big Data in E-Commerce Marketing

The impact of big data in the e-commerce industry is significant, with Amazon being a prime example. They leverage big data to provide personalized shopping experiences, forecast demand, and optimize operations:

- **Personalized shopping experience.** Amazon uses big data to track the browsing habits, past purchases, and preferences of its users to provide personalized product recommendations (Leskovec et al., 2014). This strategy enhances the shopping experience and helps to increase the conversion rate.

- **Demand forecasting.** Amazon uses big data to analyze historical purchase patterns, website traffic, and other external factors (e.g., holidays, promotions) to accurately forecast demand and manage inventory. This approach helps in minimizing stockouts and overstocks, thereby optimizing operational efficiency and customer satisfaction.

- **Operational optimization.** Amazon uses big data to optimize various aspects of its operations, such as warehouse management, logistics, and customer service. For instance, they use machine learning algorithms to predict the optimal locations for storing products in their warehouses, reducing the time it takes to retrieve an item and improving operational efficiency (Broussard, 2018).

11.3   DISTRIBUTED COMPUTING FRAMEWORKS

11.3.1   Overview of Distributed Computing Frameworks

Distributed computing frameworks, such as Hadoop and Spark, have revolutionized the way we process and analyze large volumes of data.

Hadoop, developed by Apache Software Foundation, is an open-source framework designed for storing and processing massive amounts of data across clusters of computers. Hadoop employs a distributed file system (HDFS) that allows data to be stored in an easily accessible format across a network of connected systems. Its processing model, MapReduce, enables the efficient processing of large datasets by dividing the workload and processing data in parallel (White, 2012).

Spark, also developed by Apache, is a fast and general-purpose cluster computing system. Although it also supports distributed data processing, Spark is known for its in-memory computing capabilities, which significantly speed up iterative algorithms or interactive data mining tasks. Spark supports a wide array of operations such as SQL queries, streaming data, machine learning, and graph processing, which are essential in handling various big data workloads (Zaharia et al., 2016).

These distributed computing frameworks have become essential in the big data ecosystem due to their ability to handle vast volumes of structured and unstructured data, their scalability, and their fault tolerance.

11.3.2 Basics of Distributed Computing and Its Necessity

Distributed computing, at its core, is a field of computer science that focuses on the design and implementation of systems that divide tasks and process data on multiple machines or nodes (Coulouris et al., 2005). This methodology stands in stark contrast to the traditional approach of using a single computer or system to perform tasks or run applications.

The fundamental necessity for distributed computing arises from myriad challenges:

- **Scale and complexity.** With the digital era ushering in massive amounts of data, traditional single-computer systems often hit processing and storage bottlenecks (Tanenbaum, 2007). Distributed systems, however, can scale out, meaning they can add more nodes to the system to manage increased load.
- **Fault tolerance and reliability.** Distributed systems are designed to be robust. Even if one or multiple nodes fail, the system, as a whole, continues to operate, ensuring that there is no single point of failure (Coulouris et al., 2005).
- **Resource sharing and collaboration.** Distributed systems enable a cohesive and efficient sharing of resources—be it computational power, data, or files— across a wide geographical area. This facilitates collaboration between entities located at distant places (Tanenbaum, 2007).

With the rise of big data, the adoption of distributed computing has become indispensable for businesses and researchers alike.

11.3.3 Introduction to Hadoop: Hadoop Distributed File System and MapReduce

Hadoop, developed by the Apache Software Foundation, is a seminal framework designed for distributed storage and processing of vast datasets. It has two primary components:

- **HDFS.** HDFS is the storage component of Hadoop, and it provides a distributed and scalable file system structure. The data in HDFS is broken down into blocks, typically of 128 MB or 256 MB, which are then replicated across multiple nodes, ensuring data durability and fault tolerance (Shvachko et al., 2010).

■ **MapReduce.** MapReduce is the computational paradigm of Hadoop, enabling it to process large datasets. It operates in two phases: the Map phase and the Reduce phase. The Map phase processes data and produces intermediate key-value pairs. These pairs are then processed by the Reduce phase to generate the desired output (Dean & Ghemawat, 2008). This model ensures parallel processing and offers scalability.

Hadoop's combination of HDFS and MapReduce provides an efficient framework to tackle large datasets, capitalizing on distributed computing's potential (see Figure 11.2).

11.3.4 Introduction to Apache Spark: Resilient Distributed Datasets, Spark Streaming, and Machine Learning Library

Apache Spark, another project under the Apache Software Foundation, is a fast and general-purpose cluster computing system. It offers a more advanced solution than Hadoop in certain contexts and brings a suite of libraries and features (see Figure 11.3):

■ **RDDs (resilient distributed datasets).** RDD is the foundational data structure of Spark. It is an immutable distributed collection of object that can be processed in parallel. RDDs offer fault tolerance by remembering the sequence of transformations applied to the base dataset, enabling it to rebuild lost data (Zaharia, Chowdhury, et al., 2012).

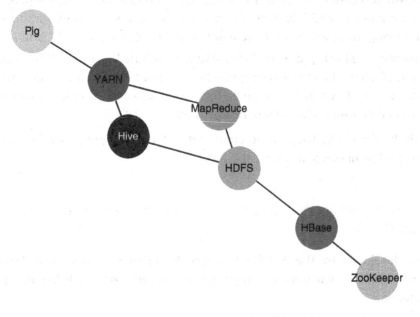

Figure 11.2 The Hadoop Ecosystem, Including Hadoop Distributed File System and MapReduce.

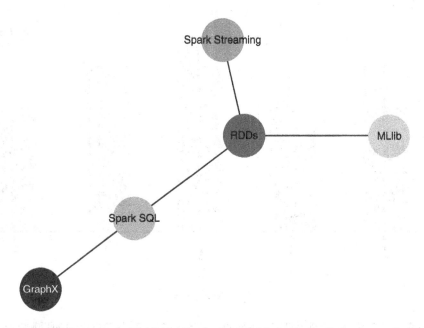

Figure 11.3 Apache Spark, Highlighting Resilient Distributed Datasets, Spark Streaming, and Machine Learning Library.

- **Spark streaming.** This is a feature that enables the processing of live data streams in real time. Data can be ingested from various sources, processed, and then pushed to databases, dashboards, or other systems (Zaharia et al., 2010).

- **MLlib.** MLlib stands for machine learning library, which is Spark's built-in library for machine learning tasks. It offers multiple algorithms and utilities, making it easier to implement machine learning on large datasets (Meng et al., 2016).

11.3.5 Choosing the Right Framework: Comparing Hadoop and Spark for Different Tasks

When it comes to choosing between Hadoop and Spark, the decision often boils down to the specific requirements of the task at hand (see Figure 11.4):

- **Data processing speed.** Although Hadoop and Spark offer distributed processing, Spark often outperforms Hadoop in terms of speed, primarily due to its in-memory computing capabilities. Hence, for tasks that require real-time processing, Spark is generally more suitable (Zaharia, Chowdhury, et al., 2012).

- **Ease of use.** Spark, with its high-level application programming interface, is considered more developer-friendly than Hadoop's MapReduce. It supports multiple languages such as Java, Scala, and Python, offering versatility in development (Zaharia et al., 2016).

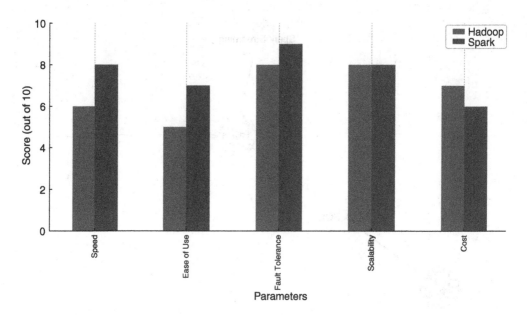

Figure 11.4 Comparison Between Hadoop and Spark, Focusing on Speed, Ease of Use, Fault Tolerance, and Other Parameters.

- **Cost-efficiency.** Hadoop's HDFS is a disk-based storage system, so it can sometimes be more cost-effective for storing massive datasets compared to Spark's in-memory approach (White, 2012).
- **Task complexity.** For complex, iterative tasks, especially in the domain of machine learning, Spark, with its MLlib, provides more advanced and efficient solutions. However, for simpler data processing and storage tasks, Hadoop can suffice (Meng et al., 2016).
- **Integration and compatibility.** Hadoop and Spark are compatible with each other. Spark can use HDFS for storage, and Hadoop can leverage Spark for computation. This flexibility enables organizations to choose the best of both worlds, depending on their specific needs.

In summary, Hadoop and Spark offer unique advantages. The choice between them should be based on the specific requirements of the data processing task, the scale of data, and the desired outcomes.

11.3.6 Key Concepts in Distributed Computing Frameworks

Several key concepts underpin the operation and functionality of distributed computing frameworks such as Hadoop and Spark:

- **Distributed storage.** This is the principle of storing data across multiple nodes in a network, rather than in a centralized database. In Hadoop, this is achieved through the HDFS. HDFS splits large data files into smaller blocks, distributes them across the nodes in the cluster, and maintains redundancy for fault tolerance (Shvachko et al., 2010).

- **MapReduce.** This is a programming model for processing large datasets with a parallel, distributed algorithm on a cluster. The Map function processes a block of data and generates a set of intermediate key-value pairs. The Reduce function merges all intermediate values associated with the same key (Dean & Ghemawat, 2008).

- **In-memory computing.** Spark uses in-memory computing, which stores data in RAM across a distributed network, enabling faster data retrieval and analysis compared to disk-based storage. This is especially effective for iterative algorithms in machine learning and interactive data mining tasks (Zaharia, Chowdhury, et al., 2012).

- **Fault tolerance.** Hadoop and Spark are designed to be fault-tolerant. This means they can continue operating even if individual nodes fail. Hadoop achieves this through data replication in HDFS, and Spark uses RDDs that track data lineage information to rebuild lost data (Zaharia, Chowdhury, et al., 2012).

- **Scalability.** Distributed computing frameworks can easily scale to handle more data by adding more nodes to the network. This ability to expand capacity makes these frameworks suitable for big data processing.

11.3.7 Cloud Technologies in Big Data and Real-time Analytics

The advent and evolution of cloud technologies have been a game-changer in how big data is managed, processed, and analyzed. Cloud platforms such as Amazon Web Services (AWS), Microsoft Azure, and Google Cloud Platform (GCP) have democratized access to high-performance computing resources, enabling businesses of all sizes to leverage big data analytics and real-time processing without significant upfront investments in infrastructure (Marston et al., 2011).

AWS offers a suite of services designed for big data solutions, such as Amazon S3 for storage, Amazon Redshift for data warehousing, and Amazon Kinesis for real-time data streaming and analytics (Jang et al., 2015). These services are scalable and can handle vast amounts of data, providing businesses the flexibility to pay for only what they use.

Microsoft Azure provides a similar range of services, with Azure Blob Storage for data storage, Azure Synapse Analytics for big data analysis, and Azure Stream Analytics for real-time event processing. Azure's integrated environment enables seamless hybrid data analytics, combining on-premises and cloud data.

GCP is noted for its BigQuery service, a serverless, highly scalable, and cost-effective multi-cloud data warehouse that enables super-fast SQL queries using the processing power of Google's infrastructure (Tigani & Naidu, 2014). Additionally, GCP's Pub/Sub and Dataflow services offer robust capabilities for real-time analytics pipelines.

Cloud technologies have also significantly affected real-time analytics by providing tools that can process and analyze data streams with minimal latency. These tools enable businesses to make data-driven decisions more rapidly, often in real time, thus opening up opportunities for instant personalization and dynamic customer engagement strategies (Li et al., 2010).

The advantages of cloud technologies in big data and real-time analytics include the following:

- **Scalability.** Cloud services can scale up or down based on demand, which is ideal for big data applications that may have variable workloads (Hashem et al., 2015).

- **Cost-effectiveness.** With pay-as-you-go pricing models, companies can optimize costs without compromising on computing capabilities (Mell & Grance, 2011).

- **Performance.** Cloud providers invest heavily in the latest technologies and infrastructure, ensuring high performance and availability (Armbrust et al., 2010).

- **Accessibility.** Cloud platforms make it easier for businesses to access and collaborate on big data projects globally (Hashem et al., 2015).

In summary, the integration of cloud technologies has become essential in the landscape of big data and real-time analytics, driving innovation and providing scalable, cost-effective solutions for businesses. The elastic nature of cloud resources aligns with the dynamic requirements of big data processing, whereas the advanced analytics services available on the cloud empower organizations to gain actionable insights faster than ever before.

By leveraging the robust infrastructure and services provided by major cloud providers such as AWS, Microsoft Azure, and GCP, businesses can focus on deriving value from their data rather than managing the underlying technology. This shift not only enhances operational efficiency but also accelerates the path from data to decision, enabling real-time personalization and responsive marketing strategies.

The evolution toward cloud-based big data solutions represents a paradigm shift in how data is processed, stored, and analyzed, marking a new era of agility and innovation in the marketing domain. As cloud technologies continue to evolve, they will undoubtedly form the backbone of marketing analytics, driving insights that are more predictive, actionable, and personalized than ever before.

11.3.8 Practical Example: Using Hadoop and Spark for Marketing Analytics

Hadoop and Spark are frequently used to handle and process vast amounts of data in marketing analytics. They can deliver valuable insights that could help in optimizing marketing strategies.

For instance, an international retail company might collect customer data from multiple channels, including online shopping platforms, in-store purchases, social media engagement, and customer service interactions. This data can be in different formats, such as text, images, and structured data. The data volume could easily reach several terabytes or even petabytes, making it a perfect use case for Hadoop's distributed storage capability.

First, the raw data is stored in the HDFS, where it's broken down into manageable blocks and distributed across the nodes in the Hadoop cluster (Shvachko et al., 2010). This system offers redundancy and fault tolerance, ensuring that no data is lost even if one or more nodes fail.

Next, the company uses MapReduce in Hadoop to preprocess and clean the data. For example, the Map function can be used to filter out irrelevant data, while the Reduce function can summarize the data into a more manageable format, such as daily sales totals for each store.

After the preprocessing and cleaning stage, the company uses Spark to perform more complex analyses. Thanks to Spark's in-memory computing capability, it can quickly process large datasets to deliver real-time insights. For example, the company might use Spark's MLlib to build a customer segmentation model, grouping customers based on their purchasing behavior, browsing history, and demographic information (Zaharia, Das, et al., 2012).

By leveraging Hadoop and Spark, the company can turn its massive customer data into actionable insights, such as identifying the most valuable customer segments, tailoring marketing campaigns to target specific groups, and optimizing product offerings based on customer preferences.

11.4   REAL-TIME ANALYTICS TOOLS AND TECHNIQUES

11.4.1   Overview of Real-Time Analytics

Real-time analytics is the use of advanced technology and methods to analyze data as soon as it is produced or collected. Unlike traditional analytics, which often involves analyzing historical data, real-time analytics enables immediate interpretation and action, offering businesses a significant competitive advantage.

Real-time analytics has become increasingly important as the volume, velocity, and variety of data have exploded in recent years (Chen et al., 2014). With the advent of the Internet of Things (IoT), social media, and other digital technologies, businesses can now collect vast amounts of data at an unprecedented speed. This data, when analyzed in real time, can provide valuable insights into customer behavior, market trends, and operational efficiency.

Several sectors, including finance, health care, manufacturing, and marketing, have embraced real-time analytics. In marketing, for example, real-time analytics enables marketers to monitor customer behavior and engagement in real time, enabling them to personalize marketing messages, optimize campaign performance, and improve customer service.

Real-time analytics can be facilitated by various tools and technologies. For instance, stream processing platforms such as Apache Kafka can process high-velocity data in real time, and real-time business intelligence tools can provide real-time analytics and visualization. In addition, machine learning and artificial intelligence (AI) techniques can be used to analyze complex data patterns and make predictions in real time.

Despite its benefits, real-time analytics also poses several challenges, including data privacy and security concerns, the need for robust and scalable IT infrastructure, and the requirement for advanced analytical skills (Chen et al., 2014).

11.4.2   Tools and Platforms: Kafka, Storm, and Elasticsearch

Real-time analytics necessitates the use of sophisticated tools and platforms that can handle the velocity, volume, and complexity of data streams. Among the array of available platforms, Kafka, Storm, and Elasticsearch have emerged as some of the leading solutions in the domain:

- **Kafka.** Developed by LinkedIn and later contributed to the Apache Software Foundation, Kafka is a distributed event streaming platform designed for high-throughput, fault-tolerance, and scalability (Kreps et al., 2011). Primarily employed for building real-time data pipelines and streaming applications, Kafka works by enabling producers to send messages to specific topics, which consumers can then subscribe to, facilitating real-time communication and data streaming between systems.

- **Storm.** Apache Storm is a distributed real-time computation system that enables processing of large volumes of high-velocity data (Toshniwal et al., 2014). With its ability to process streams of data, Storm is apt for real-time analytics, monitoring, and extract, transform, and load tasks. Its model is based on spouts (data sources) and bolts (data processors), enabling developers to set up topologies for data transformation and processing.

- **Elasticsearch.** An open-source search and analytics engine, Elasticsearch is adept at handling real-time indexing and searching tasks (Gormley & Tong, 2015). Built on top of the Lucene library, Elasticsearch is commonly employed for log or event data analysis due to its capability to query vast amounts of structured and unstructured data rapidly.

The combination of these tools provides a powerful suite for real-time analytics. For instance, one might use Kafka to stream log data, process it in real time using Storm, and then index and query it using Elasticsearch.

11.4.3 Implementing Real-Time Dashboards and Alerts

Real-time dashboards and alerts are crucial components for businesses that need instant insights and timely responses. They offer a visual representation of streaming data, enabling stakeholders to make informed decisions instantaneously.

- **Building real-time dashboards.** Leveraging platforms such as Elasticsearch with Kibana, a user can implement real-time dashboards. These dashboards can visualize various metrics, from system performance indicators to customer engagement metrics (Gormley & Tong, 2015). The key to an effective dashboard is not only the real-time data display but also the ease of interpretation, ensuring that stakeholders can immediately comprehend the data's significance.

- **Setting up alerts.** In tandem with real-time analytics, the capability to set up immediate alerts is crucial. For instance, using Storm's real-time computation potential, a system can monitor data streams for anomalies or particular events (Toshniwal et al., 2014). Once such events are detected, alerts can be triggered, sending notifications to relevant stakeholders via SMS, email, or other communication methods (see Figure 11.5).

11.4.4 Challenges in Real-Time Data Processing and Analysis

Although real-time data processing and analysis offer significant advantages, they also present challenges:

- **Data volume and velocity.** One of the primary challenges is the sheer scale of data streaming in real time. Systems must be equipped to handle massive data flows, ensuring that no data is lost and that processing occurs without lags (Chen et al., 2014).

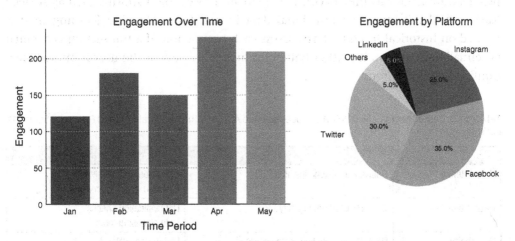

Figure 11.5 A Real-Time Dashboard Displaying Analytics from Social Media Marketing.

- **Data quality and veracity.** Real-time data streams might carry inconsistencies, noise, or errors. Implementing effective data cleaning and validation mechanisms in real time becomes paramount to ensure accurate analytics (Wang, 1998).

- **Infrastructure scalability.** The infrastructure must scale dynamically with fluctuating data loads. Static systems might struggle during peak data influx, potentially leading to data loss or system crashes (Kreps et al., 2011).

- **Complex event processing.** Identifying patterns or specific events within data streams, especially when they're spread across multiple streams, is a complex task. Systems need to be designed for such complex event processing to extract meaningful insights instantaneously (Cugola & Margara, 2012).

- **Security and privacy concern.** Real-time processing means data often gets transmitted between systems or over networks. Ensuring the security of this data and addressing privacy concerns become crucial, especially with regulatory frameworks such as GDPR emphasizing data protection (Wang et al., 2011).

Addressing these challenges necessitates a combination of robust infrastructure, efficient algorithms, and effective data management strategies (see Table 11.2).

11.4.5   Case Studies in Real-Time Analytics

11.4.5.1   Case Study 1: Real-Time Fraud Detection in Finance

The financial industry is a prime target for fraudsters, particularly in the domain of online transactions. As digital transactions have increased, so has the sophistication of fraudulent tactics. Traditional fraud detection systems that rely on historical data can lag behind and might not detect novel fraud patterns quickly enough.

A leading bank implemented a real-time analytics system to identify and halt suspicious transactions as they occur. Using stream processing platforms such as Apache Kafka, the bank ingests transactional data in real time. Machine learning models trained on historical fraud patterns assess each transaction. If a transaction is deemed potentially fraudulent, it's either halted for manual review or the user is immediately notified for verification.

Table 11.2 Challenges in Real-Time Data Processing and Analysis, Their Implications, and Proposed Solutions or Workarounds.

Challenge	Implications	Solutions/Workarounds
Data latency	Delays in real-time insights	Optimized data pipelines Reduced data transformation
Data integrity	Compromised data quality	Data validation checks Data cleansing tools
Scalability	Unable to handle high data volumes	Distributed systems Horizontal scaling
Data security	Potential data breaches	Data encryption Regular security audits

By implementing this real-time analytics system, the bank saw a significant reduction in fraudulent activities. Customers appreciated the immediate feedback, which protected their funds and enhanced their trust in the bank's security measures. Additionally, the system enabled the bank to adapt quickly to new fraud patterns, offering a dynamic defense mechanism rather than a static one.

11.4.5.2 Case Study 2: Real-Time Supply Chain Optimization in Manufacturing

In manufacturing, delays or inefficiencies in the supply chain can result in significant financial losses. Traditional supply chain management systems, which often work on historical data, may not react quickly enough to sudden changes or disruptions.

A global manufacturing company integrated real-time analytics into its supply chain management. IoT sensors were placed on equipment and in warehouses to track product levels, equipment efficiency, and shipment status. As data streamed in, real-time analytics tools processed this information, predicting potential bottlenecks, maintenance needs, or stock shortages. Alerts were sent to managers immediately on the detection of any potential issue.

The manufacturing company experienced several benefits from this system. There was a noticeable reduction in equipment downtime due to predictive maintenance alerts. Stock levels were optimized, reducing carrying costs and preventing production halts due to material shortages. The company was also better positioned to react to external disruptions, such as transportation delays, by adjusting production schedules or sourcing alternative suppliers in real time. This proactive approach led to smoother operations and cost savings.

11.4.6 Key Concepts in Real-Time Analytics

There are several key concepts and components that underpin the functioning of real-time analytics:

- **Data streaming.** Data streaming involves the continuous flow of data from various sources such as social media, website clickstream, IoT sensors, and so on. This data is processed sequentially and incrementally on a record-by-record basis or over sliding time windows (Kreps et al., 2011).
- **Real-time data processing.** The goal of real-time data processing is to take an action in response to an event within a set time frame, often within a few seconds or less. This can involve complex event processing, in which multiple streams of data from various sources are analyzed to identify meaningful events or patterns (Cugola & Margara, 2012).
- **Stream analytics.** Stream analytics involves the analysis of real-time data streams for decision-making purposes. It's essential for real-time customer engagement, fraud detection, and operational optimization.
- **In-memory computing.** In-memory computing stores data in RAM across a distributed network enables fast, real-time processing and analysis. It is a critical

component of real-time analytics because it enables high-speed data processing (Sakr et al., 2011).

■ **Event-driven architecture.** Event-driven architecture is a system design paradigm in which real-time decisions are made based on the detection of complex event patterns.

Understanding these concepts is crucial for implementing real-time analytics in marketing and other business applications, enabling organizations to respond quickly to changing market conditions and customer behaviors.

11.4.7 Practical Example: Real-Time Analytics in Social Media Marketing

One of the best illustrations of real-time analytics can be found in the realm of social media marketing. Social media platforms generate a wealth of data that is continuously updated, making it an ideal setting for real-time analytics.

For instance, consider a global company launching a new product and using a hashtag-based marketing campaign on X (formerly Twitter). The company can use real-time analytics to track the use and spread of the hashtag. They can monitor how quickly it is being shared, where it is being shared from, and by whom. This can enable them to adjust their marketing strategy in real time, capitalizing on what's working and addressing any areas of concern (Stieglitz et al., 2018).

Furthermore, real-time analytics can also be used for sentiment analysis. The company can monitor the overall sentiment of the tweets containing the campaign hashtag. If the sentiment begins to turn negative, they can quickly identify the issue and address it before it escalates.

Additionally, real-time analytics can be used to identify influential social media users who are interacting with the campaign. The company can then engage with these influencers in real time, potentially leveraging their reach for further campaign spread.

Real-time analytics tools for social media marketing can range from built-in tools in social media platforms such as Facebook Insights and Twitter Analytics to more sophisticated standalone platforms such as Brandwatch and Hootsuite, which provide more comprehensive and granular real-time analysis.

11.5 PERSONALIZATION AND REAL-TIME MARKETING

11.5.1 Overview of Personalization and Real-Time Marketing

Personalization and real-time marketing have emerged as vital strategies in the digital marketing landscape. They represent a shift from a one-size-fits-all approach to a more customized and real-time interaction with customers (Li & Kannan, 2014).

Personalization refers to the strategy of tailoring products, services, and communication to individual customers based on their preferences, behavior, and real-time information. It is often driven by data and predictive analytics and can be applied to various aspects of marketing, from personalized product recommendations and targeted advertising to personalized emails and website content.

Real-time marketing, however, involves brands reacting to events, customer interactions, or trends in real time, often through social media or digital channels. This form of marketing is spontaneous and immediate, designed to connect with customers at the right moment with the right message. It often requires the ability to analyze and act on data in real time.

The integration of personalization and real-time marketing can lead to highly effective marketing strategies. For instance, a customer browsing a company's website can receive personalized product recommendations based on their browsing behavior, and these recommendations can be updated in real time as the customer interacts with the website.

This approach can lead to increased customer engagement, improved customer satisfaction, and ultimately, higher conversion rates and increased revenue. Furthermore, it enables companies to differentiate themselves in a crowded market and build stronger relationships with their customers.

11.5.2 The Need for Real-Time Personalization

In today's digital age, consumers are surrounded by a plethora of information and options. Their attention spans have shortened, and their expectations for relevance have heightened. Real-time personalization addresses this challenge head-on. It's a method of tailoring the content, products, or service recommendations to individual users in real time based on their current behavior, past interactions, and other contextual information (Li & Kannan, 2014).

The benefits of real-time personalization are multifaceted. First, it enhances the user experience. When users feel that the content is tailored specifically for them, it leads to a more engaging and meaningful interaction (Tam & Ho, 2006). Furthermore, real-time personalization can significantly affect the bottom line. By presenting users with products or services they are more likely to be interested in at that very moment, companies can boost conversion rates, increase average transaction values, and foster customer loyalty (Moe & Fader, 2004).

Moreover, in an environment where customer preferences can shift rapidly, and external factors such as current events or trends can influence behavior, real-time personalization ensures that businesses remain agile, adapting their offerings in tune with the evolving consumer landscape.

11.5.3 Techniques for On-the-Fly Segmentation and Targeting

On-the-fly segmentation and targeting involve classifying users into specific segments based on real-time data and then providing tailored content or offers to those

Table 11.3 Techniques for On-the-Fly Segmentation and Targeting, Along with Their Pros, Cons, and Ideal Use Cases.

Technique	Pros	Cons	Ideal Use Cases
Behavioral tracking	Real-time user insights Personalized content	Privacy concerns Data storage challenges	E-commerce websites Content platforms
Predictive analysis	Forecast user behavior Enhanced user engagement	Requires historical data Model inaccuracies	E-mail marketing Product recommendations
Location-based targeting	Geographically relevant content Increased conversion	Requires location access Privacy intrusion	Local deals/promotions Travel apps

segments immediately (see Table 11.3). Machine learning models, particularly clustering algorithms, have become instrumental in achieving this (Chen et al., 2012). For instance, unsupervised machine learning techniques can analyze user behavior during a session and place them into a segment that has displayed similar behaviors in the past.

Another technique involves analyzing the user's journey or click path in real time to determine their intent and then delivering content or product recommendations that align with that intent (Montgomery et al., 2004). For example, if a user on an e-commerce site checks out several product reviews and then moves to the price comparison page, they might be closer to making a purchase decision.

11.5.4 Using Real-Time Data for Dynamic Content Optimization

Dynamic content optimization refers to adjusting website or app content in real time based on user behavior, preferences, or external factors. One prominent method involves A/B testing in which different versions of content are presented to users, and their reactions are measured in real time (Kohavi et al., 2009). The version that results in better user engagement or conversions becomes the preferred choice.

Another approach involves using predictive analytics to determine what content a particular user is most likely to engage with and then presenting that content dynamically. For instance, if an online news portal understands from past behavior that a user is interested in technology and sports news, the front page for that user might prioritize articles from these categories.

Real-time feedback loops, in which user interactions with content are immediately analyzed to refine and adjust content strategies, are also crucial. For instance, if a piece of content is generating high levels of engagement, it can be promoted more prominently.

11.5.5 Case Studies: Successful Real-Time Marketing Campaigns

- **Oreo's Super Bowl tweet.** During the 2013 Super Bowl, there was an unexpected power outage. Seizing the moment, Oreo tweeted, "You can still dunk in the dark," which became a sensation (Rooney, 2013). This real-time marketing reaction showcased the brand's agility and ability to connect with a massive audience during a live event.

- **Netflix's personalized thumbnails.** Netflix's recommendation engine is well regarded, but they took personalization a step further with dynamic thumbnail optimization (Gomez-Uribe & Hunt, 2015). By analyzing viewing history, Netflix adjusts the thumbnails of shows and movies to cater to individual user preferences, increasing click-through rates.
- **Spotify's "Year in Music" campaign.** Leveraging user data, Spotify provides its users with a personalized "Year in Music" recap, detailing their most played songs, genres, and total listening time. This personalized touch fosters a deeper connection between the user and the platform.

These case studies underline the potency of real-time marketing and personalization and how they can foster genuine connections, increase brand loyalty, and drive user engagement.

11.5.6 Key Concepts in Personalization and Real-Time Marketing

Several key concepts underpin the effective execution of personalization and real-time marketing strategies:

- **Customer segmentation.** This involves grouping customers based on various factors such as demographics, behaviors, interests, and more. It is a fundamental aspect of personalization because it enables targeted marketing efforts (Wedel & Kannan, 2016).
- **Behavioral tracking.** This includes monitoring customer behavior across various channels, such as websites, social media, and email. The data gathered provides valuable insights for personalization.
- **Dynamic content.** This is content that changes based on the user's behavior, preferences, or real-time factors. It's crucial for personalization and real-time marketing.
- **Predictive analytics.** This is the use of data, statistical algorithms, and machine learning techniques to identify the likelihood of future outcomes. It can be used to predict customer behavior and enable more effective personalization.
- **Real-time data analysis.** This involves the processing and analysis of data as it is generated or received. It enables businesses to respond immediately to emerging trends or customer actions, which is essential for real-time marketing.
- **Trigger-based marketing.** This refers to marketing actions that are triggered by specific customer behaviors or events. It's an important component of real-time marketing.
- **Omnichannel marketing.** This is the practice of integrating and coordinating marketing efforts across multiple channels. It's crucial for ensuring a consistent and personalized customer experience.
- **A/B testing.** This is a method of comparing two versions of a web page, ad, or other marketing material to see which performs better. It's essential for refining and optimizing personalization and real-time marketing strategies.

11.5.7 Practical Example: Personalization and Real-Time Marketing for an Online Retailer

Consider a large online retailer, similar to Amazon, which employs personalization and real-time marketing strategies to enhance customer experience and boost sales by enhancing the user experience of its younger audience segment (Campaign A) (see Figure 11.6):

- **Personalization.** The retailer uses a variety of data, including past purchases, browsing history, and customer demographics, to tailor the shopping experience for its Campaign A. For example, when a customer logs into their account, they are greeted by name and presented with a home page filled with product recommendations that align with their tastes and preferences. This personalization extends to marketing communications, in which customers receive emails or push notifications featuring products they may be interested in based on their past behavior (Xu et al., 2014).

- **Real-time marketing.** The retailer takes advantage of real-time data to react instantly to customer behavior in Campaign A. For instance, if a customer adds an item to their cart but doesn't complete the purchase, the retailer may send an email reminder or offer a time-limited discount to encourage the purchase. During significant events or holidays, the retailer may adjust their home page

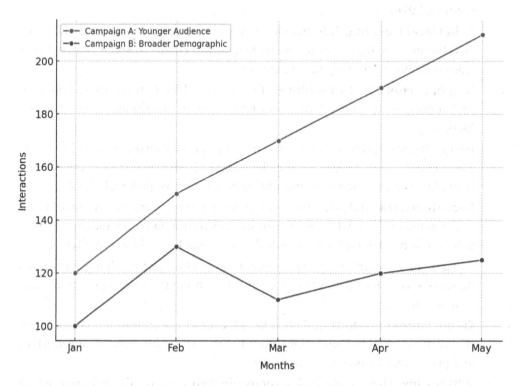

Figure 11.6 Younger Audience (Campaign A) Interactions Compared to the Broader Demographic (Campaign B).

and promotions in real time to reflect the occasion and capitalize on increased customer interest.

- ▪ **Implementation.** To support these strategies, the retailer uses advanced data analytics platforms and machine learning algorithms. These systems process massive amounts of data in real time, enabling instant personalization and marketing responses. A/B testing is continually used to refine strategies, ensuring the most effective personalization and real-time marketing tactics are employed.

- ▪ **Outcomes.** As a result of these strategies, the retailer experiences increased customer engagement, interactions, higher conversion rates, and improved customer loyalty from customers in Campaign A compared to the broader demographic (Campaign B).

11.6 CONCLUSION

The integration of big data and real-time analytics stands as one of the most transformative advancements in the modern digital era. This chapter delved deep into understanding the foundational technologies, tools, and methods that underpin this integration, unveiling the vast potentials and challenges in the realm of marketing data science.

One of the primary takeaways from this exploration is the sheer magnitude and complexity of big data. As the name suggests, big data isn't just about volume; it encompasses a diverse range of data sources, structures, and velocities. Its ubiquity in our interconnected world underscores the essence of modern business: every interaction, every transaction, and every touchpoint is an opportunity for data-driven insight. Technologies such as Hadoop and Spark have emerged as cornerstones in managing and processing this deluge, enabling businesses to make sense of the seemingly insurmountable.

Yet, it's not just the accumulation of data that's transformative; it's the capability to analyze this data in real time that's revolutionizing industries. Real-time analytics, facilitated by tools such as Kafka and Storm, empowers businesses to move from a reactive stance to a proactive one. In the world of marketing, this means engaging with consumers at the right moment, with the right message, in the right context. Such immediacy was once a luxury; today, it's a necessity to remain competitive and relevant.

However, with these advancements come significant challenges. The scale of big data mandates rigorous data governance, ensuring accuracy, security, and ethical use. Moreover, real-time analytics, although powerful, demands a robust infrastructure and a skilled workforce adept in the technical and business facets.

One must also acknowledge the dynamic nature of this field. The technologies and tools we've dissected in this chapter are continually evolving, driven by the relentless pace of innovation. As marketers, data scientists, and business leaders, there is a perpetual need for learning, adapting, and iterating.

In summation, big data technologies and real-time analytics are more than just buzzwords or fleeting trends; they represent the nexus of modern business strategy and technological prowess. Embracing them is not an option but a mandate for any enterprise aiming for sustainable growth and customer-centricity in this data-driven age. The future beckons a landscape where these tools are not mere facilitators but integral components of business strategy, steering the course of marketing endeavors across the globe.

11.7 REFERENCES

Armbrust, M., Fox, A., Griffith, R., Joseph, A. D., Katz, R., Konwinski, A., . . . & Zaharia, M. (2010). A view of cloud computing. *Communications of the ACM, 53*(4), 50–58.

Broussard, M. (2018). *Artificial unintelligence: How computers misunderstand the world.* MIT Press.

Chen, C. P., & Zhang, C. Y. (2014). Data-intensive applications, challenges, techniques and technologies: A survey on big data. *Information Sciences, 275,* 314–347.

Chen, H., Chiang, R. H., & Storey, V. C. (2012). Business intelligence and analytics: From big data to big impact. *MIS Quarterly,* 1165–1188.

Chen, M., Mao, S., & Liu, Y. (2014). Big data: A survey. *Mobile networks and Applications, 19,* 171–209.

Coulouris, G. F., Dollimore, J., & Kindberg, T. (2005). *Distributed systems: Concepts and design.* Pearson Education.

Cugola, G., & Margara, A. (2012). Processing flows of information: From data stream to complex event processing. *ACM Computing Surveys (CSUR), 44*(3), 1–62.

Davenport, T. (2014). *Big data at work: Dispelling the myths, uncovering the opportunities.* Harvard Business Review Press.

Dean, J., & Ghemawat, S. (2008). MapReduce: Simplified data processing on large clusters. *Communications of the ACM, 51*(1), 107–113.

Gandomi, A., & Haider, M. (2015). Beyond the hype: Big data concepts, methods, and analytics. *International Journal of Information Management, 35*(2), 137–144.

Gomez-Uribe, C. A., & Hunt, N. (2015). The Netflix recommender system: Algorithms, business value, and innovation. *ACM Transactions on Management Information Systems (TMIS), 6*(4), 1–19.

Gormley, C., & Tong, Z. (2015). *Elasticsearch: The definitive guide; A distributed real-time search and analytics engine.* O'Reilly Media.

Han, J., Haihong, E., Le, G., & Du, J. (2011, October). Survey on NoSQL database. *2011 6th International Conference on Pervasive Computing and Applications* (pp. 363–366).

Hashem, I.A.T., Yaqoob, I., Anuar, N. B., Mokhtar, S., Gani, A., & Khan, S. U. (2015). The rise of "big data" on cloud computing: Review and open research issues. *Information Systems, 47,* 98–115.

Jagadish, H. V., Gehrke, J., Labrinidis, A., Papakonstantinou, Y., Patel, J. M., Ramakrishnan, R., & Shahabi, C. (2014). Big data and its technical challenges. *Communications of the ACM, 57*(7), 86–94.

Jang, S. M., & Hart, P. S. (2015). Polarized frames on "climate change" and "global warming" across countries and states: Evidence from Twitter big data. *Global Environmental Change, 32,* 11–17.

Kohavi, R., Longbotham, R., Sommerfield, D., & Henne, R. M. (2009). Controlled experiments on the web: Survey and practical guide. *Data Mining and Knowledge Discovery, 18*, 140–181.

Kreps, J., Narkhede, N., & Rao, J. (2011, June). Kafka: A distributed messaging system for log processing. *Proceedings of the NetDB* (Vol. 11, No. 2011, pp. 1–7).

Laney, D. (2001). 3D data management: Controlling data volume, velocity and variety. *META Group Research Note, 6*(70), 1.

Leppäniemi, M., & Karjaluoto, H. (2008). Mobile marketing: From marketing strategy to mobile marketing campaign implementation. *International Journal of Mobile Marketing, 3*(1).

Leskovec, J., Rajaraman, A., & Ullman, J. D. (2014). *Mining of massive datasets*. Cambridge University Press.

Li, A., Yang, X., Kandula, S., & Zhang, M. (2010, November). CloudCmp: Comparing public cloud providers. *Proceedings of the 10th ACM SIGCOMM Conference on Internet Measurement* (pp. 1–14).

Li, H., & Kannan, P. K. (2014). Attributing conversions in a multichannel online marketing environment: An empirical model and a field experiment. *Journal of Marketing Research, 51*(1), 40–56.

Lohr, S. (2015). *Data-ism: The revolution transforming decision making, consumer behaviour, and almost everything else*. Harper Collins.

Lu, H., Li, Y., Chen, M., Kim, H., & Serikawa, S. (2018). Brain intelligence: Go beyond artificial intelligence. *Mobile Networks and Applications, 23*, 368–375.

Marston, S., Li, Z., Bandyopadhyay, S., Zhang, J., & Ghalsasi, A. (2011). Cloud computing—The business perspective. *Decision Support Systems, 51*(1), 176–189.

McAfee, A., Brynjolfsson, E., Davenport, T. H., Patil, D. J., & Barton, D. (2012). Big data: The management revolution. *Harvard Business Review, 90*(10), 60–68.

Mell, P., & Grance, T. (2011). *The NIST definition of cloud computing*. NIST.

Meng, X., Bradley, J., Yavuz, B., Sparks, E., Venkataraman, S., Liu, D., . . . & Xin, D. (2016). MLlib: Machine learning in Apache Spark. *Journal of Machine Learning Research, 17*(1), 1235–1241.

Moe, W. W., & Fader, P. S. (2004). Dynamic conversion behavior at e-commerce sites. *Management Science, 50*(3), 326–335.

Moniruzzaman, A.B.M., & Hossain, S. A. (2013). NoSQL database: New era of databases for big data analytics-classification, characteristics and comparison. *arXiv*:1307.0191.

Montgomery, A. L., Li, S., Srinivasan, K., & Liechty, J. C. (2004). Modeling online browsing and path analysis using clickstream data. *Marketing Science, 23*(4), 579–595.

Redman, T. C. (2013). Data's credibility problem. *Harvard Business Review, 91*(12), 84–88.

Romanosky, S., Telang, R., & Acquisti, A. (2011). Do data breach disclosure laws reduce identity theft? *Journal of Policy Analysis and Management, 30*(2), 256–286.

Rooney, J. (2013). Behind the scenes of Oreo's real-time Super Bowl slam dunk. *Forbes*. Retrieved from https://www.forbes.com/sites/jenniferrooney/2013/02/04/behind-the-scenes-of-oreos-real-time-super-bowl-slam-dunk/

Rust, R. T., & Huang, M. H. (2014). The service revolution and the transformation of marketing science. *Marketing Science, 33*(2), 206–221.

Sakr, S., Liu, A., Batista, D. M., & Alomari, M. (2011). A survey of large scale data management approaches in cloud environments. *IEEE Communications Surveys & Tutorials, 13*(3), 311–336.

Shvachko, K., Kuang, H., Radia, S., & Chansler, R. (2010, May). The Hadoop distributed file system. *2010 IEEE 26th Symposium on Mass Storage Systems and Technologies (MSST)* (pp. 1–10).

Siegel, E. (2013). *Predictive analytics: The power to predict who will click, buy, lie, or die*. Wiley.

Stieglitz, S., Mirbabaie, M., Ross, B., & Neuberger, C. (2018). Social media analytics–Challenges in topic discovery, data collection, and data preparation. *International Journal of Information Management, 39,* 156–168.

Stonebraker, M., & Çetintemel, U. (2018). "One size fits all": An idea whose time has come and gone. In *Making databases work: The pragmatic wisdom of Michael Stonebraker* (pp. 441–462). ACM.

Tam, K. Y., & Ho, S. Y. (2006). Understanding the impact of web personalization on user information processing and decision outcomes. *MIS Quarterly, 30*(4), 865–890.

Tanenbaum, A. S. (2007). *Distributed systems principles and paradigms.* CreateSpace Independent Publishing Platform.

Tigani, J., & Naidu, S. (2014). *Google BigQuery analytics.* Wiley.

Toshniwal, A., Taneja, S., Shukla, A., Ramasamy, K., Patel, J. M., Kulkarni, S., . . . & Ryaboy, D. (2014, June). Storm@ twitter. *Proceedings of the 2014 ACM SIGMOD International Conference on Management of Data* (pp. 147–156).

Wang, L., Zhan, J., Shi, W., & Liang, Y. (2011). In cloud, can scientific communities benefit from the economies of scale? *IEEE Transactions on Parallel and Distributed Systems, 23*(2), 296–303.

Wang, R. Y. (1998). A product perspective on total data quality management. *Communications of the ACM, 41*(2), 58–65.

Wedel, M., & Kannan, P. K. (2016). Marketing analytics for data-rich environments. *Journal of Marketing, 80*(6), 97–121.

White, T. (2012). *Hadoop: The definitive guide.* O'Reilly Media.

Xu, L., Duan, J. A., & Whinston, A. (2014). Path to purchase: A mutually exciting point process model for online advertising and conversion. *Management Science, 60*(6), 1392–1412.

Zaharia, M., Chowdhury, M., Das, T., Dave, A., Ma, J., McCauly, M., . . . & Stoica, I. (2012). Resilient distributed datasets: A {Fault-Tolerant} abstraction for {In-Memory} cluster computing. *9th USENIX Symposium on Networked Systems Design and Implementation (NSDI 12)* (pp. 15–28).

Zaharia, M., Chowdhury, M., Franklin, M. J., Shenker, S., & Stoica, I. (2010). Spark: Cluster computing with working sets. *2nd USENIX Workshop on Hot Topics in Cloud Computing (HotCloud 10).*

Zaharia, M., Das, T., Li, H., Shenker, S., & Stoica, I. (2012). Discretized streams: An efficient and {Fault-Tolerant} model for stream processing on large clusters. *4th USENIX Workshop on Hot Topics in Cloud Computing (HotCloud 12).*

Zaharia, M., Xin, R. S., Wendell, P., Das, T., Armbrust, M., Dave, A., . . . & Stoica, I. (2016). Apache Spark: A unified engine for big data processing. *Communications of the ACM, 59*(11), 56–65.

Zikopoulos, P., & Eaton, C. (2011). *Understanding big data: Analytics for enterprise class Hadoop and streaming data.* McGraw-Hill Osborne Media.

CHAPTER **12**

Generative Artificial Intelligence and Its Applications in Marketing

12.1 INTRODUCTION

Artificial intelligence (AI) is a broad field that encompasses various subfields, such as machine learning, computer vision, natural language processing, and more. Among these subfields, generative AI is one of the most exciting and innovative areas of research and development. Generative AI refers to algorithms that can generate new data samples based on a given dataset, such as images, text, audio, or video. These algorithms can learn from existing data and create novel and realistic content that mimics the original data distribution (Goodfellow et al., 2014).

Generative AI has many potential applications across different domains and industries, such as art, entertainment, education, health care, and more. One of the industries that can benefit greatly from generative AI is marketing. As discussed through this text marketing is the process of creating, communicating, and delivering value to customers and stakeholders. It involves understanding customer needs and preferences, designing and developing products and services, creating and distributing content, and measuring and optimizing marketing performance (Kotler & Keller, 2015). These algorithms have evolved significantly since the initial breakthroughs with generative adversarial networks (GANs) (Goodfellow et al., 2014) and variational autoencoders (VAEs) (Kingma & Welling, 2013), moving toward more sophisticated architectures that can generate increasingly complex and high-resolution outputs.

Generative AI can help marketers in various aspects of their work, such as content creation, personalization, segmentation, prediction, and optimization. By using generative AI, marketers can not only automate some of the tedious and repetitive tasks but also enhance their creativity and innovation. Moreover, generative AI can enable marketers to generate more relevant and engaging content for individual customers, as well as to model and anticipate customer behavior more accurately. This can lead to improved customer satisfaction, loyalty, retention, and lifetime value (Kingma & Welling, 2013).

Recent developments in transformer models, especially GPT-4 and its forerunners, have significantly affected generative AI, leading to revolutionary capabilities in text generation and comprehension (Brown et al., 2020). These advancements have paved the way for generative AI to play a transformative role in marketing, which at its core, seeks to create, communicate, and deliver value to customers (Kotler & Keller, 2015).

However, generative AI also poses some challenges and ethical issues that need to be addressed by marketers and businesses. Some of these issues include data quality, privacy, consent, ownership, authenticity, accountability, fairness, transparency, and social impact. For example, generative AI can create fake or misleading content that can harm the reputation or credibility of a brand or a person. It can also violate the privacy or consent of customers or users by using their personal data without their knowledge or permission. Furthermore, generative AI can introduce biases or discrimination in the data or the algorithms that can affect the outcomes or decisions of marketing activities (Žliobaitė & Custers, 2016). Marketers and businesses must navigate issues of authenticity, ownership, and social impact with diligence, adhering to emerging guidelines and frameworks put forth by governing bodies (European Commission, 2021).

Therefore, it is essential for marketers and businesses to be aware of the benefits and risks of generative AI and to use it responsibly and ethically. This requires following some best practices and guidelines that can ensure the quality, reliability, security, fairness, transparency, and accountability of generative AI applications in marketing (Chen et al., 2015).

In this chapter, we will explore the basics and principles of generative AI, its potential applications in marketing with some examples and case studies from different sectors and regions, and the ethical considerations that come with its adoption. As the technology continues to evolve and improve rapidly (such as with ChatGPT-4), it is important for marketers and businesses to stay updated about the latest advancements and understand how they can leverage them for enhancing their marketing outcomes while adhering to responsible practices.

12.2 UNDERSTANDING GENERATIVE ARTIFICIAL INTELLIGENCE: BASICS AND PRINCIPLES

12.2.1 Introduction to Generative Models

Generative AI encompasses machine learning techniques that aim to generate new data samples reflective of the training data's inherent distribution. The objective transcends replication; it's to grasp the training set's distribution intricacies to spawn new, variant-rich data points (Goodfellow et al., 2014).

Distinct from discriminative models, which discern class boundaries, generative models internalize class distributions. Their mastery in spawning novel data points underpins their nomenclature (Ng & Jordan, 2001). GANs, a prominent generative model subclass, embody a dualistic architecture—a generator that forges data instances and a discriminator that discerns between generated and authentic instances, enabling the generator to refine through iterative feedback (Goodfellow et al., 2014).

Generative models have burgeoned beyond GANs. VAEs have undergone significant refinement, allowing for more stable and controlled generation processes (Kingma & Welling, 2013). Furthermore, transformer-based models have brought forth a renaissance in generative tasks, especially in text generation, with models such as OpenAI's GPT-4 demonstrating unprecedented versatility and coherence across diverse domains (Brown et al., 2020).

In marketing, the potential of generative AI has magnified. It has ventured into the creation of hyper-realistic visual content for advertising, AI-driven copywriting tools that draft marketing copy varying in style and tone, and sophisticated prediction models for consumer behavior forecasting. These tools are now foundational in synthesizing realistic customer personas, thus refining segmentation, targeting, and positioning strategies (Smith & Linden, 2017).

Recent trends have seen the emergence of AI-driven design platforms that integrate with generative models, revolutionizing product design, packaging, and visual marketing materials. Companies are harnessing these platforms to iterate designs at a fraction of the time and cost required for traditional methods.

The burgeoning field of reinforcement learning also finds synergy with generative models, particularly in dynamic pricing and inventory management, by adapting to changing market conditions and consumer responses in real time.

Given the rapid evolution of generative AI, marketers must remain vigilant to the ethical implications. As AI-generated content becomes increasingly indistinguishable from human-generated content, the demand for transparency and authenticity escalates. The need for frameworks governing the responsible use of generative AI in marketing is not just prudent but necessary to sustain consumer trust and regulatory compliance (Diakopoulos, 2016).

12.2.2 Key Techniques: Generative Adversarial Networks, Variational Autoencoders, and Beyond

Generative AI encompasses a suite of AI technologies that synthesize data that is statistically similar to the training set. Predominant among these are generative adversarial networks (GANs) and variational autoencoders (VAEs) but recent advancements have broadened the spectrum:

- **GANs.** GANs, introduced by Goodfellow et al. in 2014, have continued to evolve, with newer architectures such as progressive GANs and StyleGANs enhancing the quality and resolution of generated images, as well as expanding into domains such as video and three-dimensional object generation. These innovations have further refined GANs' applicability in marketing for creating hyper-realistic product mock-ups and visual content for advertising (Karras et al., 2019, 2020).

- **VAEs.** Although VAEs are adept at generating complex data distributions, recent developments have focused on improving their stability and sample quality. Introduction of hierarchical VAEs and the employment of more powerful posterior inference mechanisms have made them even more robust in generating coherent and diversified outputs (Zhao et al., 2017).

- **Transformer-based models.** Transformer architectures, particularly in language generation tasks, have greatly affected generative AI with their ability to produce contextually relevant and syntactically coherent text. Marketing applications have immensely benefited from this for creating product descriptions, chatbots, and AI copywriting (Vaswani et al., 2017).

- **Applications of generative AI in marketing.** Generative AI can be used in various marketing applications, including content creation, personalization, predictive analytics, and customer behavior modeling. For instance, it can generate personalized emails, social media posts, or advertisements based on patterns it has learned from past marketing campaigns. Beyond content creation and personalization, generative AI's role in marketing now extends to creating synthetic datasets for market research, simulating economic and market scenarios, and generating interactive customer experiences through virtual realities and augmented reality applications.

- **Evaluation of generative AI models.** The performance of generative AI models is usually evaluated using metrics such as the inception score (IS) and the fréchet inception distance (FID). These metrics assess the diversity and quality of the generated samples compared to the original data.

- **Evaluation of generative AI models.** Although IS and FID, which are metrics that can assess the diversity and quality of the generated samples compared to the original data, remain standard metrics, there is a growing preference for more nuanced and application-specific metrics that can better evaluate the utility of generated samples in realistic settings, such as precision and recall metrics, and user studies for subjective assessment (Sajjadi et al., 2018).

12.2.3 Strengths and Limitations of Generative Artificial Intelligence

Generative models in AI, such as GANs and VAEs, have become bastions of innovation, offering a plethora of creative applications across various sectors, including the dynamic field of marketing (Goodfellow et al., 2014; Kingma & Welling, 2013). These models excel in synthesizing high-fidelity data, which has proven invaluable in the creation of digital art, music, and especially in the generation of realistic marketing content (Creswell et al., 2018). Their ability to augment data enriches the dataset available for training other machine learning models, a significant advantage in scenarios where data scarcity is a bottleneck (Antoniou et al., 2017). Real-time content generation is another forte of these models, enabling marketers to tailor dynamic advertising and content strategies that respond instantaneously to the changing landscape of consumer preferences (Radford et al., 2015). The evolution of personalization capabilities through generative AI has been transformative, leading to a new era of targeted marketing that caters to individualized consumer experiences at scale (Zhu et al., 2017).

However, the deployment of generative models is not without its challenges. The requirement for extensive computational resources can pose a significant hurdle, especially for organizations with limited capacity, potentially leading to a digital divide in marketing technology utilization (Brock et al., 2018). The reliance on the quality of training data is another critical aspect, in which biases or inadequacies in the dataset can lead to outputs that are less than realistic or even ethically problematic (Salimans et al., 2016). Assessing the quality of generated content remains a complex issue because conventional performance metrics fall short in capturing the nuanced aspects of quality and diversity in generative models, necessitating new evaluative frameworks (Borji,

2019). The potential misuse of generative AI, such as in the creation of deepfakes or the propagation of misinformation, presents a significant ethical concern, raising questions about the governance and oversight of this powerful technology (Chesney & Citron, 2019; see Table 12.1).

12.2.4   A Glimpse at Cutting-Edge Research in Generative Artificial Intelligence

The field of generative AI continues to grow at an unprecedented pace, with research advancements consistently breaking new ground. Updates in this vibrant research landscape often focus on improving the sophistication, efficiency, and accessibility of generative models. Here are some developments that could be integrated into this section to reflect the most current state of the field:

- **Advanced StyleGAN developments.** The progression from StyleGAN to StyleGAN2 and StyleGAN3 by Karras et al. has provided enhancements in image quality, removing artifacts, and introducing temporal consistency for video generation. These advancements have pushed the limits of what can be considered distinguishably different from actual photographs or videos (Karras et al., 2020, 2021).

- **Diffusion models.** Another notable advancement in generative AI is the emergence of diffusion models, such as denoising diffusion probabilistic models. These models, which gradually transform noise into structured data, have been applied to produce images of comparable fidelity to those generated by GANs, often with improved training stability and sample diversity (Ho et al., 2020).

- **Multimodal generative AI.** Research has also expanded into multimodal generative models, which can understand and generate content across different modalities, such as DALL-E by OpenAI for text-to-image generation and RAG (retrieval-augmented generation) for enhanced natural language understanding and generation by incorporating document retrieval into the generative process (Lewis et al., 2020; Ramesh et al., 2021).

- **Scalability and efficiency improvements.** There is a continual push toward making generative models more scalable and efficient. Innovations such as sparse transformers and distillation techniques enable the training of large-scale

Table 12.1 The Strengths and Limitations of Generative Artificial Intelligence.

Strengths	Limitations
High adaptability for creative applications	High computational and data requirements
Capacity for significant data augmentation	Outputs possibly unrealistic without proper training
Real-time content generation capabilities	Evaluation metrics for quality complex
Enhanced personalization for marketing content	Ethical concerns including potential for misuse

models with billions of parameters more feasibly, enhancing their performance and reducing computational requirements (Child et al., 2019; Hinton et al., 2015).

- **On-device and edge AI advancements.** Beyond Qualcomm's efforts, there's significant progress in the domain of on-device and edge AI, enabling powerful generative models to run on consumer-grade hardware. This includes advancements in model quantization and network pruning, which allow complex models to be compressed into a more efficient form without substantial loss in performance (Hubara et al., 2017).

- **Applications in marketing.** The utility of generative AI in marketing has continued to broaden, with AI not just personalizing content but also optimizing marketing funnels, improving customer journey simulations, and aiding in dynamic pricing strategies. AI-generated content has become increasingly indistinguishable from human-created content, enabling more automated and personalized customer interactions (Gentsch, 2018).

In summary, generative AI is not just a tool for creating realistic images or text but is rapidly becoming a multifunctional asset that can operate across different media, improve efficiency, and even run on consumer devices. These models are instrumental in crafting immersive experiences that have a growing impact on marketing, design, and creative industries.

12.2.5 Practical Example: Generative Artificial Intelligence in Content Creation and Personalization

Consider a company named *RetailX*, a major online retailer that has a wide range of products across multiple categories. They are facing the daunting task of creating and personalizing marketing content for millions of unique customers, with a diversity of preferences and shopping behaviors. To meet this challenge, RetailX decides to implement generative AI techniques.

They first collect a large amount of data about their customers, including past purchase history, browsing behavior, and personal details provided by the customers themselves. This data forms the foundation for the generative AI model.

The team decides to use a GAN model, which has shown promising results in creating personalized content. They train the GAN on the collected customer data. The generator part of the GAN uses this training data to create new, hypothetical customer profiles and their associated shopping behaviors. The discriminator part then evaluates these generated profiles for authenticity, helping the generator improve its output over time (Goodfellow et al., 2014).

After training the GAN, RetailX uses it to generate personalized marketing content for their customers. For example, they generate unique product descriptions and recommendations for each customer based on their hypothetical profile. They also use the GAN to create personalized email campaigns, where the subject line, content, and product recommendations are tailored to each individual customer.

Over time, they observe a significant increase in customer engagement and conversion rates. The personalized marketing content created by the generative AI model resonates with customers, leading to higher click-through rates and ultimately higher sales.

In this way, RetailX leverages the power of generative AI to automate and optimize their content creation and personalization process, achieving better marketing results and a more personalized shopping experience for their customers.

12.3 IMPLEMENTING GENERATIVE ARTIFICIAL INTELLIGENCE IN CONTENT CREATION AND PERSONALIZATION

12.3.1 Generative Artificial Intelligence for Content Generation: Text, Images, and Videos

Generative AI is an exciting and rapidly growing field of machine learning. It uses algorithms to generate content such as text, images, and music based on the patterns they learn from data. This innovative use of AI has started to revolutionize many areas, including content creation and personalization in marketing (Goodfellow et al., 2014).

In marketing, content is king. Creating personalized content that appeals to various customer segments can be a laborious and complex task. But with generative AI, we can automate this process and generate personalized content at scale, thus enhancing marketing efforts.

Generative AI has been used to write product descriptions, email content, social media posts, and even articles. In addition, it can create personalized product recommendations for individual users based on their preferences and past behavior. This increases engagement and click-through rates while improving the overall customer experience.

For example, AI writing assistant tools can help marketers draft more effective content by suggesting ways to improve clarity, conciseness, and tone. It can also generate unique and creative copies for advertising campaigns, catering to different customer personas.

Although the technology holds immense potential, there are challenges to be addressed. The quality of generated content heavily depends on the quality and amount of data fed into the AI system. The systems can sometimes generate inappropriate content, and there are ethical concerns surrounding the use of AI in content creation (Radziwill & Benton, 2017).

However, with further research and development, generative AI is set to become a game-changer in the field of content marketing.

12.3.2 Personalizing User Experiences with Generative Models

The world of marketing thrives on personalization. Generative AI extends this personal touch, offering bespoke experiences to users:

- **Hyper-personalized content.** Generative models can churn out content tailored to individual user preferences, from personalized emails to curated product suggestions, elevating user experience and potentially boosting conversions.
- **User interaction and feedback.** Some advanced systems can adapt in real time based on user interaction, ensuring the content remains relevant and appealing, further enhancing engagement rates.
- **Ethical considerations.** As personalization deepens, the thin line between curated experiences and invasive marketing blurs. It's imperative to approach AI-driven personalization with respect to privacy norms and user comfort (Voigt & Von dem Bussche, 2017).

12.3.3 Case Studies: Successful Generative Artificial Intelligence Marketing Campaigns

Several brands have embraced generative AI for pioneering campaigns:

- **Bespoke fashion designs.** Brands like StitchFix use generative models to forecast fashion trends, producing designs that resonate with current user preferences.
- **Music creation.** Companies like Amper Music employ AI to generate unique music tracks for advertising campaigns, ensuring they always have a fresh soundtrack (Briot et al., 2017).

12.3.4 Tools and Platforms for Generative Content Creation

For businesses keen on exploring generative AI, various tools and platforms simplify the journey:

- **OpenAI's GPT series.** This suite, especially the later versions, facilitates high-quality text generation, suitable for a plethora of content needs (Brown et al., 2020).
- **Runway ML.** This is an intuitive platform that brings the capabilities of generative models to visual content creation, from images to videos.
- **DeepArt.io.** Leveraging neural style transfer, this tool enables brands to craft unique visual content inspired by iconic art styles, adding a touch of class to campaigns.

12.3.5 Key Concepts

When considering the implementation of generative AI in content creation and personalization, several key concepts need to be understood:

- **Generative models.** Generative models, such as GANs or VAEs, are types of AI algorithms that generate new data instances similar to the input data. They're used to produce diverse and creative content, from synthetic images to text (Goodfellow et al., 2014).

- **Personalization.** In the context of content creation, personalization refers to tailoring the content to fit the individual needs and preferences of each user. This process improves user engagement and satisfaction. Personalization is often performed based on user profiles, behavior, and feedback, and with generative AI, it's possible to generate hyper-personalized content at scale.

- **AI creativity.** This concept refers to the ability of AI systems to generate content that is not only new but also creative and novel. Although this is a complex and subjective field, recent advances in generative AI have shown promising results in producing AI-created music, art, and text that is perceived as creative by humans (Elgammal et al., 2017).

- **Data privacy.** In the context of personalization, data privacy is a key concern. Data protection regulations such as GDPR impose strict rules on how personal data can be used, and it's important to ensure that generative AI applications respect these regulations (Voigt & Von dem Bussche, 2017).

12.3.6 Practical Example

Consider a retail brand that wants to improve its content creation and personalization strategies. Let's name the brand RetailXYZ. To keep up with the fast-paced retail industry, RetailXYZ needed a way to create a large amount of personalized content quickly and efficiently. They turned to generative AI to help meet these goals.

First, RetailXYZ used a generative AI model to create unique product descriptions. By feeding the model with data about product category, features, and existing product descriptions, the AI was able to generate thousands of unique descriptions in a fraction of the time it would have taken a human. It helped streamline the process and improve the consistency and quality of the descriptions across their entire catalog.

Next, RetailXYZ used generative AI to create personalized email marketing campaigns. The model was trained on past email campaigns and customer data to generate email content tailored to each customer's preferences and behavior. This resulted in higher open and click-through rates as the content was highly relevant to each recipient.

Finally, RetailXYZ harnessed the power of generative AI for social media marketing. They used the model to generate creative and engaging posts for different customer personas based on their interests and interactions with the brand on social media.

Despite initial challenges in refining the AI model to align with the brand's voice and ensuring it created appropriate content, RetailXYZ found significant success with generative AI. It not only improved efficiency but also enabled a higher degree of personalization in their marketing efforts.

This case study illustrates the power of generative AI in marketing. By automating the creation of personalized content, companies like RetailXYZ can more effectively engage their customers and enhance their marketing strategies.

12.4 GENERATIVE ARTIFICIAL INTELLIGENCE IN PREDICTIVE ANALYTICS AND CUSTOMER BEHAVIOR MODELING

12.4.1 Overview

Predictive analytics and customer behavior modeling have long been critical components of marketing strategy, enabling marketers to anticipate future trends, understand customer behavior, and make informed decisions. With the advent of generative AI, these fields are experiencing a paradigm shift.

Generative AI models can generate new data instances that resemble the training data. This has profound implications for predictive analytics and customer behavior modeling. In essence, generative AI can create synthetic datasets that mirror real-world scenarios, enabling marketers to simulate different marketing strategies and gauge customer responses without having to implement them in reality.

For instance, generative AI can simulate customer reactions to a new product launch or a pricing change, providing invaluable insights before the actual implementation. This can help marketers fine-tune their strategies, anticipate potential pitfalls, and optimize for maximum customer satisfaction and revenue growth.

Moreover, generative AI can also aid in understanding and visualizing complex customer behaviors. For example, generative models such as GANs can learn the distribution of customer behaviors and generate new instances that help in understanding the underlying patterns and trends.

Notably, generative AI is a powerful tool in the era of big data, where traditional predictive analytics techniques may falter due to the sheer volume and complexity of data. With its ability to work with large and complex datasets, generative AI provides an effective way to leverage big data for predictive analytics and customer behavior modeling.

12.4.2 Enhancing Predictive Models Using Generative Techniques

Generative AI techniques, especially those anchored in deep learning, have unlocked a new dimension in predictive modeling. Instead of solely leveraging existing datasets to make predictions, generative techniques enable the augmentation and enrichment of these datasets, facilitating better model training and more nuanced predictions. This section explores how generative techniques can enhance traditional predictive models, leading to better decision-making in the marketing realm.

12.4.2.1   Augmenting Data for Better Training

One of the fundamental challenges in predictive modeling is the scarcity of data. For instance, in customer behavior analysis, certain behaviors may be underrepresented due to their rarity. Generative models, particularly GANs, can be employed to generate synthetic data samples, ensuring that the model gets a holistic training experience (Wang et al., 2020).

12.4.2.2   Scenario Simulation

Generative models, by virtue of their data-generating capacity, can simulate diverse scenarios. A marketer wondering about the potential impact of a new pricing strategy can use these models to simulate customer responses, thereby gaining insights before actual implementation (Deng et al., 2016).

12.4.2.3   Data Imputation and Denoising

In many datasets, missing values or noisy data can compromise the predictive power of models. Generative techniques, especially VAEs, have shown potential in filling missing values based on the learned data distribution, thereby enhancing the quality of the dataset and, subsequently, the predictive outcomes (Lu et al., 2015).

12.4.2.4   Feature Generation

Generative techniques can also be instrumental in creating new features that might enhance the predictability of models. By learning complex patterns within the data, generative models can identify and generate features that might be nonobvious but significant for prediction tasks (Yoon et al., 2018).

12.4.2.5   Model Robustness

Predictive models can sometimes be vulnerable to slight perturbations in the input data, leading to erratic predictions. Generative models can be used to generate perturbed or augmented versions of the training data, thereby training predictive models to be more robust and consistent in their predictions (Zheng et al., 2016).

12.4.2.6   Understanding Complex Interactions

Many customer behaviors result from intricate interactions between multiple variables. Traditional predictive models might struggle to encapsulate these interactions, but generative models, with their capacity to understand data distributions, can capture and model these complex interactions, leading to more nuanced predictions (Choi et al., 2016).

In conclusion, the integration of generative techniques with predictive modeling heralds a new era in predictive analytics. By enabling data augmentation, scenario simulation, and a deep understanding of intricate patterns, generative techniques are poised to significantly enhance the accuracy and applicability of predictive models in marketing contexts.

12.4.3 Simulating Customer Journeys and Behaviors

The incorporation of generative AI into the simulation of customer journeys and behaviors opens up a new realm of possibilities. By creating hypothetical but realistic customer journeys, businesses can gain an in-depth understanding of potential paths a customer might take and make proactive decisions.

12.4.3.1 Virtual A/B Testing

Generative models can simulate the outcome of different marketing strategies on synthetic customer profiles. Instead of implementing strategies in real time and waiting to gather results, businesses can virtually test multiple campaigns on these generated profiles, enabling them to choose the most effective campaign beforehand.

12.4.3.2 Dynamic Customer Personas

Traditional customer personas are static. With generative AI, marketers can have dynamic personas that evolve with time, giving real-time insights into changing customer preferences. For instance, a dynamic persona might reflect how a customer's preferences change after major life events, such as marriage or the birth of a child.

12.4.3.3 Scenario Planning

Companies can use generative AI to simulate various scenarios, such as a new product launch or changes in market dynamics, to gauge potential customer reactions. This aids in risk mitigation, ensuring businesses are prepared for a wide range of outcomes (Ribeiro et al., 2016).

12.4.4 Potential Pitfalls and Misuses of Generative Predictions

Although generative AI offers a wealth of benefits, it is not devoid of potential pitfalls (see Table 12.2):

- **Overreliance.** The potential risk lies in over-relying on AI-generated simulations and predictions without considering real-world unpredictabilities. Generative models, after all, base their predictions on historical data, which might not always account for sudden changes in market dynamics.

Table 12.2 Potential Pitfalls and Misuses of Generative Predictions with Examples and Consequences.

Pitfalls/Misuses	Examples	Consequences
Generating misleading content	Generating fake product reviews	Misguiding customers Legal actions
Creating deepfakes for misinformation	Creating videos with fake endorsements	Spreading falsehoods Damaging reputation
Over-reliance on AI-generated predictions	Ignoring human judgment in crucial decisions	Potential business losses
Ignoring ethical considerations	Using generative AI without user consent	Loss of customer trust Legal issues

- **Ethical concerns.** Creating hyper-realistic customer profiles might border on intruding into customer privacy. Moreover, if the generated data is misunderstood as real data, it can lead to misguided marketing strategies or even legal implications (Žliobaitė & Custers, 2016).

- **Data bias.** If the training data has inherent biases, the generative models can reproduce and even amplify those biases, leading to skewed and potentially harmful predictions (Buolamwini & Gebru, 2018).

12.4.5 Future Avenues for Generative Predictive Analytics

The field of generative predictive analytics is ripe for innovation, and future advancements will likely be based on these enhancements:

- **Integration with other AI technologies.** Merging generative models with other AI systems such as reinforcement learning could pave the way for more adaptive and responsive marketing models that can react to real-time feedback (Arulkumaran et al., 2017).

- **More ethical generative models.** With increasing concerns over privacy and consent, we might see a push toward models that prioritize ethical considerations, leading to more transparent and responsible AI (Jobin et al., 2019).

- **Granular personalization.** As generative models become more sophisticated, the level of personalization they offer will become more nuanced, potentially enabling businesses to tailor content to individual moods, moments, or even physiological states (Brown et al., 2020).

- **Holistic customer understanding.** The future might see generative models that don't just predict buying behavior but also offer insights into a customer's entire lifestyle, from dietary habits to entertainment preferences, providing a holistic understanding of the modern consumer.

In conclusion, generative AI in marketing is an evolving domain that promises a blend of innovative possibilities and challenges. As the landscape continues to shift, the need for ethical considerations, robust methodologies, and a balanced human-machine collaboration will become even more pronounced.

12.4.6 Key Concepts

- **Generative models in predictive analytics.** Generative models, as opposed to discriminative models, do not just learn the boundaries between different classes of data but also the actual distribution of the data. This makes them ideal for tasks such as anomaly detection, where the goal is to identify data points that deviate from the norm. In predictive analytics, this could mean identifying unusual customer behavior or forecasting future sales based on historical trends (Goodfellow et al., 2016).

- **Customer behavior modeling.** Generative models can be used to simulate customer behavior. The model learns the behavior of customers from historical data and can generate new data that follows the same patterns. This can be particularly useful in scenario testing and decision-making. For instance, a company can use a generative model to predict the impact of a new marketing strategy on customer behavior.

- **Data imputation.** Missing data is a common problem in customer behavior analytics. Generative models such as VAEs can be used to generate missing data based on the patterns it learned from the available data. This can result in more robust predictive models and better insights into customer behavior.

- **Temporal modeling.** Many customer behaviors are time dependent, such as purchasing patterns. Generative models can be used to model these time dependencies, helping companies to predict future customer behaviors and optimize their marketing strategies accordingly.

12.4.7 Practical Example: Generative Artificial Intelligence in Predictive Analytics for a Retail Company

To bring the concept of generative AI in predictive analytics and customer behavior modeling to life, let's consider a real-world example of a multinational retail company. This retail company, let's call it RetailX, operates physical stores and an online platform. RetailX has a vast amount of customer behavior data from its loyalty program, which includes information such as frequency of purchases, amount spent, and products bought. The company wishes to better understand its customers and predict their future behavior to optimize marketing strategies.

RetailX employs generative AI, specifically a type of model known as a *GAN*, to learn the distribution of customer behaviors. After training on historical purchase data, the GAN can generate synthetic customer profiles that match the behavior patterns of real customers. This synthetic data serves as an expanded dataset for modeling, enabling RetailX to simulate a much larger customer base and predict various future behavior scenarios.

Furthermore, RetailX uses a type of generative AI model called *VAEs* to impute missing data in its customer behavior dataset. VAEs learn the distribution of observed data and can generate likely values for missing data points, making the customer behavior data more complete and reliable for further analysis and predictive modeling.

The use of generative AI models in predictive analytics and customer behavior modeling enables RetailX to better understand its customers, anticipate their needs, and tailor marketing strategies accordingly.

12.5 ETHICAL CONSIDERATIONS AND FUTURE PROSPECTS OF GENERATIVE ARTIFICIAL INTELLIGENCE IN MARKETING

12.5.1 Overview

As powerful as generative AI can be in enhancing marketing practices, it doesn't come without its ethical considerations and challenges. This goes beyond the usual concerns about data privacy and security, though these are still very relevant, to include novel issues unique to the power and capability of generative AI.

One of the main ethical considerations is the potential for misuse of generative AI in creating misleading or even harmful content. Deepfakes, a notable example of generative AI technology, have been used to create fake news and spread disinformation, posing serious threats to individuals and societies (Chesney & Citron, 2019). Similarly, in marketing, there is a potential for generating misleading or deceptive ads, leading to consumer distrust and damage to brand reputation.

Another ethical concern lies in the opacity of generative AI models. These models, being highly complex, often lack transparency and explainability, making it hard to interpret their outputs or the processes that led to them (Arrieta et al., 2020). This opacity could lead to unintentional bias, unfairness, and discrimination in marketing practices.

The future prospects of generative AI in marketing, however, are highly promising. It's expected to drive more personalized and engaging marketing experiences, streamline content creation processes, and provide deeper insights into customer behaviors and preferences. Furthermore, advancements in AI ethics and regulation, along with ongoing research into making AI more transparent and interpretable, are expected to address many of the ethical concerns associated with generative AI (Mehrabi et al., 2021).

12.5.2 Ethical Challenges: Deepfakes, Misinformation, and More

The rapid evolution of generative AI has brought with it myriad ethical challenges. Deepfakes, which use GANs to create hyper-realistic but entirely fictitious video content, are perhaps the most well-known menace. Such technologies, in the hands of those with malicious intent, can misrepresent events, undermine reputations, or even manipulate public opinion and political processes.

Moreover, misinformation is not limited to deepfakes. Generative AI has the capability to create false news articles, fake images, or counterfeit voices. The dissemination of such false content can erode trust in reputable news sources, thereby destabilizing societal structures (Zellers et al., 2019).

12.5.3 Responsible Use of Generative Artificial Intelligence in Marketing

Marketing professionals must navigate this new landscape with a keen ethical compass. The power of generative AI should be used responsibly (see Table 12.3):

- **Transparency and disclosure.** Companies should disclose when they employ generative AI, especially when creating promotional content. Being transparent about the use of these technologies not only fosters trust but also maintains the integrity of the brand.
- **Ethical data collection and use.** Marketers should ensure that any data used to train generative models are obtained ethically, respecting privacy rights and data protection regulations.
- **Avoidance of misleading representations.** Generative AI should not be used to fabricate testimonials, reviews, or endorsements. Authenticity remains paramount in building and maintaining brand loyalty.

12.5.4 The Future of Generative Artificial Intelligence: What's on the Horizon?

Generative AI's future holds immense promise. We anticipate advancements in the refinement of deepfake detection tools, leveraging the "arms race" between generators and detectors. Additionally, as AI continues to understand human behaviors and preferences better, we might see the development of more personalized and efficient marketing campaigns.

Innovations are also on the horizon in terms of real-time content generation. Imagine a world where marketing campaigns are dynamically created in real time based on current events, consumer sentiment, or even weather patterns.

Table 12.3 Best Practices for Responsible Use of Generative Artificial Intelligence in Marketing.

Best Practices	Reasoning
Always disclose AI-generated content to users	Builds trust and maintains transparency
Refrain from generating misleading content	Prevents legal issues and maintains integrity
Conduct regular audits of AI models	Ensures model accuracy and ethical use
Stay updated with ethical guidelines	Aligns with industry standards and best practices
Ensure transparency in AI processes	Helps in stakeholder communication and trust building

12.5.5 Preparing for a Generative Artificial Intelligence-Dominated Marketing Landscape

To thrive in an AI-dominated landscape, marketing professionals must do the following:

- **Embrace continuous learning.** The field is rapidly evolving, and professionals need to stay updated with the latest tools, techniques, and ethical guidelines.

- **Invest in tools and platforms.** Companies should invest in platforms that enable them to harness the power of generative AI responsibly and effectively.

- **Engage in ethical discussions.** Marketers should participate in broader societal and industry-wide conversations about the ethical implications and guidelines for the use of these potent technologies.

In conclusion, although the growth and capabilities of generative AI present challenges, they also offer unprecedented opportunities for innovation and connection in the world of marketing.

12.5.6 Key Concepts

- **Misuse and misinformation.** As highlighted by Chesney and Citron (2019), the capabilities of generative AI have led to the creation of deepfakes, which have the potential to mislead consumers and the public. Marketers must be aware of the implications of creating content that can be mistaken for authentic human-generated content, including the potential to mislead consumers and damage brand credibility.

- **Transparency and opacity.** Generative AI models, similar to many machine learning models, can be opaque, making it difficult to understand how they make decisions or produce outputs. This opacity raises ethical issues about fairness, bias, and accountability (Arrieta et al., 2020).

- **Bias and fairness.** Generative AI models can inadvertently learn and propagate biases present in their training data. These biases can lead to unfair or discriminatory outcomes when used in marketing applications (Mehrabi et al., 2021).

- **Regulation and governance.** As the use of generative AI in marketing becomes more prevalent, there will be a growing need for regulations and governance mechanisms to ensure ethical and fair use. This includes mechanisms for data privacy, transparency, accountability, and consent.

- **The future of generative AI in marketing.** Despite these ethical considerations, the future of generative AI in marketing is bright. It has the potential to revolutionize content creation, personalization, and customer engagement, as well as provide deeper insights into customer behaviors and preferences. However, the ethical considerations and challenges will need to be addressed to fully realize this potential.

12.5.7 Practical Example

Let's consider the case of an online fashion retailer that uses generative AI to create personalized advertisements. The AI analyzes data about a customer's past purchases, browsing history, and stated preferences, and then uses this data to generate highly customized ads, including creating digital images of outfits it predicts the customer will like.

This application of generative AI has several ethical implications that the retailer must consider:

- **Transparency and misinformation.** The generated ads could be so realistic that customers might mistake them for actual products available for purchase. If not properly disclosed, this could be seen as misleading. As suggested by Chesney and Citron (2019), it's important that the company clearly indicates the AI-generated images to maintain transparency and avoid misinformation.

- **Bias and fairness.** Suppose the retailer's generative AI has been trained on historical data that predominantly includes young, thin models. The AI might then generate images that perpetuate these body types, resulting in a biased portrayal of beauty standards. As noted by Mehrabi et al. (2021), to prevent this, the retailer should ensure that the training data is representative of diverse body types and that the AI doesn't unfairly exclude or stereotype certain groups.

- **Data privacy.** The retailer must be mindful of data privacy regulations when collecting and using customer data for AI. As per Goodman and Flaxman (2017), the company must ensure that the customer data used to personalize ads is collected and stored in accordance with regulations such as GDPR and CCPA.

- **Future prospects.** Looking forward, as the retailer improves its generative AI capabilities and addresses these ethical considerations, it could create even more personalized shopping experiences. For instance, the AI could generate images showing how clothes would look on the customer's own body or in their own home. However, ethical considerations, especially about data privacy and transparency, will continue to be a top priority.

12.6 CONCLUSION

Generative AI stands at the forefront of a transformative wave in marketing, poised to redefine the realms of creativity, efficiency, and hyper-personalization. It promises to enrich consumer interactions, crafting content that resonates on a deeply individual level. Nevertheless, such power carries substantial ethical implications. The potential for generative technologies to undermine public trust through misuse or overuse is a pressing concern, and missteps could prompt skepticism or even provoke regulatory action.

The increasingly indistinct boundary between content created by humans and that generated by AI amplifies the importance of authenticity in marketing strategies. Transparency in the use of AI will be essential for brands that aim to maintain a sincere connection with their customers. Authenticity in marketing transcends mere honesty; it's about forging and cultivating genuine relationships.

As generative AI becomes more entrenched, the marketing industry will see a surge in demand for professionals who can adeptly weave AI into marketing strategies while navigating the ethical quandaries it presents. The emerging skill set will demand a hybrid of technological acumen and ethical discernment.

Businesses that strategically leverage generative AI, although conscientiously addressing ethical concerns and emphasizing authentic consumer rapport, will distinguish themselves. Success in this new era will not solely be measured by conversion metrics but also by the depth and durability of customer relationships in a digital-first marketplace.

12.7 REFERENCES

Antoniou, A., Storkey, A., & Edwards, H. (2017). Data augmentation generative adversarial networks. *arXiv*:1711.04340.

Arrieta, A. B., Díaz-Rodríguez, N., Del Ser, J., Bennetot, A., Tabik, S., Barbado, A., . . . & Herrera, F. (2020). Explainable artificial intelligence (XAI): Concepts, taxonomies, opportunities and challenges toward responsible AI. *Information Fusion, 58*, 82115.

Arulkumaran, K., Deisenroth, M. P., Brundage, M., & Bharath, A. A. (2017). Deep reinforcement learning: A brief survey. *IEEE Signal Processing Magazine, 34*(6), 26–38.

Borji, A. (2019). Pros and cons of GAN evaluation measures. *Computer Vision and Image Understanding, 179*, 41–65.

Briot, J. P., Hadjeres, G., & Pachet, F. D. (2017). Deep learning techniques for music generation—A survey. *arXiv*:1709.01620.

Brock, A., Donahue, J., & Simonyan, K. (2018). Large-scale GAN training for high fidelity natural image synthesis. *arXiv*:1809.11096.

Brown, T., Mann, B., Ryder, N., Subbiah, M., Kaplan, J. D., Dhariwal, P., . . . & Amodei, D. (2020). Language models are few-shot learners. *Advances in Neural Information Processing Systems, 33*, 1877–1901.

Buolamwini, J., & Gebru, T. (2018, January). Gender shades: Intersectional accuracy disparities in commercial gender classification. *Conference on Fairness, Accountability and Transparency* (pp. 77–91). PMLR.

Chen, L., Mislove, A., & Wilson, C. (2015, October). Peeking beneath the hood of uber. *Proceedings of the 2015 Internet Measurement Conference* (pp. 495–508).

Chesney, B., & Citron, D. (2019). Deep fakes: A looming challenge for privacy, democracy, and national security. *California Law Review, 107*, 1753.

Child, R., Gray, S., Radford, A., & Sutskever, I. (2019). Generating long sequences with sparse transformers. *arXiv*:1904.10509.

Choi, E., Bahadori, M. T., Schuetz, A., Stewart, W. F., & Sun, J. (2016, December). Doctor AI: Predicting clinical events via recurrent neural networks. *Machine Learning for Healthcare Conference* (pp. 301–318). PMLR.

Creswell, A., White, T., Dumoulin, V., Arulkumaran, K., Sengupta, B., & Bharath, A. A. (2018). Generative adversarial networks: An overview. *IEEE Signal Processing Magazine, 35*(1), 53–65.

Deng, S., Huang, L., Xu, G., Wu, X., & Wu, Z. (2016). On deep learning for trust-aware recommendations in social networks. *IEEE Transactions on Neural Networks and Learning Systems, 28*(5), 1164–1177.

Diakopoulos, N. (2016). Accountability in algorithmic decision making. *Communications of the ACM, 59*(2), 56–62.

Elgammal, A., Liu, B., Elhoseiny, M., & Mazzone, M. (2017). Can creative adversarial networks, generating "art" by learning about styles, and deviating from style norms? *arXiv*:1706.07068.

European Commission. (2021). Data protection in the EU. Retrieved from https://ec.europa.eu/info/law/law-topic/data-protection/data-protection-eu_en

Gentsch, P. (2018). *AI in marketing, sales and service: How marketers without a data science degree can use AI, big data and bots*. Springer.

Goodfellow, I., Bengio, Y., & Courville, A. (2016). *Deep learning*. MIT Press.

Goodfellow, I., Pouget-Abadie, J., Mirza, M., Xu, B., Warde-Farley, D., Ozair, S., Courville, A., & Bengio, Y. (2014). Generative adversarial networks. In M. I. Jordan, Y. LeCun, & S. A. Solla (Eds.), *Advances in neural information processing systems* (pp. 2672–2680). MIT Press.

Goodman, B., & Flaxman, S. (2017). European Union regulations on algorithmic decision-making and a "right to explanation." *AI Magazine, 38*(3), 50–57.

Hinton, G., Vinyals, O., & Dean, J. (2015). Distilling the knowledge in a neural network. *arXiv*:1503.02531.

Ho, J., Jain, A., & Abbeel, P. (2020). Denoising diffusion probabilistic models. *Advances in Neural Information Processing Systems, 33*, 6840–6851.

Hubara, I., Courbariaux, M., Soudry, D., El-Yaniv, R., & Bengio, Y. (2017). Quantized neural networks: Training neural networks with low precision weights and activations. *The Journal of Machine Learning Research, 18*(1), 6869–6898.

Jobin, A., Ienca, M., & Vayena, E. (2019). The global landscape of AI ethics guidelines. *Nature Machine Intelligence, 1*(9), 389–399.

Karras, T., Aittala, M., Laine, S., Härkönen, E., Hellsten, J., Lehtinen, J., & Aila, T. (2021). Alias-free generative adversarial networks. *Advances in Neural Information Processing Systems, 34*, 852–863.

Karras, T., Laine, S., & Aila, T. (2019). A style-based generator architecture for generative adversarial networks. *Proceedings of the IEEE/CVF Conference on Computer Vision and Pattern Recognition* (pp. 4401–4410).

Karras, T., Laine, S., Aittala, M., Hellsten, J., Lehtinen, J., & Aila, T. (2020). Analyzing and improving the image quality of StyleGAN. *Proceedings of the IEEE/CVF Conference on Computer Vision and Pattern Recognition* (pp. 8110–8119).

Kingma, D. P., & Welling, M. (2013). Auto-encoding variational bayes. *arXiv*:1312.6114.

Kotler, P., & Keller, K. L. (2015). *Framework for marketing management*. Pearson.

Lewis, P., Perez, E., Piktus, A., Petroni, F., Karpukhin, V., Goyal, N., . . . & Kiela, D. (2020). Retrieval-augmented generation for knowledge-intensive NLP tasks. *Advances in Neural Information Processing Systems, 33*, 9459–9474.

Lu, J., Behbood, V., Hao, P., Zuo, H., Xue, S., & Zhang, G. (2015). Transfer learning using computational intelligence: A survey. *Knowledge-Based Systems, 80*, 14–23.

Mehrabi, N., Morstatter, F., Saxena, N., Lerman, K., & Galstyan, A. (2021). A survey on bias and fairness in machine learning. *ACM Computing Surveys (CSUR), 54*(6), 1–35.

Ng, A., & Jordan, M. (2001). On discriminative vs. generative classifiers: A comparison of logistic regression and naive Bayes. *Advances in Neural Information Processing Systems, 14.*

Radford, A., Metz, L., & Chintala, S. (2015). Unsupervised representation learning with deep convolutional generative adversarial networks. *arXiv*:1511.06434.

Radziwill, N. M., & Benton, M. C. (2017). Evaluating quality of chatbots and intelligent conversational agents. *arXiv*:1704.04579.

Ramesh, A., Pavlov, M., Goh, G., Gray, S., Voss, C., Radford, A., . . . & Sutskever, I. (2021, July). Zero-shot text-to-image generation. *International Conference on Machine Learning* (pp. 8821–8831). PMLR.

Ribeiro, M. T., Singh, S., & Guestrin, C. (2016, August). "Why should I trust you?" Explaining the predictions of any classifier. *Proceedings of the 22nd ACM SIGKDD International Conference on Knowledge Discovery and Data Mining* (pp. 1135–1144).

Sajjadi, M. S., Bachem, O., Lucic, M., Bousquet, O., & Gelly, S. (2018). Assessing generative models via precision and recall. *Advances in Neural Information Processing Systems, 31.*

Salimans, T., Goodfellow, I., Zaremba, W., Cheung, V., Radford, A., & Chen, X. (2016). Improved techniques for training GANS. *Advances in Neural Information Processing Systems, 29.*

Smith, B., & Linden, G. (2017). Two decades of recommender systems at Amazon. com. *IEEE Internet Computing, 21*(3), 12–18.

Vaswani, A., Shazeer, N., Parmar, N., Uszkoreit, J., Jones, L., Gomez, A. N., . . . & Polosukhin, I. (2017). Attention is all you need. *Advances in Neural Information Processing Systems, 30.*

Voigt, P., & Von dem Bussche, A. (2017). *The EU general data protection regulation (GDPR): A practical guide.* Springer International Publishing.

Wang, Y., Yao, Q., Kwok, J. T., & Ni, L. M. (2020). Generalizing from a few examples: A survey on few-shot learning. *ACM Computing Surveys (CSUR), 53*(3), 1–34.

Yoon, J., Jordon, J., & Schaar, M. (2018, July). Gain: Missing data imputation using generative adversarial nets. *International Conference on Machine Learning* (pp. 5689–5698). PMLR.

Zellers, R., Holtzman, A., Rashkin, H., Bisk, Y., Farhadi, A., Roesner, F., & Choi, Y. (2019). Defending against neural fake news. *Advances in Neural Information Processing Systems,* p. 32.

Zhao, S., Song, J., & Ermon, S. (2017). Learning hierarchical features from generative models. *arXiv*:1702.08396.

Zheng, S., Song, Y., Leung, T., & Goodfellow, I. (2016). Improving the robustness of deep neural networks via stability training. *Proceedings of the IEEE Conference on Computer Vision and Pattern Recognition* (pp. 4480–4488).

Zhu, J. Y., Park, T., Isola, P., & Efros, A. A. (2017). Unpaired image-to-image translation using cycle-consistent adversarial networks. *Proceedings of the IEEE International Conference on Computer Vision* (pp. 2223–2232).

Žliobaitė, I., & Custers, B. (2016). Using sensitive personal data may be necessary for avoiding discrimination in data-driven decision models. *Artificial Intelligence and Law, 24*, 183–201.

CHAPTER 13

Ethics, Privacy, and the Future of Marketing Data Science

13.1 INTRODUCTION

The digital era has brought forth an explosion of data, reshaping the landscape of marketing. As businesses delve deeper into the world of marketing data science to harness the power of this data, they navigate an intricate web of opportunities and challenges. The vast potential of data-driven insights promises enhanced customer experiences, precise targeting, and innovative marketing strategies. However, the same tools and techniques that empower these advances also give rise to complex ethical, privacy, and transparency issues.

In the race to gain a competitive edge, it's paramount that businesses remain cognizant of the profound responsibilities that accompany the use of personal and sensitive data. Beyond mere regulatory compliance, there's an ethical imperative to handle data with care, ensuring the respect and protection of individuals' privacy rights. This delicate balancing act between leveraging data and maintaining trust is pivotal because missteps can lead to not just legal repercussions but also eroded customer trust and brand damage.

In this chapter, we delve deep into the intertwined realms of ethics, privacy, and the future prospects of marketing data science. We explore the critical ethical considerations surrounding data use, dissect key privacy regulations such as the General Data Protection Regulation (GDPR) and California Consumer Privacy Act (CCPA), and ruminate on the emerging trends that are poised to define the next frontier of data-driven marketing. Through a mix of theoretical insights, practical examples, and case studies, this chapter illuminates the path for businesses and data scientists, guiding them through the ethical quandaries and opportunities that lie ahead in the evolving domain of marketing data science.

13.2 ETHICAL CONSIDERATIONS IN MARKETING DATA SCIENCE

13.2.1 Overview of Ethical Considerations

Marketing data science involves working with vast amounts of personal and sensitive data, raising numerous ethical considerations. These ethical issues primarily are based on the responsible use of data and the protection of consumer privacy and rights (Martin, 2015).

First, the concept of informed consent is a key ethical concern. Informed consent ensures that customers understand how their data will be used before they provide it. This concept includes providing clear and transparent privacy policies that the average customer can understand (Martin, 2015). It also requires businesses to respect the customer's choice if they decide not to share their data.

Second, the principle of data minimization comes into play, which states that only the data necessary for the stated purpose should be collected and processed. This principle helps to reduce the risk of data breaches and misuse of data.

Finally, the issue of data accuracy and integrity is another significant ethical concern. Maintaining data accuracy ensures that decisions made based on the data are reliable and fair. Misrepresentation or inaccuracies can lead to unfair treatment of customers and potentially harm the reputation of the company (Custers et al., 2018).

Several key concepts underpin ethical considerations in marketing data science (see Figure 13.1):

- **Informed consent.** This is the practice of getting explicit permission from consumers before collecting, using, or sharing their data (Martin, 2015). It involves clearly explaining the intended use of the data and the potential implications of data sharing. This respect for autonomy helps build trust between businesses and customers.

- **Data minimization.** This principle suggests that organizations should only collect and retain data necessary for their stated purpose. It is seen as a key practice in respecting consumer privacy and reducing the risk of data breaches.

- **Data accuracy.** Ensuring that the data used in analytics processes are accurate and up-to-date is critical for fair and effective decision-making. Inaccurate data can lead to unfair or discriminatory outcomes (Custers et al., 2018).

- **Privacy-by-design.** This concept proposes that privacy considerations should be embedded into the design of systems and practices right from their inception, rather than being added on as an afterthought (Cavoukian, 2009).

- **Transparency.** This involves clearly communicating with consumers about data collection practices, data uses, and data protection measures in place. Transparency fosters trust and enables consumers to make informed decisions about data sharing (Martin, 2015).

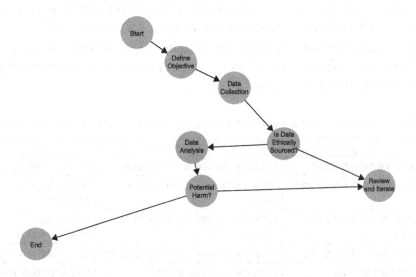

Figure 13.1 The Ethical Decision-Making Process in Data Science.

■ **Accountability.** Companies should be accountable for their data practices, including compliance with privacy laws and regulations, and implementing data protection measures (Bennett, 2012).

13.2.2 The Importance of Ethics in Data Handling

The digital age brings with it unprecedented access to data, a lot of which is personal. Although this access provides numerous opportunities for businesses to enhance their marketing strategies and customer experiences, it also poses significant ethical challenges. Ethics in data handling pertains to the moral principles and standards that guide actions when collecting, storing, processing, and sharing data (Zwitter, 2014). The consequences of not upholding these standards can be damaging both to individuals whose data is mishandled and to the businesses responsible for the mishandling.

Problems such as data breaches can lead to financial losses, damage to reputation, and potential legal consequences for businesses (Romanosky, 2016). For individuals, the misuse of personal data can result in loss of privacy, financial repercussions, or discrimination (Mittelstadt et al., 2016). Hence, adhering to ethical guidelines is not just a regulatory requirement but also a social responsibility for businesses.

13.2.3 Potential Misuses of Data and Analytics

The vast quantities of data available to marketers and the advanced analytical tools at their disposal can sometimes lead to unintended consequences. Potential misuses include the following (see Table 13.1):

■ **Data discrimination.** Algorithms might unintentionally favor one group over another. For instance, an ad-targeting system might disproportionately show high-paying job ads to men more than women (Datta et al., 2015).

■ **Invasion of privacy.** Marketers might collect more data than necessary or use data in ways that customers haven't consented to, leading to potential privacy violations (Tene & Polonetsky, 2012).

Table 13.1 Common Misuses of Data with Corresponding Consequences and Ethical Considerations.

Misuses of Data	Consequences	Ethical Considerations
Data snooping without consent	Legal consequences and loss of trust	Respect for privacy
Selling personal data to third parties	Loss of customer trust and potential legal action	Respect for privacy and honesty
Using data to discriminate against certain groups	Public backlash and potential legal consequences	Fairness and nondiscrimination
Misrepresentation of data results	Misguided decisions and loss of credibility	Honesty and accuracy
Ignoring data privacy laws	Heavy fines and legal actions	Respect for laws and regulations

- **Misleading advertising.** Using data analytics to manipulate consumer behavior by pushing products or services they might not need, or using psychological tricks, can be considered unethical (Susser et al., 2019).

- **Data reselling.** Selling user data to third parties without explicit consent can lead to unwanted marketing and potential breaches of user trust (Schreurs et al., 2008).

13.2.4 Balancing Personalization and Intrusiveness

A major application of marketing data science is personalization, tailoring content and experiences to individual users based on their preferences and behaviors. Although personalization can enhance user experiences, it's essential to strike a balance so that it doesn't come off as intrusive or creepy (Zuboff, 2019).

A study by Marreiros et al. (2017) found that users can feel violated when personalization is too precise, especially if they are not aware of the data that's been collected about them. For businesses, it's crucial to ensure that personalization strategies are transparent, and users are made aware of how their data is used. Offering users control over their data and its uses can also help in striking the right balance (Martínez-Alemán & Wartman, 2008).

Practitioners should consider the following strategies on how this balance can be achieved (see Figure 13.2):

- **Prioritize transparency:**
  - **Information clarity.** Always make sure that any data collection process is explained in simple terms, without hiding behind jargons. A user should be able to easily understand what data is being collected and for what purpose.
  - **Consent mechanisms.** Explicitly ask for consent before collecting personal data and allow users to opt out anytime. A just-in-time notification, which provides information as it becomes relevant, can also be beneficial.

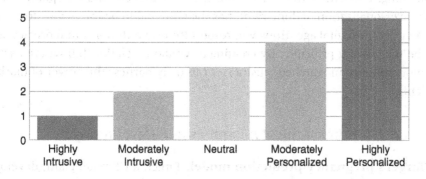

Figure 13.2 The Balance Between Personalization and Intrusiveness in Marketing Campaigns.

- **Give control to the user:**
  - **Data access.** Allow users to view the data that's been collected about them. This not only builds trust but also provides an opportunity for data correction, ensuring more accurate personalization.
  - **Customization options.** Let users decide the degree of personalization they're comfortable with. Some might prefer broader categories, and others might appreciate detail-oriented personalization.
- **Limit data retention:**
  - **Retention policies.** Implement strict policies about how long data will be retained and stick to them. This reduces the potential for misuse and is often viewed positively by consumers.
- **Educate users:**
  - **Awareness campaigns.** Conduct campaigns to educate users about data collection practices, the benefits of personalization, and potential risks. A well-informed user is more likely to trust and engage with personalized content.
  - **Feedback loops.** Regularly collect feedback on personalization strategies to understand user sentiments and adjust strategies accordingly.
- **Anonymize data:**
  - **Data masking.** Whenever possible, anonymize the data to ensure that even if it's accessed, it doesn't harm the individual's privacy.
- **Monitor and adjust:**
  - **Dynamic algorithms.** Employ algorithms that dynamically adjust the level of personalization based on user feedback and engagement. If users consistently ignore or dislike certain personalized content, the system should learn and adapt.
  - **Regular audits.** Conduct regular audits to ensure that personalization strategies align with ethical guidelines and user preferences.

Although the technological prowess to personalize exists, it's the human touch, understanding, and ethics that determine the effectiveness and acceptance of such strategies. Personalization, if done right, has the potential to be the cornerstone of user engagement in the digital age. However, respect for user autonomy and privacy should always be the guiding principle. By creating a symbiotic relationship where users feel understood rather than watched, businesses can truly harness the power of marketing data science.

13.2.5 Case Studies: Ethical Dilemmas and Resolutions

- **Target's pregnancy prediction model.** Target, a US retail giant, developed a model to predict the pregnancy status of its customers based on their shopping patterns. However, the model inadvertently revealed a teen's pregnancy to her father by sending her maternity product coupons, leading to a public relations debacle (Duhigg, 2013). This case underscores the need for companies to be cautious when using predictive analytics, especially when dealing with sensitive information.

- **Resolution.** After the incident, Target became more subtle in its marketing. Instead of only sending maternity product coupons, they mixed them with other unrelated offers to make it less obvious (Duhigg, 2013).

- **Strava heat maps.** In 2018, Strava, a fitness tracking app, released a global heat map showcasing popular running routes. However, the map unintentionally revealed the locations of military bases and the routines of soldiers, posing potential security threats (Hern, 2018).

  - **Resolution.** Strava responded by emphasizing user privacy settings and pledging to work with military and government officials to address sensitive areas on the map (Strava, 2018).

These case studies emphasize the importance of ethical considerations in marketing data science. They demonstrate that even with the best intentions, data can be misused or mishandled, leading to unintended consequences. As the field of marketing data science continues to grow, companies must be vigilant and prioritize ethical considerations in their data practices.

Building on the discussion of ethical challenges, Table 13.2 delves deeper by presenting additional case studies that highlight specific ethical dilemmas encountered in marketing data science, along with the possible solutions implemented and their respective outcomes, illustrating the complex nature of ethical decision-making in this field.

Table 13.2 Additional Case Studies Highlighting the Ethical Dilemmas Faced, Possible Solutions, and Outcomes.

Case Studies	Ethical Dilemmas	Possible Solutions	Outcomes
Study A: Targeted ads based on health data	Privacy concerns regarding sensitive health data	Anonymize data and obtain explicit consent	Enhanced user trust and better ad engagement
Study B: Personalized shopping experience using facial recognition	Privacy invasion and potential misuse of facial data	Notify customers and provide opt-out options	Mixed reception; some appreciated, others opted out
Study C: Selling user data to insurance companies	Potential misuse leading to unfair premiums	Ensure data is anonymized and not used for discriminatory pricing	Faced backlash and revised its policies
Study D: Predictive policing using demographic data	Potential racial bias and discrimination	Use nondiscriminatory data sources and regular audits	Reduced crime rates but faced criticism for potential bias

13.2.6 Practical Example: Ethical Considerations in Social Media Marketing

Social media marketing provides a rich source of data about customer preferences, behaviors, and sentiments. However, the use of this data must be balanced with ethical considerations.

For instance, Cambridge Analytica, a British political consulting firm, was found to have harvested the personal data of millions of people's Facebook profiles without their consent and used it for political advertising purposes (Cadwalladr & Graham-Harrison, 2018). This case raised serious ethical concerns about informed consent and privacy in data collection and use. It also sparked a global debate about the responsibility of social media platforms to protect user data.

By contrast, consider Patagonia, an outdoor clothing company known for its ethical business practices. In their social media marketing, they prioritize transparency and informed consent. They clearly communicate how they collect and use customer data, and they provide options for customers to control their data (Patagonia, 2021). By doing so, they foster trust and loyalty among their customers while respecting their privacy.

These examples highlight the importance of ethical considerations in marketing data science. Companies that prioritize ethical data practices not only comply with regulations but also build trust with their customers, which can lead to long-term business success.

13.3 DATA PRIVACY REGULATIONS

13.3.1 Overview of Data Privacy Regulations

As data has become a critical asset in the digital economy, concerns about data privacy have spurred the creation of various regulations worldwide to protect consumers' personal information. The most notable of these are GDPR in the European Union and the CCPA in the United States (see Table 13.3).

GDPR, which came into effect in May 2018, is a comprehensive data protection law that regulates the processing of personal data of individuals within the EU and the European Economic Area. It gives individuals more control over their personal data and imposes strict rules on those hosting and processing this data, no matter where they are based (European Commission, 2021).

On the other side of the Atlantic, the CCPA, which came into effect in January 2020, provides California residents with specific rights over their personal information, including the right to know about the personal information a business collects about them and the right to delete personal information collected from them (with some exceptions). It also provides the right to opt out of the sale of their personal information (State of California, 2021).

Table 13.3 Major Data Privacy Regulations (GDPR, CCPA) Showcasing Their Primary Objectives, Covered Entities, and Penalties.

Regulation	Primary Objectives	Covered Entities	Penalties
GDPR (General Data Protection Regulation)	Protect individual rights regarding personal data and reshape the approach of organizations to data privacy	All companies processing the personal data of subjects residing in the EU, regardless of the company's location	Up to €20 million or 4% of annual global turnover, whichever is higher
CCPA (California Consumer Privacy Act)	Grant California consumers the right to know what personal data is collected, deny the sale of their personal data, and access their personal data	Businesses that serve California residents and have at least $25 million in annual revenue	Up to $7,500 for each intentional violation and $2,500 for each unintentional violation

These regulations reflect a global trend toward strengthening data protection rights, with other regions and countries such as Brazil, India, and China also implementing or planning similar laws. This trend has significant implications for marketing data science because it affects how marketers can collect, store, process, and use consumer data.

13.3.2 Implications for Data Collection and Processing

The evolution of data privacy regulations worldwide has profound implications for how businesses approach data collection and processing in their marketing initiatives (see Figure 13.3):

- **Scope of data collection.** Regulations such as GDPR mandate that data should be collected for a specific purpose and should be limited to what is necessary for that purpose (European Commission, 2021). This means marketers need to be

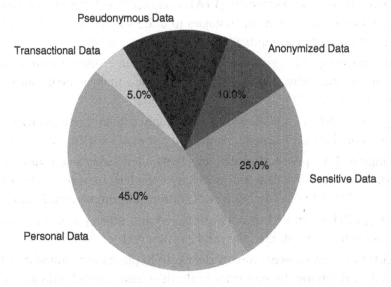

Figure 13.3 The Percentage of Data Types Affected by Regulations.

precise about why they are collecting data and ensure that data redundancy is minimized.

- **Data retention.** Data can no longer be held indefinitely. Businesses must have clear data retention policies, where data is deleted or anonymized after its intended purpose has been served (ICO, 2018).

- **Consent management.** Implicit or assumed consent is no longer sufficient. Regulations demand explicit consent, which has led to a surge in opt-in forms and cookie consent banners on websites. Moreover, businesses must provide mechanisms for users to withdraw their consent at any time easily.

- **Data accuracy.** Regulations underscore the importance of data accuracy. Individuals have the right to correct inaccuracies in their personal data, putting an onus on organizations to implement processes that facilitate such corrections (European Commission, 2021).

- **Data security.** With data breaches being a prime concern, companies are now required to have robust data security measures in place, with penalties for lapses (State of California, 2021).

13.3.3 Achieving Compliance: Best Practices and Checklists

Ensuring compliance with evolving data privacy regulations requires a proactive and systematic approach. Here are some best practices:

- **Awareness and training.** Regularly educate and train staff members, especially those handling data, on the importance of data protection and compliance (ICO, 2018).

- **Privacy impact assessments (PIA).** Conduct PIAs before embarking on new projects or adopting new technologies to understand the potential privacy risks and address them preemptively (Clarke & Moses, 2014).

- **Data mapping.** Understand where personal data resides in your systems, who has access, and why. This aids in effective data management and compliance (Kuner et al., 2017).

- **Regular audits.** Periodically review and audit data processing activities to identify potential areas of noncompliance (Kuner et al., 2017).

- **Engage a data protection officer (DPO).** For larger organizations or those involved in extensive data processing, it's beneficial to have a DPO, a role mandated by GDPR for certain businesses (European Commission, 2021).

- **Clear policies.** Draft clear data protection and privacy policies, making them accessible to both staff members and customers (ICO, 2018).

- **Incident management.** Have a clear plan in place for handling data breaches, including notifying the necessary authorities and affected individuals (State of California, 2021).

Checklist

- ☐ Regular training sessions scheduled
- ☐ PIA conducted for new projects
- ☐ Data map updated
- ☐ Audit conducted in the past six months
- ☐ Data protection policies in place and reviewed
- ☐ Incident management plan prepared

13.3.4 The Global Landscape: Differences and Commonalities in Regulations

Data protection regulations vary across the globe, reflecting cultural, social, and political differences. However, they often share common principles:

- **Rights of individuals.** Most regulations grant individuals rights over their data, including access, correction, deletion, and sometimes portability (Bygrave, 2014).
- **Accountability and governance.** Organizations are generally held accountable for protecting data, necessitating governance mechanisms such as data protection impact assessments and appointing data protection officers (Bennett, 2012).
- **International data flows.** Regulations frequently address the transfer of personal data across borders, ensuring that data remains protected when transferred internationally (Kuner, 2013).
- **Consent.** The need for explicit consent before data collection and processing is a recurring theme across regulations, though the exact nature and requirements around consent might vary (Bygrave, 2014).

Differences arise in the nuances, with some regions placing more emphasis on certain principles over others (see Table 13.4). For instance, the EU's GDPR places strong

Table 13.4 Differences and Commonalities Among Global Data Privacy Regulations.

Aspect	GDPR	CCPA	Commonalities
Scope	Applies to all organizations processing data of EU residents, irrespective of location	Applies to businesses that collect data of California residents and meet certain criteria	Both aim to protect the privacy rights of individuals.
Rights of data subjects	Right to be forgotten, data portability, access, rectification, and objection	Right to know, opt out, and data deletion	Both grant rights to access and delete personal data.
Data breach notification	72 hours from the knowledge of the breach	Not specifically defined	Both require organizations to notify in the event of a data breach.
Fines	Up to 4% of annual global turnover or €20 million, whichever is higher	Up to $7,500 for intentional violations and $2,500 for unintentional violations	Both impose penalties for violations.

emphasis on individual rights, whereas the United States has a sectoral approach to data protection, with different rules for health data, financial data, and so forth (Schwartz & Solove, 2014). Asia-Pacific countries, such as Japan and Australia, have their unique blends of principles, reflecting both Western and regional influences (Greenleaf, 2017).

In conclusion, although there are specific nuances and requirements under each jurisdiction, the foundational principles of data protection remain similar, emphasizing individual rights, accountability, and the ethical use of data.

13.3.5 Key Concepts in Data Privacy Regulations

Understanding the key concepts of data privacy regulations such as GDPR and CCPA is critical for organizations to ensure compliance and to avoid substantial penalties:

- **Personal data.** Under GDPR, *personal data* refers to any information relating to an identified or identifiable natural person. This includes name, identification number, location data, online identifier or to one or more factors specific to the physical, physiological, genetic, mental, economic, cultural, or social identity of that natural person (European Commission, 2021). Similarly, CCPA refers to **personal information** as information that identifies, relates to, describes, is reasonably capable of being associated with, or could reasonably be linked, directly or indirectly, with a particular consumer or household (State of California, 2021).

- **Consent.** GDPR and CCPA require businesses to obtain explicit consent from individuals before collecting and processing their personal data. The consent must be freely given, specific, informed, and unambiguous (ICO, 2018).

- **Right to access and right to erasure.** Both regulations provide individuals with the right to access their personal data held by an organization and the right to request the erasure of their personal data under certain circumstances.

- **Data protection officer (DPO).** GDPR requires organizations to appoint a DPO if they conduct large scale systematic monitoring or process a lot of sensitive personal data. The DPO oversees data protection strategy and implementation to ensure compliance with GDPR requirements.

- **Data breach notification.** Under GDPR, organizations must report certain types of personal data breaches to the relevant supervisory authority within 72 hours of becoming aware of the breach, if feasible.

By understanding these key concepts, organizations can navigate the complex landscape of data privacy regulations and build trust with their customers.

13.3.6 Practical Example: GDPR Compliance in Email Marketing

GDPR compliance is a crucial aspect of email marketing. Many companies have had to adjust their email marketing practices to comply with the new regulation.

Let's consider an example of how a retail company adheres to GDPR in its email marketing practices:

- **Opt in.** The first step in GDPR compliance is ensuring that all email recipients have given explicit consent to receive marketing emails. This is typically done through an opt-in process. For example, when a user creates an account or makes a purchase, the retail company might include a checkbox that the user must click to opt into email marketing. This box cannot be prechecked; the user must take a clear and affirmative action to give consent (Mailjet, 2021).

- **Unambiguous consent.** Under GDPR, the consent must be specific and unambiguous. This means the retail company must clearly state what the user is consenting to. For instance, the opt-in box might say, "Yes, I want to receive promotional emails about your products and services."

- **Withdrawal of consent.** GDPR also requires that it must be as easy to withdraw consent as it was to give it. Therefore, every marketing email sent by the retail company includes an unsubscribe link at the bottom. If a user clicks this link, they must be able to easily and immediately unsubscribe from future emails.

- **Data minimization.** The retail company adheres to the principle of data minimization, which means they only collect the data necessary for the email marketing. They don't ask for or store any extraneous personal data from their subscribers.

- **Data protection.** The company also implements robust security measures to protect the personal data of its subscribers, such as encryption and regular security audits, to prevent data breaches.

This example illustrates how GDPR affects email marketing practices. Although GDPR compliance requires some changes and ongoing diligence, it ultimately helps build trust and better relationships with customers.

13.4   BIAS, FAIRNESS, AND TRANSPARENCY

13.4.1   Overview of Bias, Fairness, and Transparency

Bias, fairness, and transparency are critical considerations in marketing data science. With the increasing use of machine learning (ML) and artificial intelligence (AI) in marketing, these aspects have become even more significant.

- **Bias** in data science refers to the systematic error introduced by the data collection, data processing, or algorithm that makes the results skew in a specific direction (Hajian et al., 2016). For instance, if a recommendation algorithm is trained on data from a specific demographic group, it may not perform well for other groups, creating a bias. This can lead to unfair outcomes and can harm certain groups of customers.

- **Fairness** in data science means that the outcomes of an algorithm do not discriminate against certain groups based on sensitive attributes such as race, gender, age, and so on. It's important to ensure that the models used in marketing do not inadvertently lead to unfair treatment of certain customer groups (Grgić-Hlača et al., 2018).
- **Transparency** in data science refers to the ability to understand and interpret the workings and decisions made by an algorithm (Goodman & Flaxman, 2017). This is particularly important in marketing, where decisions made by algorithms can have a significant impact on customers. Transparency also helps build trust with customers because they understand how their data is being used.

In the context of marketing data science, ensuring bias mitigation, fairness, and transparency is not just about complying with regulations or avoiding public relations disasters. It's about building trust with customers, which can lead to better customer relationships and ultimately a competitive advantage.

13.4.2   Recognizing and Addressing Bias in Data and Models

Bias is an innate risk when dealing with data collection and model creation in marketing data science. It's essential to recognize that bias can manifest at any stage: from the data collected to the algorithms developed. For instance, if a dataset predominantly consists of one demographic group, insights derived might not be applicable to a broader audience (O'neil, 2017). To address this, businesses need to do the following.

13.4.2.1   Audit the Data

Before model development, evaluate the data's representativeness. Ensure that it captures diverse perspectives and doesn't inadvertently exclude significant segments (Barocas & Selbst, 2016).

13.4.2.2   Use Diverse Training Data

In ML, the training data determines the model's understanding. Incorporating diverse data helps in developing a more generalized and less biased model (Buolamwini & Gebru, 2018).

13.4.2.3   Regularly Reevaluate Models

Continual assessment of models for potential biases and refining them ensures that they remain relevant and accurate over time (Danks & London, 2017; see Table 13.5).

Table 13.5 Common Sources of Bias in Data and Corresponding Methods to Address Them.

Sources of Bias	Methods to Address
Sampling	Use stratified sampling and ensure representative samples
Measurement	Regularly calibrate measurement tools and train data collectors
Confirmation	Seek external audits and reviews Challenge and validate assumptions
Algorithmic	Use interpretable models and validate against various demographic groups
Cultural	Diverse team composition and periodic training on cultural awareness

13.4.3 Principles of Algorithmic Fairness

Algorithmic fairness seeks to ensure that models do not produce discriminatory or unjust results based on certain attributes such as race, gender, or age. The key principles include the following reasons:

- **Demographic parity.** Parity ensures that decisions made by an algorithm give equal positive outcomes across different groups (Hardt et al., 2016).
- **Equalized odds.** This means that the algorithm's error rates should be consistent across groups. This ensures that no group is disproportionately affected by mistakes the algorithm might make (Zafar et al., 2017).
- **Individual fairness.** Each individual who is similar in relevant aspects should be treated similarly by the algorithm (Dwork, 2008). It's a granular approach, focusing on the individual level rather than the group level.

13.4.4 Importance of Model Transparency and Explainability

With the rise of complex models, especially in deep learning, understanding why a model makes certain decisions can be elusive. However, transparency and explainability are crucial because of the following reasons:

- **Trust.** Consumers and stakeholders are more likely to trust a model if they understand its workings and the rationale behind its decisions (Ribeiro et al., 2016).
- **Regulatory compliance.** Regulations such as GDPR provide individuals with the right to an explanation when algorithmic decisions affect them, making transparency nonnegotiable (Goodman & Flaxman, 2017).
- **Ethical considerations.** A transparent model enables ethical oversight, ensuring that it operates within accepted societal norms (Wachter et al., 2017).

13.4.5   Tools and Techniques for Fair and Transparent Modeling

Several tools and techniques can be employed to build fair and transparent models:

- **Interpretation libraries.** Tools such as LIME (local interpretable model-agnostic explanations) or SHAP (Shapley additive explanations) can help elucidate why a model is making particular predictions, making complex models more interpretable (Lundberg & Lee, 2017).

- **Bias detection tools.** Platforms such as IBM's AI Fairness 360 or Google's What-If Tool can help in identifying and mitigating biases in models.

- **Regularization techniques.** These can be employed in ML to avoid overfitting, ensuring that the model doesn't just memorize the training data but generalizes well to new, unseen data (Ng, 2004).

- **Differential privacy.** This is a technique that adds noise to data, ensuring privacy while still allowing for meaningful analysis (Dwork, 2008).

In the realm of marketing data science, the recognition of bias, commitment to algorithmic fairness, and emphasis on transparency are nonnegotiable tenets. As businesses become increasingly data-driven, they must ensure that the models they deploy are powerful and principled.

13.4.6   Key Concepts in Bias, Fairness, and Transparency

In the realm of marketing data science, a few key concepts are central to understanding and addressing bias, ensuring fairness, and promoting transparency.

- **Algorithmic bias.** Algorithmic bias occurs when an algorithm systematically produces outcomes that are skewed in a specific direction, often resulting in unfair treatment of certain groups (Barocas & Selbst, 2016). For example, a loan approval algorithm might be biased against certain demographics if the data used to train it were historically biased. In marketing, this could manifest as certain customer groups being unfairly excluded from promotional campaigns.

- **Fairness metrics.** There are various metrics and techniques that can be used to assess the fairness of algorithms, such as demographic parity, equal opportunity, and individual fairness (Verma & Rubin, 2018). These metrics ensure that the algorithm's outcomes are fair across different groups and individuals. In the context of marketing, this could involve assessing whether a product recommendation algorithm gives equitable recommendations across different demographics.

- **Explainability and interpretability.** These terms refer to the ability to understand the inner workings of an algorithm and explain its decisions (Doshi-Velez & Kim, 2017). Explainability is crucial in marketing data science because it enables marketers to understand why certain recommendations or decisions were made, which can help improve future campaigns and build customer trust.

- **Privacy-preserving algorithms.** With growing concerns about data privacy, there has been a surge in the development of algorithms that can work with encrypted or anonymized data, such as differential privacy algorithms (Dwork, 2008). These algorithms can help marketers use customer data for insights while respecting their privacy.

13.4.7 Practical Example: Ensuring Fairness and Transparency in Personalization Algorithms

To illustrate the application of fairness and transparency in marketing data science, let's consider an online retail company that uses a personalization algorithm to recommend products to its customers.

The algorithm was initially developed using historical purchase data, and over time, the company noticed that it was recommending certain types of products more frequently to males than to females, potentially indicating a gender bias.

To address this, the company decided to take a two-step approach:

1. **Bias detection and mitigation.** The company used fairness metrics such as demographic parity to assess whether the recommendations were indeed biased (Verma & Rubin, 2018). On confirming the bias, they implemented a bias-correction algorithm to adjust the recommendations and ensure a more equal distribution across different demographic groups (Kearns et al., 2018).
2. **Transparency and explainability.** To improve transparency, the company adopted an interpretable ML approach, where the model's predictions can be easily understood by humans (Ribeiro et al., 2016). This enabled them to explain to customers why they were receiving certain recommendations, increasing customer trust and satisfaction.

This example highlights the importance of continuously monitoring and adjusting algorithms to ensure fairness, and providing transparency in how decisions are made.

13.5 EMERGING TRENDS AND THE FUTURE OF MARKETING DATA SCIENCE

13.5.1 Overview of Emerging Trends and the Future

The field of marketing data science is rapidly evolving, driven by a variety of emerging trends and technologies. Here are a few key areas to watch (see Table 13.6):

- **AI and ML.** AI and ML are no longer just buzzwords; they're becoming integral parts of marketing strategies. These technologies can help businesses automate processes, gain insights, and enhance personalization, leading to improved customer experiences (Russell, 2016).

Table 13.6 Emerging Trends in Marketing Data Science Along with Their Potential Impact on Businesses.

Emerging Trends	Potential Impact on Businesses
Quantum computing in marketing analytics	Significantly faster data processing and enhanced analytical capabilities
Use of augmented reality for product trials	Enhanced customer engagement and improved online shopping experience
Virtual reality marketing experiences	Immersive brand experiences leading to deeper customer loyalty
Convergence of offline and online marketing realms	Unified customer journey tracking and holistic marketing strategies
Advanced AI-driven customer segmentation	Highly personalized marketing campaigns with improved ROI

- **Customer data platforms.** These platforms are software that consolidate customer data from multiple sources into a unified database, making it easier for marketers to segment their audience and deliver personalized experiences.

- **Predictive analytics.** The use of predictive analytics in marketing is expected to increase, enabling businesses to anticipate customer behaviors and trends and to optimize their marketing efforts accordingly.

- **Privacy-enhancing technologies.** With the growing emphasis on data privacy, technologies that help businesses protect customer information while still gaining insights from it will become increasingly important (Danezis & Gürses, 2010).

Looking to the future, marketers will need to stay abreast of these developments and be prepared to integrate them into their data-driven strategies.

13.5.2 Evolution of Marketing Analytics: Past, Present, Future

Marketing analytics has undergone considerable transformation over the years, adapting to the evolving landscape of technology and consumer behavior (see Figure 13.4):

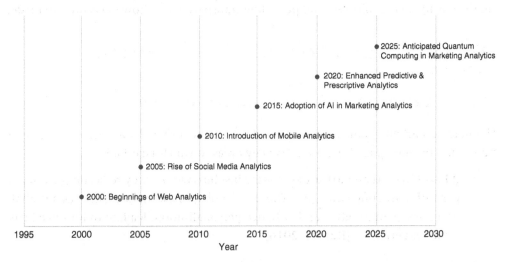

Figure 13.4 The Evolution of Marketing Analytics over the Years and Potential Future Direction.

- **Past.** The genesis of marketing analytics was in direct response advertising in print media, where marketers could track response rates to specific ads. As technology advanced, databases became popular, enabling the storage and retrieval of customer information, heralding the onset of database marketing.

- **Present.** The explosion of digital platforms and social media has presented marketers with vast amounts of data. The use of ML and predictive analytics has become commonplace, enabling businesses to target and personalize their messaging with unprecedented precision (Provost & Fawcett, 2013).

- **Future.** As the Internet of Things continues to expand, there will be even more touchpoints for collecting data. Marketers are expected to leverage this, coupled with the power of AI, to anticipate customer needs before they even arise, creating a more proactive approach to marketing.

13.5.3 The Role of Quantum Computing and Advanced AI in Marketing

Quantum computing, with its potential to process vast amounts of data exponentially faster than classical computers, is poised to revolutionize marketing analytics. Tasks such as optimization of marketing strategies, which currently take substantial computational time, can be reduced significantly using quantum algorithms (Aaronson, 2013). Meanwhile, advanced AI can synthesize and analyze complex patterns in consumer behavior, enabling more sophisticated segmentation and personalization strategies.

13.5.4 Integrating Virtual Reality and Augmented Reality in Marketing Strategies

Virtual reality (VR) and augmented reality (AR) technologies offer marketers immersive mediums to engage consumers. Brands have started to leverage VR to provide virtual showrooms, offering a tactile shopping experience from the comfort of a consumer's home. However, AR apps on smartphones can overlay product information and virtual try-ons, enriching the in-store shopping experience. Such integrative experiences are not only novel but can significantly boost engagement and purchase intent.

13.5.5 The Ongoing Fusion of Offline and Online Marketing Realms

The once distinct realms of offline (physical) and online (digital) marketing are rapidly converging. The prevalence of omnichannel strategies epitomizes this merger. Consumers today may begin their shopping journey online via social media or an e-commerce platform, visit a physical store to try a product, and then complete their purchase on a mobile app. Marketers are thus tasked with ensuring consistent branding and seamless transitions between these channels. This fusion also presents opportunities for leveraging data from one realm (e.g., online browsing behavior) to enhance experiences in the other (e.g., in-store personalized offers) (Verhoef et al., 2015).

In conclusion, the landscape of marketing continues to evolve rapidly, driven by technological advancements and changing consumer behaviors. As new tools and strategies emerge, marketers must remain agile, always adapting to best serve and engage their target audiences.

13.5.6   Key Concepts in Emerging Trends and the Future

The future of marketing data science will be shaped by several key concepts that are emerging from current trends:

- **Explainable AI**. As AI becomes more prevalent in marketing, there is an increasing demand for transparency and interpretability of AI systems. Explainable AI aims to make the decision-making process of AI systems understandable to humans (Adadi & Berrada, 2018).
- **Privacy by design.** With the advent of stringent data privacy regulations, the concept of integrating privacy into the design of systems and practices from the outset is becoming more important. This concept ensures privacy and data protection compliance from the start (Cavoukian, 2009).
- **Omnichannel marketing.** The future of marketing lies in the integration of customer experiences across all channels. Marketers are increasingly looking to create seamless customer experiences, whether the customer is shopping online from a mobile device, a laptop, or in a brick-and-mortar store (Verhoef et al., 2015).
- **Hyper-personalization.** Personalization in marketing is not new, but with advances in AI and ML, hyper-personalization, which involves real-time personalization based on customer behavior, is becoming possible (Li & Kannan, 2014).
- **Ethical AI.** As AI and ML are increasingly being applied in marketing, there is a growing recognition of the need for ethical considerations in their use, such as fairness, accountability, and transparency (Jobin et al., 2019).

13.5.7   Practical Example: AI in Personalized Marketing

AI has been increasingly used in personalized marketing efforts. An instance of this application can be seen in the case of Netflix, a leading streaming platform.

Netflix uses AI to personalize its user experience extensively. Based on the individual user's viewing history, Netflix recommends shows and movies that the user is likely to watch and enjoy (Gomez-Uribe & Hunt, 2015). This personalized recommendation engine is driven by sophisticated ML algorithms that predict user preferences based on past behavior.

The AI system at Netflix uses a technique called *collaborative filtering*. This technique takes into account not only the individual user's behavior but also the behavior of other users with similar preferences. For example, if two users have watched and liked a similar set of movies, and one of them watches and likes a new movie, the system will recommend this new movie to the other user (Bell & Koren, 2007).

Netflix's use of AI in personalized marketing has been very successful. Their recommendation engine, which is a significant component of their marketing strategy, is estimated to save them $1 billion a year by reducing the rate of subscription cancellations (Amatriain & Basilico, 2012).

13.6 CONCLUSION

In today's digital age, the confluence of marketing and data science provides unparalleled opportunities for businesses to understand their consumers and personalize experiences. However, with great power comes great responsibility. Chapter 13 has underscored the criticality of ethical considerations, privacy concerns, and regulatory adherence in the realm of marketing data science.

At its core, ethical practice in marketing data science is not merely about compliance, but about forging trust. Consumers, more than ever, are cognizant of their digital footprints. As businesses harness data for insights, there is a moral imperative to ensure that such data is not misused, misrepresented, or mishandled. Ethical lapses can irrevocably damage a brand's reputation, consumer trust, and the broader ecosystem's integrity.

Privacy, intertwined with ethics, has emerged as a cornerstone of modern marketing practices. The intricate balance between personalization and privacy is a tightrope that marketers must tread carefully on. Ensuring data anonymity, adhering to data minimization principles, and maintaining transparency in data collection and use are nonnegotiables in the current landscape.

Regulations, such as GDPR and CCPA, although seen by some as stringent, are emblematic of society's push for a more controlled, transparent, and consumer-centric data environment. These regulations underscore the rights of individuals over their data, compelling businesses to adopt a more respectful and cautious approach to data collection and use.

Moreover, as technology continues its relentless march forward—bringing forth tools such as AI and quantum computing—the ethical, privacy, and regulatory considerations will only magnify in their importance. The onus is on the present and future marketers, data scientists, and businesses to be proactive, constantly updating their knowledge, revisiting their practices, and engaging in open dialogues about the evolving challenges and opportunities.

In essence, although the amalgamation of marketing and data science offers a promising frontier for businesses, it is imperative to navigate this domain with a compass grounded in ethics, respect for privacy, and a keen understanding of regulations. Only by doing so can businesses truly harness the transformative power of marketing data science in a sustainable and consumer-centric manner.

13.7 REFERENCES

Aaronson, S. (2013). *Quantum computing since Democritus*. Cambridge University Press.

Adadi, A., & Berrada, M. (2018). Peeking inside the black-box: A survey on explainable artificial intelligence (XAI). *IEEE Access, 6*, 52138–52160.

Amatriain, X., & Basilico, J. (2012). Netflix recommendations: Beyond the 5 stars (part 1). *Netflix Tech Blog*, p. 6.

Barocas, S., & Selbst, A. D. (2016). Big data's disparate impact. *California Law Review*, pp. 671–732.

Bell, R. M., & Koren, Y. (2007). Lessons from the Netflix prize challenge. *ACM SIGKDD Explorations Newsletter, 9*(2), 75–79.

Bennett, C. J. (2012). The accountability approach to privacy and data protection: Assumptions and caveats. In D. Guagnin, L. Hempel, C. Ilten, I. Kroener, D. Neyland, & H. Postigo (Eds.), *Managing privacy through accountability* (pp. 33–48). Palgrave Macmillan UK.

Buolamwini, J., & Gebru, T. (2018, January). Gender shades: Intersectional accuracy disparities in commercial gender classification. *Conference on Fairness, Accountability and Transparency* (pp. 77–91). PMLR.

Bygrave, L. A. (2014). *Data privacy law: An international perspective*. Oxford University Press.

Cadwalladr, C., & Graham-Harrison, E. (2018). Revealed: 50 million Facebook profiles harvested for Cambridge Analytica in major data breach. *The Guardian, 17*(1), 22.

Cavoukian, A. (2009). Privacy by design: The 7 foundational principles. *Information and Privacy Commissioner of Ontario, Canada, 5*, 12.

Clarke, R., & Moses, L. B. (2014). The regulation of civilian drones' impacts on public safety. *Computer Law & Security Review, 30*(3), 263–285.

Custers, B., Calders, T., Schermer, B., Zarsky, T., & Schermer, B. (2018). *Discrimination and privacy in the information society: Data mining and profiling in large databases* (Vol. 3). Springer Science & Business Media.

Danezis, G., & Gürses, S. (2010). A critical review of 10 years of privacy technology. *Proceedings of Surveillance Cultures: A Global Surveillance Society* (pp. 1–16).

Danks, D., & London, A. J. (2017, August). Algorithmic bias in autonomous systems. *Proceedings of the 26th International Joint Conference on Artificial Intelligence (IJCAI 2017), 17* (2017), 4691–4697.

Datta, A., Tschantz, M. C., & Datta, A. (2015). Automated experiments on ad privacy settings. *Proceedings of Privacy Enhancing Technologies* (pp. 92–112).

Doshi-Velez, F., & Kim, B. (2017). Towards a rigorous science of interpretable machine learning. *arXiv*:1702.08608.

Duhigg, C. (2013). How companies learn your secrets. In D. Starkman, M.M. Hamilton, R. Chittum, & F. Salmon (Eds.), *The best business writing 2013* (pp. 421–444). Columbia University Press.

Dwork, C. (2008, April). Differential privacy: A survey of results. *International Conference on Theory and Applications of Models of Computation* (pp. 1–19). Springer Berlin Heidelberg.

European Commission. (2021). Data protection in the EU. Retrieved from https://ec.europa.eu/info/law/law-topic/data-protection/data-protection-eu_en

Gomez-Uribe, C. A., & Hunt, N. (2015). The Netflix recommender system: Algorithms, business value, and innovation. *ACM Transactions on Management Information Systems (TMIS), 6*(4), 1–19.

Goodman, B., & Flaxman, S. (2017). European Union regulations on algorithmic decision-making and a "right to explanation." *AI Magazine, 38*(3), 50–57.

Greenleaf, G. (2017). Global data privacy laws 2017: 120 national data privacy laws, including Indonesia and Turkey. *UNSW Law Research Paper No. 17–45*, 10–13.

Grgić-Hlača, N., Zafar, M. B., Gummadi, K. P., & Weller, A. (2018, April). Beyond distributive fairness in algorithmic decision making: Feature selection for procedurally fair learning. *Proceedings of the AAAI Conference on Artificial Intelligence* (Vol. 32, No. 1).

Hajian, S., Bonchi, F., & Castillo, C. (2016, August). Algorithmic bias: From discrimination discovery to fairness-aware data mining. *Proceedings of the 22nd ACM SIGKDD International Conference on Knowledge Discovery and Data Mining* (pp. 2125–2126).

Hardt, M., Price, E., & Srebro, N. (2016). Equality of opportunity in supervised learning. *Advances in Neural Information Processing Systems, 29*.

Hern, A. (2018). Fitness tracking app Strava gives away location of secret US army bases. *The Guardian*. Retrieved from https://www.theguardian.com/world/2018/jan/28/fitness-tracking-app-gives-away-location-of-secret-us-army-bases

ICO. (2018). Data Protection Act. Retrieved from https://www.legislation.gov.uk/ukpga/2018/12/contents/enacted

Jobin, A., Ienca, M., & Vayena, E. (2019). The global landscape of AI ethics guidelines. *Nature Machine Intelligence, 1*(9), 389–399.

Kearns, M., Neel, S., Roth, A., & Wu, Z. S. (2018, July). Preventing fairness gerrymandering: Auditing and learning for subgroup fairness. *International Conference on Machine Learning* (pp. 2564–2572). PMLR.

Kuner, C. (2013). *Transborder data flows and data privacy law*. Oxford University Press.

Kuner, C., Svantesson, D.J.B., Cate, F. H., Lynskey, O., & Millard, C. (2017). Machine learning with personal data: Is data protection law smart enough to meet the challenge? *International Data Privacy Law, 7*(1), 1–2.

Li, H., & Kannan, P. K. (2014). Attributing conversions in a multichannel online marketing environment: An empirical model and a field experiment. *Journal of Marketing Research, 51*(1), 40–56.

Lundberg, S. M., & Lee, S. I. (2017). A unified approach to interpreting model predictions. *Advances in Neural Information Processing Systems, 30*.

Mailjet. (2021). GDPR & email marketing: The definitive guide. Retrieved from https://www.mailjet.com/gdpr/email-marketing/

Marreiros, H., Tonin, M., Vlassopoulos, M., & Schraefel, M. C. (2017). "Now that you mention it": A survey experiment on information, inattention and online privacy. *Journal of Economic Behavior & Organization, 140*, 1–17.

Martin, K. (2015). Ethical issues in the big data industry. *MIS Quarterly Executive, 14*, 2.

Martínez-Alemán, A. M., & Wartman, K. L. (2008). *Online social networking on campus: Understanding what matters in student culture*. Routledge.

Mittelstadt, B. D., Allo, P., Taddeo, M., Wachter, S., & Floridi, L. (2016). The ethics of algorithms: Mapping the debate. *Big Data & Society, 3*(2), 2053951716679679.

Ng, A. Y. (2004, July). Feature selection, L 1 vs. L 2 regularization, and rotational invariance. *Proceedings of the Twenty-First International Conference on Machine Learning* (p. 78).

O'neil, C. (2017). *Weapons of math destruction: How big data increases inequality and threatens democracy*. Crown.

Patagonia. (2021). Privacy policy. Retrieved from https://www.patagonia.com/privacy-policy.html

Provost, F., & Fawcett, T. (2013). *Data science for business: What you need to know about data mining and data-analytic thinking.* O'Reilly Media.

Ribeiro, M. T., Singh, S., & Guestrin, C. (2016, August). "Why should I trust you?" Explaining the predictions of any classifier. *Proceedings of the 22nd ACM SIGKDD international conference on knowledge discovery and data mining* (pp. 1135–1144).

Romanosky, S. (2016). Examining the costs and causes of cyber incidents. *Journal of Cybersecurity,* *2*(2), 121–135.

Russell, S. (2016). *Artificial intelligence: A modern approach.* Pearson Education.

Schreurs, W., Hildebrandt, M., Kindt, E., & Vanfleteren, M. (2008). Cogitas, ergo sum: The role of data protection law and non-discrimination law in group profiling in the private sector. *Profiling the European citizen: Cross-disciplinary perspectives* (pp. 241–270). Springer.

Schwartz, P. M., & Solove, D. J. (2014). Reconciling personal information in the United States and European Union. *California Law Review, 102,* 877.

State of California. (2021). California Consumer Privacy Act (CCPA). Retrieved from https://oag.ca.gov/privacy/ccpa

Strava. (2018). Strava responds to security concerns with new privacy settings. Retrieved from https://blog.strava.com/press/strava-responds-to-security-concerns-with-new-privacy-settings-13329/

Susser, D., Roessler, B., & Nissenbaum, H. (2019). Online manipulation: Hidden influences in a digital world. *Georgetown Law Technology Review, 4,* 1.

Tene, O., & Polonetsky, J. (2012). Big data for all: Privacy and user control in the age of analytics. *Northwestern Journal of Technology and Intellectual Property, 11,* 239.

Verhoef, P. C., Kannan, P. K., & Inman, J. J. (2015). From multi-channel retailing to omni-channel retailing: Introduction to the special issue on multi-channel retailing. *Journal of Retailing, 91*(2), 174–181.

Verma, S., & Rubin, J. (2018, May). Fairness definitions explained. *Proceedings of the International Workshop on Software Fairness* (pp. 1–7).

Wachter, S., Mittelstadt, B., & Floridi, L. (2017). Why a right to explanation of automated decision-making does not exist in the general data protection regulation. *International Data Privacy Law, 7*(2), 76–99.

Zafar, M. B., Valera, I., Rogriguez, M. G., & Gummadi, K. P. (2017, April). Fairness constraints: Mechanisms for fair classification. *Artificial intelligence and statistics* (pp. 962–970). PMLR.

Zuboff, S. (2019). *The age of surveillance capitalism: The fight for a human future at the new frontier of power.* Profile Books.

Zwitter, A. (2014). Big data ethics. *Big Data & Society, 1*(2), 2053951714559253.

About the Website

Thank you for purchasing *Mastering Marketing Data Science: A Comprehensive Guide for Today's Marketers*. To enhance your learning experience and provide practical application of the concepts discussed in this book, a range of complementary resources are available online here: www.wiley.com/go/Brown/MasteringMarketing DataScience.

Available Resources:

The following are the resources provided to complement the content of the book:

1. **Datasets for Hands-On Practice (Chapters 2-10):**

   Each chapter comes with corresponding datasets, enabling you to apply the concepts and techniques in practical, real-world scenarios.

2. **Exercise Files in Python and SAS (Chapters 2-10):**

   To reinforce your understanding, exercises are included. These exercises are available in both Python and SAS, catering to different preferences and skill levels in programming.

3. **Code Snippets and Scripts in Python and SAS (Chapters 2-10):**

   You will find practical code examples in both Python and SAS. These scripts illustrate the implementation of various data science techniques discussed in the book, making them accessible to both beginners and experienced data scientists.

We trust that these resources will significantly aid you in mastering the intricate field of marketing data science.

Index